Lecture Notes of the Institute for Computer Sciences, Social Informatics and Telecommunications Engineering 531

The LNICST series publishes ICST's conferences, symposia and workshops.

LNICST reports state-of-the-art results in areas related to the scope of the Institute.
The type of material published includes

- Proceedings (published in time for the respective event)
- Other edited monographs (such as project reports or invited volumes)

LNICST topics span the following areas:

- General Computer Science
- E-Economy
- E-Medicine
- Knowledge Management
- Multimedia
- Operations, Management and Policy
- Social Informatics
- Systems

Nguyen-Son Vo · Hoai-An Tran
Editors

Industrial Networks and Intelligent Systems

9th EAI International Conference, INISCOM 2023
Ho Chi Minh City, Vietnam, August 2–3, 2023
Proceedings

Springer

Editors
Nguyen-Son Vo 🆔
Duy Tan University
Da Nang, Vietnam

Hoai-An Tran
Vietnam Aviation Institute
Ho Chi Minh City, Vietnam

ISSN 1867-8211   ISSN 1867-822X (electronic)
Lecture Notes of the Institute for Computer Sciences, Social Informatics
and Telecommunications Engineering
ISBN 978-3-031-47358-6   ISBN 978-3-031-47359-3 (eBook)
https://doi.org/10.1007/978-3-031-47359-3

This Springer imprint is published by the registered company Springer Nature Switzerland AG
The registered company address is: Gewerbestrasse 11, 6330 Cham, Switzerland

Paper in this product is recyclable.

Preface

We are delighted to introduce the proceedings of the 9th European Alliance for Innovation (EAI) International Conference on Industrial Networks and Intelligent Systems (INISCOM 2023). This conference brought together researchers, developers and practitioners from around the world who are leveraging and developing industrial networks and intelligent systems. The focus of INISCOM 2023 was the state of the art in all types of big data, AI and 6G networks: technologies, services and applications.

The technical program of INISCOM 2023 consisted of 23 full papers in oral presentation sessions at the main conference tracks. There were four conference tracks: Track1 – Telecommunications Systems and Networks; Track2 – Information Processing and Data Analysis; Track 3 – Industrial Networks and Intelligent Systems; and Track 4 – Security and Privacy. Aside from the high-quality technical paper presentations, the technical program also featured a keynote speech about "Edge Intelligence URLLC for 6G Digital Twin: Joint Communications and Computation Design" given by Trung Q. Duong (Queen's University Belfast, UK) and Saeed Khosravirad (Nokia Bell Labs, USA) and a tutorial speech about "Digital Twin for 6G ORAN: Taxonomy, Research Challenges, and the Road Ahead" given by Antonino Masaracchia (Queen's University Belfast, UK).

Coordination with the steering chair, Imrich Chlamtac, was essential for the success of the conference. We sincerely appreciate his constant support and guidance. It was also a great pleasure to work with such an excellent Organizing Committee team and we thank them for their hard work in organizing and supporting the conference. Particular thanks go to the Technical Program Committee (TPC), who completed the peer-review process for the technical papers and put together a high-quality technical program. We are also grateful to the conference manager, Veronika Kissova, for her support and to all the authors who submitted their papers to INISCOM 2023.

We strongly believe that INISCOM provides a good forum for all researchers, developers and practitioners to discuss all science and technology aspects that are relevant to industrial networks and intelligent systems. We also expect that the future editions of INISCOM will be as successful and stimulating as this year's conference, as indicated by the contributions presented in this volume.

August 2023

Nguyen-Son Vo
Hoai-An Tran

Organization

Steering Committee

Imrich Chlamtac   University of Trento, Italy

Organizing Committee

General Chair

Nguyen-Son Vo   Duy Tan University, Vietnam

General Co-chair

Tran Hoai An   Vietnam Aviation Academy, Vietnam

TPC Chair and Co-chairs

Zhichao Sheng   Shanghai University, China
Muhammad Fahim   Queen's University Belfast, UK
Van-Phuc Hoang   Le Quy Don Technical University, Vietnam

Sponsorship and Exhibit Chairs

Chinmoy Kundu   University College Dublin, Ireland
Thanh-Minh Phan   Vietnam Aviation Academy, Vietnam

Local Chairs

Bui Nhat Vuong   Vietnam Aviation Academy, Vietnam
Thanh-Minh Phan   Vietnam Aviation Academy, Vietnam

Workshops Chair

To Ba Lam   Vietnam Aviation Academy, Vietnam

Publicity and Social Media Chair

Antonino Masaracchia   Queen's University Belfast, UK

Publications Chair

Nguyen-Son Vo   Duy Tan University, Vietnam

Web Chair

Pham Cong Thanh   Vietnam Aviation Academy, Vietnam

Posters and PhD Track Chair

Nguyen Luong Anh Tuan   Vietnam Aviation Academy, Vietnam

Panels Chair

James Adu Ansere   Sunyani Technical University, Ghana

Demos Chair

Bhaskara Narottama   Kumoh National Institute of Technology, South Korea

Tutorials Chair

Nguyen Huu Chan Thanh   Vietnam Aviation Academy, Vietnam

Technical Program Committee

Nguyen-Son Vo	Duy Tan University, Vietnam
Zhichao Sheng	Shanghai University, China
Muhammad Fahim	Queen's University Belfast, UK
Antonino Masaracchia	Queen's University Belfast, UK
To Ba Lam	Vietnam Aviation Academy, Vietnam
James Adu Ansere	Sunyani Technical University, Ghana
Bhaskara Narottama	Kumoh National Institute of Technology, South Korea
Tat-Bao-Thien Nguyen	Vietnam Aviation Academy, Vietnam

Minh-Phung Bui	Van Lang University, Vietnam
Thanh-Minh Phan	Vietnam Aviation Academy, Vietnam
Chinmoy Kundu	University College Dublin, Ireland
Dac-Binh Ha	Duy Tan University, Vietnam
Long Nguyen	Dong Nai University, Vietnam
Van-Phuc Hoang	Le Quy Don Technical University, Vietnam
Cheng Yin	Queen's University Belfast, UK
Dang Huynh	Queen's University Belfast, UK
Trung Q. Duong	Queen's University Belfast, UK
Tan Do-Duy	HCMC University of Technology and Education, Vietnam
Quoc Tuan Vien	Middlesex University London, UK
Van Nhan Vo	Duy Tan University, Vietnam
Hoang Trang	Ho Chi Minh City University of Technology, Vietnam
Ha Quang Thinh Ngo	Ho Chi Minh City University of Technology, Vietnam
Tran Trung Duy	Posts and Telecommunications Institute of Technology, Vietnam
Muhammad Azhar Iqbal	Lancaster University, UK
Pham Ngoc Son	Ho Chi Minh City University of Technology and Education, Vietnam

Contents

Information Processing and Data Analysis

Industrial Networks and Intelligent Systems

Security and Privacy

Telecommunications Systems
and Networks

A Smart Agriculture Solution Includes Intelligent Irrigation and Security

Tang Nguyen-Tan[1,2], Chien Dang-Ngoc[1,2], and Quan Le-Trung[1,2(✉)]

[1] Faculty of Computer Networks and Communications, University of Information Technology, Ho Chi Minh City, Vietnam
{19522181,19520424}@gm.uit.edu.vn, quanlt@uit.edu.vn
[2] Vietnam National University, Ho Chi Minh City, Vietnam

Abstract. One of the key roles of a smart agricultural system is irrigation, which is carried out automatically, optimally, and at each stage of the growth of each crop. The optimal soil moisture data for each plant at each stage of growth that have been stored in the database, along with two forecasts of the weather and the soil moisture level for the next hour, are incorporated to propose an autonomous irrigation solution in this paper. Two Transformer deep-learning models were used to train forecasts of the weather and soil moisture. The test results demonstrate that the Transformer model is able with the same accuracy of 91.41% on the weather forecast test set and 82.06% on the soil moisture forecast test set despite having 40.62% fewer training variables than the LSTM model. As an Internet of Things system, the smart agriculture system must be safeguarded against eavesdropping, attacks that spoof control commands, and machine learning models that are poisoned with false data. In this research, we have also proposed an end-to-end encryption and authentication solution using AES 256-bit, HMAC, along with a safe CRYSTALS-Kyber key exchange technique in the quantum age. The evaluation results show that the proposed solution can be deployed on IoT devices similar to Arduino, STM32, and Raspberry Pi 4.

Keywords: Smart Agricultural · Time-series Forecasting · Transformer · IoT Security

1 Introduction

Smart agriculture is the term used to refer to the application of technology to improve efficiency and productivity in agricultural activities. Smart irrigation is an Internet of Things (IoT) system comprising a sensor network, irrigation control components, and software for monitoring and remotely controlling the system. It is one of many uses of intelligent agriculture. Nowadays, irrigation systems are either manually controlled by the farmer or provide automatic irrigation through a timer; however, the farmer must analyze factors including soil moisture, weather, and the optimal environmental conditions for each stage of

N.-S. Vo and H.-A. Tran (Eds.): INISCOM 2023, LNICST 531, pp. 3–18, 2023.
https://doi.org/10.1007/978-3-031-47359-3_1

the plant's growth to set the right time for the timer. That inconvenience has contributed to our motivation to perform this research and use deep learning techniques to propose an appropriate autonomous irrigation system for each stage of crop growth.

Predicting soil moisture levels with machine learning algorithms is one way to enhance the performance of smart irrigation systems, making them more efficient and precise [1]. Numerous researchers from around the world have proposed the strategy of using deep learning models to optimize smart agricultural systems. The authors of a research paper proposed a method for predicting soil moisture levels in smart irrigation systems using fog computing, which involves combining multiple deep learning models such as Long Short-Term Memory Networks (LSTM), Recurrent Neural Networks (RNN), and General Deep Regression (GDR) [2]. The predicted soil moisture level will be obtained by running the K-Nearest Neighbor (KNN) algorithm on the output data of the three aforementioned deep-learning models. Reinforcement learning has been applied to automate the scheduling of irrigation for a tomato field, and the results have shown that the LSTM model is effective in reducing water usage, with savings ranging from 18% to 30% [3]. Another research employed a combination of LSTM, KNN, and Gradient Boosting-based Tree (GBT) models to forecast weather for optimizing irrigation water usage [4].

A smart agricultural system is an Internet of Things (IoT) system, which means it needs protection from network attacks. These attacks can include spoofing sensor data or control commands, as well as eavesdropping on the information. Such attacks can cause the system to malfunction, which could seriously affect the crop's growth. The article [5] proposes an authentication and key agreement protocol for IoT devices to update the secret key using the HMAC hash function. This protocol is designed to protect the system from eavesdropping and data tampering. The CRYSTALS-Kyber is a key encapsulation mechanism (KEM) that provides quantum-safe security with IND-CCA2 security. In the article [6], the first fine-grained implementation of the post-quantum CRYSTALS-Kyber KEM on a GPU is proposed, which can be utilized to offer key encapsulation and decapsulation for IoT systems. Another research found that it was possible to load and run the Kyber768 CPAPKE algorithm on the MULTOS Trust-Anchor for IoT [7], but there were performance issues due to polynomial multiplication and reduction operations. While the current performance may be adequate for machine-to-machine scenarios, further optimization studies are recommended to ensure the intended strength of the algorithm. However, it is challenging to put the aforementioned research into reality because they are purely theoretical.

In this work, we indicate a smart agriculture approach that combines deep learning and security technologies. Based on time series containing information on air temperature, air humidity, sunlight, pressure, wind speed, and time values, we trained two Transformer models to forecast weather and soil moisture in the upcoming hour. These two models were converted to TensorFlow Lite and deployed on a Raspberry Pi 4 that serves as a LoRa Gateway in our designed system. In addition, we have proposed employing CRYSTALS-Kyber KEM for key exchange, HMAC for authentication, and AES for data encryption to increase the system's security. Our security solution will be used in the connection at the edge network as well as the connection over the internet between the system's devices, such as IoT devices (Arduino), the LoRa Gateway (Raspberry Pi), and Backend servers,...

This paper has the following structure: Sect. 1 introduces the overview of current research, motivation, and purpose of this study, and Sect. 2 will demonstrate the challenges encountered in constructing a practical smart Smart agriculture system in practice system. The IoT reference model and the network context of the system are described in detail in Sect. 3. In Sect. 4, we propose an automatic irrigation solution using two Transformer models to forecast weather and soil moisture. The end-to-end encryption and authentication solutions for the system are proposed in Sect. 5. The results of the two Transformer models' accuracy and the system's performance after the proposed security solution was applied are shown in Sect. 6. Section 7 ends this paper with a conclusion and future development directions.

2   Related Work

An overview of current smart agricultural innovations and the challenges involved in bringing them into use will be provided in this section.

2.1   Smart Agriculture System in Practice

In order to increase productivity and product quality in agricultural production, smart agricultural systems have received extensive research and practical application in developed countries. These systems are frequently constructed using local servers on a farm or centralized servers in the cloud. Wi-fi, NB-IoT, LoRa, Zigbee, Cellular, and other network technologies are frequently used for transmitting and receiving sensor data and control orders [8].

The majority of automatic irrigation systems only function according to the farmer's predetermined schedule; therefore, the best irrigation depends on the farmer's irrigation schedule. One drawback of existing smart irrigation systems is that an internet connection is required to access the server performing data review or rescheduling. This problem will be solved with the system model proposed in this study by placing the server in the internal network. When we need remote access to the server, we have set up a Zero-trust communication tunnel from the farmer's terminal software to the server, moreover, the farmers may still use their private network to access the web dashboard and manage the system even if their internet connection is down.

2.2   Security Challenge for IoT Systems

When bringing an IoT system into practice, the problem of securing the system to ensure it works properly is a huge challenge. If we only mention the system we built in this study, the remote sensing data from the sensors can be spoofed, leading to the system making wrong decisions that seriously affect the growth of the crops. In addition, control commands can also be eavesdropped and then retransmitted in a control command spoofing attack. Typically, these issues only arise at the edge network layer, where very few security solutions are currently in use.

Because there are so many security issues with IoT systems in practice, in conjunction with the issues we highlight here, an article outlines those issues [9]. This research direction has received the attention of many researchers around the world, but the results from that research are difficult to apply in practice. The research applying the blockchain network technique has a disadvantage in that the cost of deploying and operating the system is very high, in addition, device authentication using the blockchain technique increases the latency of the system due to the call to execute smart contracts [10]. Another way is to use ECC in key exchange and authentication of edge devices, but this solution is not secure in the quantum era [11,12]. The solution proposed by us in this study will solve those problems.

3   IoT Reference Model

The IoT reference model that we use as the basis for constructing a security and deep learning solution is described in depth in this section. It is shown in Fig. 1. Sensors mounted on front-end IoT devices (Arduino or Waspmote block) help gather data on air temperature, air humidity, soil moisture, wind speed, etc. during remote sensing. In this case, the LoRa Gateway and Edge server is deployed in a 2-in-1 form on a Raspberry Pi 4 so that the collected data is transmitted to it through a LoRa connection. Then, the data will be stored in the local database as time series. During remote control, the LoRa connection is also used to forward commands to control the water pump and grow lights via the LoRa Gateway. The data stored in the local database will be aggregated, filtered with the necessary information, and periodically updated to the global database at the backend server using an internet connection.

The end user remote control the system through an application on the end device and the control command will be forwarded to the LoRa Gateway using the MQTT protocol via the MQTT Broker in the Edge server. In addition, the MQTT protocol is also used to update sensor data in real time to the end-user application. Since our system was developed via the agent application approach, each tenant will have their own Edge server. We have created a tunnel so that the tenant using our developed application can access the Edge server where the Web dashboard is installed to monitor and operate the system. We choose to deploy the system according to that model so that the Edge server can be placed in the internal network to help the system's services remain highly available when the internet connection is lost.

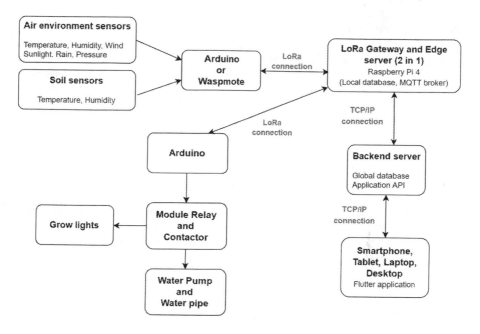

Fig. 1. IoT Reference Model.

4   Intelligent Irrigation Using Transformer Models

This section proposes two Transformer deep learning models that can be deployed on a Raspberry Pi 4 acting as a LoRa Gateway and Edge server in the IoT reference model above. The first model is used to forecast the weather, while the second model is used to forecast the soil moisture level after one hour. Both of these forecast values will then be used to schedule automatic irrigation and update the automatic irrigation schedule every five minutes. In recent years, the transformer model has attracted the attention of researchers and has been employed in much recent research to forecast time series [13–17]. We decided on using Transformer for this research rather than more traditional models like LSTM and GRU since that is a cutting-edge network architecture, even if the forecasts, in this case, are based on time series data.

4.1   Soil Moisture and Weather Forecasting

The challenge with automatic irrigation systems is to keep the soil moisture level suitable for every stage of the plant's growth. This challenge was resolved by constructing the Transformer model to forecast the next hour's soil mois-ture level based on five-time series containing information on soil moisture, air temperature, air humidity, air pressure, and luminosity of sunlight collected in the previous hour. The remaining Transformer model will be used to forecast the weather for the upcoming hour because irrigation scheduling is based on both soil moisture levels and weather conditions. The weather condition will be forecasted based on five-time series that carry information on air humidity, air temperature, air pressure, wind speed, and weather conditions that were collected at previous timestamps. The forecasted value of soil moisture level and weather conditions will be used to schedule irrigation automatically.

Datasets Description

The dataset used during training and evaluation of our proposed Transformer model to forecast soil moisture is provided by SMART FASAL. This dataset of precision agriculture consists of several agricultural parameters like soil moisture, air humidity, air temperature, air pressure, and luminosity of sunlight. The interval between timestamps in the dataset ranges from one to two minutes. The dataset is conveniently available at http://smartfasal.in/ftp-dataset-portal/. In addition to forecasting soil moisture, we also construct an extra model for forecasting the weather. The dataset used to train and evaluate this Transformer model was scraped from https://www.wunderground.com with three locations in western Vietnam: Ca Mau, Rach Gia, and Can Tho City. We scraped hourly data on air temperature, air humidity, air pressure, wind speed, and weather conditions for all three locations starting on January 1, 2020, and ending on February 23, 2023, using Python and the Selenium library. The dataset is conveniently available at the Google Drive link.

Transformer Model

We constructed and trained two Transformer models based on the two datasets mentioned earlier to forecast soil moisture content and weather for the upcoming hour. The detailed structure of the two Transformer models we proposed is shown in Fig. 2. Two models are implemented based on the paper "Attention is all you need" [18] using Tensorflow with Keras modules.

Five-time series having sixty timestamps and the time signal with sixty values corresponding to those sixty timestamps serve as the input data for the soil moisture level forecasting model. The output of this model is the forecast value of the next hour's soil moisture level. In our case research, we employ sixty timestamps to forecast soil moisture levels because the interval between timestamps is between one and two minutes. The input five-time series contains data collected in the preceding hour on soil moisture, air temperature, air humidity, air pressure, and sunlight luminosity. The values of the time signal in the case of soil moisture forecasting represent the influence of the time of day on the rate of change of soil moisture.

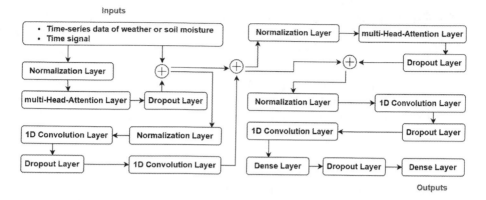

Fig. 2. Transfomer model for soil moisture and weather forecasting.

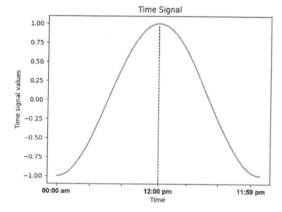

Fig. 3. The time signal.

The time signal is calculated through the formula 1 and shown in Fig. 3. In formula 1:

$$T_S = -\cos\left(\frac{60H + M + \frac{S}{60}}{1440} 2\pi\right) \quad (1)$$

- T_S is a time signal whose value ranges from -1 to 1.
- The time of day is represented by the numbers H, M, and S, respectively.

The input data of the weather forecasting model also includes the five-time series and the time signal. Five-time series containing data on weather conditions, wind speed, air pressure, air temperature, and air humidity were gathered at six timestamps earlier. The formula $T_S = \frac{N_{day}}{365}$ is used to calculate the six-time signal values matching the six timestamps in the five-time series. N_{day} is the number of days from the beginning of the year to the current time. The output of the weather forecasting model is the weather condition in the upcoming hour. Since the timestamps in the data we gathered are one hour apart, we make use of six timestamps to forecast the weather.

Following the schematic diagram of the Transformer model structure that we propose (shown in Fig. 2), the multi-Head-Attention layer in our model is multi-Self-Attention, it is used for aggregating information between timestamps while the 1D convolution layer is used for feature extraction at each timestamp. When each key's dimension is d_k and the output of the normalization layer is $\widehat{Y}$, the query, key, and value matrices are called Q, K, and V, respectively. Each

Self-Attention in our multi-Head-Attention layer is followed as formulas 2 and 3.

$$Q = \widehat{Y}W_Q \quad K = \widehat{Y}W_K \quad V = \widehat{Y}W_V \qquad (2)$$

$$\textbf{Self-Attention}(Q, K, V) = \textbf{Softmax}(\frac{QK^T}{\sqrt{d_k}}V) \qquad (3)$$

Two soil moisture and weather forecasting models were implemented, trained using Tensorflow, and then converted into Tensorflow Lite for deployment on Raspberry Pi 4 to carry out autonomous irrigation scheduling.

4.2   Automatic Irrigation Scheduling

This sub-section will propose an automatic irrigation scheduling technique that applies the two proposed deep learning models above. In Fig. 4, we have illustrated the specifics of the automatic scheduling method. The Raspberry Pi 4 is used to execute the diagram's orange blocks.

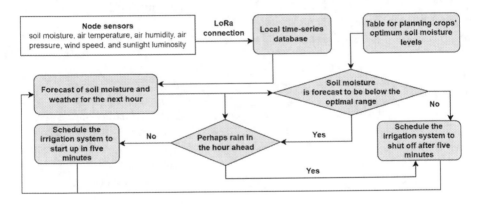

Fig. 4. Automatic irrigation scheduling diagram.

The irrigation schedule will be updated every five minutes based on the new forecast value of the weather condition and soil moisture level. When the previously scheduled time is reached, the Raspberry Pi 4 will send a corresponding control command to turn on or off the irrigation system via the LoRa connection. In addition, the end user can actively turn the irrigation system on or off via a Flutter application, shown inside the IoT reference model in Fig. 1. In case the forecasts give wrong results leading to incorrect scheduling, when the end user makes adjustments by actively turning the irrigation system on or off, the input data of the forecasts, the results of the forecasts, the scheduling results, and the control commands of the end users will be recorded and sent to the Backend server to serve the training process and improve the model.

5   End-to-End Encryption and Authentication

The intelligent irrigation method we proposed above is likely one of many other intelligent features built into contemporary smart agriculture systems that help boost efficiency and productivity in the production of agriculture. However, when implementing the system in practice, intelligent features are not enough for such an IoT system, it must be protected from spoofing attacks on sensor data, control commands, and eavesdropping data. In this section, an End-to-End encryption and authentication solution is proposed by us to apply to smart agriculture systems and can be extended to apply to other IoT systems. Our goal in our research is to deliver level 5 security in the age of quantum technology with 256 bits of safety and security. Our solution is designed to be applied synchronously on all devices of the system such as IoT devices (Arduino), Gateway (Raspberry Pi), Edge server, Cloud (Backend server), and Application.

IoT devices such as Arduino or Waspmote of Libelium, STM32 are embedded devices equipped with Micro Controller Unit (MCU) with RAM size from a few Kilobytes to several hundred Kilobytes, therefore we propose using HMAC hash with SHAKE-256 for authentication computations. There is no need to encrypt sensor data in our system because it is merely remote sensing information about the condition of the environment. However, to authenticate node sensors, we compute a digital signature and attach it to each sent data frame. Control command encryption makes little sense because they are frequently very brief and have a predetermined value, such as ON or OFF, thus we chose to add a digital signature to the control command frame as a means of authenticating its origin. The HMAC hash with SHAKE-256 is used to compute the attached digital signature in both of the sent frames stated. Authentication is necessary because our system uses LoRa waves to communicate at the edge layer. Control commands transmitted in the air environment with a radius of 3 km can be eavesdropped, and collected to perform command spoofing attacks to make the system work at the will of the attacker. The strategy of authenticating data frames exchanged between Edge Server and IoT devices is shown in Fig. 5.

Since our system was developed via the agent application approach, each tenant will have their own Edge server. Cloud not only provides data storage and backup features but also acts as an intermediary to maintain the tunnel between the edge server and the application. It is necessary to encrypt and authenticate all data transfers between the cloud, the edge server, and the application. In this case, we propose using CRYSTALS-Kyber as the encapsulation and key exchange algorithm, AES 256 bits for data encryption, and digital signature authentication using HMAC hash with SHAKE-256. We decided to use CRYSTALS-Kyber because it is a key encapsulation method (KEM) designed to be resistant to cryptanalytic attacks with future powerful quantum computers. The key exchange technique to encrypt and authenticate all data transfers between the edge server, the cloud, and the application is shown in Fig. 6.

Details of the symbols we use are shown in Table 1, the 256-byte Entropy Vector (EV) represents random values that were initially stored in the EEPROM memory of the IoT device and Edge server during system setup. The Entropy

Table 1. Symbols used in diagrams.

Symbols	Description
ID_u, ID_e, ID_c, ID_a	The identifier of IoT devices, Edge servers, Cloud, and Applications
EV_u	The 256-byte Entropy Vector
T_i	The 4-byte integer representing the time
p	The random padding
e, eu	The public entropy used to exchange a session key
K_{eu}	The shared session key between the Edge server and IoT device
SD	Data collected by sensors
CC	Control commands
tag, sig	The digital signatures
PK_c, SK_c	Cloud's public key and private key
PK_e, SK_e	Edge's public key and private key
PK_a, SK_a	Application's public key and private key
C_a	the ciphertext containing the shared session key encapsulated by the Application using Kyber
C_e	the ciphertext containing the shared session key encapsulated by the Edge server using Kyber
K_{ec}	The shared session key between the Edge server and Cloud
K_{ac}	The shared session key between the Application and Cloud
K_{ae}	The shared session key between the Application and the Edge server

Vector is random and is not the same between IoT devices so for these devices, the EV is secret and is used to compute the shared session key with the Edge server. The shared session keys are then used as input to the HMAC hash function to generate a digital signature attached to each data frame sent. T_i is a time variable used to handle data frame duplication and to generate different digital signatures for each transmission to thwart attempts to spoof sensor data and control commands.

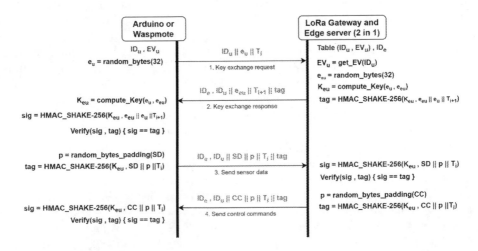

Fig. 5. Authentication strategy between the IoT device and Edge server.

In both Figs. 5 and 6 The black text denotes the node's processing tasks, the red text is the payload of the sent data frame, and the blue text is the data

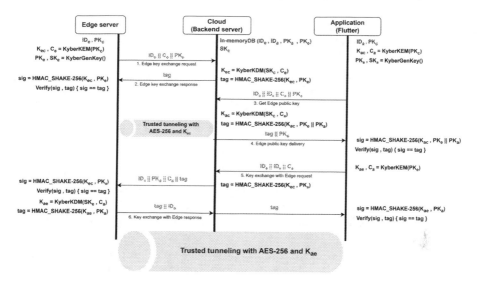

Fig. 6. Authentication and key exchange technique between Edge server, Cloud, and Application.

that has been pre-stored at the node. The following two functions are used to calculate the shared key and padding:

```
typedef unsigned char Byte

Byte* compute_Key(Byte* e, Byte* eu, Byte* EV) {
    Byte* pk = new Byte[64];
    for (int i = 0; i <= 32; i++) {
        pk[i] = EV[e[i]];    pk[i+32] = EV[eu[i]];
    }
    return SHAKE_256(pk);
}

Byte^ random_bytes_padding(Byte* data) {
    size_t length = length(data);
    if (length < 64) return random_bytes(64-length);
    return nullptr;
}
```

In addition to being utilized for end-to-end encryption of the data sent over the tunnel, K_{ec} and K_{ae} are employed to create digital signatures for end-to-end authentication. Every time a new session through the tunnel is formed, both of these keys are updated by using Kyber key encapsulation technique (Kyber KEM) with PK_e and PK_a.

We developed a C++ library using the CRYSTALS-Kyber official documentation [19] to implement the solution we proposed. The source code of the library we have developed can be accessed at this GitHub repository https://github. com/tangnguyendeveloper/KyberKEM_1024. In addition, we also utilized the Crypto library developed and optimized for microcontrollers like Arduino for the HMAC hash implementation with SHAKE-256, etc.

6   Experimental Results

The accuracy of the two Transformer models proposed in Sect. 4 will be evaluated along with the training outcomes in this section. Additionally, we demonstrate in this section the system's performance evaluation findings after implementing the end-to-end encryption and authentication technique we proposed in Sect. 5. Both of the early transformer models were built and trained by us with TensorFlow and then migrated to TensorFlow Lite for deployment on a Raspberry Pi 4 serving as an Edge server. The two proposed Transformer models are compared with two LSTM models that are similarly constructed to forecast soil moisture levels and weather conditions for the upcoming hour. For end-to-end encryption and authentication, we implement and evaluate the performance on devices such as Arduino uno R3, STM32F407VET6 ARM Cortex-M4, Raspberry Pi 4 Model B, Laptop (Ubuntu server 22.04 LTS), Xiaomi Redmi Note 7 (Android 10).

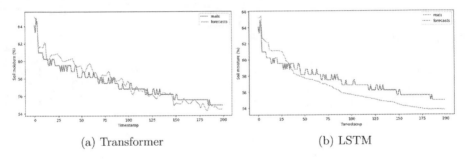

(a) Transformer   (b) LSTM

Fig. 7. Compare the outcomes of the transformer model and the LSTM model forecasting soil moisture levels.

The Transformer model used to forecast soil moisture level is trained and evaluated by us on the dataset provided by SMART FASAL. Thirty percent of the samples are used by us for the accuracy evaluation, and seventy percent of the samples are used for training. Figure 7 shows the difference between the forecasted soil moisture level value with that value in the practice when getting the outcome of the Transformer model and the LSTM. Additionally, Fig. 8 depicts the distribution of the difference between the predicted value and the actual value.

We use our scraping dataset for the training and evaluation of Transformer and LSTM models for the instance of the weather forecast. The data samples

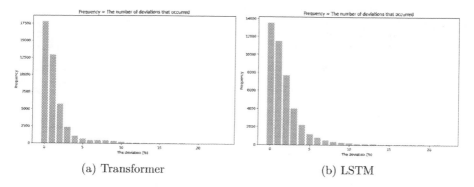

(a) Transformer   (b) LSTM

Fig. 8. Compare the frequency of the deviations for the Transformer model and LSTM model forecasts of soil moisture levels.

acquired in Rach Gia, Vietnam are utilized as the test set while the data samples collected in Can Tho and Ca Mau, Vietnam, are used in the training process. Figures 9 and 10 show the findings of a comparison of the accuracy and loss between the Transformer model and the LSTM model used for forecasting the weather conditions of the upcoming hour.

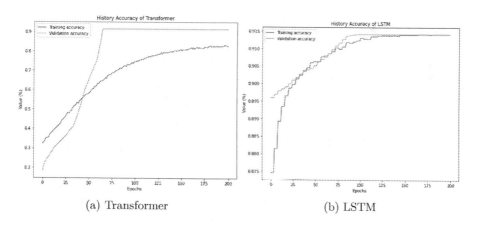

(a) Transformer   (b) LSTM

Fig. 9. Compare the accuracy of the Transformer model and the LSTM model forecasting the weather conditions.

The results of evaluating the accuracy and performance of Raspberry Pi 4 when performing soil moisture forecasting and weather forecasting are shown in Table 2.

The end-to-end encryption and authentication technique proposed in this research has been implemented and evaluated by us on real devices. We used the libraries mentioned in Sect. 5 to do that, the performance benchmarks on each device are shown in Table 3. RF UART Lora SX1278 433Mhz modules were

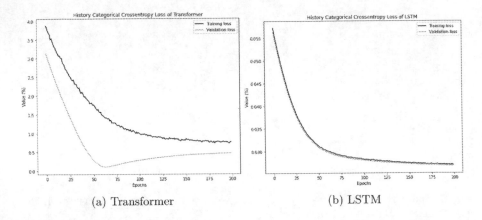

(a) Transformer   (b) LSTM

Fig. 10. Compare the Categorical Cross entropy loss of the Transformer model and the LSTM model forecasting the weather conditions.

Table 2. Summarizes the results of evaluating the accuracy and performance of soil moisture and weather forecasting models.

Model	Trainable params	epochs	Training accuracy	Testing accuracy	Performance on Raspberry Pi 4
Transformer soil moisture	30441	120	79.52%	82.06%	52 ms/sample
LSTM soil moisture	51265	120	80.17%	79.63%	108 ms/sample
Transformer weather	15306	200	82.06%	91.41%	34 ms/sample
LSTM weather	29954	200	91.41%	91.41%	71 ms/sample

Table 3. Performance benchmarks of end-to-end encryption and authentication.

	Arduino uno R3	STM32	Raspberry Pi4	Laptop	Redmi Note 7
RAM	2 KB	192 KB	8 GB	10 GB	4 GB
CPU speed	16 MHz	168 MHz	1.5 GHz	3.5 GHz	1.25 GHz
HMAC SHAKE-256	67.821 ms	7.483 ms	5.36 ns	0.627 ns	12.74 ns
Kyber1024 generate key	NaN	NaN	1.6 s	482 ms	2.217 s
Kyber1024 key encapsulation	NaN	NaN	2.235 s	739 ms	2.538 s
Kyber1024 key decapsulation	NaN	NaN	2.720 s	916 ms	3.11 s

used to implement LoRa connections for data transmission and receive in this research.

7   Conclusion and Future Work

In this research, two Transformer models were proposed to forecast soil moisture and weather conditions in the next hour to automatically schedule irrigation. The test results demonstrate that the Transformer model is able with the same accuracy of 91.41% on the weather forecast test set and 82.06% on the soil moisture forecast test set despite having 40.62% fewer training variables than the LSTM model. Not only that, an end-to-end encryption and authentication technique has also been proposed to help improve the security and reliability of the system, protecting it from sensor data spoofing, control command spoofing, and eavesdropping attacks. In addition, we have also successfully developed a C++ library to implement the encryption and authentication technique proposed in this study. In the future, we will carry out the implementation of the proposals in this research on a practical smart agricultural system, thereby evaluating the effectiveness of the proposed solutions.

Acknowledgement. This research is funded by the Faculty of Computer Networks and Communications, University of Information Technology, Vietnam National University Ho Chi Minh City, Vietnam.

References

1. Togneri, R., et al.: Soil moisture forecast for smart irrigation: the primetime for machine learning. Expert Syst. Appl. **207**, 117653 (2022)
2. Cordeiro, M.: Towards Smart Farming: Fog-enabled intelligent irrigation system using deep neural networks. Futur. Gener. Comput. Syst. **129**, 115–124 (2022)
3. Alibabaei, K., Gaspar, P.D., Assunção, E., Alirezazadeh, S., Lima, T.M.: Irrigation optimization with a deep reinforcement learning model: case study on a site in Portugal. Agric. Water Manag. **263**, 107480 (2022)
4. Vianny, D.M.M., John, A., Mohan, S.K., Sarlan, A., Ahmadian, A.: Water optimization technique for precision irrigation system using IoT and machine learning. Sustainable Energy Technol. Assess. **52**, 102307 (2022)
5. Nakkar, M., AlTawy, R., Youssef, A.: Lightweight broadcast authentication protocol for edge-based applications. IEEE Internet Things J. **7**(12), 11766–11777 (2020)
6. Lee, W.K., Hwang, S.O.: High throughput implementation of post-quantum key encapsulation and decapsulation on GPU for Internet of Things applications. IEEE Trans. Serv. Comput. **15**(6), 3275–3288 (2021)
7. Mayes, K.: Performance evaluation and optimisation for kyber on the MULTOS IoT trust-anchor. In: 2020 IEEE International Conference on Smart Internet of Things (SmartIoT), pp. 1–8. IEEE, August 2020
8. Qazi, S., Khawaja, B.A., Farooq, Q.U.: IoT-equipped and AI-enabled next generation smart agriculture: a critical review, current challenges and future trends. IEEE Access **10**, 21219–21235 (2022)
9. Vangala, A., Das, A.K., Chamola, V., Korotaev, V., Rodrigues, J.J.: Security in IoT-enabled smart agriculture: architecture, security solutions and challenges. Cluster Comput. **26**, 1–24 (2022)
10. Khashan, O.A., Khafajah, N.M.: Efficient hybrid centralized and blockchain-based authentication architecture for heterogeneous IoT systems. J. King Saud Univ.-Comput. Inf. Sci. **35**(2), 726–739 (2023)
11. Kumar, P., Bhushan, S., Kumar, M., Alazab, M.: Secure key management and mutual authentication protocol for wireless sensor network by linking edge devices using hybrid approach. Wirel. Pers. Commun., 1–23 (2023)
12. Nakkar, M., AlTawy, R., Youssef, A.: GASE: a lightweight group authentication scheme with key agreement for edge computing applications. IEEE Internet Things J. **10**(1), 840–854 (2022)
13. Zeng, A., Chen, M., Zhang, L., Xu, Q.: Are transformers effective for time series forecasting? arXiv preprint arXiv:2205.13504 (2022)

14. Woo, G., Liu, C., Sahoo, D., Kumar, A., Hoi, S.: ETSformer: exponential smoothing transformers for time-series forecasting. arXiv preprint arXiv:2202.01381 (2022)
15. Wen, Q., et al.: Transformers in time series: a survey. arXiv preprint arXiv:2202.07125 (2022)
16. Zhou, H., et al.: Informer: beyond efficient transformer for long sequence time-series forecasting. In: Proceedings of the AAAI Conference on Artificial Intelligence, vol. 35, no. 12, pp. 11106–11115, May 2021
17. Wu, N., Green, B., Ben, X., O'Banion, S.: Deep transformer models for time series forecasting: The influenza prevalence case. arXiv preprint arXiv:2001.08317 (2020)
18. Vaswani, A., et al.: Attention is all you need. In: Advances in Neural Information Processing Systems, vol. 30 (2017)
19. Avanzi, R., et al.: CRYSTALS-Kyber algorithm specifications and supporting documentation. NIST PQC Round **2**(4), 1–43 (2019)

Integrated Intelligent Agent for SNMP-Based Network Management System

Dung Ong Mau[✉]

Industrial University of Ho Chi Minh City, Faculty of Electronics Technology,
Ho Chi Minh City, Vietnam
ongmaudung@iuh.edu.vn

Abstract. This paper proposes intelligent Simple Network Management Protocol (i-SNMP) agents, which add intelligent functions to the network routers, help routers know the most updated status of the whole network, and efficiently improve the performance as well as the stability of network devices. i-SNMP agents are able to monitor the network nodes, collect real-time network data, and communicate with the SNMP manager in the community. The SNMP manager can also diagnose and analyze the collected operational data and identify network anomalies. Then, proper actions can be taken to correct the network faults. OPNET Modeler is used in our research as the simulated network environment. By using OPNET Modeler, we describe the design and implementation of i-SNMP agents for managing the network and detecting network faults successfully.

Keywords: Network Management System · Simple Network Management Protocol · OPNET Modeler

1 Introduction

As the network becomes more complex, maintaining fast and reliable network communication becomes an important task for network management. Identifying network failures for effective network management is very important to ensure real-time performance. Routers play an important role in network management since they make decisions about which of several possible network paths data should follow, whether routers can arrive at the right decision will have a great impact on the network's performance [1]. But most of the routers on the market haven't sophisticated diagnosis abilities that can lead them to arrive at intelligent decisions, even for those intelligent routers. Routers are limited to global information about the network environment, only getting information from surrounding routers. One of the reasons is that as the router travels further into a geographic area, more data must be processed and analyzed, causing the router's speed to slow [2,3].

© ICST Institute for Computer Sciences, Social Informatics and Telecommunications Engineering 2023
Published by Springer Nature Switzerland AG 2023. All Rights Reserved
N.-S. Vo and H.-A. Tran (Eds.): INISCOM 2023, LNICST 531, pp. 19–33, 2023.
https://doi.org/10.1007/978-3-031-47359-3_2

There have been several discussions and implementations of intelligent agents. They pointed out that intelligent agents hold the most promise in bringing maverick equipment from outside organizations into the network-monitoring fold. There are various intelligent agent implementations, and most of the existing approaches emphasize the management of the network. These approaches could not solve the problem those routers have a limited view of the entire network environment [4–6]. Our goal is to get a global picture that can help the routers make more intelligent decisions about how to direct network traffic and at the same time avoid slowing down the speed of the router.

For this reason, we decided to build an intelligent agent, which sits beside the router and collects information from geographically dispersed servers using Simple Network Management Protocol (SNMP) application. It also should be able to analysis the information collected and provide the analysis result of the current status for network component to the router so that the router can make more intelligent decisions. We choose to use the SNMP application because SNMP is a widely used network management protocol. Another reason is that the connection-less communication feature and simple frame structure of SNMP have greatly promoted its applications. The two main components of SNMP (agents and manager) have independent operating mechanisms. Even though agents may fail and stop working, manager can continue to work normally.

In order to design and implement our proposed i-SNMP, an Ethernet LAN environment is created in OPNET Modeler [7,8]. Various kinds of traffic are implemented, and network fault scenarios are simulated. The i-SNMP agent is implemented on each router based on the SNMPv2 architecture. The SNMP manager is created to poll each agent and receive network data through SNMP packets. Data are processed, and analysis is done on the SNMP manager to detect network faults. The OPNET simulation results show that the i-SNMP agent is able to monitor the status of routers, identify network abnormalities such as heavy congestion and transient errors that are difficult to detect by network devices alone, and improve the performance of routers. The i-SNMP agent can be implemented on other network nodes, such as switches or servers. Because of the distributed agent architecture, the i-SNMP agent is able to monitor and manage networks at both small and large scales.

The remaining paper divides into the following primary sections: Sect. 2 highlights our proposed i-SNMP architecture. Section 3 describes the network system in OPNET Modeler in detail. Section 4 describes scenario simulations and results. Finally, the paper concludes in Sect. 5.

2   i-SNMP Architecture

The two key components in the project are the i-SNMP agent and SNMP agent manager. i-SNMP agents are responsible for monitoring the network nodes, collecting real-time network data, and communicating with the intelligent agent (SNMP manager) in the same community. SNMP manager receives information from the agents, analyzes the collected operational data, diagnoses the network fault, and reports the status of the network components [9].

2.1 Client and Server Architecture

The SNMP application is developed in a client/server architecture to implement SNMP version 2 and for network management. The SNMP application is based on the generic application model of OPNET Modeler, which models the detailed behaviors of the SNMP application [10,11].

The client and the server are the two major roles in the application architecture. In this paper, the agent manager is a workstation, which is running the SNMP application as a client, and the intelligent router is a network router, which is running the SNMP application as a server.

2.2 SNMP Message Exchange Architecture

The agent manager and the intelligent routers have different functions for network communication and data analysis. The agent manager is able to send *getRequest* packets to the router, receive *getResponse* packets, store the information in its database, analyze the information, and detect network faults. Similarly, the intelligent router is able to receive *getRequest* packets from the agent manager and send *getResponse* packets with its current information.

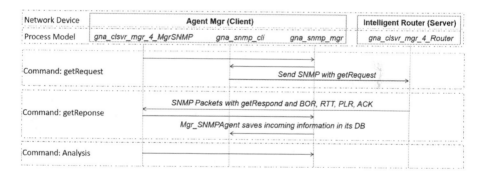

Fig. 1. Three scenarios of the SNMP application.

In order to illustrate the SNMP application for network management, we divided it into three scenarios. They are the *getRequest* scenario, the *getResponse* scenario, and the analysis scenario. Figure 1 illustrates these three scenarios for the SNMP application for network management. In the *getRequest* scenario, the agent manager sends *getRequest* packets to the intelligent routers to request their current status. In the *getResponse* scenario, the intelligent routers send the *getResponse* packets to the agent manager with their real-time status, such as Buffer Occupancy Rate (BOR), Round-Trip Time (RTT), Packet Loss Rate (PLR), and Acknowledgement (ACK). The agent manager receives *getResponse* packets and saves the information to its database. In the Analysis scenario, the agent manager analyzes the operational data of intelligent routers in time series and detects the three kinds of network faults: congestion, equipment failure, and transient error.

To achieve these three scenarios of the SNMP application, four process models were created. The process models of *gna-clsvr-mgr4-MgrSNMP*, *gna-snmp-mgr*, and *gna-snmp-cli* are developed for the agent manager, and *gna-clsvr-mgr4-Router* is implemented for the intelligent router. The agent manager invokes three different process models to complete three scenarios, and the intelligent router invokes one process model to respond to the requests from the agent manager.

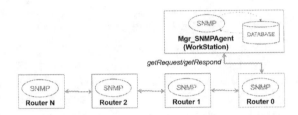

Fig. 2. SNMP message exchange mechanism and architecture.

Figure 2 illustrates the SNMP message exchange mechanism. The agent manager and the intelligent routers are running the SNMP application. They exchange SNMP messages by sending and receiving packets. The agent manager maintains a database for all the collected information from the intelligent agents.

This SNMP application is integrated into the network routers of OPNET Modeler to implement SNMP for network management. By adding these process models into the process architecture of routers, the routers can support SNMP. By running the SNMP applications on the agent manager and the intelligent routers, the agent manager can easily monitor the distributed intelligent routers, which are located in different subnets. And by analyzing the current information from intelligent routers, the agent manager can immediately detect four network faults. The network administrator and other applications can acquire the status of network routers in real time.

3   Network System in OPNET Modeler

3.1   SNMP Agent Implementation

We created a new process model supported by *gna-clsvr-mgr4-Router* that was based on the application model of OPNET Modeler to support SNMP. This process model is able to process both the regular packets and the *getRequest* and *getResponse* packets. By embedding SNMP messages inside the Generic Network Application (GNA) packet, it can also exchange SNMP messages between the client and server at the application layer by sending GNA packets.

Version	Community	PDUType	ReqestID	ErrStatus	ErrID	objectValue
BOR	RTT	PLR	ACK			

Fig. 3. SNMP message exchange mechanism and architecture.

The SNMP message format was created for exchanging messages between the agent manager and the intelligent routers. The SNMP *getRequest* and *getResponse* messages, embedded in the GNA packet, can be exchanged between the agent manager and the intelligent routers. Figure 3 shows the design of the SNMP message format. There are 11 columns in the message format, and they support SNMP version 2. The agent manager can exchange information with the intelligent routers using the SNMP message format.

The clients and server in this application use the GNA packet format to exchange messages at the application layer of OPNET Modeler. In order to exchange SNMP message information, the SNMP message was embedded in the data field of the GNA messages, which are supported in the OPNET Modeler. Figure 4 shows the SNMP message embedded in the GNA packet of OPNET Modeler.

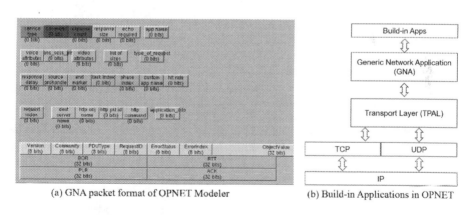

(a) GNA packet format of OPNET Modeler   (b) Build-in Applications in OPNET

Fig. 4. GNA packet format of OPNET Modeler.

The *gna-clsvr-mgr4-Router* is depicted in Fig. 5(a). This process model parses *getRequest* packets in the Arrival process and sends *getResponse* packets to the agent manager by invoking the *gna-clsvr-mgr-getRespond-packet-send* function. The write-stat process is used to record the current operational data of a router. In order to support the SNMP application for a router, this SNMP-Application process model was added to the process model architecture of a router and connected to the Transport Layer (TPAL) process model with two stream wires. As shown in Fig. 5(b), four statistic wires were created to collect the operational data of a router, such as BOR, RTT, PLR, and ACK.

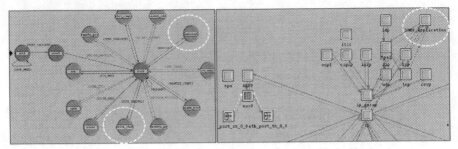

(a) Process model of *gna_clsvr_mgr_4_Router*   (b) Model of the intelligent router

Fig. 5. Process and model for i-SNMP integrated in the Router.

3.2   SNMP Agent Manager Implementation

In this session, three new process models were created: *gna-clsvr-mgr4-MgrSNMP*, *gna-snmp-mgr*, and *gna-snmp-cli* for the agent manager to support the SNMP application. These three process models deal with sending and receiving regular packets as well as SNMP *getRequest* and *getResponse* packets between a client and server at the application layer, saving information on intelligent routers, and analyzing the real-time status of the intelligent routers. The *gna-clsvr-mgr4-MgrSNMP* is depicted in Fig. 6(a). This process model of the agent manager is used for processing the GNA packets at the application layer. This process model is modified to support the SNMP application based on the process model *gna-clsvr-mgr* of OPNET Modeler. Figure 6(b) shows the complete design of the *gna-snmp-mgr* process model. This process model has four functions: send, receive, analysis, and end.

- In the send and receive functions, the sub-process *gna-snmp-cli* is invoked to send *getRequest* packets and receive *getResponse* packets every 10 s.
- The analysis function retrieves collected data from its database every 30 s, analyzes the current status of intelligent routers, and detects the three network faults of intelligent routers.
- The end function closes the session between the client and server after it receives a packet with a close command. The design of the *gna-snmp-cli* process model is shown in Fig. 6(c).

This process model has three functions: open, send, and closed. It helps the process model of *gna-snmp-mgr* carry out the task of sending and receiving packets.

- The open function sends *getRequest* packets to the intelligent routers.
- The send function is invoked to receive the *getResponse* packets from the intelligent routers and save the information to the database of the agent manager.
- At last, the closed function closes the session between the client and server after it receives a packet that contains a close command.

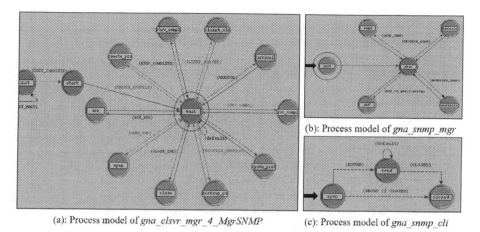

(a): Process model of *gna_clsvr_mgr_4_MgrSNMP*   (c): Process model of *gna_snmp_cli*

(b): Process model of *gna_snmp_mgr*

Fig. 6. Process model of SNMP Agent Manager.

Figure 7 illustrates the database table of the agent manager. There are nine columns that keep the information of intelligent routers, such as "Version", "Community", "PDUType", "RequestID", "TimeStamp", "BOR", "RTT", "PLR" and "ACK". The agent manager retrieves the information from its database, analyzes the real-time status of the intelligent routers, and detects the four network faults of the intelligent routers.

Version	Community	PDUType	ReqestID	TimeStamp	BOR	RTT	PLR	ACK

Fig. 7. Database table of the agent manager.

The network environment setup focuses on showing the ability of the agent manager to monitor the status of a group of distributed intelligent routers by using SNMP. In this paper, the network topology was designed to be a single network community with three subnets. Three intelligent routers connect three subnets using 10Mbps Ethernet connections. Figure 8 illustrates that three intelligent routers are distributed in three different subnets. In Subnet-0, the agent manager monitors the three intelligent routers and maintains a database that keeps the information collected from all three intelligent routers.

In order to simulate the regular network traffic, an application server and an HTTP server were set up to provide the network clients with applications such as HTTP and databases. The network node "Application Configuration" of OPNET Modeler is used for configuring the applications on the server side, and "Profile Configuration" is used for configuring the profiles on the client side.

The network topology is depicted in Fig. 9(a). There are three distributed subnets and three configuration nodes. Subnet0's topology is depicted in Fig. 9(b). There are five network devices in this subnet. The agent manager

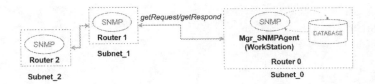

Fig. 8. Distributed network routers and agent manager.

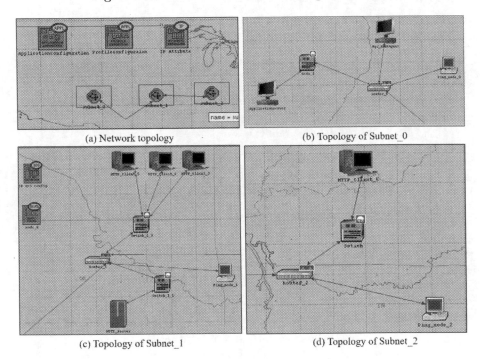

is located in this subnet. Subnet1's topology is depicted in Fig. 9(c). There are eight network devices and two network configuration nodes in this subnet. The simulation of network faults is configured by the "IP QoS Config" and the "Traffic Config". Subnet2's topology is depicted in Fig. 9(d). There are four network devices in this subnet.

4   Scenario Simulations and Results

In this session, four scenarios are simulated to test and demonstrate the SNMP intelligent agent's ability to detect network faults. The SNMP agent manager sends out requests to get information from network nodes and gets back SNMP messages that contain the data. The data are then written to the database, which is a generic data file. An Analysis process is added to perform the analysis task.

The analysis process analyzes the collection of data for RTT, acknowledge, BOR, and PLR; diagnoses the status of the router; sets the router information; writes the router information to the database; and returns a pointer to the router information with the router's most current status.

The router information can be used by other applications that need to know the current status of network nodes. To discover the status of the router, the analysis process first compares the data with the lower limits to see if there is any sign of a problem. If PLR, BOR, and RTT are smaller than the lower limit, there is no sign that a problem occurred. If any of these are above the limit, the analysis process would look at the slope of the ten most recent records and calculate the slope of the regression line, with the horizontal data being the time stamp of the SNMP message and the vertical data being the data, such as BOR. If the slope of the regression line is less than the threshold of slope, the analysis process would consider that a normal condition. Otherwise, further investigation is needed to determine if there is a network fault. We will discuss the different patterns that appear on the operational data when network faults occur in the following.

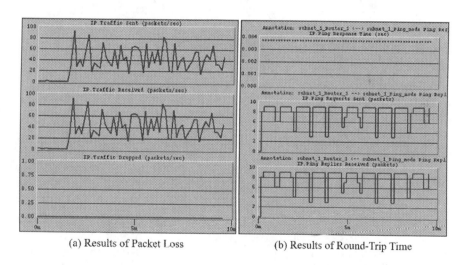

(a) Results of Packet Loss   (b) Results of Round-Trip Time

Fig. 10. Packet Loss and RTT results for Normal Traffic.

4.1   Scenario1: Regular Traffic

Scenario Description: In subnet-1, a few HTTP-client nodes are added. A ping-node is added and connected to Router-1. HTTP-client workstations that run the HTTP (heavy) profile, which accesses the HTTP server in the same network as HTTP client/server applications, are analogous to how workstations and servers run applications in real life. Between Router-1 and Ping-node, the

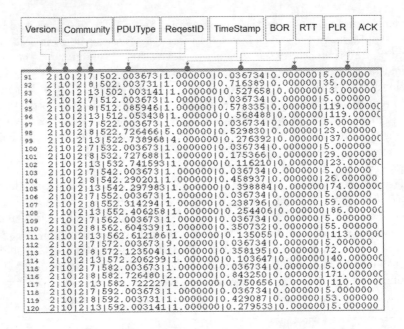

Fig. 11. Node Information for Normal Traffic.

PING pattern uses *PacketSize* 1024. This pattern will not cause network congestion because of its small packet size and long timeout. Inter-repetition time is set to 7.0 s, meaning a PING packet is sent out every 7 s. The maximum repetition count is unlimited, meaning PING traffic will last as long as the simulation runs. Subnet-2 is similarly configured. The HTTP clients in Subnet-2 access the HTTP server in Subnet-1, and PING traffic in Router-2 is set up the same way as in Router-1.

Scenario Results: As shown in Fig. 10(a), the simulation result indicates that IP traffic on Router-1 is stable and does not vary dramatically. Packet loss on Router-1 is zero. There is no congestion; all IP packets are delivered, and replies are received. In Fig. 10(b), this result showed that the PING response time, which is the RTT, is constant. It was also noted that the PING requests sent, and PING replies received were almost identical, which meant the traffic was normal and no congestion occurred. For this reason, there is no increase in the buffer occupancy of the FIFO queue.

Analysis Result: In the database of the SNMP agent manager, as shown in Fig. 11, the BOR is less than 10, the RTT is less than 1, the PLR is 0, and the ACK is mostly constant. The analysis showed that all three routers are in normal condition.

4.2   Scenario2: Highly Congestion

Scenario Description: HTTP clients and the server still run the same traffic as in a regular traffic scenario, but the setting for PING traffic on Router-1 is different. In the first six minutes (360 s), it runs the same light PING traffic as in regular traffic. It runs heavy PING traffic after 360 s. The very-big-packet-size PING pattern is used. The packet size in this pattern is very large (10000), and the timeout is only 2.0 s. With large packets like this, it's very likely to cause congestion in the network. The processing speed of the router on the interface, which generates and receives the PING traffic, is also slowed down to exaggerate the congestion. Running regular traffic in the first six minutes gives a comparison between regular traffic and congestion traffic.

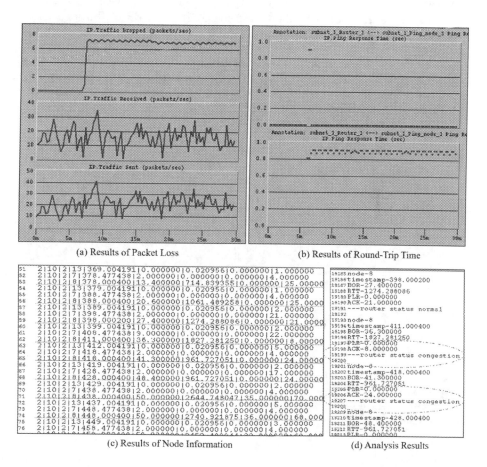

(a) Results of Packet Loss   (b) Results of Round-Trip Time

(c) Results of Node Information   (d) Analysis Results

Fig. 12. PLR and RTT results for highly congestion traffic.

Scenario Results: Fig. 12(a) shows that after six minutes (360 s), the IP traffic dropped, which is the packet lost, increases dramatically. Because the processing speed cannot match the speed at which packets are linked to this interface, the BOR increases from 360 s. Packets have to remain in queue for a longer time. Those packets with short timeout limits will be lost. As a result, the RTT after 6 min has increased significantly, as illustrated in Fig. 12(b).

Analysis Result: In this scenario, the slopes of PLR, BOR, and RTT are bigger than the thresholds, and ACK is constant or decreasing. The analysis process determines that there is traffic congestion. In another case, if PLR, BOR, and RTT are bigger than the upper limits, it's identified as a congestion condition because the slope at a certain point will flatten and will not increase significantly anymore. Figures 12(c) and (b) show that the BOR and PLR of Router-1 (node ID: 8) are increasing, indicating traffic congestion, based on node information.

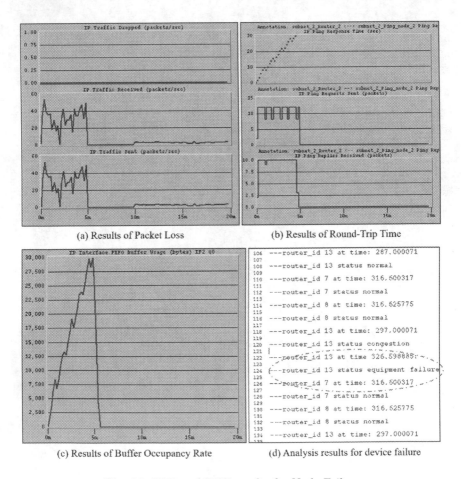

(a) Results of Packet Loss   (b) Results of Round-Trip Time

(c) Results of Buffer Occupancy Rate   (d) Analysis results for device failure

Fig. 13. PLR and RTT results for Node Failure.

4.3   Scenario3: Node Failure

Scenario Description: The device node failure scenario is set up in the following way: on Router-2, node failure is simulated in subnet-2. Subnet2's traffic setup is the same as that in Scenario 1. To configure a node failure, a Failure/Recovery config node is added. The attribute is specified in the node failure and recovery specification. A node failure and recovery have to be entered in pairs. It specifies the start time of failure and the start time of recovery for a particular node. The time interval in between is the duration of the failure. In this scenario, Subnet-2 and Router-2 will fail for five minutes, which is from 300 s to 600 s.

Scenario Results: As shown in Fig. 13(a), the result indicates that IP traffic sent and received drop to zero after five minutes in this simulation; packet loss drops to zero because the device is down and then comes up a little after the 5 min down time. As shown in Fig. 13(b), the RTT increases in the first five minutes. Because Router-2 is down, the RTT drops to zero after five minutes. The BOR increases in the first five minutes, as shown in Figs. 13(c) and (d). Then, it drops to zero after five minutes because this device is down. According to the analysis results, Router-2 (node ID 13) has a device failure after five minutes.

4.4   Scenario4: Transient Error

Scenario Description: A timestamp is set up for the start point of any error that occurs. If the problem persists longer than the time frame for a transient error, it is identified as a persistent error. Otherwise, it is identified as a transient error. Subnet-1 simulates a link failure for the link Ping-node-1 and Router-1. Traffic is configured the same as in Scenario Regular Traffic. In order to simulate link failure, a Failure/Recovery Config node is added. Failure and recovery are added in pairs. The time when failure occurs at the link is specified as 360 s. The time when the link will be recovered is specified as 380 s. The duration of the failure will be 20 s. From 360 s to 380 s, the link between Ping-node-1 and Router-1 in subnet-2 fails.

Scenario Results: As shown in Fig. 14, the RTT is high only for a short period of time after six minutes when the link is broken. And the analysis result identifies the transient error at Router-1 (the node ID is 8) after six minutes.

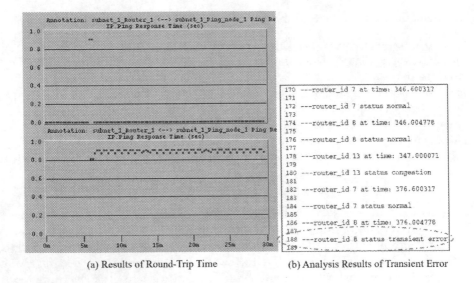

(a) Results of Round-Trip Time   (b) Analysis Results of Transient Error

Fig. 14. RTT and analysis results for Transient Error.

5   Conclusions

Various traffic combinations can be configured in OPNET Modeler to simulate different scenarios in the network environment. Results show that our proposed i-SNMP agent and the SNMP agent manager are able to collect these simulation statistics, perform analysis, and pinpoint the network faults. The SNMP process is implemented in a way that is easy to configure, automatically starts, and requires little maintenance. It can be added to all kinds of network nodes that support TCP/IP and client/server application processes. Both the SNMP agent and SNMP manager processes can be easily implemented and configured in future research.

References

1. Cisco, Network Management System: Best Practices White Paper, Technology White Paper, August 2018
2. Roquero, P., Aracil, J.: On performance and scalability of cost-effective SNMP managers for large-scale polling. IEEE Access **9**, 7374–7383 (2021)
3. Pallmann, D.: Network query language (NQL). Wiley, New York (2002)
4. Safrianti, E., Sari, L.O., Sari, N.A.: Real-time network device monitoring system with simple network management protocol (SNMP) Model. In: 2021 3rd International Conference on Research and Academic Community Services (ICRACOS), IEEE (2021)
5. Helali, S.: Monitoring systems and networks. In: Systems and Network Infrastructure Integration: Design, Implementation, Safety and Supervision, Wiley, pp. 157–171 (2020)

6. Aweya, J.: Designing Switch/Routers: Architectures and Applications. CRC Press, Boca Raton (2022)
7. OPNET Technologies Inc, Opnet Modeler. http://www.opnet.com
8. Smera, C., Sandeep, J.: Networks Simulation: research based implementation using tools and approaches. In: 2022 IEEE 3rd Global Conference for Advancement in Technology (GCAT). Bangalore, India, pp. 1–7 (2022)
9. Yang, B.: Research on simulation system of information management construction based on computer internet technology. In: Proceedings of the 7th International Conference on Cyber Security and Information Engineering (2022)
10. Chen, M., Miao, Y., Humar, I.: OPNET IoT Simulation. Springer, Singapore (2019). https://doi.org/10.1007/978-981-32-9170-6
11. Chen, M.: OPNET Network Simulation, Press of Tsinghua University, ISBN 7-302-08232-4 (2004)

Genetic Algorithms for Storage- and Energy-Aware Caching and Trajectory Optimisation Problem in UAV-Assisted Content Delivery Networks

Thuong C. Lam[1], Nguyen-Son Vo[2(✉)], Thanh-Hieu Nguyen[3],
Thanh-Minh Phan[4], and De-Thu Huynh[5]

[1] HUTECH University, Ho Chi Minh City, Vietnam
lc.thuong@hutech.edu.vn
[2] Institute of Fundamental and Applied Sciences, Duy Tan University,
Ho Chi Minh City, Vietnam
vonguyenson@duytan.edu.vn
[3] Ho Chi Minh City University of Transport, Ho Chi Minh City, Vietnam
thanhhieu.nguyen@ut.edu.vn
[4] Vietnam Aviation Academy, Ho Chi Minh City, Vietnam
minhpt@vaa.edu.vn
[5] The Saigon International University, Ho Chi Minh City, Vietnam
huynhdethu@siu.edu.vn

Abstract. Trajectory and caching optimisation design is a promising joint solution for enhancing the quality of services in unmanned aerial vehicle (UAV) assisted content delivery networks (CDNs). In this paper, we review the problem of which contents to cache in the UAV and which trajectory to fly, i.e., where to stop and how to gain the shortest path over the stops, under the constraints of caching storage and energy resources, namely storage- and energy-aware caching and trajectory optimisation (SECTO) problem. The SECTO problem in UAV-assisted CDNs is formulated and solved by applying genetic algorithms (GAs) to maximise the content delivery capacity while minimising the flying distance. The simulation results are shown to demonstrate the benefits of GAs in terms of accuracy and time complexity performance compared to other conventional solutions such as exhausted and greedy search algorithms.

Keywords: Content delivery network · Genetic algorithm · travelling salesman problem · UAV caching · UAV trajectory

1 Introduction

One of the most important missions of 6 G networks is to take the non-terrestrial networks (NTNs) into account [1]. The NTNs enable a flying platform of satellites and unmanned aerial vehicles (UAVs) to connect more things in every remote

N.-S. Vo and H.-A. Tran (Eds.): INISCOM 2023, LNICST 531, pp. 34–50, 2023.
https://doi.org/10.1007/978-3-031-47359-3_3

corner on the earth. And thus, the physical, cyber, and biological worlds can further flourish in the era of 6G thanks to the present of flexible access points, relays, contents, helps, and many advanced applications and services (AASs) from the sky [2–6]. In this scenario, the models, techniques, and AASs of UAV caching and trajectory in content delivery networks (CDNs) have drawn a numerous studies from both industrial and academic sectors [7]. These studies demonstrate that UAV caching networks are able to partially alternate the CDNs so as to not only mitigate the workload of the terrestrial stations but also provide the end users (EUs) with better AASs by exploiting shorter and line-of-sight (LoS) transmission.

In UAV caching networks, the UAVs have to select a set of contents to cache in advance. It then flies to deliver the contents to the EUs in the error-prone areas in which, for example, the workload of the terrestrial stations is extremely high, the wireless links are not good due to high and dense obstacles, and the emergency communications are required for rescue operations and safety public activities. To serve the EUs the highest quality of service (QoS) while utilising the resources of UAVs, the optimal set of contents and the optimal trajectory must be found simultaneously. This so-called resource-aware caching and trajectory optimisation problem in UAV-assisted CDNs has been studied in the literature by different approaches from objective functions, constraints, to algorithms and solutions [8–12].

Particularly, the work in [8] proposed a storage- and energy-aware caching and trajectory optimisation (SECTO) problem to maximise the content delivery capacity while minimising the flight distance under the caching storage and energy consumption constraints. The SECTO is solved by using exhausted and greedy search algorithms. In [9], the authors tried to minimise only the delay under the constraint of caching storage by solving a tractable semi-definite programming problem reformulated from an original intractable distributionally robust stochastic optimization problem. Besides caching in the UAVs, the authors in [10] considered caching in the EUs to establish a cache-enabling UAV-device-to-device (UAV-D2D) network. A joint caching placement in UAV-D2D network and UAV trajectory optimization (CTO) problem under the constraint of caching storage is formulated for maximising the cache utility. The CTO problem, which is a mixed integer nonlinear programming problem, is decomposed into three sub-problems for being solved by a low complexity iterative algorithm. Interestingly, reinforcement learning approach is applied to minimise the sum content acquisition delay of EUs by jointly optimising the multiple EUs' association, cache placement, UAV trajectory, and transmission power [11,12].

We can see that the aforementioned optimisation solutions are for whether multiple objective functions of very high time complexity but exact results [8] or single objective function of lower time complexity with approximate results by reformulating and decomposing the original problems into solvable sub-problems [9–12]. However, these solutions are not flexible in terms of balancing the trade-off between accuracy and time complexity in accordance with the

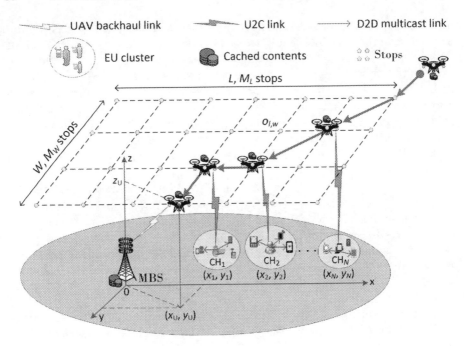

Fig. 1. UAV-assisted content delivery networks [8].

diverse requirements of AASs, especially in solving the complicated SECTO problem with multiple objective functions studied in [8].

In this paper, the typical SECTO problem is studied and then efficiently solved by applying genetic algorithms (GAs). The benefit of GAs is that they can capture the evolutionary principles of natural selection and genetic variation to find the exactly or approximately global optimal results without considering the fact that if the search space is unimodal or multimodal. To make the GAs more feasible to solve the SECTO problem with respect to two types of variables, i.e., 1) binary variables for caching decision and stop index and 2) integer variables for trajectory, we divide each original chromosome into two sub-chromosomes. The left sub-chromosome and the right sub-chromosome represent the binary variables and the integer variables, respectively. Each sub-chromosome is applied it own crossover and mutation operations with different probabilities. The performance of GAs is investigated in terms of flexible implementation, accuracy, and time complexity compared to other conventional exhausted and greedy search algorithms.

The rest of this paper is organised as follows. We introduce the UAV-assisted CDNs and describe how it works in Sect. 2. In Sect. 3, we review the SECTO problem formulations studied in [8] for the ease of following the GAs solution. Section 4 presents the GAs solution for SECTO optimisation problem. The GAs and system performance metrics are investigated in Sect. 5. Finally, Sect. 6 is dedicated to concluding the paper.

2 UAV-Assisted Content Delivery Networks

In this paper, we consider the model of UAV-assisted CDNs as shown in Fig. 1 [8]. The model consists of one MBS, one UAV, I contents, and N EU clusters. The clusters are established by applying the device-to-device (D2D) clustering scheme [13]. In each cluster, the EUs, who are interested in the same content, are represented by a cluster head (CH). The CHs, which are in charge of forwarding the contents to their EU members, are selected based on their powerful capacity of computing, storage, and energy. The MBS is able to acknowledge all the information of UEs for clustering, then formulating and solving the SECTO optimisation problem. After solving the SECTO optimisation, the UAV realises 1) the optimal set of contents for caching and 2) the optimal trajectory, i.e., optimal set of stops and optimal stop sequence, for flying and delivering. As a result, the content delivery capacity is maximised, meanwhile the flight distance is minimised. In addition, we further consider the constraints of storage and energy resources of the UAV to make the SECTO solution more efficient.

To fly, we assume that the UAV is placed at the horizontal coordinate of $o_U = (x_U, y_U)$ while the vertical coordinate is fixed at $z_U = h_U$. We then limit the flight area by defining a smallest rectangular, a length of L (m), and a width of W (m) that covers all the CHs. The rectangular is divided into a grid topology of $M_L \times M_W$ stops as shown in Fig. 1. The horizontal coordinates of the UAV's stops are $o_U = o_{l,w} = (x_l, y_w), l = 1, 2, ..., M_L, w = 1, 2, ..., M_W$. Furthermore, we define a $F_{M_L \times M_W}$ binary matrix in which each pair of row and column is represented by a binary stop index $f(o_{l,w})$. The UAV stops at $o_{w,l}$ if $f(o_{l,w}) = 1$, otherwise $f(o_{l,w}) = 0$. So, given N_T stops, we can find a proper stop sequence T for the UAV to fly throughout with minimum distance.

3 SECTO Problem Formulations

In this section, we review the system formulations studied in [8] for the ease of following. Based on these formulations, we then introduce the SECTO optimisation problem that can be solved by using GAs.

3.1 Content Popularity

It is certain that each content has its own access rate depending on the EUs' behavior, and thus a given set of I contents follows a popularity pattern. In this paper, we assume that the popularity pattern is modeled by Zipf-like distribution [14]. In this distribution, the content i is ranked in accordance with its popularity expressed as

$$p_i = \frac{i^{-\alpha}}{\sum_{i=1}^{I} i^{-\alpha}},\tag{1}$$

where α is the coefficient reflecting the skewness of the content popularity preference, i.e., $\alpha = 0$ means that there is no popularity skewness among different contents, while the higher value of α makes the first contents much higher popularity than the last ones.

3.2   Caching, Requesting, and UAV-Cluster Association Index

Due to the storage limit, the UAV is capable of caching a proper number of contents which are frequently requested by the EUs in different clusters. So, the UAV has to decide which contents to be cached before flying to deliver. We define a binary variable c_i for cache decision in which $c_i = 1$ indicates that the content i is cached, otherwise $c_i = 0$. Meanwhile, the number of clusters requesting the content i, which is directly proportional to the popularity p_i is given by

$$N_i = \lceil p_i N \rfloor, \tag{2}$$

where the operator $\lceil . \rfloor$ is used to round an arbitrary value the nearest integer.

However, this way may cause $\sum_{i=1}^{I} N_i \neq N$ due to the round operator. To make the equality held, without loss of generality, we do the following adjustment

- If $\sum_{i=1}^{I} N_i < N$, then the first smallest value in the array $\{N_i, i = 1, 2, ..., I\}$ is increased by 1.
- If $\sum_{i=1}^{I} N_i > N$, then the last highest value in the array $\{N_i, i = 1, 2, ..., I\}$ is decreased by 1.

To obtain the UAV-cluster association index, let $r_{i,n}$ be the requesting index to indicate that $r_{i,n} = 1$ if there is at least one EU in the cluster n requesting the content i ($r_{i,n} = 1$), otherwise $r_{i,n} = 0$. Obviously, we have

$$N_i = \sum_{n=1}^{N} r_{i,n}, \tag{3}$$

and

$$N = \sum_{n=1}^{N} \sum_{i=1}^{I} r_{i,n}. \tag{4}$$

So far, we define the UAV-cluster association index as below

$$a_{i,n} = c_i r_{i,n}. \tag{5}$$

The UAV-cluster association index $a_{i,n} \in \{0, 1\}$ is used to match the content i cached in the UAV and the cluster n. This association index enables us to establish the transmission channel, and thus derive the delivering capacity between the UAV and the cluster n presented in the following subsections.

3.3   Content Delivery Capacity

Following the UAV-cluster association, we further compute the average delivery capacity which is obtained based on the wireless channel model from the UAV to the CHs in different clusters. The UAV utilises the licensed frequency band for backhaul link, while stipulating the unlicensed Industrial, Scientific, Medical

(ISM) WiFi band, i.e.,2.4 GHz with 802.11 b/g/n devices and 5 GHz with 802.11 a/n/ac devices, for communicating with the CH in each cluster [15]. By dominating the LoS links [16,17], the signal-to-noise ratio of the channel for delivering the content i from the UAV located at $o_{l,w}$ to the CH n in the cluster n located at o_n is given by

$$\gamma_{l,w}^{i,n} = \frac{a_{i,n} P_{\mathrm{T}} \beta_0^{\mathrm{U}} (d_{l,w}^n)^{-2}}{\sigma^2},$$ (6)

where P_{T} is the transmission power of the UAV, β_0^{U} is the channel power gain at the reference distance of 1m, σ^2 is the additive white Gaussian noise power, and $d_{l,w}^n$, which is the distance between the UAV and the CH n, is computed as

$$d_{l,w}^n = \sqrt{h_{\mathrm{U}}^2 + \|o_{l,w} - o_n\|^2},$$ (7)

where $\|.\|$ is the Euclidean norm.

From Eq. (6), we have the corresponding delivery capacity expressed as

$$C_{l,w}^{i,n} = B \log_2(1 + \gamma_{l,w}^{i,n}),$$ (8)

where B is the system bandwidth.

Finally, the overall average delivery capacity from the UAV to the CHs in all clusters, which is the objective function of the SECTO optimisation problem, is given by

$$\overline{C} = \frac{1}{N} \sum_{n=1}^{N} \sum_{l=1}^{M_L} \sum_{w=1}^{M_W} \sum_{i=1}^{I} p_i f(o_{l,w}) C_{l,w}^{i,n},$$ (9)

where $f(o_{l,w}) \in \{0,1\}$ is the stop index used to indicate that if $f(o_{l,w}) = 1$, the UAV stops at $o_{l,w}$, otherwise $f(o_{l,w}) = 0$, it does not stop. And thus, the number of stops is expressed as

$$N_T = \sum_{l=1}^{M_L} \sum_{w=1}^{M_W} f(o_{l,w}).$$ (10)

In Eq. (9) and Eq. (10), $\overline{C}$ is the function of caching index (c_i) and the flying strategy $f(o_{l,w})$. So, besides finding the optimal caching index, the SECTO finds the optimal flying strategy via $f(o_{l,w})$, which includes: 1) where to stop among N_T out of N stops ($N_T \leq N$) to maximise $\overline{C}$ and 2) how to fly throughout N_T stops to minimise the distance for energy saving.

3.4   Storage and Energy Consumption

Storage Consumption. Given the caching index c_i and the size s_i of the content i, the total caching storage consumed is given by

$$S = \sum_{\substack{i=1 \\ r_{i,n}=1,\forall n}}^{I} c_i s_i.$$ (11)

Energy Consumption. The energy is consumed by transmission and flying. To compute the total energy consumption, we need to derive the transmission duration and flying duration. It is noted that when flying, the UAV must stop to transmit the contents, and thus the standstill duration is actually equal to the transmission duration. We first compute the transmission/standstill duration at the stop $o_{l,w}$ for transmitting the content i to the CH n which is given by

$$t_{l,w}^{i,n} = \frac{a_{i,n} f(o_{l,w}) s_i}{\max\{\epsilon, C_{l,w}^{i,n}\}}, \tag{12}$$

where the infinitesimal value ϵ is added to avoid the situation of dividing by zero if $C_{l,w}^{i,n} = 0$. And then, the total transmission/standstill duration is

$$t_{\mathrm{T}} = \sum_{n=1}^{N} \sum_{l=1}^{M_{\mathrm{L}}} \sum_{w=1}^{M_{\mathrm{W}}} \sum_{i=1}^{I} t_{l,w}^{i,n}. \tag{13}$$

For the flying duration, given a minimum distance $d_{\min}$ found by solving the SECTO optimisation problem (23) for minimum value of d (17) and a fixed flying velocity V, it is simply expressed by

$$t_{\mathrm{F}} = d_{min}/V. \tag{14}$$

Finally, the total energy consumption is given by

$$E = P_{\mathrm{F}} t_{\mathrm{F}} + (P_{\mathrm{S}} + P_{\mathrm{T}}) t_{\mathrm{T}}, \tag{15}$$

where P_{F}, P_{S}, and P_{T} are the transmission powers used for flight, standstill, and transmission, respectively.

3.5   SECTO Optimisation Problem

As aforementioned, the SECTO solution includes 1) which contents to cache and where to stop (WCS) for maximising the average content delivery capacity and 2) how to fly over the stops for minimising the distance, i.e., the shortest path (STP) or travelling salesman problem. So, we first present the two STP and WCS optimisation subproblems separately and then we combine them to formulate the SECTO optimisation problem as below.

For the STP optimisation problem, given a set of $N_{\mathcal{T}}$ valid stops $\mathcal{T}_s = \{1, 2, ..., N_{\mathcal{T}}\}$, $\mathcal{T}$ is the set of stop sequence (order) to fly, i.e., $\mathcal{T}$ is an arbitrary combination of $\mathcal{T}_s$. For example, if $\mathcal{T}_s = \{1, 2, 3\}$, $\mathcal{T} = \{2, 1, 3\}$, i.e., $\mathcal{T}_1 = 2, \mathcal{T}_2 = 1, \mathcal{T}_3 = 3$, is a valid stop sequence, meaning that the UAV flies to the stop 2 first, then to the stop 1, and finally to the stop 3. The distance to fly from the stop $n - 1$ to the stop n is expressed as

$$d_n = \begin{cases} d(\mathcal{T}_{n-1}, \mathcal{T}_n), \text{if } \mathcal{T}_n \in \mathcal{T}_s, \mathcal{T}_s = \mathcal{T}_s \setminus \mathcal{T}_n, \\ 0, \text{if } \mathcal{T}_n \notin \mathcal{T}_s. \end{cases} \tag{16}$$

It is noted in (16) that if $\mathcal{T}_n \in \mathcal{T}_s$, after flying to the n-th stop with an actual distance added, and then this stop is removed from the set of valid stops. Otherwise, the UAV cannot fly to the n-th stop, and thus no distance is added but with violence. For example, considering an invalid stop sequence $\mathcal{T} = \{1, 1, 3\}$, it is easy to see that the violence occurs when $n = 2$ at $\mathcal{T}_2$. Consequently, the total distance for the UAV to fly over $N_{\mathcal{T}}$ stops is given by

$$d = \sum_{n=1}^{N_{\mathcal{T}}} d_n. \tag{17}$$

For the ease of grasping the violence degree of (16) if $\mathcal{T}_n \notin \mathcal{T}_s$, we further add an independent penalty function βd_p to (17); where $\beta > 0$ is the violent degree and d_p starts with 0, then increases by 1 if the violence occurs. So, the minimum value of d holds since $d_p = 0$. The STP integer combination problem is formulated as

$$\min_{\mathcal{T}} (d + \beta d_p). \tag{18}$$

For the WCS optimisation problem, we take into account the constraints of caching storage (S), energy consumption (E), and number of stops ($N_{\mathcal{T}}$), it is formulated as below

$$\max_{c_i, f(o_{l,w})} \overline{C} \tag{19a}$$

$$\text{s.t.} \qquad S \leq S^* \tag{19b}$$

$$E \leq E^* \tag{19c}$$

$$N_{\mathcal{T}} \leq N \tag{19d}$$

Aiming at maximising the average content delivery capacity (19) and minimising the distance (18) simultaneously, the SECTO optimisation problem is formulated as

$$\max_{c_i, f(o_{l,w}), \mathcal{T}} \left[\overline{C} - (\gamma d + \beta d_p) \right], \tag{20}$$

$$\text{s.t. } (19b), (19c), (19d),$$

where $\gamma > 0$ is used to adjust the balance between the two objective functions $\overline{C}$ and d; and S^* and E^* are to limit the caching storage and energy consumption.

4   GAs for SECTO Optimisation Problem

In this paper, we apply GAs [18] to solve the SECTO optimisation problem. To do so, we apply penalty function [19] which requires to rewrite (19b), (19c), and

(19d) as below

$$\begin{cases} \Delta S = S^* - S \geq 0, \\ \Delta E = E^* - E \geq 0, \\ \Delta N = N - N_T \geq 0. \end{cases} \tag{21}$$

As we have mentioned that βd_p in (18) is the penalty function, thus we extract it from (20), and then add it to the whole penalty function of (22) which is given by

$$F = \lambda_1 \left(\min\{0, \Delta S\}\right)^2 + \lambda_2 \left(\min\{0, \Delta E\}\right)^2 + \lambda_3 \left(\min\{0, \Delta N\}\right)^2 + \beta d_p, \tag{22}$$

where λ_1, λ_2, and λ_3 are the constraint violation degrees which are properly selected to punish the individuals in the current generation if they violate the constraints.

Finally, the GAs can be used to solve the unconstrained SECTO optimisation problem given by

$$\max_{c_i, f(o_{l,w}), T} \overline{C}_F = \overline{C} - (\gamma d + F). \tag{23}$$

In (23), if d is minimised and too small (~ 0), the UAV flies over small number of stops or even it stops at the original location to transmit the contents. This makes the capacity significantly decreased. Inversely, if d is minimised but too large, the capacity increases but limited by E^*. The balance of maximum value of $\overline{C}$ and minimum value of d yields maximum value of $\overline{C}_F$ when F approaches 0. So, together with λ_1, λ_2, and λ_3, γ is used to balance the impact of F and d on the process of maximising the fitness function $\overline{C}_F$.

To implement GAs, it is noted that the SECTO optimisation problem has two different types of variables. The binary variables (c_i and $f(o_{l,w})$) for caching and stop indexes, and meanwhile the integer variables (T) for stop sequence. These two types have different requirements of crossover and mutation, i.e., different operations and probabilities. So, we use two chromosome types, one for binary variables and the other for integer variables. Correspondingly, we have to create two separated binary and integer populations, each of the same number of individuals is performed by its own crossover and mutation operations.

In the SECTO optimisation problem, because the binary variables are c_i and $f(o_{l,w})$ of length $I + M_L \times M_W$ bits, each individual represented by a binary chromosome (binary string) has $N_B = I + M_L \times M_W$ bits. The maximum number of stops in the sequence T is $N_T = N$, each individual represented by an integer chromosome (integer string) therefore has $N_I = N$ integers. When GAs terminate, the first N_T stops in the final T are derived for the optimal stop sequence. The detailed implementation of GAs is shown in Algorithm 1. In Algorithm 1, GAs terminate if one of the three following conditions of TC holds: 1) $F = 0$ in 3 successive generations, 2) $\overline{C}_F$ does not change while $F \leq 10^{-3}$ in 3 successive generations, and 3) $gen = N_G$.

Algorithm 1. GAs implementation

Input: System parameters listed in Table 1

$N_P = 10,000$: Number of individuals in both the binary and integer populations

$N_B = I + M_L \times M_W$: Number of binary variables (bits) for each binary individual

$N_I = N$: Number of integer variables for each integer individual

$N_G = 100$: Number of generations

$P_G = 0.8$: Generation gap

$P_{CB} = 0.6$: Crossover probability for binary individuals

$P_{CI} = 0.9$: Crossover probability for integer individuals

$P_{MB} = 10^{-6}$: Mutation probability for binary individuals

$P_{MI} = 10^{-10}$: Mutation probability for integer individuals

$\beta = 1$: Violence degree applied if $\mathcal{T}$ is invalid

$\gamma = 0.1$: Coefficient used to balance the two objective functions $\overline{C}$ and d

$\{\lambda_{1,2,3}\} = \{1, 10^3, 1\}$: The method to choose the proper λs is presented in [20]

TC: Termination conditions

$Gen = 1$: Generation count

Output: $\overline{C}_F^*$ and X^*

1: Randomly generating N_P binary strings, each of length N_B bits to represent the individual k ($\{X_B^k\}$), $k = 1, 2, ..., N_P$

2: Randomly generating N_P integer strings, each of length N_I integers to represent the individual k ($\{X_I^k\}$)

3: Mapping $\{X_B^k\}$ into the binary variables c_i^k and $f(o_{l,w}^k)$ and mapping $\{X_I^k\}$ into the integer variables $\mathcal{T}^k$

4: Calculating N_P fitness values $\overline{C}_F\big(c_i^k, f(o_{l,w}^k), \mathcal{T}^k\big)$

5: **while** TC does not hold **do**

6:    Putting $\{X_B^k\}$, $\{X_I^k\}$, and $\overline{C}_F\big(c_i^k, f(o_{l,w}^k), \mathcal{T}^k\big)$ in the mating pool for ranking

7:    Selecting $N_G = N_P \times P_G$ better individuals with higher $\overline{C}_F\big(c_i^k, f(o_{l,w}^k), \mathcal{T}^k\big)$ for breeding the next generation by using stochastic universal sampling operator [18]

8:    Dividing the selected individuals into a set of N_G binary individuals $\{X_B^{k,*}\}$ and a set of N_G integer individuals $\{X_I^{k,*}\}$

9:    Selecting a pair of parents to make a pair of offsprings by using 1) multiple point crossover with probability P_{CB} for $\{X_B^{k,*}\}$ and 2) single point crossover with probability P_{CI} for $\{X_I^{k,*}\}$ [18]

10:    Mutating the offsprings of $\{X_B^{k,*}\}$ with probability P_{MB} and the offsprings of $\{X_I^{k,*}\}$ with probability P_{MI}, to recover the good genetic materials likely lost in the previous operations

11:    Merging the two sets of offsprings into one, evaluating the fitness values of the merged set, reinserting it into the present generation

12:    $Gen = Gen + 1$

13: **end while**

14: Finding the best fitness value $\overline{C}_F^*$ with respect to the best individual X^* in the last generation

---

5 Performance Evaluation

5.1 GAs Performance

To evaluate the performance of GAs, we compare it to the other two search algorithms namely exhausted - exhausted (EE) search algorithm and exhausted - greedy (EG) search algorithm which are corresponding to TSM and NSH respectively studied in [8]. We deploy GAs, EE, and EG by a desktop computer with detailed information listed in Table 2. The CHs are randomly distributed within a circle of 100-meter radius. The UAV is originally located at $(x_U, y_U) = (100\text{m},$ 100m) and its vertical coordinate is fixed at $h_U = 50\text{m}$.

We first evaluate the convergence rate of GAs by considering 100 generations. Figure 2 plots the results of the best fitness value $\overline{C}_F^*$, the mean of all the fitness values with respect to all individuals in each generation, and the penalty value (F). The results show that the convergence situation of GAs starts from the 35-th generation when the mean value is closer to the best value and $F = 0$. It indicates that all the individuals become better after each generation while ensuring the given constraints for optimal solutions.

The performance of GAs is further evaluated by investigating the accuracy and time complexity in comparison with EG and EE. The Algorithm 1 is exe-

Table 1. Parameters setting.

Symbols	Specifications
$\{N, I\}$	$\{10$ clusters, 5 videos$\}$
s_i	$[300, 100, 200, 400, 900]$ Mbits
S^*	1000 Mbits
α	1
V	$15\,\text{m/s}$
$\{P_T, P_F, P_S\}$	$\{0.5, 50, 0.25 \times P_F\}$ W
E^*	5000 Joules
B	$10\,\text{MHz}$
β_0^U	10^{-5}
σ^2	10^{-13} W

Table 2. Computer information.

Processor	Intel(R) Core(TM) i7-7700 CPU @ 3.60 GHz, 3601 Mhz
Processor type	x64-based PC
Processor cores	4
Logical processors	8
Total PHY memory	15,9 GB
Operating System	Windows 10

cuted versus different population sizes N_P from 1000 to 20,000. For each population size, the Algorithm 1 is repeated 50 times, and then we calculate the average of 50 optimal results of $\overline{C}$ and d in accordance with the average of time complexities. As shown in Table 3, the accuracy of GAs increases if N_P increases. We select $N_P = 10,000$ for obtaining the optimal results because if $N_P > 10,000$, the accuracy does not increase significantly but time complexity becomes too high, i.e., up to 1,009.36 s. At $N_P = 10,000$, GAs provide a reasonable accuracy of 99.69% for $\overline{C}$ and 99.51% for d compared to EE. However, GAs have a much less time complexity of 356.01 s compared to that of 1,320.17 s introduced by EE. Related to EG, although it can provide the exact result of $\overline{C}$ thanks to using exhausted search algorithm, the accuracy of d is lower than GAs done at $N_P \geq 5,000$. We can see that the accuracy and time complexity of EG is equivalent to GAs done at $N_P = 5,000$. So, GAs are flexible to obtain the exact or approximate optimal results with reasonable accuracy and time complexity.

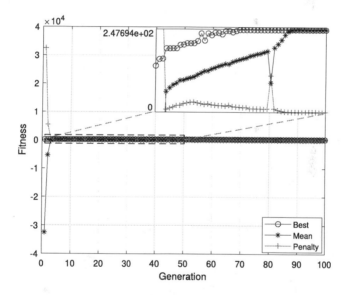

Fig. 2. Convergence rate of GAs.

Table 3. Accuracy and time complexity comparison

Metric	N_P (GAs)					EG	EE
	1,000	5,000	10,000	15,000	20,000		
$\overline{C}$ (Mbps)	310.55	310.91	310.97	311.14	311.15	311.95	311.95
Accuracy of $\overline{C}$ (%)	99.55	99.67	99.69	99.74	99.74	100.00	100.00
d (m)	696.26	653.93	645.64	641.25	641.94	657.93	642.53
Accuracy of d (%)	91.64	98.22	99.51	99.80	99.91	97.60	100.00
Time (s)	19.23	117.55	356.01	635.52	1,009.36	111.65	1,320.17

5.2   System Performance Metrics

Storage-Aware Results. To have the storage-aware results, we run the Algorithm 1 by changing the skewness coefficient of content popularity preference α with different values of caching storage constraint S^* (19b). As shown in Fig. 3, if S^* is large enough ($S^* \geq 400$ Mbits), $\overline{C}$ increases with respect to the increase of α commonly (Fig. 3(a)), meanwhile d is mostly kept the same to provide the highest value of $\overline{C}$ (Fig. 3(b)). It is noted that when α is high, the results become

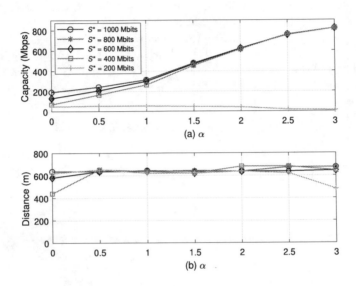

Fig. 3. Capacity and distance versus α with different S^*.

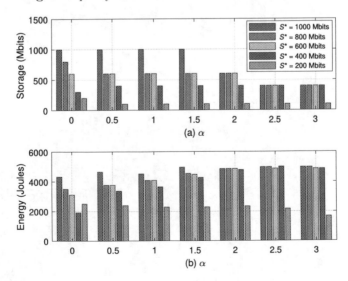

Fig. 4. Storage and energy consumption versus α with different S^*.

equally saturated because the system just focuses on less contents with higher popularity to serve the CHs for the highest capacity performance. However, if S^* is too small ($S^* = 200$ Mbits), it is clear that $\overline{C}$ significantly decreases since the UAV cannot cache the most popular contents with $s_i > 200$ Mbits, e.g., $s_1 = 300$ Mbits.

Figure 4 plots the storage and energy consumption which strictly satisfies the constraints (19b) and (19c). In Fig. 4(a), if α is high enough, i.e., $\alpha \geq 2.5$,

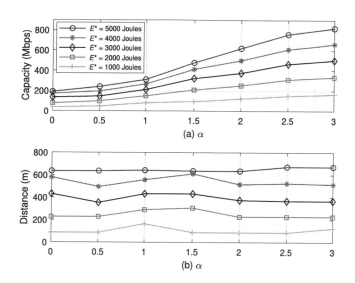

Fig. 5. Capacity and distance versus α with different E^*.

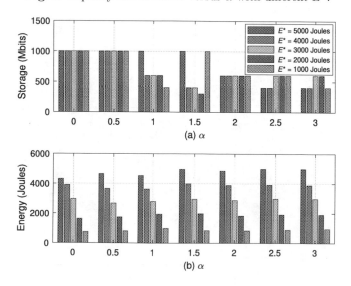

Fig. 6. Storage and energy consumption versus α with different E^*.

the system just focuses on less contents with higher popularity as we mentioned earlier, thus the caching storage consumption decreases. However, the energy consumption increases if α increases because more CHs request the most popular content with relatively large size, i.e., $s_1 = 300$ Mbits, leading to the fact that the transmission and standstill duration becomes longer requiring higher energy consumption (Fig. 4(b)), except for $S^* = 200$ Mbits making the distance decreased.

Energy-Aware Results. To have the energy-aware results, we run the Algorithm 1 by changing the skewness coefficient of content popularity preference α with different values of energy constraint E^* (19c). As shown in Fig. 5, the decrease of E^* significantly reduces both capacity and distance. The results of caching storage and energy consumption in Fig. 6 always satisfy the constraints (19b) and (19c). The behavior of all the system performance metrics is similar to that of the storage-aware results with respect to α.

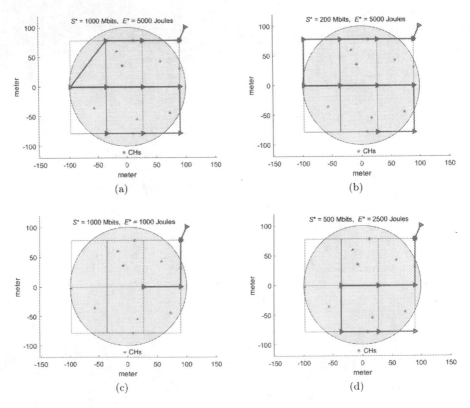

Fig. 7. Optimal trajectories with different constraints of S^* and E^*.

Optimal Trajectories. Figure 7 depicts the optimal trajectories of the UAV when $\alpha = 1$ versus different constraints of S^* and E^*. Figure 7(a) shows the optimal trajectory when S^* and E^* are relaxed to 1000 Mbits and 5000 Joules, respectively. In Fig. 7(b), if we strictly limit the caching storage constraint S^* to 200 Mbits, the UAV has to change the caching policy, and thus change the set of stops to serve the CHs with a different optimal trajectory. The trajectories significantly change to the short flight distances if we further limit the energy constraint E^* or/and the caching storage constraint S^* as plotted in Fig. 7(c) and Fig. 7(d).

6   Conclusion

In this paper, we have introduced GAs to solve the SECTO problem for UAV-assisted CDNs to maximise the content delivery capacity while minimising the flight distance. Unlike other common optimisation problem having only one objective function with respect to (w.r.t) only one type of variable, i.e., binary, real, or integer variable, the SECTO problem consists of two objective functions w.r.t both binary and integer variables. To solve the SECTO problem, we modify the GAs by applying penalty method and separating the whole string (chromosome) of each individual into binary sub-string and integer sub-string. These sub-strings are applied different crossover and mutation schemes (operations and probabilities). The results are shown to demonstrate the benefits of GAs in terms of flexible implementation, accuracy, and time complexity compared to other conventional exhausted and greedy search algorithms.

References

1. Strinati, E., et al.: 6G in the sky: on-demand intelligence at the edge of 3D networks. ETRI J. **42**, 643–657 (2020)
2. Chen, M., Mozaffari, M., Saad, W., Yin, C., Debbah, M., Hong, C.S.: Caching in the sky: proactive deployment of cache-enabled unmanned aerial vehicles for optimized quality-of-experience. IEEE J. Sel. Areas Commun. **35**, 1046–1061 (2017)
3. Zeng, Y., Wu, Q., Zhang, R.: Accessing from the sky: a tutorial on UAV communications for 5G and beyond. Proc. IEEE **107**, 2327–2375 (2019)
4. Lu, R., Zhang, R., Cheng, X., Yang, L.: Relay in the sky: a UAV-aided cooperative data dissemination scheduling strategy in VANETs. In: Proceedings IEEE International Conference on Communications (Shanghai, China), pp. 1–6 (2019)
5. Erdelj, M., Natalizio, E., Chowdhury, K.R., Akyildiz, I.F.: Help from the sky: leveraging UAVs for disaster management. IEEE Pervasive Comput. **16**, 24–32 (2017)
6. Bilen, T., Canberk, B.: Content delivery from the sky: drone-aided load balancing for mobile-CDN. EAI Endorsed Trans. Ind. Netw. Intell. Syst. **9**, 1–7 (2022)
7. Duong, T.Q., Kim, K.J., Kaleem, Z., Bui, M.-P., Vo, N.-S.: UAV caching in 6G networks: a survey on models, techniques, and applications. Phys. Commun. **51**, 1–19 (2022)

8. Vo, N.-S., Lam, T.C., Bui, M.-P., Phan, T.-M., Tran, Q.-N.: UAV assisted video multicasting in 6G networks: a joint caching and trajectory optimisation. J. Aviat. Sci. Technol. **1**, 37–42 (2022)

9. Li, X., Liu, J., Zhao, N., Wang, X.: UAV-assisted edge caching under uncertain demand: a data-driven distributionally robust joint strategy. IEEE Trans. Commun. **70**, 3499–3511 (2022)

10. Zhang, T., Wang, Y., Yi, W., Liu, Y., Nallanathan, A.: Joint optimization of caching placement and trajectory for UAV-D2D networks. IEEE Trans. Commun. **7**, 5514–5527 (2022)

11. Xu, H., Ji, J., Zhu, K., Wang, R.: Reinforcement learning for trajectory design in cache-enabled UAV-assisted cellular networks. In: Proceedings IEEE Wireless Communications and Networking Conference (Austin, TX), pp. 1–6 (2022)

12. Ji, J., Zhu, K., Cai, L.: Trajectory and communication design for cache- enabled UAVs in cellular networks: a deep reinforcement learning approach. IEEE Trans. Mob. Comput., 1–15 (2022)

13. Gyawali, S., Xu, S., Ye, F., Hu, R.Q., Qian, Y.: A D2D based clustering scheme for public safety communications. In: Proceedings of IEEE 87th Vehicular Technology Conference (Porto, Portugal), pp. 1–5 (2018)

14. Breslau, L., Cao, P., Fan, L., Phillips, G., Shenker, S.: Web caching and Zipf-like distributions: evidence and implications. In: Proceedings of IEEE International Conference on Computer Communications (INFOCOM) (New York, NY), pp. 126–134 (1999)

15. Lin, D., Zuo, P., Peng, T., Qian, R., Wang, W.: Energy-efficient UAV-based IoT communications with WiFi suppression in 5 GHz ISM bands. IEEE Trans. Veh. Technol., 1–16 (2022)

16. Xu, X., Zeng, Y., Guan, Y.L., Zhang, R.: Overcoming endurance issue: UAV-enabled communications with proactive caching. IEEE J. Sel. Areas Commun. **36**, 1231–1244 (2018)

17. Wu, H., Lyu, F., Zhou, C., Chen, J., Wang, L., Shen, X.: Optimal UAV caching and trajectory in aerial-assisted vehicular networks: a learning-based approach. IEEE J. Sel. Areas Commun., 1–14 (2020)

18. Chipperfield, A., Fleming, P., Pohlheim, H., Fonseca, C.: Genetic algorithm TOOLBOX for using with Matlab Ver 1.2 users guide. University of Sheffield (1994)

19. Fang, T., Chau, L.P.: GOP-based channel rate allocation using genetic algorithm for scalable video streaming over error-prone networks. IEEE Trans. Image Process. **15**, 1323–1330 (2006)

20. Vo, N.-S., Duong, T.Q., Tuan, H.D., Kortun, A.: Optimal video streaming in dense 5G networks with D2D communications. IEEE Access **6**, 209–223 (2017)

Joint Computation Offloading and Resource Allocation for Mobile Edge Computing

John Erskine$^{(\boxtimes)}$ ⓘ and Dang Van Huynh ⓘ

School of Electronics, Electrical Engineering and Computer Science,
Queen's University Belfast, Belfast, UK
{jerskine07,dhuynh01}@qub.ac.uk

Abstract. This paper studies joint computation offloading and communication resource allocation for mobile edge computing (MEC) systems. We aim to minimise the end-to-end (e2e) latency among users (UEs) by jointly optimising task offloading portions, frequency of UEs and edge servers, as well as transmission power of UEs with respect to the latency requirements, computing and energy budgets. To deal with this challenging optimisation problem, we propose efficient algorithms based on the alternating optimisation (AO) approach and convex optimisation. Simulation results validate the effectiveness of the proposed solutions in terms of reducing the e2e latency of UEs as well as demonstrate the impacts of involved parameters on the performance.

Keywords: Mobile Edge Computing · Task Offloading · Resource Allocation · Convex Optimisation

1 Introduction

1.1 Mobile Edge Computing

Mobile Edge Computing (MEC), is a novel technology in the field of mobile computing that allows computing, storage, and networking services to be deployed in nearby edge servers [8,19]. MEC plays an important role in 5G and beyond. Services in terms of computing perspective have strong potential to integrate with other wireless technologies as URLLC [17] and mm-wave [4] which enable new applications. The main objective of MEC is to provide ultra-low latency, high-bandwidth, secure services, and direct access to real-time network information to mobile users (UEs), by bringing the cloud to the edge of the network [17]. MEC is considered a key enabler for emerging mobile applications such as augmented reality, virtual reality, Internet of Things (IoT) and 5G services [3]. MEC provides a cost-effective solution for providing computing services to mobile users by reducing the amount of data that needs to be transmitted to the central cloud.

© ICST Institute for Computer Sciences, Social Informatics and Telecommunications Engineering 2023
Published by Springer Nature Switzerland AG 2023. All Rights Reserved
N.-S. Vo and H.-A. Tran (Eds.): INISCOM 2023, LNICST 531, pp. 51–62, 2023.
https://doi.org/10.1007/978-3-031-47359-3_4

Research in MEC has focused on several areas such as resource management, security, quality of service (QoS), energy efficiency. Resource management algorithms, such as the one in this paper, have been proposed to optimise the use of computational and storage resources at the edge of the network [16]. Quality of service is a critical aspect of MEC, as it ensures that the services provided by the edge server meet the required performance levels [6,12]. Energy efficiency is another important aspect, as it helps to reduce the energy consumption of mobile devices and edge servers [13]. MEC has the potential to revolutionise the way we use mobile devices by bringing the clouds computing power to mobile devices.

1.2 Resource Allocation

One of the key challenges in MEC is resource allocation, which involves deciding how to allocate computational and storage resources at the edge of the network to meet the demands of UEs. Resource allocation strategies in MEC are essential to optimise the use of resources, minimise energy consumption [13], and ensure that the QoS requirements of UEs are met.

Several such resource allocation strategies have been proposed in previous literature to address the challenges of resource allocation in MEC. These include centralised algorithms, distributed algorithms [18], and hybrid algorithms [14]. Centralised algorithms allocate resources based on a global view of the system, whilst decentralised algorithms allocate resources based on local information. Hybrid algorithms can combine the advantages of centralised and decentralised algorithms to provide a balance between performance and scalability. Another important aspect of resource allocation in MEC is the integration of energy efficiency. Several energy-efficient resource allocation algorithms have been proposed to address this challenge [20].

1.3 Task Offloading

Task offloading or computing offloading, involves migrating computing processes from a mobile device to a MEC server. Task offloading is performed to shorten the task response delays and save energy resources [1]. Task offloading in MEC refers to the process of transferring computationally intensive tasks from UEs to edge servers for processing. This is an important aspect of MEC as it helps to reduce the energy consumption of UEs and improves their performance. Several energy-efficient task offloading algorithms have been proposed in literature to address this challenge [20]. More importantly, task offloading in MEC has been recently integrated into other emerging technologies like UAV-based communications and digital twin [2,7] to fully realise the potential of MEC in the development of new delay-sensitive applications.

2   System Model and Problem Formulation

We consider a MEC system as illustrated in Fig. 1. In the system model, the user layer consists of many user equipment (UE) such as mobile robots, actu-

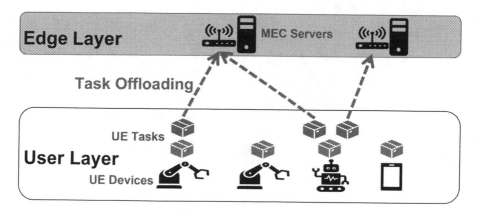

Fig. 1. An illustration of MEC System Model.

ators, sensors. The UEs have different computational tasks to execute, but the computing capacity of UEs is typically limited. Therefore, a portion of tasks can be offloaded to the edge server (MEC) on the edge layer to reduce execution time. Each UE can transmit data to multiple MECs to offload a computational task, and each MEC is available to serve all UEs with an appropriate sharing computing resource to guarantee performance.

2.1 Task Offloading Model

Let us define $\mathcal{M} = \{1, 2, ..., M\}$ and $\mathcal{K} = \{1, 2, ..K\}$ as the sets of UEs, and MECs in the system, respectively. A computational task offloaded from the m-th UE is modelled by three parameters including data size (bit), D_m, the required computation CPU cycles to execute the task, C_m (cycle), and $T_m^{\max}$ (s) is the maximum latency tolerance. Let $\mathbf{u} = \{u_m\}_{\forall m}$ be the portion of the task executed locally and $\mathbf{v} = \{v_{mk}\}_{\forall m,k}$ be the portion of the task offloaded from the m-th UE to the k-th MEC server, satisfying $0 \leq u_{mk} \leq 1$, $0 \leq v_{mk} \leq 1$. Following that definition, the constraint of each computational task can be expressed as follows

$$u_m + \sum_{k \in K} v_{mk} = 1, \forall m. \tag{1}$$

2.2 Wireless Transmission Model

Task offloading from UEs to MECs is based on wireless communications. The access points (AP) associated with MECs are equipped with L antennas to serve single-antenna UEs. The wireless channel between the m-th UE and the k-th MEC is modelled as $\mathbf{h}_{mk} = \sqrt{\gamma_{mk}}\mathbf{g}_{mk}$, where γ_{mk} is the channel path-loss and $\mathbf{g}_{mk}$ is the small-scale fading coefficients. We apply maximum ratio combining (MRC) at the AP to calculate the transmission rate for task offloading and first introduce $\varphi_{m,k,l} = \mathbf{h}_{mk}^T \mathbf{h}_{lk}^* / \|\mathbf{h}_{lk}\|$. Then, the achievable transmission rate from the m-th UE to k-th MEC can be calculated as [9]

$$R_{mk}(\mathbf{p}) = B \log_2 \left(1 + \frac{p_m |\varphi_{m,k,m}|^2}{\mathcal{I}_m(\mathbf{p}) + \sigma_k^2} \right), \tag{2}$$

where B, p_m, and σ_k^2 are the system bandwidth, transmission power of the m-th UE, and the noise variance, respectively. The expression of $\mathcal{I}_m(\mathbf{p}) = \sum_{l \in \mathcal{M}, l \neq m} p_l |\varphi_{m,k,l}|^2$ is the interference caused by other UEs. As a result, the transmission latency for task offloading from the m-th UE to the k-th MEC is expressed as

$$T_{mk}^{\text{off}}(\mathbf{p}, u_m) = \frac{v_{mk} D_m}{R_{mk}(\mathbf{p})}. \tag{3}$$

2.3   Computation and Latency Models

Let f_m^{ue} be the frequency (i.e., clock speed or processing rate) of the m-th UE (cycles/s). The latency of local execution at the m-th UE is given by

$$T_m^{\text{ue}}(u_m, f_m^{\text{ue}}) = \frac{u_m C_m}{f_m^{\text{ue}}} \tag{4}$$

Similarly, given the frequency f_k^{mec}, the latency of the k-th MEC server to execute a portion v_{mk} of the task offloaded from the m-th UE is modelled as

$$T_{mk}^{\text{mec}}(v_{mk}, f_{mk}^{\text{mec}}) = \frac{v_{mk} C_m}{f_{mk}^{\text{mec}}} \tag{5}$$

Consequently, the end-to-end (e2e) latency to complete task execution including local processing, wireless transmission, and MEC processing is expressed as following T_m^{tot}. This value cannot exceed the maximum latency requirement, T_m^{max}

$$T_m^{\text{tot}}(\mathbf{p}, u_m, v_{mk}, f_m^{\text{ue}}, f_{mk}^{\text{mec}}) = T_m^{\text{ue}}(u_m, f_m^{\text{ue}}) + \max\{T_{mk}^{\text{off}}(\mathbf{p}, v_{mk})\}$$
$$+ \max\{T_{mk}^{\text{mec}}(v_{mk}, f_{mk}^{\text{mec}})\} \leq T_m^{\text{max}}, \forall m. \tag{6}$$

It is important to note that after the MEC executes the offloaded task, the size of responses from MECs to UEs (e.g., controlled packets) are much smaller than the offloaded data size, whilst the transmission power of APs are higher than UEs. Therefore, the latency for responses from MECs to UEs is not considered in this paper [19].

2.4   Energy Consumption Model

To execute computational tasks locally, and to offload the task to APs via wireless links, UEs consume energy for computation as well as communication. We model the total energy consumption of UEs as a summation of two components including energy for computation (E_m^{cp}) and energy for communication (E_m^{cm}). As a constraint, this value must be less than or equal to the energy budget of UEs.

$$E_m^{tot}\left(u_m, p_m, f_m^{ue}\right) = E_m^{cp} + E_m^{cm}$$
$$= u_m \frac{\theta}{2} C_m (f_m^{ue})^2 + \sum_{k \in \mathcal{K}} p_m \frac{v_{mk} D_m}{R_{mk}(\mathbf{p})} \leq E_m^{max}, \forall m, \quad (7)$$

where $\theta/2$ is a constant factor to calculate the computation energy consumption of the m-th UE [15].

2.5   Problem Formulation

In this paper, we consider a min-max fairness latency minimisation problem. In particular, we aim at minimising the worst-case e2e latency among UEs subject to requirements of the latency, the UEs energy budget, the transmission power budget, the offloading policies, and the computation capacity of UEs and MECs. On this point, the optimisation problem is formulated as follows

$$\min_{\alpha, \beta, \mathbf{p}, \mathbf{f}} \max_{\forall m \in \mathcal{M}} \left\{ T_m^{tot}\left(u_m, v_{mk}, f_m^{ue}, f_{mk}^{mec}, \mathbf{p}\right) \right\} \quad (8a)$$

$$\text{s.t. } p_m \leq P_m^{max}, \forall m, \quad (8b)$$

$$u_m \in [0, 1], v_{mk} \in [0, 1], \forall m, k, \quad (8c)$$

$$R_{mk}(\mathbf{p}) \geq R_{mk}^{min}, \forall m, k, \quad (8d)$$

$$u_m f_m^{ue} \leq f_m^{max}, \forall m, \quad (8e)$$

$$\sum_{m \in \mathcal{M}} v_{mk} f_{mk}^{mec} \leq f_k^{max}, \forall k, \quad (8f)$$

$$(1), (6), (7), \quad (8g)$$

where $\mathbf{u} \triangleq \{u_m\}, \forall m \in \mathcal{M}$; $\mathbf{v} \triangleq \{v_{mk}\}, \forall m \in \mathcal{M}, \forall k \in \mathcal{K}$; $\mathbf{p} \triangleq \{p_m\} \forall m \in \mathcal{M}$; $\mathbf{f} \triangleq \{f_m^{ue}, f_{mk}^{mec}\}, \forall m \in \mathcal{M}, \forall k \in \mathcal{K}$ in their feasible domains. In (8), constraints (8b) and (8c) indicate the value range of transmission power and offloading portions of the tasks. Constraint (8d) shows the QoS requirements in terms of the transmission rate. The computation capacity of UEs and MECs is presented in (8e) and (8f), respectively. Finally, constraints (1), (6), (7) are already mentioned in above subsections.

3   Proposed Solution

It is challenging to solve the problem (8) directly with conventional approaches, due to the non-smooth and non-convex objective function, (8a) as well as non-convex constraints, i.e., (8d), (6), (7). Therefore, we propose an alternative opti-misation (AO) solution to deal with this problem. We first solve for the trans-mission power ($\mathbf{p}$) of UEs with given values of $\mathbf{u}, \mathbf{v}, \mathbf{f}$. Next, offloading portions are optimised with given $\mathbf{p}, \mathbf{f}$. Finally, the processing rate of UEs and MECs is solved to complete the AO-based algorithm. The following subsections provide the development of our proposed solution.

3.1   Optimal Transmission Power with Given $(\mathbf{u}, \mathbf{v}, \mathbf{f})$

For any given $(\mathbf{u}, \mathbf{v}, \mathbf{f})$, problem (8) can be expressed as

$$\underset{\mathbf{p}}{\text{minimise}} \ \underset{\forall m \in \mathcal{M}}{\max} \ \{T_m^{tot}(\mathbf{p})\} \tag{9a}$$

$$\text{s.t. } (8b), (8d), (6), (7). \tag{9b}$$

To deal with the problem (9), we first address the transmission rate by using the logarithmic inequality given in [10, 11], which follows from the convexity of the function $f(x, y) = \log_2\left(1 + 1/xy\right)$ as follows

$$f(x, y) = \log_2(1 + \frac{1}{xy}) \geq \hat{f}(x, y). \tag{10}$$

Given $\forall x > 0, \bar{x} > 0, y > 0, \bar{y} > 0$, by applying first-order Taylor's expansion for $f(x, y)$, we have $\hat{f}(x, y) = \log_2\left(1 + \frac{1}{\bar{x}\bar{y}}\right) + \frac{2}{(\bar{x}\bar{y}+1)} - \frac{x}{\bar{x}(\bar{x}\bar{y}+1)} - \frac{y}{\bar{y}(\bar{x}\bar{y}+1)}$. Let (i) denote the i-th iteration and substituting $x = \frac{1}{p_m|\varphi_{m,k,m}|^2}$, $y = \mathcal{I}_m(\mathbf{p}) + \sigma_k^2$, $\bar{x} = x^{(i)} = \frac{1}{p_m^{(i)}|\varphi_{m,k,m}|^2}$, and $\bar{y} = y^{(i)} = \mathcal{I}_m(\mathbf{p}^{(i)}) + \sigma_k^2$, we can obtain the approximation of wireless transmission rate for task offloading from the m-th IoT to the k-th MEC in (2) as

$$R_{mk}(\mathbf{p}) \geq \hat{R}_{mk}^{(i)}(\mathbf{p}), \forall m \in \mathcal{M}, \forall k \in \mathcal{K}, \tag{11}$$

where

$$\hat{R}_{mk}^{(i)}(\mathbf{p}) = B\left(\log_2\left(1 + \frac{1}{\bar{x}\bar{y}}\right) + \frac{2}{(\bar{x}\bar{y}+1)} - \frac{x}{\bar{x}(\bar{x}\bar{y}+1)} - \frac{y}{\bar{y}(\bar{x}\bar{y}+1)}\right). \tag{12}$$

As a result, the constraint (8d) is now equivalent to

$$\hat{R}_{mk}^{(i)}(\mathbf{p}) \geq R_{mk}^{min}, \ \forall m \in \mathcal{M}, \forall k \in \mathcal{K}. \tag{13}$$

This is now a convex constraint.

Next, to deal with the latency constraint, we introduce new variables $\mathbf{r} \triangleq \{r_{mk}\}_{\forall m,k}$ satisfying $1/\hat{R}_{mk}^{(i)}(\mathbf{p}) \leq r_{mk}, \forall m, k$. Then, the objective function $T_m^{tot}(\mathbf{p})$ can be upper-bounded as

$$T_m^{tot}(\mathbf{p}) \leq \hat{T}_m^{tot}(\mathbf{r}) = \frac{v_m C_m}{f_m + \tilde{f}_m} + \underset{k \in \mathcal{K}}{\max}\left(\frac{u_{mk} C_m}{f_{mk}^{mec} + \tilde{f}_k}\right) + \underset{k \in \mathcal{K}}{\max}\{r_{mk} u_{mk} D_m\} \tag{14}$$

Consequently, we can express (6) and (7) as

$$
\begin{cases}
\hat{T}_m^{\text{tot}}\left(\mathbf{r}\right) \leq T_m^{max}, \forall m, & (15a) \\[2mm]
v_m \dfrac{\theta}{2} C_m f_m^2 + \displaystyle\sum_{k \in \mathcal{K}} p_m r_{mk} u_{mk} D_m \leq E_m^{max}, \forall m, & (15b) \\[2mm]
\dfrac{1}{\hat{R}_{mk}^{ul(i)}(\mathbf{p})} \leq r_{mk}, \forall m, k, & (15c)
\end{cases}
$$

As we can see the constraint (15b) is still non-convex; therefore, we apply following inequality

$$
xy \leq \frac{1}{2}\left(\frac{\bar{y}}{\bar{x}}x^2 + \frac{\bar{x}}{\bar{y}}y^2\right), \tag{16}
$$

with $x = p_m$, $\bar{x} = p_m^{(i)}$, $y = r_{mk}$, $\bar{y} = r_{mk}^{(i)}$, to iteratively express (15b) as

$$
u_m \frac{\theta}{2} C_m f_m^2 + \sum_{k \in \mathcal{K}} \frac{1}{2}\left(\frac{r_{mk}^{(i)}}{p_m^{(i)}}p_m^2 + \frac{p_m^{(i)}}{r_{mk}^{(i)}}r_{mk}^2\right) v_{mk} D_m \leq E_m^{max}, \forall m, k, \tag{17}
$$

which is now a convex constraint. Problem (9) is equivalent to the following convex problem:

$$
\min_{\mathbf{p},\mathbf{r}} \max_{\forall m \in \mathcal{M}} \left\{\hat{T}_m^{\text{tot}}\left(\mathbf{r}\right)\right\}, \tag{18a}
$$

$$
\text{s.t. } (8b), (15a), (13), (15c), (17). \tag{18b}
$$

To solve problem (18), a CVX package in MATLAB is used [5]. The proposed power allocation procedure for solving problem (18) is summarised in Algorithm 1.

Algorithm 1. Proposed algorithm for solving power allocation in problem (18)

Initialisation: Set $i = 0$ and initial feasible point $\mathbf{p}^{(0)}$; set the tolerance $\varepsilon = 10^{-3}$ and the maximum number of iteration $I_{max} = 20$.
    repeat
        Solve problem (18) for the next feasible solution $(\mathbf{p}^{(i+1)})$;
        Update $i = i + 1$;
    until Convergence or $i > I_{max}$;
    Output: Optimal power allocation coefficients $(\mathbf{p}^*)$.

3.2 Optimal Offloading Portions with Given $(\mathbf{p}, \mathbf{f})$

In this subsection, we solve for the optimal offloading portion with fixed $\mathbf{p}, \mathbf{f}$. Here problem (8) solving for $(\mathbf{u}, \mathbf{v})$ can be expressed as

$$
\min_{\mathbf{u},\mathbf{v}} \max_{\forall m \in \mathcal{M}} \left\{T_m^{\text{tot}}\left(u_m, v_{mk}\right)\right\}, \tag{19a}
$$

$$
\text{s.t. } (1), (6), (7), (8c), (8e), (8f). \tag{19b}
$$

It is clearly seen that problem (19) is a standard convex program with all linear constraints that can be solved efficiently by CVX.

3.3 Optimal Frequency of UEs and MEC Servers with Given $(\mathbf{u}, \mathbf{v}, \mathbf{p})$

In this last sub-problem, we solve for the optimal frequency values of UEs and MECs, $\mathbf{f}$ with given $(\mathbf{u}, \mathbf{v}, \mathbf{p})$. To do that, we can rewrite problem (8) as follows

$$\min_{\mathbf{f}} \max_{\forall m \in \mathcal{M}} \left\{ T_m^{tot} \left(f_m^{ue}, f_{mk}^{mec} \right) \right\} \tag{20a}$$

$$\text{s.t. } (6), (7), (8e), (8f) \tag{20b}$$

As we can see from (20), the problem is also a convex program with respect to variables $\mathbf{f}$. Therefore, it can be solved efficiently by CVX to obtain optimal solutions for the frequency of UEs and MECs.

Based on the above development, we propose using an iterative optimisation algorithm to solve the computing resource optimisation of UEs and MEC servers. The iterative algorithm is provided as following Algorithm 2.

Algorithm 2. Proposed iterative optimisation algorithm for solving (8).

Initialisation: Set $i = 0$, generate initial points $(\mathbf{u}^{(0)}, \mathbf{v}^{(0)}, \mathbf{p}^{(0)}, \mathbf{f}^{(0)})$; set the error tolerance $\varepsilon = 10^{-3}$, and the maximum number of iteration $I_{max} = 20$.

  repeat

    With given $(\mathbf{u}^{(i)}, \beta^{(i)}, \mathbf{f}^{(i)})$, solve problem (18) for optimal power control coefficients $(\mathbf{p}^{(i+1)})$;

    With given $(\mathbf{p}^{(i+1)}, \mathbf{f}^{(i)})$, solve problem (19) for optimal offloading policies $(\mathbf{u}^{(i+1)}, \mathbf{v}^{(i+1)})$;

    With given $(\mathbf{u}^{(i+1)}, \mathbf{v}^{(i+1)}, \mathbf{p}^{(i+1)})$, solve problem (20) for optimal frequency $(\mathbf{f}^{(i+1)})$;

    Update $i = i + 1$;

  until Convergence or $i > I_{max}$;

  Output: Optimal solutions of $\mathbf{u}^*, \mathbf{v}^*, \mathbf{p}^*, \mathbf{f}^*$.

---

4 Numerical Results

For simulations, the parameters are set as presented in Table 1. Simulations are run on MATLAB and the convex optimisation problems are solved by CVX package.

It is clear from the results in Fig. 2 that as the computation resource limitations at the UEs increase, the worst-case latency decreases. This is because when there are more local computation resources, there is a greater ability to process tasks locally rather than offloading them to MEC servers. As a result, there is

Table 1. Parameter settings of simulations [1, 19].

Parameter	Value
Number antennas of AP	4
Channel pathloss	$140.7 + 36.7 \log_{10} d$
System bandwidth	10 MHz
Maximum transmission power	30 dBm
Noise power density	-174 dBm/Hz
Task data size	100 kB
Task complexity	$[600, 1200]$ cycles/bit
Maximum UE frequency	1 GHz
Maximum MEC frequency	20 GHz
Maximum latency requirement	1 s
UE energy budget	1.5 J
The effective capacitance coefficient	10^{-24} watt.s^3/cycle^3

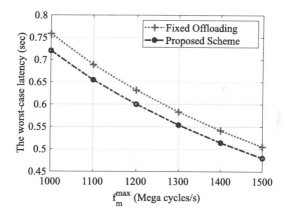

Fig. 2. Latency versus f_m^{max}.

a higher chance of reducing latency, especially when network resources are optimally allocated. The 'Proposed Scheme' uses the proposed solution written in this paper.'Fixed Offloading', uses fixed values for **u** and **v** to determine task offloading for all the UEs. The fixed values in this case are initialised values. It is clear that the optimised scheme must offload at a similar level to the initialised values, hence the difference in results of about 0.04 s.

Figure 3 demonstrates how the worst case latency changes with different values of UE task complexity (given in cycles per second). It is clear that as the task complexity increases, so does the worst case latency. This is due to both the UEs and MEC servers having to process a more complex task, which of course requires more time to do. Additionally the more complex tasks take more

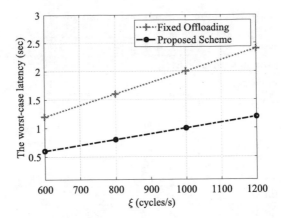

Fig. 3. Latency versus ξ.

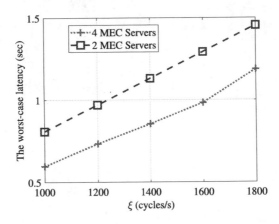

Fig. 4. Latency versus ξ with varying number of MEC Servers.

time to be offloaded, thus increasing the latency. What this figure demonstrates, is that there exists a predictable relationship, which could make guaranteeing performance simpler for end users. Once again, the proposed scheme performs better than a fixed scheme.

Figure 4 demonstrates the relationship between latency and the number of MEC servers. The worst case latency is lower with more MEC servers. As is made clear by both graphs, the latency increases as the task complexity increases, this graph also complements Fig. 3. The system with 4 MEC servers performs better to the system with 2 MEC servers.

5   Conclusion

In conclusion, we have presented a framework that assists in task offloading for IoT networks with mobile edge computing (MEC). Specifically, we have addressed the highly non-convex optimisation problem of minimising e2e latency in the system. The formulated problem has taken into account several variables such as transmission power, task offloading portions, CPU frequency of UEs and MECs subject to system budgets and QoS requirements. To evaluate the effectiveness of our proposed approach, we have conducted simulations by varying task complexity. Our simulation results clearly demonstrate that the proposed scheme outperforms the benchmark scheme, highlighting the efficacy of our approach in minimising e2e latency and improving the performance of IoT networks with MEC.

References

1. Do-Duy, T., Van Huynh, D., Dobre, O.A., Canberk, B., Duong, T.Q.: Digital twin-aided intelligent offloading with edge selection in mobile edge computing. IEEE Wirel. Commun. Lett. **11**(4), 806–810 (2022)
2. Duong, T.Q., Van Huynh, D., Li, Y., Garcia-Palacios, E., Sun, K.: Digital twin-enabled 6G aerial edge computing with ultra-reliable and low-latency communications: (invited paper). In: Proceedings of 1st International Conference on 6G Networking (6GNet), Paris, France (2022)
3. Elbamby, M.S., et al.: Wireless edge computing with latency and reliability guarantees. Proc. IEEE **107**(8), 1717–1737 (2019)
4. Elkashlan, M., Duong, T.Q., Chen, H.H.: Millimeter-wave communications for 5G - part 2: applications [guest editorial]. IEEE Commun. Mag. **53**(1), 166–167 (2015)
5. Grant, M., Boyd, S.: CVX: MATLAB software for disciplined convex programming, version 2.1, March 2014. http://cvxr.com/cvx
6. Ha, D.B., Truong, V.T., Lee, Y.: Performance analysis for RF energy harvesting mobile edge computing networks with SIMO/MISO-NOMA schemes. EAI Endorsed Trans. Ind. Netw. Intell. Syst. **8**(27), e2 (2021)
7. Li, Y., Huynh, D.V., Do-Duy, T., Garcia-Palacios, E., Duong, T.Q.: Unmanned aerial vehicle-aided edge networks with ultra-reliable low-latency communications: a digital twin approach. IET Signal Proc. **16**(8), 897–908 (2022)
8. Mao, Y., You, C., Zhang, J., Huang, K., Letaief, K.B.: A survey on mobile edge computing: the communication perspective. IEEE Commun. Surv. Tutorials **19**(4), 2322–2358 (2017)
9. Merluzzi, M., Lorenzo, P.D., Barbarossa, S., Frascolla, V.: Dynamic computation offloading in multi-access edge computing via ultra-reliable and low-latency communications. IEEE Trans. Signal Inf. Process. Netw. **6**, 342–356 (2020)
10. Nguyen, L.D., Tuan, H.D., Duong, T.Q., Dobre, O.A., Poor, H.V.: Downlink beamforming for energy-efficient heterogeneous networks with massive MIMO and small cells. IEEE Trans. Wirel. Commun. **17**(5), 3386–3400 (2018)
11. Nguyen, L.D., Tuan, H.D., Duong, T.Q., Poor, H.V.: Multi-user regularized zero-forcing beamforming. IEEE Trans. Signal Process. **67**(11), 2839–2853 (2019)
12. Nguyen, L.D., Kortun, A., Duong, T.Q.: An introduction of real-time embedded optimisation programming for UAV systems under disaster communication. EAI Endorsed Trans. Ind. Netw. Intell. Syst. **5**(17), e5 (2018)

13. Pan, Y., Chen, M., Yang, Z., Huang, N., Shikh-Bahaei, M.: Energy-efficient NOMA-based mobile edge computing offloading. IEEE Commun. Lett. **23**(2), 310–313 (2018)
14. Peng, K., Zhao, B., Qian, X., Xu, X., Zheng, L., Leung, V.C.M.: A multi-objective computation offloading method for hybrid workflow applications in mobile edge computing. In: Zhang, X., Liu, G., Qiu, M., Xiang, W., Huang, T. (eds.) Cloud-Comp/SmartGift -2019. LNICST, vol. 322, pp. 47–62. Springer, Cham (2020). https://doi.org/10.1007/978-3-030-48513-9_4
15. Sun, W., Wang, P., Xu, N., Wang, G., Zhang, Y.: Dynamic digital twin and distributed incentives for resource allocation in aerial-assisted internet of vehicles. IEEE Internet Things J. **9**(8), 5839–5852 (2021)
16. Van Huynh, D., Khosravirad, S.R., Masaracchia, A., Dobre, O.A., Duong, T.Q.: Edge intelligence-based ultra-reliable and low-latency communications for digital twin-enabled metaverse. IEEE Wireless Commun. Lett. **11**(8), 1733–1737 (2022)
17. Van Huynh, D., Nguyen, V.D., Chatzinotas, S., Khosravirad, S.R., Poor, H.V., Duong, T.Q.: Joint communication and computation offloading for ultra-reliable and low-latency with multi-tier computing. IEEE J. Sel. Areas Commun. **41**(2), 521–537 (2023)
18. Van Huynh, D., Nguyen, V.D., Khosravirad, S.R., Duong, T.Q.: Fairness-aware latency minimisation in digital twin-aided edge computing with ultra-reliable and low-latency communications: a distributed optimisation approach (invited paper). In: 2022 56th Asilomar Conference on Signals. Systems, and Computers, pp. 1045–1049, Pacific Grove, CA (2022)
19. Van Huynh, D., et al.: URLLC edge networks with joint optimal user association, task offloading and resource allocation: a digital twin approach. IEEE Trans. Commun. **70**(11), 7669–7682 (2022)
20. Xiao, Y., Krunz, M.: Distributed optimization for energy-efficient fog computing in the tactile Internet. IEEE J. Sel. Areas Commun. **36**(11), 2390–2400 (2018)

An Open Source Wireless Communication Database for Radio Access Network

Yanzan Sun[1], Shengyu Gao[1(✉)], Jun Yu[1], Yanyu Huang[1], Shunqin Zhang[1], Xiaojing Chen[1], and Ming Gan[2]

[1] Shanghai University, Shanghai 200444, China
{yanzansun,gaolegao,junyu,huangyanyu,shunqing,jodiechen}@shu.edu.cn
[2] Xintu (Wuxi) New Energy Technology Co. LTD., Wuxi 214000, China
gan.m@xjieg.com

Abstract. The research and development of wireless communication technology is inseparable from the support of experimental dataset. This paper first provides an open source multi-dimensional high-precision database of wireless communication signaling data based on the OAI platform, which can build actual communication scenarios to ensure that the dataset in this database is authentic and reliable. Second, we improve the time precision of this dataset to the millisecond level and realize multi-dimensional wireless communication signaling data collection at both of the physical layer and MAC layer, which can provide a more comprehensive and high-precision data foundation for wireless communication research. Finally, our database is applied for supporting two applications, i.e. RAN slice resource prediction and video bit rate adaptive adjustment, respectively. The experiment results show that our proposed database performs better for supporting the RAN slice resource prediction and video bit rate adaptive adjustment compared with other existing databases.

Keywords: Wireless communication · Database · OAI platform

1 Introduction

Since the advent of the first mobile communication system in the 1980s, wireless communication technology has experienced considerable development in the past few decades. Until the freezing of the 3GPP R16 standard, mobile communication technology has realized the technical iteration from the first generation to the fifth generation, and has now formed a wide range of commercial applications based on three typical application scenarios, i.e. enhanced mobile broadband (eMBB), ultra-reliable low latency communications (uRLLC), and massive machine-type communications (mMTC) [1]. The evolution of wireless communication technology from CDMA to LTE, and then to 5G NR requires a lot of technological improvements and innovations, which cannot be separated from the support of a large number of experimental datasets.

N.-S. Vo and H.-A. Tran (Eds.): INISCOM 2023, LNICST 531, pp. 63–74, 2023.
https://doi.org/10.1007/978-3-031-47359-3_5

In recent years, different types of datasets have been collected for the research of wireless communication technology. Particularly, in [2], a large amount of on-site wireless communication data was collected on the actual HRS (high-speed railway) network to evaluate the impact of frequent handover on TCP protocol deterioration, which was then solved by the proposed congestion control algorithm. Based on time-critical warning information collected from buses, such as 3D spatial information and wireless communication signal data, the authors in [3] studied the expected performance of connected vehicles in LTE networks and estimated the potential benefits of simultaneous multiple access transmission over multiple operators. A large-scale wireless communication dataset at the city level is studied in [4], where the authors measured and made public a rich open multi-source dataset in two geographic regions, namely the city of Milan and the province of Trentino, covering telecommunication, weather, news, social networking, and electricity data, providing an ideal testbed for methodologies and approaches aimed at tackling a wide range of problems such as energy consumption, urban structures and interactions. For both of 5G SA and NSA campus network, the datasets were collected from the campus network to study the packet delays and the losses of one-way transmission in [5], which informed the further development and refinement of 5G SA and NSA campus networks for industrial use cases.

Although the above research are promoting technological progress, there are still some deficiencies in the experimental dataset. First, most of the experimental research is based on the simulation data, without using the real collected data. Second, some studies only use some relevant and incomplete data as the basis for drawing research conclusions. Due to the incompleteness of experimental datasets, the accuracy of research conclusions cannot be guaranteed. Third, the granularities of most of the current datasets are not accurate enough, which inevitably leads to the neglect of features of short time scales. Last, the datasets of many experimental studies are not public due to data protection, so that it is difficult for researchers in the same direction to continue their research on the basis of their predecessors.

In view of the above issues, our work mainly focus on the following aspects:

- *Real Dataset Construction.* Different from the simulation dataset, we construct a real dataset by capturing the real signaling data in actual wireless communication scenarios, which are built by using the OAI (OpenAirInterface) platform. Then the dataset built in this way can be more authentic and reliable.
- *High-precision and Multi-dimensional Dataset Collection.* In order to enable wireless communication research more accurate and comprehensive, we improve the accuracy of the dataset to the millisecond level; meanwhile, we capture multi-dimensional wireless communication signaling dataset in both of the physical layer and the MAC layer. What's more, we open source our high-precision and multi-dimensional database to other wireless communications research peers in [6].

2 Preliminaries

To build a light-weight 5G service delivery platform across reusable software components, OAI provides a system called Mosaic5G. In radio access network, Mosaic5G is mainly composed of OAI-RAN and OAI-CN, and is equipped with network interface tools such as FlexRAN to capture, analyze and control network data in the communication system. In the following, we will describe OAI-RAN, OAI-CN and FlexRAN in detail.

Firstly, OAI-RAN is mainly composed of Openair1, Openair2, Openair3 and Common. Among them, Openair1 corresponds to 3GPP38.321 protocol and consists of the physical layer and physical layer RF simulation module to realize functions such as physical layer coding/decoding, OFDM baseband modulation and demodulation, Fourier transform and inverse transform, etc. Openair2 consists of the entire wireless communication RAN Protocol stacks of layer 2 and layer 3, such as MAC, RLC, PDCP, SDAP and RRC layers, and implements wireless communication data transmission functions including physical layer frame scheduling, radio link transmission modes definition, compression and decompression of IP header, QoS (Quality of Service) to DRB (Data Ratio Bearer) mapping, radio resource management and control, etc. Openair3 includes S1AP and GTP-U modules, and connects the communication between base station and core network in both of user plane and data plane.

Secondly, OAI-CN is for the realization of the 3GPP specifications for the 5G Core Network, and contains the following seven modules: AMF (Access and Mobility Management Function), AUSF (Authentication Server Management Function), NRF (Network Repository Function), SMF (Session Management Function), UDM (Unified Data Management), UDR (Unified Data Repository) and UPF (User Plane Function). Due to the complexity of the 5G in SA mode, the functions and modules of OAI-CN are not perfect and still being supplemented according to 3GPP standards.

Thirdly, FlexRAN platform consists of two main components, i.e. the FlexRAN service and control plane, and the FlexRAN application plane. The FlexRAN service and control plane consists of real-time controllers (RTCs) connecting to multiple underlying RAN runtimes. The separation of control and data planes is achieved through the RAN runtime environment. RAN control applications can be developed on top of the RAN runtime and RTC SDK, and allow monitoring, control and coordination of the state of the RAN infrastructure.

The development and maturity of OAI have driven the research and application in various wireless communication-related fields in both of academia and industry. For example, network slicing [7,8], internet of vehicles [9,10], non-orthogonal multiple access [11], multi-access edge computing [12,13] and other research hotspots in the field of communication are studied based on the open OAI platform, respectively.

Based on the analysis above, quite a few studies have been made based on the deployment of actual OAI systems. However, the wireless communication database research based on OAI is still lacking. Considering that wireless communication database can provide data support for more efficient research, this paper will conduct research on wireless communication dataset acquirement and construction based on the OAI system according to 3GPP series protocol standards.

3   OFDMA Based Wireless Communication Database

OAI RAN has designed a matching RAN communication architecture for different networking modes. In NSA (Non-Standalone) mode, eNB and gNB are connected through X2-C interface; eNB and EPC are connected through S1-U and S1-MME; gNB and EPC are connected through S1-U. In SA (Standalone) mode, the control plane and user plane information of gNB are connected to AMF/UPF via NG-C/U. A schematic diagram is shown in Fig. 1.

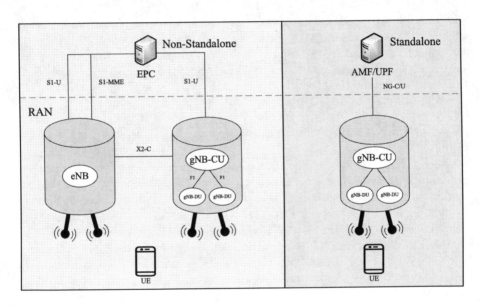

Fig. 1. RAN architecture of OAI system under the dual architecture of NSA and SA.

3.1   Software and Hardware Configuration

According to the existing version of OAI system, considering the stability and performance differences brought about by different construction methods of the OAI system, we built two sets of actual wireless communication scenarios. The first is Separate Mode, where the base station and the core network are deployed on two independent PCs, as shown in Fig. 2; the second one is All In One Mode, where the base station and the core network are deployed on the same PC. In terms of hardware, we use Intel i5 Computer as the platform for the base station and core network, use Huawei Nexus 6P for UE equipment, and adopt Ettus USRP B210 for the RF front end, respectively. AS for software, the host system equipped with the base station and the core network adopts Ubuntu16.04, and the UE system is android8.0. The details of hardware and software arrangement are summarized in Table 1.

Table 1. Details of hardware and software arrangement for wireless communication environment based on OpenAirInterface.

Component	Hardware	Software
UEs	Huawei Nexus 6P	Android 8.0
eNodeB	Intel i5 Computer with low-latency kernel 3.19	OpenAirInterface (OAI) [14]
RF Front-End	Ettus USRP B210	N/A
EPC	Intel i5 Computer with low-latency kernel 3.19	openair-cn [15]

In addition, to obtain the communication dataset under different communication scenarios, we set different service modes for different UEs, such as web browsing, SMS communication, live video with different bit rates, etc, to distinguish the service type and the load differences of UEs.

3.2   Data Collection

We will collect multi-dimensional wireless communication signaling data at both of the physical layer and MAC layer for the dataset construction. Based on the deployment of the above communication scenarios, we will focus on the data transmission of various types on the RAN side. On the one hand, since FlexRAN can directly capture the transmission data of the OAI MAC layer, we are able to capture the transmission data between the UE and the eNB during the actual communication through FlexRAN, including PDU, SUD, etc. On the other hand, by modifying the source code of the OAI MAC layer, we can further capture the physical layer parameters allocated to the UE on the eNB side, such as CQI, RBS, MCS, etc. Parts of the dataset contents are depicted in Fig. 3.

4   Database Analysis

In this section, we will compare our database with several existing wireless communication datasets in terms of time granularity, data integrity, and data authenticity, respectively.

4.1   Time Granularity

In terms of time granularity, we compare our dataset with the public Cellular dataset from Moving Buses, Telecom Italia Big Data Challenge dataset, Link Quality Estimation Data for FlockLab dataset, etc.

Fig. 2. Actual wireless communication system based on OAI in Separate Mode.

TIME	FRAME	SUBFRAME	UEID	CCID	HARQ	ROUND	RBS	CQI	MCS	RRC	TBS
1630055921267	258	2	0	0	6	8	3	15	28	4	7
1630055921348	266	3	1	0	7	8	3	15	28	4	7
1630055921387	270	2	0	0	6	8	3	15	28	4	7
1630055921468	278	3	1	0	7	8	3	15	28	4	7
1630055921507	282	2	0	0	6	8	3	15	28	4	7
1630055921588	290	3	1	0	7	8	3	15	28	4	7
1630055921627	294	2	0	0	6	8	3	15	28	4	7
1630055921708	302	3	1	0	7	8	3	15	28	4	7
1630055921747	306	2	0	0	6	8	3	15	28	4	7
1630055921828	314	3	1	0	7	8	3	15	28	4	7
1630055921844	315	9	1	0	7	8	3	15	28	4	7
1630055921867	318	2	0	0	6	8	3	15	28	4	7
1630055921874	318	9	1	0	5	8	3	15	28	4	7
1630055921906	322	1	1	0	5	8	3	15	28	4	161

Fig. 3. Part of the dataset content collected by the OAI system.

As shown in Table 2, our dataset can output wireless communication data per millisecond and then reach millisecond-level precision, embodying the advantage of features on the smallest time scale. This means that our database can provide more-different time scales data for supporting wireless communication research.

4.2   Data Integrity

In terms of dataset integrity, compared with the public Cellular Received Signal Strength Indicator, LTE Frequency Hopping dataset, etc., our dataset has more comprehensive data types, including Time, UEID, Harq, Hard Round, CQI, MCS, RBS, TBS, PDU, SDU, etc., covering both of the PYH layer and the MAC layer. Furthermore, our underlying dataset also retains the features of the raw data more comprehensively, and can provide input dimension guarantee of multi-dimensional feature input for wireless communication research.

Table 2. Comparison of different wireless communication signaling datasets in terms of time granularity.

dataset	Data Type	Time Resolution
Cellular Received Signal Strength Indicator [2]	Time, Network(2G, 3G, 4G), RSRP, RSS, RSCP, RSSI	30 min
Celluar dataset from Moving Buses [3]	GPS, RSSI, RSRP, Frequency, RSRQ, Band, Protocol, Operator	200 ms
LTE Frequency Hopping dataset [16]	Band, MCS, rblength, UEs, hopinfo	40 ms
LTE KPI [17]	eNB, LCID, RSRP, RSRQ, RSSNR, Carrier Frequency, HandoverDelay, CQI, UE Speed, UE Direction,	1 ms
Link Quality Estimation Data for FlockLab [18]	date_time, rf_channel, tx_power, payload, host_id, rand_seed	2 h
Telecom Italia Big Data Challenge dataset [4]	SMS-in activity, Call-in activity, Internet traffic activity	10 min
Ours	Time, UEID, Harq, CQI, RSRP, RSRQ, Hard Round, RBS, TBS, PDU, SDU, MCS_DL, MCS_UL	1 ms

5   Application

In this section, we use two applications to verify the effectiveness of our proposed wireless communication database.

5.1   Database for Supporting RAN Slicing

We build a RAN slice wireless communication platform, where wireless communication signaling dataset is constructed in single base station, multi-UE, and multi-slice scenarios. Based on this, prediction-based resource slicing is investigated under the premise of ensuring SLA.

The communication scenario is set up with one mini PC building the EPC and one mini PC building the eNB. An USRP B210 is connected to the eNB as a radio frequency transceiver. The terminals are two Huawei Nexus 6Ps, which are connected to the base station for video and web browsing service transmission, respectively. Through FlexRAN, two UEs are assigned to two different slices and run their respective services, where the signaling data are collected.

We set the collected CQI, TBS, MCS as the three input dimension of the CNN-LSTM neural network, to train and predict the number of PRB resources requested by different slices at the next moment. Then slice resources can be allocated in advance to reduce the service SLA level drop caused by inappropriate and untimely allocation of slice resources. Compared with the limitations of existing in dataset integrity and time granularity, we use different input feature dimensions and different time granularity as the independent variables of the experiment to study the variation of SLA satisfaction rate caused by dataset differences. Specifically, we take TBS as the one-dimension input, TBS, MCS as the two-dimension input, TBS, MCS, CQI as the three-dimension input. The time granularity is divided into 100 ms, 500 ms and 1000 ms, respectively.

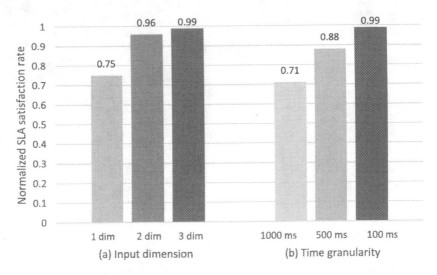

Fig. 4. Comparison of SLA satisfaction rate with different input dimensions and time granularities.

The SLA satisfaction rates with different input dimensions and time granularities are shown in Fig. 4. We can see that the three-dimension input has the highest SLA satisfaction rate and improves the SLA satisfaction rate by 24% over that of one-dimension input. This is due to the fact that a richer input dataset allows the network to learn more complete data characteristics, thereby providing more reasonable decisions for resource allocation after prediction to meet the SLA requirements. On the basis of the three-dimension input, we further compare the experimental results with different time granularities from 1000 ms to 100 ms. Compared with 1000 ms, the time granularity of 100 ms improves the SLA satisfaction rate by 28%. This is because a smaller time granularity allows the network to learn data characteristics on a smaller time scale.

5.2 Database for Supporting Video Bit Rate Adaptive Adjustment

In this subsection, we further verify the effectiveness of our proposed database for supporting video bit rate adaptive adjustment in wireless transmission. We first build a wireless air interface bandwidth prediction and optimization system through FlexRAN, where the real-time parameters data are collected by the interface function in the OAI platform from the PHY layer, the MAC layer, the PDCP layer and other layers of the OAI base station during operation in every 100 ms. In order to keep the data collection time granularity consistent with the bit rate adjustment period, we preprocessed the data, such as mean filtering, feature selection, normalization operations, etc. Second, we input the collected data into LSTM based prediction algorithm to predict the maximum available air interface bandwidth on the user side. Finally, we combine the video quality information returned by the user-side video player, such as the client video buffer, and use the DQN algorithm to optimize the video bit rate adjustment.

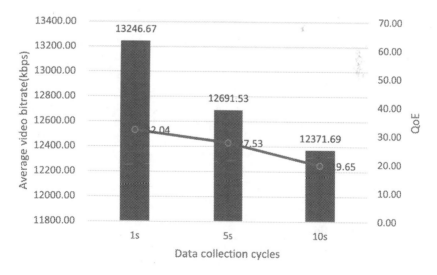

Fig. 5. Performance comparison of different data collection cycles.

The average video bit rate and QoE (Quality of Experience) versus the data collection cycles are shown in Fig. 5. We can see that the performances of the smallest data acquisition period are the best in both of the average video bit rate and QoE. This is because a smaller data acquisition period can provide conditions for a smaller code rate adjustment period. The more frequent video

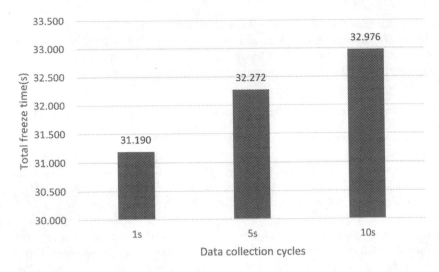

Fig. 6. Comparison of total video freeze time and different data collection cycles.

bit rate switching is also more compatible with the dynamic time-varying channel state variation, so that it can be adjusted to a video bit rate suitable for users more quickly and provide user better QoE. Compared with the 10 s data collection period, the average video bit rate/QoE performance under the 1 s data collection period is 1.07/1.63 times than that of the 10 s data collection period, respectively.

The total video freeze time versus data collection cycles is shown in Fig. 6. The total freeze time corresponding to the 1 s data collection period is 1.786 s less than the total freeze time corresponding to the 10 s data collection period. This is because a larger data collection period corresponds to a larger bit rate adjustment period, which makes The video bit rate fails to respond to the video freeze caused by channel changes in a timely manner.

6   Conclusion

In this paper, we build a real wireless communication database based on the OAI platform. By modifying the OAI source code, a millisecond-level wireless communication signaling dataset can be collected. Furthermore, we built a multi-dimensional high-precision wireless open source database including multi-dimensional wireless communication signaling data in both of the physical layer and the MAC layer. Simulation results of RAN slice resource prediction and video bit rate adaptive adjustment based on our proposed database show that our database provides a good support for wireless communication research.

Acknowledgment. This work was supported by the Innovation Program of Shanghai Municipal Science and Technology Commission under Grant 22511100604 and

20JC1416400, the National Key Research and Development Program of China under Grants 2022YFB2902005, 2022YFB2902304 and 2022YFB2902002, the National Natural Science Foundation of China (NSFC) under Grants 62071284 and 61904101, Key-Area Research and Development Program of Guangdong Province under Grants 2020B0101130012.

References

1. 3GPP: TR 21.916; Services and System Aspects; Release 16 Description; Summary of Rel-16 Work Items (Release 16) (2022)
2. Cui, L., Yuan, Z., Ming, Z., Yang, S.: Improving the congestion control performance for mobile networks in high-speed railway via deep reinforcement learning. IEEE Trans. Veh. Technol. **69**(6), 5864–5875 (2020)
3. Abdesslem, F.B., Abrahamsson, H., Ahlgren, B.: Measuring mobile network multi-access for time-critical C-its applications. In: 2018 Network Traffic Measurement and Analysis Conference (TMA), pp. 1–8 (2018). https://doi.org/10.23919/TMA.2018.8506551
4. Barlacchi, G., et al.: A multi-source dataset of urban life in the city of Milan and the province of Trentino. Sci. Data **2**(1), 1–15 (2015)
5. Rischke, J., Sossalla, P., Itting, S., Fitzek, F.H.P., Reisslein, M.: 5G campus networks: a first measurement study. IEEE Access **9**, 121786–121803 (2021). https://doi.org/10.1109/ACCESS.2021.3108423
6. LabGreat: OAI dataset. https://github.com/LabGreatOfficial/OAI. Accessed 17 Mar
7. Liu, Q., Han, T., Moges, E.: EdgeSlice: slicing wireless edge computing network with decentralized deep reinforcement learning. In: 2020 IEEE 40th International Conference on Distributed Computing Systems (ICDCS), pp. 234–244 (2020). https://doi.org/10.1109/ICDCS47774.2020.00028
8. Schmidt, R., Chang, C.Y., Nikaein, N.: FlexVRAN: a flexible controller for virtualized ran over heterogeneous deployments. In: ICC 2019–2019 IEEE International Conference on Communications (ICC), pp. 1–7 (2019). https://doi.org/10.1109/ICC.2019.8761222
9. Manco, J., Baños, G.G., Härri, J., Sepulcre, M.: Prototyping V2X applications in large-scale scenarios using OpenAirInterface. In: 2020 IEEE Vehicular Networking Conference (VNC), pp. 1–4 (2020). https://doi.org/10.1109/VNC51378.2020.9318327
10. Gill, K.S., et al.: Bumblebee-inspired C-V2X dynamic spectrum access testbed using OpenAirInterface. In: 2020 IEEE 91st Vehicular Technology Conference (VTC2020-Spring), pp. 1–5 (2020). https://doi.org/10.1109/VTC2020-Spring48590.2020.9128871
11. Wei, X., et al.: Software defined radio implementation of a non-orthogonal multiple access system towards 5G. IEEE Access **4**, 9604–9613 (2016)
12. Li, C.Y., et al.: Transparent AAA security design for low-latency MEC-integrated cellular networks. IEEE Trans. Veh. Technol. **69**(3), 3231–3243 (2020)
13. Li, C.Y., et al.: Mobile edge computing platform deployment in 4G LTE networks: a middlebox approach. In: USENIX Workshop on Hot Topics in Edge Computing (HotEdge 2018). USENIX Association, Boston, MA (2018). https://www.usenix.org/conference/hotedge18/presentation/li
14. Openairinterface repository. https://gitlab.eurecom.fr/oai/openairinterface5g. Accessed 10 Oct 2021

15. OpenAir-CN repository. https://gitlab.eurecom.fr/oai/openair-cn. Accessed 17 Oct 2021
16. Cintron, F.: Performance evaluation of LTE device-to-device out-of-coverage communication with frequency hopping resource scheduling (2018-07-23 2018). https:// doi.org/10.6028/NIST.IR.8220
17. Mohan, D., Geetha Mary, A.: LTE KPI for data mining and machine learning (2020). https://doi.org/10.17632/czkn9c4wk6.2
18. Jacob, R., Forno, R.D., Trüb, R., Biri, A., Thiele, L.: Dataset: wireless link quality estimation on FlockLab - and beyond. In: Proceedings of the 2nd Workshop on Data Acquisition to Analysis, DATA 2019, pp. 57–60. Association for Computing Machinery, New York, NY, USA (2019). https://doi.org/10.1145/3359427.3361907

Performance Analysis of RF Energy Harvesting Mobile Edge Computing Network Using NOMA Scheme with Dual Access Points

Minh-Thong Vo[1,2]($\boxtimes$), Thanh-Nam Nguyen[1,2], Van-Truong Truong[1,2], and Dac-Binh Ha[1,2]

[1] Faculty of Electrical-Electronic Engineering, Duy Tan University, Da Nang 550000, Vietnam
{nguyenthanhnam9,truongvantruong}@dtu.edu.vn, hadacbinh@duytan.edu.vn
[2] Institute of Research and Development, Duy Tan University, Da Nang 550000, Vietnam
vominhthong@dtu.edu.vn

Abstract. Mobile edge computing (MEC) is an emerging cloud computing trend that enables terminal users with limited computing ability to offload their tasks to the edge servers. In this paper, we study the performance of the MEC system using non-orthogonal multiple access (NOMA) and radio frequency energy harvesting techniques (RF EH). Specifically, a user harvests energy from a hybrid access point (HAP) and offloads tasks to the edge servers using the NOMA scheme over wireless channels. The protocol, specifically NOMA-MEC, is proposed for this considered system, and the closed-form expression of successful computation probability (SCP) is derived to evaluate the system performance. In addition, an OMA-based reference protocol, namely OMA-MEC, was used to compare with the proposed solution. The numerical results show the superior performance of NOMA-MEC over OMA-MEC in terms of SCP. Furthermore, system behaviors were clarified by investigating SCP using Monte-Carlo simulation through critical parameters such as time switching ratio, power allocation coefficient, task length, and transmit power.

Keywords: mobile edge computing · non-orthogonal multiple access · uplink NOMA · successful computation probability · multiple devices

1 Introduction

In recent decades, Cloud computing (CC) has provided resources such as software, services, and hardware to terminal users (TU) through the Internet. CC allows TUs to conveniently access any resource in the cloud (i.e., server) anytime and anywhere [1]. However, with the development of autonomous systems that require real-time processing, such as industrial IoT networks, and V2X networks,

© ICST Institute for Computer Sciences, Social Informatics and Telecommunications Engineering 2023
Published by Springer Nature Switzerland AG 2023. All Rights Reserved
N.-S. Vo and H.-A. Tran (Eds.): INISCOM 2023, LNICST 531, pp. 75–88, 2023.
https://doi.org/10.1007/978-3-031-47359-3_6

CC no longer fulfills some of the new requirements of TUs [2,3]. Mobile edge computing (MEC) networks are designed and deployed with proximity wireless servers to assist TUs in addressing real-time demanding tasks [4]. In the MEC paradigm, the computing and IT services are provided at the network edge, closest to the MEC devices. They can be smartphones, set-top boxes, IoT devices, or sensor and actuator nodes [5]. MEC can be seen as the next generation of evolution in the field of CC, helping to meet the higher requirements of TUs, especially real-time requirements. MEC ensures low latency, instant response, saves bandwidth, increases security, and good scalability [6].

Currently, the non-orthogonal multiple access (NOMA) technique is applied in MEC networks to solve the problems of many users, high communication data rate requirements, and low latency [7]. NOMA allows multi-user communications through a non-orthogonal division multiplexing technique in which TUs are distinguished based on power level. Obviously, the combination of MEC and NOMA significantly enhances the TU experience and network performance. NOMA provides outstanding advantages in improving spectrum efficiency and throughput, while MEC allows for improved overall network performance. Furthermore, MEC can widely distribute computing resources from the centralized cloud to the network's edge and immediately serve TUs. The NOMA MEC network has been proven effective in enhancing performance compared to OMA-based systems [8].

A radio frequency energy harvesting technique is used to enhance the performance of the MEC-based system further, allowing the TUs to collect energy from RF electromagnetic waves in the wireless environment to operate [9]. In this context, TUs can collect energy from power stations or hybrid access points (HAPs), thus prolonging network connectivity. Integrating these technologies in future wireless communication systems could significantly improve network performance by taking advantage of their strengths [10,11]. For instance, in the work [12], the authors investigate the MEC network using NOMA and RF EH with the power station. Specifically, the user collects radio energy from the power station and offloads the tasks to the edge servers using the NOMA technique to the two access points (APs). To the best of our knowledge, no studies have investigated the MEC network model with mixed APs combined with NOMA offloading. The main contributions of this study are as follows:

- Propose a MEC network model based on the NOMA technique and RF EH transmission from mixed APs, i.e., AP and HAP operating together in the system.
- Propose a four-phase operation protocol, namely NOMA-MEC, for the proposed system that allows radio energy transmission and offloading. In addition, an OMA-based reference protocol, namely OMA-MEC, is analyzed to clarify system performance.
- Derive the close-form expressions of the successful calculation probability (SCP) of NOMA-MEC and OMA-MEC protocol to evaluate the performance of the proposed system.

– Investigate the behavior of the proposed system according to the main parameters such as signal-to-noise ratio, time switching ratio, power allocation coefficient, and task division ratio.

The paper's layout is as follows: Section 2 presents the system model and communication protocol. Section 3 presents the performance analysis of the proposed model. Section 4 describes the numerical results. And Sect. 5 is the conclusion and future scope of the paper.

2   System Model and Communication Protocol

In this study, we investigate the RF EH NOMA MEC network system as depicted in Fig. 1. The network model consists of a user device (U) and two access points, including a hybrid access point (HAP) and a common access point (AP). Suppose the HAP can provide the RF power and offloading services to U, while the AP only provides the offloading services. The devices are equipped with a single antenna and operate in half-duplex mode. The system operates over Rayleigh fading channel.

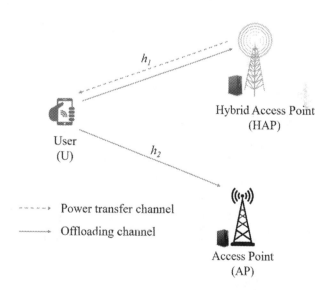

Fig. 1. System model for RF EH NOMA MEC with dual APs system

Assume that U consistently performs tasks of length L bits. Each task consists of two parts: the first L_1-bit part is designed to offload the HAP, and the second L_2-bit part reduces the load on the AP ($L_1 + L_2 = L$). Furthermore, due to the situation of limited power, U offloads its tasks by using all the energy obtained from the HAP and adopting the downlink NOMA technique. Finally, the HAP and AP feedback on the computation results to U using the uplink NOMA

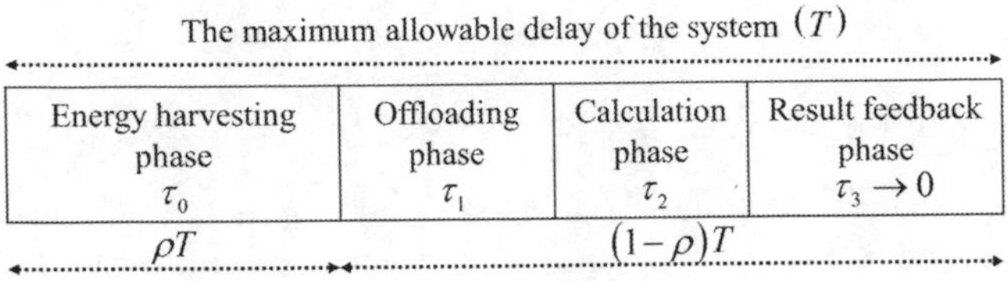

The maximum allowable delay of the system (T)

Energy harvesting phase τ_0	Offloading phase τ_1	Calculation phase τ_2	Result feedback phase $\tau_3 \to 0$
ρT		$(1-\rho)T$	

Fig. 2. Time flow chart for proposed system.

technique. This protocol, called NOMA-MEC, can be divided into four phases, as shown in the time flow diagram in Fig. 2.

We continue to present NOMA-MEC protocol for the proposed system with specific mathematical expressions as follows.

Phase 1- Energy Harvesting Phase: In this phase, U collects radio energy from the HAP in the time interval $\tau_0 = \rho T$, where ρ is the time switching ratio, $0 < \rho < 1$, and T is the block time allocated to the system or the maximum allowable delay of the system. The energy obtained by U in this phase is as follow:

$$E_U = \eta P_0 g_1 \rho T, \qquad (1)$$

where η is the energy conversion factor, $0 < \eta \leq 1$; P_0 is the transmit power of the HAP; g_1 is the channel power gain from U to the HAP.

Phase 2- Offloading Phase: During this phase, U uses all the energy collected in **Phase 1** to simultaneously offload tasks to the HAP and AP using the downlink NOMA. According to NOMA technique, U transmit the superimposed signal as follows:

$$x = \sqrt{a}x_1 + \sqrt{1-a}x_2. \qquad (2)$$

where x_1 and x_2 are L_1-bit and L_2-bit tasks respectively; a is the power allocation coefficient. Thus, the received signal at the HAP is as follow:

$$y_{HAP}^{NOMA-MEC} = h_1\sqrt{P_t}x + n_1 = h_1\sqrt{P_t}(\sqrt{a}x_1 + \sqrt{1-a}x_2) + n_1, \qquad (3)$$

where, h_1 is the channel coefficient from U to HAP, n_1 is the additive white Gaussian noise (AWGN) of the U-HAP channel. Following that, the transmit power of U is:

$$P_t = \frac{E_U}{(1-\rho)T - \tau_2} = b P_0 g_1, \qquad (4)$$

where $b \triangleq \frac{\eta \rho T}{(1-\rho)T - \tau_2}$; τ_2 is the maximum computation time at the MEC servers and is calculated by

$$\tau_2 = \max\left\{\frac{\delta_1 L_1}{f_1}, \frac{\delta_2 L_2}{f_2}\right\}, \qquad (5)$$

where δ_X $(X \in \{1,2\})$ is the number of CPU cycles required to process one input bit; f_X $(X \in \{1,2\})$ denoted the server CPU frequency at the HAP and AP, respectively.

Similarly, the received signal at the AP is as follow:

$$y_{AP}^{NOMA-MEC} = h_2\sqrt{P_t}(\sqrt{a}x_1 + \sqrt{1-a}x_2) + n_2, \tag{6}$$

where, h_2 is the channel coefficient from U to HAP, n_2 is the AWGN of the U-AP channel.

Phase 3- Calculation Phase: In this phase, assuming HAP is located closer to U than AP, thus that HAP can directly decode to get x_1 while AP uses successive interference cancelation (SIC) to decode signal x_1 first and then subtract x_1 to get x_2 signal [10,13]. Hence, the signal-to-interference noise ratio (SINR) at the HAP is as follow:

$$\gamma_1 = \frac{aP_t|h_1|^2}{(1-a)P_t|h_1|^2 + N_0} = \frac{ab\gamma_0 g_1^2}{(1-a)b\gamma_0 g_1^2 + 1}, \tag{7}$$

where $\gamma_0 = \frac{P_0}{N_0}$.

The SINR and signal-to-noise ratio (SNR) at the AP to decode x_1 and x_2 signals are:

$$\gamma_2^{x_1} = \frac{ab\gamma_0 g_1 g_2}{(1-a)b\gamma_0 g_1 g_2 + 1}, \tag{8}$$

$$\gamma_2^{x_2} = (1-a)b\gamma_0 g_1 g_2, \tag{9}$$

The capacity of U-HAP and U-AP channels is calculated according to Shannon's theorem as follows:

$$C_1 = (1-\rho)B\log_2(1+\gamma_1), \tag{10}$$

$$C_2 = (1-\rho)B\log_2(1+\gamma_2^{x_2}), \tag{11}$$

where B is the bandwidth.

The offloading time when U offloads its task to HAP and AP is calculated as follows:

$$t_1 = \frac{L_1}{C_1} = \frac{L_1}{(1-\rho)B\log_2(1+\gamma_1)}, \tag{12}$$

$$t_2 = \frac{L_2}{C_2} = \frac{L_2}{(1-\rho)B\log_2(1+\gamma_2^{x_2})}. \tag{13}$$

The maximum offload time τ of this system is:

$$\tau = \max\left\{t_1 + \frac{\delta_1 L_1}{f_1}, t_2 + \frac{\delta_2 L_2}{f_2}\right\}. \tag{14}$$

Phase 4- Result Feedback Phase: In this phase, U receives calculation results from HAP and AP in time τ_3. τ_3 is very small compared to transmission and computation time, so it can be ignored [8,10].

The power gain of the Rayleigh fading channel g_i follows an exponential distribution with the parameter λ_i, $i \in \{1, 2\}$. Therefore, the cumulative distribution function (CDF) and the probability density function (PDF) of g_i are given by following equations.

$$F_{g_i}(x) = 1 - e^{-\frac{x}{\lambda_i}}, \tag{15}$$

$$f_{g_i}(x) = \frac{1}{\lambda_i} e^{-\frac{x}{\lambda_i}}. \tag{16}$$

3   Performance Analysis

In this section, we analyze the RF EH NOMA-MEC with mixed APs system performance through the criterion of SCP, denoted by Φ_s. It is the probability that all tasks are completed within the maximum allowable delay time $T > 0$. Accordingly, Φ_s is given by the formula:

$$\Phi_s = \Pr\left(\tau < (1 - \rho)T\right). \tag{17}$$

To evaluate the system performance, we find the following theorem.

Theorem 1. *The approximation close-form expression of the SCP of the proposed system under NOMA-MEC protocol, denoted by Φ_s^{NOMA}, over Rayleigh fading channel is as follow:*

$$\Phi_s^{NOMA} = \begin{cases} 0, & \text{if } \frac{a}{1-a} \le 2^{\frac{L_1}{(1-\rho)B\Omega_1}} - 1 \\ \frac{\pi e^{-\sqrt{\beta_1}}}{2Q\lambda_1} \sum_{q=1}^{Q} t_q^{\frac{1}{\lambda_1}-1} e^{\frac{\beta_2}{\lambda_2 \ln t_q}} \sqrt{1 - x_q^2}, & \text{if } \frac{a}{1-a} > 2^{\frac{L_1}{(1-\rho)B\Omega_1}} - 1 \end{cases} \tag{18}$$

where $\beta_1 = \dfrac{2^{\frac{L_1}{(1-\rho)B\Omega_1}} - 1}{b\gamma_0 \left[a - (1-a)\left(2^{\frac{L_1}{(1-\rho)B\Omega_1}} - 1\right)\right]}$; $\beta_2 = \dfrac{2^{\frac{L_2}{(1-\rho)B\Omega_2}} - 1}{(1-a)b\gamma_0}$; $\Omega_1 = (1-\rho)T -$
$\frac{\delta_1 L_1}{f_1}$; $\Omega_2 = (1-\rho)T - \frac{\delta_2 L_2}{f_2}$; *and* $x_q = \cos\left(\frac{2q-1}{2Q}\pi\right)$; $t_q = \frac{(x_q+1)}{2} e^{-\sqrt{\beta_1}}$ *and* Q *is the trade-off coefficient between complexity and precision.*

Proof. See appendix A.

To refer to the NOMA-MEC protocol, we propose the second operating protocol system, named OMA-MEC, as follows:

Phase 1- Energy Harvesting Phase: The system works entirely similar to the NOMA-MEC protocol described above, i.e., U receives energy from HAP.

Phase 2- Offloading Phase: The task (L-bits) is offloaded to the MEC server located at the HAP in this phase. In other words, the downlink OMA scheme is applied to offload workload. Accordingly, the received signal at HAP has the form:

$$y_{HAP}^{OMA-MEC} = h_1 x_1 \sqrt{P_t^{OMA}} + n_1, \tag{19}$$

where $P_t^{OMA} = \frac{E_U}{(1-\rho)T - \tau_2^{OMA}} = b^{OMA} P_0 g_1$; $b^{OMA} \triangleq \frac{\eta \rho T}{(1-\rho)T - \tau_2^{OMA}}$; $\tau_2^{OMA} = \frac{\delta_1 L}{f_1}$.

Phase 3- Calculation Phase: The SNR at the HAP to decode the signal is as follow:

$$\gamma_1^{OMA} = \frac{P_t^{OMA}|h_1|^2}{N_0} = b^{OMA} \gamma_0 g_1^2, \tag{20}$$

Phase 4- Result Feedback Phase: In this phase, U receives calculation results from HAP for the rest of the time.

Accordingly, we state Theorem 2, describing the system SCP of the OMA-MEC protocol as follow.

Theorem 2. *The exact close-form expression of the SCP of the proposed system under OMA-MEC protocol, denoted by Φ_s^{OMA} over Rayleigh fading channel is as follow:*

$$\Phi_s^{OMA} = \Pr(\tau_1^{OMA} + \tau_2^{OMA} \leq (1-\rho)T)$$
$$= e^{-\frac{\sqrt{\beta_3}}{\lambda_1}}, \tag{21}$$

where $\beta_3 = \frac{2^{\frac{L}{(1-\rho)B\Omega_3}} - 1}{b^{OMA}\gamma_0}$; $\Omega_3 = (1-\rho)T - \frac{\delta_1 L}{f_1}$; $\tau_1^{OMA} = \frac{L}{C^{OMA}}$; $C^{OMA} = \frac{L}{(1-\rho)B\log_2(1+b^{OMA}\gamma_0 g_1^2)}$.

Proof. See appendix B.

4   Numerical Results and Discussion

In this section, we present the numerical results of the SCP of the proposed system. We use the Monte Carlo simulation method and the Matlab tool to drive simulations and evaluate the correctness of the system analysis. At the same time, the system behavior is investigated under NOMA-MEC and OMA-MEC protocols according to critical parameters such as signal-to-noise ratio, time-switching ratio, power allocation coefficient, and task division ratio. The parameters used in the detailed simulation are shown in Table 1 [14].

In the first experiment, we compared the SCP system under NOMA-MEC and OMA-MEC protocols, as Fig. 3. The SCP curves for the two protocols show similar upward or downward trends. However, it is easy to see that the SCP when the system uses the NOMA-MEC protocol is always higher than the OMA-MEC. This result was investigated when setting the computing capability of the two MEC servers to be the same. Accordingly, the task offloaded for two MECs in the NOMA-MEC protocol will have a shorter execution time than the case of using only one HAP in the OMA-MEC protocol. We conclude that the proposed NOMA-MEC protocol helps the system perform better than the OMA-MEC protocol. This result is repeated when performing investigations with different parameters; therefore, we only evaluate system performance under the NOMA-MEC protocol in subsequent experiments.

Table 1. Simulation Parameters.

Parameters	Notation	Typical Values
Environment		Rayleigh
Transmit power	P_0	$-10 \rightarrow 30\,\text{dB}$
Time switching ratio	ρ	0.4
CPU-cycle frequency of MEC server deployed in HAP	f_1	10 GHz
CPU-cycle frequency of MEC server deployed in AP	f_2	10 GHz
Channel bandwidth	B	100 MHz
The threshold of latency	T	0.5 s
The number of data bits offloaded to HAP	L_1	0.6 Mbits
The number of data bits offloaded to AP	L_2	0.6 Mbits
Power allocation coefficient	a	0.7
Energy conversion factor	η	0.75

Figure 4 examines the SCP of the system according to the transmitted power with the power allocation coefficient values of 0.6, 0.75, and 0.9, respectively. In all three cases, the descriptive curve Φ_s shows that the larger the transmit power, the better the system performance. This is entirely consistent with formulas (7), (8), and (9); that is, when the transmit power increases, the average transmit SNR increases, leading to an increase in the SINR and SNR values at the HAP and AP, thereby improving the SCP of the system. One note is that with significant transmit power levels (>20 dB), Φ_s reaches saturation value. Therefore, there should be a consideration during system design to ensure system performance at a reasonable energy cost.

Figure 5 depicts the SCP of the system according to the power allocation coefficient with different task division ratios. In which the task division ratio is denoted by ε, $\varepsilon = \frac{L_1}{L}$. Based on the similar form of all three different ε cases, we conclude that there exists an optimal power allocation coefficient (a^*) such that the system performance stands at the maximum. Indeed, Φ_s has a small value when a is small; then Φ_s gradually increases to a maximum value as a increases; and finally, Φ_s tends to decrease as a increase to 1. It shows that the system performance depends essentially on a. Therefore when designing the system, it is necessary to design suitable optimization algorithms so that a^* can be determined to optimize the SCP. Furthermore, there exists a unique point on the graph, which we call the transition point (TP), which has the coordinate a_{TP}. For the values a, which are smaller than a_{TP}, lower ε leads to higher Φ_s. Conversely, when a is larger than a_{TP}, the higher ε is, the better the system performance is.

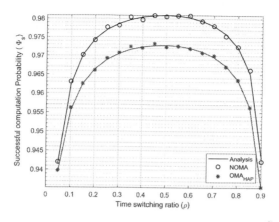

Fig. 3. System performance comparison under the NOMA-MEC and OMA-MEC protocols.

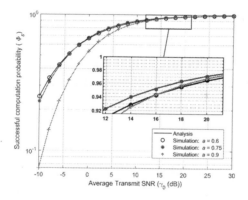

Fig. 4. SCP vs. the average transmit SNR with different power allocation coefficients.

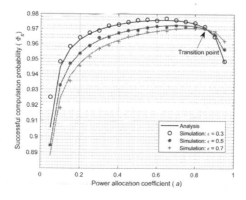

Fig. 5. SCP vs. the power allocation coefficient with different task division ratios.

Figure 6 examines the SCP of the system according to the task division ratio and the time switching ratio. In all three survey cases, when ε increases from 0.05 to 0.95, i.e., the L_1 task length increases and L_2 task length decreases, the system performance degrades from 1% to 2%. Another remark is that an extreme value of Φ_s exists according to the time switching ratio because Φ_s at $\rho = 0.4$ is better than the two cases $\rho = 0.1$ and $\rho = 0.7$.

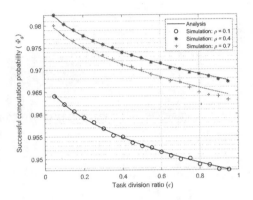

Fig. 6. SCP vs. the task division ratio with different time switching ratios.

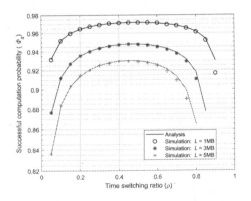

Fig. 7. SCP vs. the time switching ratio with different the task lengths.

Figure 7 examines the SCP of the system according to the time switching ratio with different task sizes. Specifically, when ρ is low, Φ_s is low. When ρ increases to the optimal value (ρ^*), Φ_s reaches its maximum value. When $\rho > \rho^*$, Φ_s tends to decrease. It is imaginable because when ρ is small ($\rho < 0.2$), the time spent in the energy-harvesting phase is narrow, resulting in a low transmit power of U. Thus, the SCP of the system will be low. Meanwhile, when ρ is large ($\rho > 0.8$), although the transmit power of U is significant, the time spent on offloading and calculation phases is deficient, resulting in a low value of Φ_s. Therefore, designing the system with the optimal time-switching ratio is essential for maximum system performance. Another observation is that task length has a significant effect on system performance. When L increases from 1 MB to 5 MB, the system performance degrades by approximately 10%. Therefore, designing the task of appropriate length in MEC-based networks is one of the basic requirements to ensure system performance.

The simulation results (Simulation) and analytical calculations (Analysis) are consistent in the above experiments, showing our research's correctness.

5   Conclusion

In this paper, we have investigated the system performance of a MEC network that harvests radio energy using NOMA and two access points. One of these two APs is the HAP, and the other is the standard AP. We propose the NOMA-MEC protocol for this network and derive a closed-form expression for the system SCP. To evaluate the NOMA-MEC protocol, we compare it with the OMA-MEC protocol. The results show the superiority of our approach. We used Monte Carlo simulation to verify the correctness of the mathematical analysis results and investigate the system's performance through critical parameters such as transmit power, time switching ratio, power allocation coefficient, and task division ratio. The results show that the performance of the proposed system depends on the main parameters mentioned above. To improve the system performance, we can determine one of the methods: (i) increase the transmit power, (ii) select the optimal time switching ratio, power allocation coefficient, and task division ratio. We will propose an algorithm to find these optimal coefficients in future work.

Acknowledgment. This research is funded by Vietnam National Foundation for Science and Technology Development (NAFOSTED) under grant number 102.04-2021.11.

APPENDIX A: PROOF OF THEOREM 1

In this section, we prove Theorem 1. From the fomular (12) to (14), and (17), we rewrite the SCP of the proposed system as follows:

$$
\begin{aligned}
\Phi_s^{NOMA} &= \Pr\left(\frac{L_1}{C_1} + \frac{\delta_1 L_1}{f_1} \leq (1-\rho)\,T,\quad \frac{L_2}{C_2} + \frac{\delta_2 L_2}{f_2} \leq (1-\rho)\,T\right) \\
&= \Pr\left((1-\rho)\,B\log_2\left[1 + \frac{ab\gamma_0 g_1^2}{(1-a)b\gamma_0 g_1^2 + 1}\right] \geq \frac{L_1}{\Omega_1},\ (1-\rho)\,B\log_2\left[1 + (1-a)b\gamma_0 g_1 g_2\right] \geq \frac{L_2}{\Omega_2}\right) \\
&= \Pr\left(\frac{ab\gamma_0 g_1^2}{(1-a)b\gamma_0 g_1^2 + 1} \geq 2^{\frac{L_1}{\Omega_1(1-\rho)B}} - 1,\ (1-a)b\gamma_0 g_1 g_2 \geq 2^{\frac{L_2}{\Omega_2(1-\rho)B}} - 1\right) \\
&= \begin{cases}
0, & \text{if } \frac{a}{1-a} \leq 2^{\frac{L_1}{(1-\rho)B\Omega_1}} - 1 \\
\Pr\left(g_1 \geq \sqrt{\beta_1},\, g_2 \geq \frac{\beta_2}{g_1}\right), & \text{if } \frac{a}{1-a} > 2^{\frac{L_1}{(1-\rho)B\Omega_1}} - 1
\end{cases} \\
&= \begin{cases}
0, & \text{if } \frac{a}{1-a} \leq 2^{\frac{L_1}{(1-\rho)B\Omega_1}} - 1 \\
\underbrace{\int_{\sqrt{\beta_1}}^{\infty} \left[1 - F_{g_2}\left(\frac{\beta_2}{x}\right)\right] f_{g_1}(x)dx}_{I}, & \text{if } \frac{a}{1-a} > 2^{\frac{L_1}{(1-\rho)B\Omega_1}} - 1
\end{cases}
\end{aligned}
$$

$$\tag{22}$$

We focus on the case $\frac{a}{1-a} > 2^{\frac{L_1}{(1-\rho)B\Omega_1}} - 1$. The integral I is calculated as:

$$
\begin{aligned}
I &= \int_{\sqrt{\beta_1}}^{\infty} \left[1 - F_{g_2}\left(\frac{\beta_2}{x}\right)\right] f_{g_1}(x)dx \\
&= \frac{1}{\lambda_1} \int_{\sqrt{\beta_1}}^{\infty} e^{-\frac{x}{\lambda_1} - \frac{\beta_2}{\lambda_2 x}} dx \\
&\overset{(*)}{=} \frac{1}{\lambda_1} \int_{0}^{e^{-\sqrt{\beta_1}}} t^{\frac{1}{\lambda_1} - 1} e^{\frac{\beta_2}{\lambda_2 \ln t}} dt \\
&\overset{(**)}{=} \frac{\pi e^{-\sqrt{\beta_1}}}{2Q\lambda_1} \sum_{q=1}^{Q} t_q^{\frac{1}{\lambda_1} - 1} e^{\frac{\beta_2}{\lambda_2 \ln t_q}} \sqrt{1 - x_q^2}.
\end{aligned}
$$

$$\tag{23}$$

where step $(*)$ is obtained by putting $t = e^{-x}$. The step $(**)$ is achieved by applying the Gauss-Chebyshev quadrature approximation. Here, Theorem 1 has been proved.

APPENDIX B: PROOF OF THEOREM 2

We continue to demonstrate Theorem 2 in this section. From the definition formula, Φ_s^{OMA} is implemented as follows:

$$
\begin{aligned}
\Phi_s^{OMA} &= \Pr\left(\frac{L}{(1-\rho)B\log_2(1 + b^{OMA}\gamma_0 g_1{}^2)} + \frac{\delta_1 L}{f_1} \leq (1-\rho)T \right) \\
&= \Pr\left(\frac{L}{(1-\rho)B\log_2(1 + b^{OMA}\gamma_0 g_1{}^2)} \leq \underbrace{(1-\rho)T - \frac{\delta_1 L}{f_1}}_{\Omega_3} \right) \\
&= \Pr\left(\underbrace{\frac{2^{\frac{L}{(1-\rho)B\Omega_3}} - 1}{b\gamma_0}}_{\beta_3} \leq g_1{}^2 \right) \\
&= 1 - F_{g_1}(\sqrt{\beta_3}) \\
&= e^{-\frac{\sqrt{\beta_3}}{\lambda_1}}
\end{aligned}
\tag{24}
$$

We have completed the proof of Theorem 2.

References

1. Zhou, Y., Zhang, D., Xiong, N.: Post-cloud computing paradigms: a survey and comparison. Tsinghua Sci. Technol. **22**(6), 714–732. https://doi.org/10.23919/TST.2017.8195353
2. Hou, X., Ren, Z., Yang, K., Chen, C., Zhang, H., Xiao, Y.: IIoT-MEC: a novel mobile edge computing framework for 5G-enabled IIoT. In: Proceedings 2019 IEEE Wireless Communications and Networking Conference (WCNC), pp. 1–7 (2019). https://doi.org/10.1109/WCNC.2019.8885703
3. Ma, H., Li, S., Zhang, E., Lv, Z., Hu, J., Wei, X.: Cooperative autonomous driving oriented MEC-aided 5G–V2X: prototype system design, field tests and AI-based optimization tools. IEEE Access **8**, 54288–54302 (2020). https://doi.org/10.1109/ACCESS.2020.2981463
4. Mao, Y., You, C., Zhang, J., Huang, K., Letaief, K.B.: A survey on mobile edge computing: the communication perspective. IEEE Commun. Surveys Tut. **19**(4), 2322–2358 (2017)
5. Mach, P., Becvar, Z.: Mobile edge computing: a survey on architecture and computation offloading. IEEE Commun. Surveys Tut. **19**(3), 1628–1656 (2017)
6. Mehrabi, M., You, D., Latzko, V., Salah, H., Reisslein, M., Fitzek, F.H.P.: Device-enhanced MEC: multi-access edge computing (MEC) aided by end device computation and caching: a survey. IEEE Access **7**, 166079–166108 (2019). https://doi.org/10.1109/ACCESS.2019.2953172
7. Truong, T.P., Nguyen, T.V., Noh, W., Cho, S., et al.: Partial computation offloading in NOMA-assisted mobile-edge computing systems using deep reinforcement learning. IEEE Internet Things J. **8**(17), 13196–13208 (2021)

8. Ha, D.-B., Truong, V.-T., Ha, D.-H.: A novel secure protocol for mobile edge computing network applied downlink NOMA. In: Vo, N.-S., Hoang, V.-P. (eds.) INISCOM 2020. LNICST, vol. 334, pp. 324–336. Springer, Cham (2020). https://doi.org/10.1007/978-3-030-63083-6_25

9. Nguyen, M.T., Tran, H.T., Nguyen, C.V., Ala, G., Viola, F., Colak, I.: A novel framework of hybrid harvesting mechanisms for remote sensing devices. In: 2022 IEEE 21st Mediterranean Electrotechnical Conference (MELECON) (IEEE), pp. 1007–1012 (2022)

10. Truong, V.-T., Vo, M.-T., Ha, D.-B.: Performance analysis of mobile edge computing network applied uplink NOMA with RF energy harvesting. In: Vo, N.-S., Hoang, V.-P., Vien, Q.-T. (eds.) INISCOM 2021. LNICST, vol. 379, pp. 57–72. Springer, Cham (2021). https://doi.org/10.1007/978-3-030-77424-0_6

11. Nguyen, M.T., Nguyen, C.V., Tran, H.T., Viola, F.: Energy harvesting for mobile agents supporting wireless sensor networks. Energy Harvesting Syst. (2022)

12. Truong, V.T., Ha, D.B.: Secured scheme for RF energy harvesting mobile edge computing networks based on NOMA and access point selection. In: Proceedings 2020 7th NAFOSTED Conference on Information and Computer Science (NICS), pp. 7–12 (2020). https://doi.org/10.1109/NICS51282.2020.9335833

13. Zhu, B., Chi, K., Liu, J., Yu, K., Mumtaz, S.: Efficient offloading for minimizing task computation delay of NOMA-based multiaccess edge computing. IEEE Trans. Commun. **70**(5), 3186–3203 (2022)

14. Truong, V.T., Ha, D.B., So-In, C., et al.: On the system performance of mobile edge computing in an uplink NOMA WSN with a multiantenna access point over Nakagami-m fading. IEEE/CAA J. Automatica Sinica **9**(4), 668–685 (2022)

Joint Design of Reflection Coefficients and Beamforming in Double RIS-Assisted System

Qiangqiang Yang[1], Yufeng Chen[1], Hongwen Yu[1], Guannan Tan[2], Antonino Masaracchia[3], and Yong Fang[1(✉)]

[1] Shanghai University, Shanghai 200444, China
{yangqq,cyf119,hw_yu,yfang}@shu.edu.cn
[2] Huizhou Speed Wireless Technology Company, Huizhou 516000, China
[3] Queen's University Belfast, Belfast BT7 1NN, UK
a.masaracchia@qub.ac.uk

Abstract. Reconfigurable intelligent surfaces (RISs) offer a cost-effective approach to creating adaptable wireless communication environments. This study focuses on a double-RIS assisted multi-user network, deploying two RISs near a multi-antenna base station (BS) and a cluster of nearby users. The communication occurs through a cascaded double-reflection link: BS-RIS 1-RIS 2-users. Our objective is to optimize beamforming at the BS and quantized programmable reflecting elements of the RISs to maximize the geometric mean of users' rates. We present an efficient algorithm that generates improved feasible solutions using closed-form methods. Simulations confirm the algorithm's effectiveness in enhancing rate fairness among users.

Keywords: Reconfigurable intelligent surface · transmit beamforming · programmable reflecting elements · geometric mean maximization · nonconvex optimization algorithm

1 Introduction

As the deployment of fifth-generation (5G) networks progresses, researchers are increasingly focusing on the advancement of the upcoming sixth-generation (6G) technologies, with significant attention from both academia and industry [1]. In this context, reconfigurable intelligent surface (RIS) has been proposed as a revolutionary technology to support faster and more reliable data transmissions while maintaining at a low cost and energy consumption. An RIS consists of an array of small, cost-effective, and almost passive scattering elements, alongside a programmable controller. This controller is capable of adjusting the phase of the metasurface, thereby altering the reflective properties of an incoming wave [2–4]. Hence, researchers have extensively explored the benefits of efficient energy

Supported by Technology Key Project of Guangdong Province, China (HZJBGS-2021001).

N.-S. Vo and H.-A. Tran (Eds.): INISCOM 2023, LNICST 531, pp. 89–103, 2023.
https://doi.org/10.1007/978-3-031-47359-3_7

utilization, improved spectrum utilization, cost-effective implementation, and flexible deployment of RIS [5–7].

Previous research on double-RIS has predominantly focused on wireless communication systems aided by two distributed RISs [8–11]. Each RIS independently enhances the communication of its nearby multi-antenna base station (BS) or a cluster of nearby users. Nonetheless, these studies are not applicable to practical scenarios where a single RIS's reflected signal cannot completely overcome all major obstacles. The initial attempt to jointly design passive beamforming for a wireless communication system assisted by a double-RIS was undertaken by the authors in [12]. However, their approach is not suitable for general scenarios involving multi-antenna BS/users. Another study [13] explored a double RIS-assisted communication system, aiming to optimize the average achievable rate through cooperative passive beamforming. Nevertheless, the algorithm proposed in [13] was computationally intensive due to the utilization of semidefinite relaxation (SDR) and Gaussian randomization techniques. Consequently, only 6 reflecting elements were considered in the simulations.

This study aims to enhance the spectral efficiency in a multi-user context by optimizing the geometric mean (GM) of user rates within a double-RIS framework. We present a low-complexity optimization algorithm for jointly designing beamforming and the quantized programmable reflecting elements (PREs) of RISs to maximize the GM rate. Our algorithm, based on a closed-form approach utilizing the Lagrange multiplier method and linear optimization, provides optimal solutions. Compared to conventional sum rate (SR) based algorithms, our GM rate-based algorithm offers notable advantages. It ensures a fair and equitable distribution of rates among all users without imposing any minimum user-rate constraints. Notably, the proposed GM rate descent algorithm effectively avoids zero-rate users (ZR-UEs), showcasing the efficiency of our approach. We substantiate our claims with simulation results, highlighting the effectiveness of our GM rate-based strategy.

The structure of the remaining sections in this paper is as follows. In Sect. 2, we present the system model for the double RIS-assisted wireless communication system and provide an outline of the optimization problem formulation. In Sect. 3, we present our efficient algorithm designed to tackle the formulated problems within the framework of the double-RIS system. Section 4 presents numerical results to validate the performance of the proposed GM descent algorithm. Lastly, Sect. 5 serves as the conclusion of this paper.

2   Signaling Model

We analyze a downlink communication network assisted by two RISs, as depicted in Fig. 1. This network comprises a BS equipped with N antennas and K individual users, where RIS 1 and RIS 2, each composed of M_1 and M_2 elements respectively, are strategically positioned in proximity to the BS and users. We denote $\overline{h}_R \in \mathbb{C}^{1 \times M_2}$, $\overline{h}_B \in \mathbb{C}^{M_1 \times N}$, and $\overline{D} \in \mathbb{C}^{M_2 \times M_1}$ as the channels for the communication links from RIS 2 to user k, from BS to RIS 1, and from RIS 1

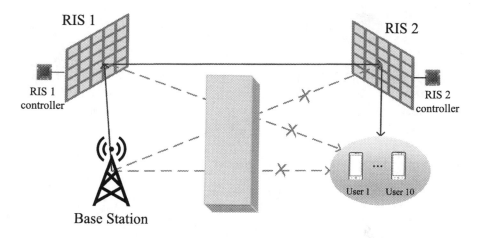

Fig. 1. A MISO wireless communication system assisted by a double-RIS framework.

to RIS 2, with $k \in \mathcal{D} \triangleq \{1, \ldots, K\}$, respectively, all of which are modelled by Rician fading. In this research, we assume perfect acquisition of channel state information (CSI) at the BS to demonstrate the enhancement in the performance of the proposed system, as discussed in previous works [14,15].

The effective channel connecting the BS to user k is represented as

$$\bar{\mathcal{H}}_k(\varphi_1, \varphi_2) \triangleq \bar{h}_R \boldsymbol{\Phi}_2 \overline{D} \boldsymbol{\Phi}_1 \bar{h}_B \in \mathbb{C}^{1 \times N}, \tag{1}$$

for

$$\begin{aligned}
\boldsymbol{\Phi}_1 &= \mathrm{diag}(e^{j\bar{\psi}_1}) = \mathrm{diag}(e^{j\bar{\psi}_{1,1}}, e^{j\bar{\psi}_{1,2}}, \ldots, e^{j\bar{\psi}_{1,M_1}}), \bar{\psi}_1 \in [0, 2\pi]^{M_1}, \\
\boldsymbol{\Phi}_2 &= \mathrm{diag}(e^{j\bar{\psi}_2}) = \mathrm{diag}(e^{j\bar{\psi}_{2,1}}, e^{j\bar{\psi}_{2,2}}, \ldots, e^{j\bar{\psi}_{2,M_2}}), \bar{\psi}_2 \in [0, 2\pi]^{M_2},
\end{aligned} \tag{2}$$

where $\boldsymbol{\Phi}_1 \in \mathbb{C}^{M_1 \times M_1}$ and $\boldsymbol{\Phi}_2 \in \mathbb{C}^{M_2 \times M_2}$ denote the PREs associated with RIS 1 and RIS 2, respectively.

We optimize PREs quantized by b-bit resolutions i.e.

$$\begin{aligned}
\bar{\psi}_{1,m_1}, \bar{\psi}_{2,m_2} &\in \Delta \triangleq \left\{ \delta \frac{2\pi}{2^b}, \delta = 0, 1, \ldots, 2^b - 1 \right\}, \\
m_1 &\in \mathcal{F}_1 \triangleq \{1, \ldots, M_1\}, m_2 \in \mathcal{F}_2 \triangleq \{1, \ldots, M_2\}.
\end{aligned} \tag{3}$$

Subsequently, the projection of $\xi \in [0, 2\pi)$ onto the set Δ, denoted as $\lfloor \xi \rfloor_b$, signifies its approximation with b bits:

$$\lfloor \xi \rfloor_b = \delta_\xi \frac{2\pi}{2^b} \tag{4}$$

with

$$\delta_\xi \triangleq \arg \min_{\delta = 0, 1, \ldots, 2^b - 1} \left| \delta \frac{2\pi}{2^b} - \xi \right|, \tag{5}$$

which can be easily determined, as we have $\delta_\xi \in \delta, \delta + 1$ for $\xi \in [\delta \frac{2\pi}{2^b}, (\delta + 1)\frac{2\pi}{2^b}]$. When $b = \infty$, it is true that

$$\xi = \lfloor \xi \rfloor_\infty. \tag{6}$$

Consider $s_k \in \mathcal{C}(0, 1)$ as the information symbol designated for user k, which is directed through beamforming by $\bar{\mathbf{w}}_k \in \mathbb{C}^M$. The signal x transmitted from the BS is denoted as

$$x = \sum_{k \in \mathcal{D}} \bar{\mathbf{w}}_k s_k. \tag{7}$$

The received signal at user k can be represented as follows:

$$\bar{y}_k = \bar{\mathcal{H}}_k(\bar{\psi}_1, \bar{\psi}_2) \sum_{k \in \mathcal{D}} \bar{\mathbf{w}}_k s_k + n_k, \tag{8}$$

where $n_k \in \mathcal{C}(0, \sigma)$ represents the background noise at user k.

We define the set $\bar{\mathbf{w}}$ as $\mathbf{w} \triangleq \{\bar{\mathbf{w}}_k, k \in \mathcal{D}\}$. The rate at user k can be expressed as

$$r_k(\bar{\mathbf{w}}, \bar{\psi}_1, \bar{\psi}_2) = \ln\left(1 + \frac{|\bar{\mathcal{H}}_k(\bar{\psi}_1, \bar{\psi}_2)\bar{\mathbf{w}}_k|^2}{\sum_{k' \in \mathcal{D}\setminus\{k\}} |\bar{\mathcal{H}}_k(\bar{\psi}_1, \bar{\psi}_2)\bar{\mathbf{w}}_{k'}|^2 + \sigma}\right). \tag{9}$$

3　GM-Rate Optimization

We express the cooperative optimization of the beamforming vector $\bar{\mathbf{w}}$ for the BS and the PREs $\bar{\psi}_1$ and $\bar{\psi}_2$ to optimize the GM of users' rates in the following manner:

$$\max_{\bar{\mathbf{w}}, \bar{\psi}_1, \bar{\psi}_2} \left(\prod_{k \in \mathcal{D}} r_k(\bar{\mathbf{w}}, \bar{\psi}_1, \bar{\psi}_2)\right)^{1/K} \quad \text{s.t.} \tag{10a}$$

$$\sum_{k \in \mathcal{D}} \|\bar{\mathbf{w}}_k\|^2 \leq P, \tag{10b}$$

while subjecting to a given transmit power P. This issue can be equivalently expressed as the following:

$$\min_{\bar{\mathbf{w}}, \bar{\psi}_1, \bar{\psi}_2} g\left(r_1\left(\bar{\mathbf{w}}, \bar{\psi}_1, \bar{\psi}_2\right), \ldots, r_K\left(\bar{\mathbf{w}}, \bar{\psi}_1, \bar{\psi}_2\right)\right) \triangleq \frac{1}{\left(\prod_{k \in \mathcal{D}} r_k(\bar{\mathbf{w}}, \bar{\psi}_1, \bar{\psi}_2)\right)^{1/K}}$$

$$\text{s.t.} \quad (10b). \tag{11}$$

The problem becomes non-convex due to the inherent non-convexity of the function $r_k(\bar{\mathbf{w}}, \bar{\varphi}_1, \bar{\varphi}_2)$ for $k \in \mathcal{D}$. Let us denote $(\bar{w}^{(\iota)}, \bar{\psi}_1^{(\iota)}, \bar{\psi}_2^{(\iota)})$ as a feasible point of (11), which can be derived from the $(\iota - 1)$-th iteration

$$g'(\bar{\mathbf{w}}, \bar{\psi}_1, \bar{\psi}_2) = -\frac{g(r_1(\bar{\mathbf{w}}, \bar{\psi}_1, \bar{\varphi}_2), \ldots, r_K(\bar{\mathbf{w}}, \bar{\psi}_1, \bar{\psi}_2))}{K \sum_{k \in \mathcal{D}} r_k(\bar{\mathbf{w}}, \bar{\psi}_1, \bar{\psi}_2)}, \tag{12}$$

The gradient of $g(\bar{\mathbf{w}}, \bar{\psi}_1, \bar{\psi}_2)$ is (12), so the linearized function of $g(\bar{\mathbf{w}}, \bar{\psi}_1, \bar{\psi}_2)$ at $(r_1(\bar{w}^{(\iota)}, \bar{\psi}_1^{(\iota)}, \bar{\psi}_2^{(\iota)}), \ldots, r_K(\bar{w}^{(\iota)}, \bar{\psi}_1^{(\iota)}, \bar{\psi}_2^{(\iota)}))$ is given by

$$2g\left(r_1(\bar{w}^{(\iota)}, \bar{\psi}_1^{(\iota)}, \bar{\psi}_2^{(\iota)}), \ldots, r_K(\bar{w}^{(\iota)}, \bar{\psi}_1^{(\iota)}, \bar{\psi}_2^{(\iota)})\right) - g(r_1(\bar{w}^{(\iota)}, \bar{\psi}_1^{(\iota)}, \bar{\psi}_2^{(\iota)}), \ldots,$$

$$r_K(\bar{w}^{(\iota)}, \bar{\psi}_1^{(\iota)}, \bar{\psi}_2^{(\iota)})) \frac{1}{K} \sum_{k \in \mathcal{D}} \frac{r_k(\bar{\mathbf{w}}, \bar{\psi}_1, \bar{\psi}_2)}{r_k(\bar{w}^{(\iota)}, \bar{\psi}_1^{(\iota)}, \bar{\psi}_2^{(\iota)})}. \quad (13)$$

Considering that $g\left(r_1(\bar{w}^{(\iota)}, \bar{\psi}_1^{(\iota)}, \bar{\psi}_2^{(\iota)}), \ldots, r_K(\bar{w}^{(\iota)}, \bar{\psi}_1^{(\iota)}, \bar{\psi}_2^{(\iota)})\right) > 0$, we employ the steepest descent method to address the convex function $g(r_1, \ldots, r_K)$, leading to the derivation of the subsequent feasible point $(\bar{w}^{(\iota+1)}, \bar{\psi}_1^{(\iota)}, \bar{\psi}_2^{(\iota)})$ [16,17].

$$\max_{\bar{\mathbf{w}}, \bar{\psi}_1, \bar{\psi}_2} \frac{1}{K} \sum_{k \in \mathcal{D}} \frac{r_k(\bar{\mathbf{w}}, \bar{\psi}_1, \bar{\psi}_2)}{r_k(\bar{w}^{(\iota)}, \bar{\psi}_1^{(\iota)}, \bar{\psi}_2^{(\iota)})} g(r_1(\bar{w}^{(\iota)}, \bar{\psi}_1^{(\iota)}, \bar{\psi}_2^{(\iota)}), \ldots, r_K(\bar{w}^{(\iota)}, \bar{\psi}_1^{(\iota)}, \bar{\psi}_2^{(\iota)}))$$

$$\text{s.t.} \quad (10b), (14)$$

which is equivalent to the subsequent problem:

$$\max_{\bar{\mathbf{w}}, \bar{\psi}_1, \bar{\psi}_2} g^{(\iota)}(\bar{\mathbf{w}}, \bar{\psi}_1, \bar{\psi}_2) \triangleq \sum_{k \in \mathcal{D}} \eta_k r_k(\mathbf{w}, \bar{\psi}_1, \bar{\psi}_2) \quad \text{s.t.} \quad \sum_{k \in \mathcal{D}} \|\bar{\mathbf{w}}_k\|^2 \leq P. \quad (15)$$

for

$$\eta_k \triangleq \frac{g\left(r_1(\bar{w}^{(\iota)}, \bar{\psi}_1^{(\iota)}, \bar{\psi}_2^{(\iota)}), \ldots, r_K(\bar{w}^{(\iota)}, \bar{\psi}_1^{(\iota)}, \bar{\psi}_2^{(\iota)})\right)}{r_k(\bar{w}^{(\iota)}, \bar{\psi}_1^{(\iota)}, \bar{\psi}_2^{(\iota)})}, k = 1, \ldots, K. \quad (16)$$

3.1   Beamforming Descent Iteration

First, we consider the subproblem of optimizing the beamforming $\bar{\mathbf{w}}$ with given $\bar{\psi}_1$ and $\bar{\psi}_2$, and obtain $\bar{w}^{(\iota+1)}$ such that

$$g^{(\iota)}(\bar{w}^{(\iota+1)}, \bar{\psi}_1^{(\iota)}, \bar{\psi}_2^{(\iota)}) > g^{(\iota)}(\bar{w}^{(\iota)}, \bar{\psi}_1^{(\iota)}, \bar{\psi}_2^{(\iota)}). \quad (17)$$

Using the inequality [18]

$$\ln \left| I_2 + [\mathbf{P}]^2 (\mathbf{Q})^{-1} \right| \geq \ln \left| I_2 + [\bar{P}]^2 (\bar{Q})^{-1} \right|$$
$$- \langle [\bar{P}]^2 (\bar{Q})^{-1} \rangle + 2\Re\{\langle \bar{P}^H (\bar{Q})^{-1} \mathbf{P} \rangle\}$$
$$- \langle (\bar{Q})^{-1} - (\bar{Q} + [\bar{P}]^2)^{-1}, [\mathbf{P}]^2 + \mathbf{Q} \rangle,$$
$$\forall \, \mathbf{P}, \mathbf{Q} \succ 0 \quad \& \quad \bar{P}, \bar{Q} \succ 0, \quad (18)$$

we derive a concave quadratic function by approximating $r_k^{(\iota)}(\bar{\mathbf{w}})$ as follows:

$$r_k(\bar{\mathbf{w}}, \bar{\psi}_1^{(\iota)}, \bar{\psi}_2^{(\iota)}) \geq r_k^{(\iota)}(\bar{\mathbf{w}})$$
$$\triangleq \bar{x}_k^{(\iota)} + 2\Re\{\langle y_k^{(\iota)}, \mathbf{w}_k \rangle\} - \bar{z}_k^{(\iota)} \sum_{k' \in \mathcal{D}} |\bar{\mathcal{H}}_k(\bar{\psi}_1^{(\iota)}, \bar{\psi}_2^{(\iota)}) \bar{\mathbf{w}}_{k'}|^2, (19)$$

with $\bar{x}_k^{(\iota)} \triangleq r_k(\bar{w}^{(\iota)}, \bar{\psi}_1^{(\iota)}, \bar{\psi}_2^{(\iota)}) - |\bar{\mathcal{H}}_k(\bar{\psi}_1^{(\iota)}, \bar{\psi}_2^{(\iota)})\bar{w}_k^{(\iota)}|^2/a_k^{(\iota)} - \sigma a_k^{(\iota)}$, $y_k^{(\iota)} \triangleq \bar{\mathcal{H}}_k^H(\bar{\psi}_1^{(\iota)}$
$,\bar{\psi}_2^{(\iota)})\bar{\mathcal{H}}_k(\bar{\psi}_1^{(\iota)}, \bar{\psi}_2^{(\iota)})\bar{w}_k^{(\iota)}/a_k^{(\iota)}$, $a_k^{(\iota)} \triangleq \sum_{k' \in \mathcal{D}\backslash\{k\}} |\bar{\mathcal{H}}_k(\bar{\psi}_1^{(\iota)}, \bar{\psi}_2^{(\iota)})\bar{w}_{k'}^{(\iota)}|^2 + \sigma$, $0 <$
$\bar{z}_k^{(\iota)} \triangleq |\bar{\mathcal{H}}_k(\bar{\psi}_1^{(\iota)}, \bar{\psi}_2^{(\iota)})\bar{w}_k^{(\iota)}|^2/ \left[a_k^{(\iota)} \left(a_k^{(\iota)} + |\bar{\mathcal{H}}_k(\bar{\psi}_1^{(\iota)}, \bar{\psi}_2^{(\iota)})\bar{w}_k^{(\iota)}|^2 \right) \right]$.

Therefore, we determine the value of $\bar{w}^{(\iota+1)}$ by solving the following problem during the ι-th iteration:

$$\max_{\bar{\mathbf{w}}} \, g_1^{(\iota)}(\bar{\mathbf{w}}) \quad \text{s.t.} \quad (10b), \tag{20}$$

where

$$g_1^{(\iota)}(\bar{\mathbf{w}}) \triangleq \sum_{k \in \mathcal{D}} \eta_k^{(\iota)} r_k^{(\iota)}(\bar{\mathbf{w}})$$

$$= \sum_{k \in \mathcal{D}} \eta_k^{(\iota)} \bar{x}_k^{(\iota)} + 2 \sum_{k \in \mathcal{D}} \Re\{\langle \eta_k^{(\iota)} y_k^{(\iota)}, \bar{\mathbf{w}}_k \rangle\} - \sum_{k=1}^{K} (\bar{\mathbf{w}}_k)^H \Omega^{(\iota)} \bar{\mathbf{w}}_k, \tag{21}$$

with $0 \preceq \Omega^{(\iota)} \triangleq \sum_{k' \in \mathcal{D}} \eta_j^{(\iota)} \bar{z}_{k'}^{(\iota)} \bar{\mathcal{H}}_{k'}^H(\bar{\psi}_1^{(\iota)}, \bar{\psi}_2^{(\iota)})\bar{\mathcal{H}}_{k'}(\bar{\psi}_1^{(\iota)}, \bar{\psi}_2^{(\iota)})$.

By employing the Lagrangian multiplier method, the optimal solution for (20) can be expressed in closed form as follows:

$$\bar{w}_k^{(\iota+1)} = \begin{cases} (\Omega^{(\iota)})^{-1}\eta_k^{(\iota)}y_k^{(\iota)} & \text{if} \sum_{k \in \mathcal{D}} ||(\Omega^{(\iota)})^{-1}\eta_k^{(\iota)}y_k^{(\iota)}||^2 \leq P \\ \left(\Omega^{(\iota)} + \rho I_N\right)^{-1} \eta_k^{(\iota)}y_k^{(\iota)} & \text{otherwise,} \end{cases} \tag{22}$$

where $\rho > 0$ is determined through a bisection process to satisfy the condition: $\sum_{k \in \mathcal{D}} || \left(\Omega^{(\iota)} + \rho I_N \right)^{-1} \eta_k^{(\iota)}y_k^{(\iota)} ||^2 = P$.

3.2   PREs of RIS 1 Descent Iteration

Next, our objective is to optimize the subproblem related to the reflecting elements $\bar{\psi}_1$, while considering the given beamforming $\mathbf{w}$ and $\bar{\psi}_2$. To achieve this, we aim to find the updated iteration point $\psi_1^{(\iota+1)}$ that satisfies the following:

$$g^{(\iota)}(\bar{w}^{(\iota+1)}, \bar{\psi}_1^{(\iota+1)}, \bar{\psi}_2^{(\iota)}) > g^{(\iota)}(\bar{w}^{(\iota+1)}, \bar{\psi}_1^{(\iota)}, \bar{\psi}_2^{(\iota)}). \tag{23}$$

By applying the inequality (18),

$$r_k(\bar{w}^{(\iota+1)}, \bar{\psi}_1, \bar{\psi}_2^{(\iota)}) \geq \bar{r}_{1k}^{(\iota)}(\bar{\psi}_1)$$
$$\triangleq 2\Re\{(\bar{w}_k^{(\iota+1)})^H \bar{\mathcal{H}}_k^H(\bar{\psi}_1^{(\iota)}, \bar{\psi}_2^{(\iota)})\bar{\mathcal{H}}_k(\bar{\psi}_1)\bar{w}_k^{(\iota+1)}\}/a_k^{(\iota+1)} + \bar{x}_{1k}^{(\iota)}$$
$$- \bar{z}_{1k}^{(\iota)} \sum_{k' \in \mathcal{D}} |\bar{\mathcal{H}}_k(\bar{\psi}_1)\bar{w}_{k'}^{(\iota+1)}|^2, \tag{24}$$

with $\bar{x}_{1k}^{(\iota)} \triangleq r_k(\bar{w}^{(\iota+1)}, \bar{\psi}_1^{(\iota)}, \bar{\psi}_2^{(\iota)}) - \sigma a_{1k}^{(\iota+1)} - |\bar{\mathcal{H}}_k(\bar{\psi}_1^{(\iota)}, \bar{\psi}_2^{(\iota)})\bar{w}_k^{(\iota+1)}|^2/a_{1k}^{(\iota+1)}$, $a_{1k}^{(\iota+1)}$
$\triangleq \sum_{k' \in \mathcal{D}\backslash\{k\}} |\bar{\mathcal{H}}_k(\bar{\psi}_1^{(\iota)}, \bar{\psi}_2^{(\iota)})\bar{w}_{k'}^{(\iota+1)}|^2 + \sigma$, $0 < \bar{z}_{1k}^{(\iota)} \triangleq |\bar{\mathcal{H}}_k(\bar{\psi}_1^{(\iota)}, \bar{\psi}_2^{(\iota)})\bar{w}_k^{(\iota+1)}|^2/(a_{1k}^{(\iota+1)}$
$(\bar{\mathcal{H}}_k(\bar{\psi}_1^{(\iota)}, \bar{\psi}_2^{(\iota)})\bar{w}_k^{(\iota+1)}|^2 + a_{1k}^{(\iota+1)}))$.

We use $\varXi_{m_1}$ to represent a matrix of dimensions $M_1 \times M_1$, where only the element in the (m_1, m_1) position is 1, and all other elements are 0. This matrix is employed to denote as

$$\boldsymbol{\Phi}_1 = \text{diag}(e^{\jmath \bar{\psi}_1}) = \sum_{m_1 \in \mathcal{F}_1} e^{\jmath \bar{\psi}_{1,m_1}} \varXi_{m_1}. \tag{25}$$

Using (1), we have (26),

$$
\begin{aligned}
&(\bar{w}_k^{(\iota+1)})^H \bar{\mathcal{H}}_k^H(\bar{\psi}_1^{(\iota)}, \bar{\psi}_2^{(\iota)}) \bar{\mathcal{H}}_k(\bar{\psi}_1) \bar{w}_k^{(\iota+1)} \\
&= (\bar{w}_k^{(\iota+1)})^H \bar{\mathcal{H}}_k^H(\bar{\psi}_1^{(\iota)}, \bar{\psi}_2^{(\iota)}) \bar{h}_R \Phi_2 \overline{D} \Phi_1 \bar{h}_B \bar{w}_k^{(\iota+1)} \\
&= (\bar{w}_k^{(\iota+1)})^H \bar{\mathcal{H}}_k^H(\bar{\psi}_1^{(\iota)}, \bar{\psi}_2^{(\iota)}) \bar{h}_R \text{diag}(e^{\jmath \bar{\psi}_2^{(\iota)}}) \overline{D} \text{diag}(e^{\jmath \bar{\psi}_1}) \bar{h}_B \bar{w}_k^{(\iota+1)} \\
&= \sum_{m_1 \in \mathcal{F}_1} (\bar{w}_k^{(\iota+1)})^H \bar{\mathcal{H}}_k^H(\bar{\psi}_1^{(\iota)}, \bar{\psi}_2^{(\iota)}) \bar{h}_R \text{diag}(e^{\jmath \bar{\psi}_2^{(\iota)}}) \overline{D} \varXi_{m_1} \bar{h}_B \bar{w}_k^{(\iota+1)} e^{\jmath \bar{\psi}_{1,m_1}} \\
&= \sum_{m_1 \in \mathcal{F}_1} \bar{y}_{1k}^{(\iota)}(m_1) e^{\jmath \bar{\psi}_{1,m_1}}. \tag{26}
\end{aligned}
$$

---

with $\bar{y}_{1k}^{(\iota)}(m_1) = (\bar{w}_k^{(\iota+1)})^H \bar{\mathcal{H}}_k^H(\bar{\psi}_1^{(\iota)}, \bar{\psi}_2^{(\iota)}) \bar{h}_R \text{diag}(e^{\jmath \bar{\psi}_2^{(\iota)}}) \overline{D} \, \varXi_{m_1} \bar{h}_B \bar{w}_k^{(\iota+1)}$, $m_1 = 1, \ldots M_1$.

Furthermore,

$$
\begin{aligned}
|\bar{\mathcal{H}}_k(\bar{\psi}_1) \bar{w}_{k'}^{(\iota+1)}|^2 &= \left| \bar{h}_R \Phi_2 \overline{D} \Phi_1 \bar{h}_B \bar{w}_{k'}^{(\iota+1)} \right|^2 \\
&= \left| \bar{h}_R \text{diag}(e^{\jmath \bar{\psi}_2^{(\iota)}}) \overline{D} \text{diag}(e^{\jmath \bar{\psi}_1}) \bar{h}_B \bar{w}_{k'}^{(\iota+1)} \right|^2. \tag{27}
\end{aligned}
$$

Hence

$$\bar{h}_R \text{diag}(e^{\jmath \bar{\psi}_2^{(\iota)}}) \overline{D} \text{diag}(e^{\jmath \bar{\psi}_1}) \bar{h}_B \bar{w}_{k'}^{(\iota+1)} = \sum_{m_1 \in \mathcal{F}_1} b_{1k,k'}^{(\iota+1)}(m) e^{\jmath \bar{\psi}_{1,m_1}}, \tag{28}$$

for $b_{1k,k'}^{(\iota+1)}(m) = \bar{h}_R \text{diag}(e^{\jmath \bar{\psi}_2^{(\iota)}}) \overline{D} \varXi_{m_1} \bar{h}_B \bar{w}_{k'}^{(\iota+1)}$, $m = 1, \ldots, M$.

Based on (24), (26), (27) and (28), we obtain

$$
\begin{aligned}
\bar{r}_{1k}^{(\iota)}(\bar{\psi}_1) &= \bar{x}_{1k}^{(\iota)} + 2\Re\left\{ \sum_{m_1 \in \mathcal{M}_1} \bar{y}_{1k}^{(\iota+1)}(m_1) e^{\jmath \bar{\psi}_{1,m_1}} \right\} - \bar{z}_{1k}^{(\iota)} \sum_{k' \in \mathcal{D}} \left| \sum_{m_1 \in \mathcal{M}_1} b_{1k,k'}^{(\iota+1)}(m_1) e^{\jmath \bar{\psi}_{1,m_1}} \right|^2 \\
&= \bar{x}_{1k}^{(\iota)} + 2\Re\left\{ \sum_{m_1 \in \mathcal{F}_1} \bar{y}_{1k}^{(\iota+1)}(m_1) e^{\jmath \bar{\psi}_{1,m_1}} \right\} - \bar{z}_{1k}^{(\iota)} \sum_{k' \in \mathcal{D}} (e^{\jmath \bar{\psi}_1})^H \Psi_{1k,k'}^{(\iota+1)} e^{\jmath \bar{\psi}_1}, \tag{29}
\end{aligned}
$$

where $\bar{y}_{1k}^{(\iota+1)}(m_1) \triangleq \bar{y}_{1k}^{(\iota)}(m_1)/a_k^{(\iota+1)}$ and $\Psi_{1k,k'}^{(\iota+1)}(m_1, n_1) \triangleq (b_{1k,k'}^{(\iota+1)}(m_1))^* b_{1k,k'}^{(\iota+1)}(n_1)$, $m_1 = n_1 = 1, \ldots, M_1$.

Note that $\Psi_{1k,k'}^{(\iota+1)} \succeq 0$. Then,

$$
\begin{aligned}
g_2^{(\iota)}(\bar{\psi}_1) &\triangleq \sum_{k \in \mathcal{D}} \eta_k^{(\iota)} \bar{r}_{1k}^{(\iota)}(\bar{\psi}_1) \\
&= \bar{x}_1^{(\iota+1)} + 2\Re\{ \sum_{m_1 \in \mathcal{M}_1} \bar{y}_1^{(\iota+1)}(m_1) e^{\jmath \bar{\psi}_{1,m_1}} \} - (e^{\jmath \boldsymbol{\theta}_1})^H \Psi_1^{(\iota+1)} e^{\jmath \bar{\psi}_1}, (30)
\end{aligned}
$$

for $\bar{x}_1^{(\iota+1)} \triangleq \sum_{k \in \mathcal{D}} \eta_k^{(\iota)} \bar{x}_{1k}^{(\iota)}$, $\bar{y}_1^{(\iota+1)}(m_1) \triangleq \sum_{k \in \mathcal{D}} \eta_k^{(\iota)} \bar{y}_{1k}^{(\iota+1)}(m_1)$, $m_1 = 1, \dots, M_1$, $0 \preceq \Psi_1^{(\iota+1)} \triangleq \sum_{k \in \mathcal{D}} \sum_{j \in \mathcal{D}} \eta_k^{(\iota)} \bar{z}_{1k}^{(\iota)} \Psi_{1k,j}^{(\iota+1)}$.

Therefore, we obtain the value of $\bar{\psi}_1^{(\iota+1)}$ by solving the following problem:

$$
\max_{\bar{\varphi}_1} g_2^{(\iota)}(\bar{\varphi}_1), \tag{31}
$$

$g_2^{(\iota)}(\bar{\varphi}_1)$ is equivalent to (33). Using the inequality

$$
\mathbf{ABA}^H \succeq \bar{A}\bar{B}\mathbf{A}^H + \mathbf{A}\bar{B}\bar{A}^H - \bar{A}\bar{B}\mathbf{B}^{-1}\bar{B}\bar{A}^H, \forall\, \mathbf{B} \succ 0\,,\ \bar{B} \succ 0, \tag{32}
$$

we have (34).

$$
\begin{aligned}
g_2^{(\iota)}(\bar{\psi}_1) &= \bar{x}_1^{(\iota+1)} + 2\Re\{ \sum_{m_1 \in \mathcal{M}_1} \bar{y}_1^{(\iota+1)}(m_1) e^{\jmath \bar{\psi}_{1,m_1}} \} - (e^{\jmath \bar{\psi}_1})^H (\Psi_1^{(\iota+1)} - \lambda_{\max}(\Psi_1^{(\iota+1)}) I_{M_1}) \\
&\quad e^{\jmath \psi_1} - \lambda_{\max}(\Psi_1^{(\iota+1)})(e^{\jmath \bar{\psi}_1})^H I_{M_1} e^{\jmath \bar{\psi}_1} \\
&= \bar{x}_1^{(\iota+1)} + 2\Re\{ \sum_{m_1 \in \mathcal{M}_1} \bar{y}_1^{(\iota+1)}(m_1) e^{\jmath \bar{\psi}_{1,m_1}} \} - (e^{\jmath \psi_1})^H (\Psi_1^{(\iota+1)} - \lambda_{\max}(\Psi_1^{(\iota+1)}) I_{M_1}) \\
&\quad e^{\jmath \bar{\psi}_1} - \lambda_{\max}(\Psi_1^{(\iota+1)}) M_1. \tag{33}
\end{aligned}
$$

$$
\begin{aligned}
\bar{g}_2^{(\iota)}(\bar{\psi}_1) &\triangleq \bar{x}_1^{(\iota+1)} + 2\Re\{ \sum_{m_1 \in \mathcal{M}_1} \bar{y}_1^{(\iota+1)}(m_1) e^{\jmath \psi_{1,m_1}} \} - [2\Re\{ (e^{\jmath \bar{\psi}_1^{(\iota)}})^H (\Psi_1^{(\iota+1)} - \lambda_{\max}(\Psi_1^{(\iota+1)}) \\
&\quad I_{M_1}) e^{\jmath \bar{\psi}_1} \} - (e^{\jmath \bar{\psi}_1^{(\iota)}})^H (\Psi_1^{(\iota+1)} - \lambda_{\max}(\Psi_1^{(\iota+1)}) I_{M_1}) e^{\jmath \bar{\psi}_1^{(\iota)}}] - \lambda_{\max}(\Phi_1^{(\iota+1)}) M_1 \\
&= 2\Re\{ \sum_{m_1 \in \mathcal{M}_1} (\bar{y}_1^{(\iota+1)}(m_1) - \sum_{n_1 \in \mathcal{M}_1} e^{-\jmath \bar{\psi}_{1,n_1}^{(\iota)}} \Psi_1^{(\iota+1)}(n_1, m_1) + \lambda_{\max}(\Psi_1^{(\iota+1)}) e^{-\jmath \bar{\psi}_{1,m_1}^{(\iota)}}) \\
&\quad e^{\jmath \bar{\psi}_{1,m_1}} \} + \bar{x}_1^{(\iota+1)} - (e^{\jmath \bar{\psi}_1^{(\iota)}})^H \Psi_1^{(\iota+1)} e^{\jmath \bar{\psi}_1^{(\iota)}} - 2\lambda_{\max}(\Psi_1^{(\iota+1)}) M_1. \tag{34}
\end{aligned}
$$

Hence, we can solve the following problem:

$$
\max_{\bar{\psi}_1} \bar{g}_2^{(\iota)}(\bar{\psi}_1). \tag{35}
$$

Therefore, the optimal solution of equation (35) in closed-form is given by:

$$
\begin{aligned}
\bar{\psi}_{1,m_1}^{(\iota+1)} &= -\left\lfloor \angle (\bar{y}_1^{(\iota+1)}(m_1) - \sum_{n_1 \in \mathcal{F}_1} \Psi_1^{(\iota+1)}(n_1, m_1) e^{-\jmath \bar{\psi}_{1,n_1}^{(\iota)}} + \lambda_{\max}(\Psi_1^{(\iota+1)}) e^{-\jmath \bar{\psi}_{1,m_1}^{(\iota)}}) \right\rceil_b, \\
&\qquad m_1 = 1, \dots, M_1. \tag{36}
\end{aligned}
$$

3.3   PREs of RIS 2 Descent Iteration

We turn our attention to the subproblem of optimizing the reflecting elements $\bar{\psi}_2$ while considering the given beamforming $\bar{w}$ and $\bar{\varphi}_1$. We aim to find the next iterative point $\bar{\psi}_2^{(\iota+1)}$ that satisfies:

$$g^{(\iota)}(w^{(\kappa+1)},\bar{\psi}_1^{(\iota+1)},\bar{\psi}_2^{(\iota+1)}) > g^{(\iota)}(w^{(\iota+1)},\bar{\psi}_1^{(\iota+1)},\bar{\psi}_2^{(\iota)}). \tag{37}$$

Continuing with similar steps as in (24) - (33) and using the inequalities (18) and (32), we can derive $\bar{\psi}_2^{(\iota+1)}$ to solve the following problem:

$$\max_{\psi_2} \bar{g}_3^{(\iota)}(\bar{\varphi}_2). \tag{38}$$

Hence, the similar solution of (38) is given by

$$\bar{\psi}_{2,m_2}^{(\iota+1)} = -\left\lfloor \angle(\bar{y}_2^{(\iota+1)}(m_2) - \sum_{n_2 \in \mathcal{M}_2} \Psi_2^{(\iota+1)}(n_2,m_2)e^{-\jmath\bar{\psi}_{2,n_2}^{(\iota)}} + \lambda_{\max}(\Psi_2^{(\iota+1)})e^{-\jmath\bar{\psi}_{2,m_2}^{(\iota)}}) \right\rceil_b,$$
$$m_2 = 1,\ldots,M_2. \tag{39}$$

3.4   Algorithm

Algorithm 1 GM descent algorithm

1: **Initialization:**Randomly generate $(\bar{\mathbf{w}}^{(0)},\bar{\psi}_1^{(0)},\bar{\psi}_2^{(0)})$ that satisfies the constraint (10b), and define $\eta^{(0)}$ according to (16). Initialize ι as 0.
2: **Repeat until convergence of the objective function in (11):** Generate $w^{(\iota+1)}$ by solving the convex problem (20), and $\bar{\psi}_1^{(\iota+1)}$ by solving the convex problem (35), and $\bar{\psi}_2^{(\iota+1)}$ by (38). Reset $\iota \leftarrow \iota+1$.
3: **Output** $(\bar{w}^{(\iota)},\bar{\psi}_1^{(\iota)},\bar{\psi}_2^{(\iota)})$ and $r_k(\bar{w}^{(\iota)},\bar{\psi}_1^{(\iota)},\bar{\psi}_2^{(\iota)})$, $k = 1,\ldots,K$ with their GM rate $(\prod_{k \in \mathcal{D}} r_k(\bar{w}^{(\iota)},\bar{\psi}_1^{(\iota)},\bar{\psi}_2^{(\iota)}))^{1/K}$.

---

4   Numerical Results

This section is dedicated to presenting simulation results that evaluate the effectiveness of the proposed GM descent algorithm in the context of the double RIS system. The simulations are conducted in a three-dimensional coordinate system, where the BS, RIS 1, and RIS 2 are positioned at coordinates $(1,0,2)$, $(0,0.5,1)$, and $(0,49.5,1)$ in meters (m), respectively, as illustrated in Fig. 1. Furthermore, the users are randomly distributed within a circular region centered at $(1,50,0)$ with a radius of 10 meters.

The azimuth angles of RIS 1 and RIS 2 relative to the x-axis are configured as $\pi/4$ and $3\pi/4$, respectively. For our simulation, we adopt a distance-dependent channel path loss model, which is represented as follows:

$$P(d) = G(d/d_0)^{-\alpha}, \tag{40}$$

G represents the reference channel power gain at a distance of $d_0 = 1$ meter, which is configured as -30dB for the simulation. The variable d corresponds to the path's link distance, while α signifies the path loss exponent. In our simulation, we set α to 2.2 for the link between users/BS and their nearby serving RIS, and 3 for the link between RIS 1 and RIS 2. Furthermore, we incorporate Rician fading in our simulation, where the Rician factor is set at 20dB. We establish the bandwidth as 1 MHz, and the noise power density is set to -174 dBm/Hz.

Unless specified, we assume that the number of antennas $N = 10$, transmit power $P = 20$dBm, RIS 1 elements $M_1 = 50$, RIS 2 elements $M_2 = 50$, and resolution $b = 3$. Additionally, it's important to note that all simulation outcomes presented in this study are based on an average of 30 channel realizations.

- GM Double-RIS RT: This result evaluates the performance of the GM descent algorithm under the assumption of random phase coefficients ψ_1 and ψ_2 at the RISs in the double-RIS system.
- 3-bit GM Double-RIS RT: This result assesses the performance of the GM descent algorithm with random phase coefficients ψ_1 and ψ_2 at the RISs in the double-RIS system, considering a resolution of $b = 3$.
- SR Double-RIS: This result analyzes the performance of the SR algorithm in the Double-RIS system, with η_k set to 1.
- 3-bit SR Double-RIS: This result examines the performance of the SR algorithm in the Double-RIS system, with both η_k and the resolution b set to 1 and 3, respectively.

The sum rates of the proposed algorithms are examined in Fig. 2. It is evident that SR Double-RIS and 3-bit SR Double-RIS outperform GM Double-RIS and 3-bit GM Double-RIS, respectively, in terms of cumulative rates. Notably, GM Double-RIS exhibits superior performance compared to 3-bit SR Double-RIS when the number of antennas N is greater than or equal to 8. As expected, the figure shows an upward trend with the increment in the number of antennas N at the BS, attributable to the enhanced spatial diversity.

Figure 3 illustrates the rate distribution among the proposed algorithms within the double-RIS system. It is evident from Fig. 3 that the introduced GM descent algorithms possess the capability to prevent the occurrence of zero rate assignments, showcasing their superior performance in this regard.

In order to provide empirical evidence for the susceptibility of SR-based algorithms to zero rate allocations, Table 1 presents the average count of ZR-UEs across varying numbers of antennas N. As depicted in Table 1, the count of ZR-UEs demonstrates an upward trend with the reduction of N across all proposed algorithms. Furthermore, the data in Table 1 consistently indicates the presence of ZR-UEs within SR-based algorithms.

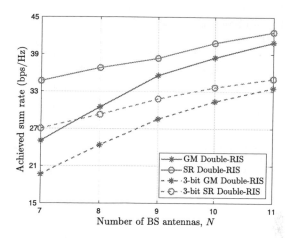

Fig. 2. Achieved SR versus the number of antennas N.

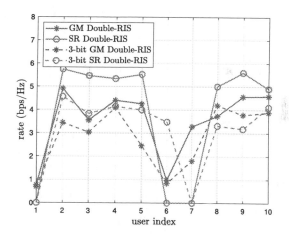

Fig. 3. Rate distribution.

Table 1. The average number of ZR-UEs versus the number of antennas N.

	$N = 7$	$N = 8$	$N = 9$	$N = 10$	$N = 11$
GM Double-RIS	0	0	0	0	0
SR Double-RIS	3.27	2.67	2.33	1.77	1.47
3-bit GM Double-RIS	0	0	0	0	0
3-bit SR Double-RIS	3.10	2.10	1.50	1.17	0.77

Figure 4 illustrates the achieved GM rate in relation to the number of antennas N. The figure highlights the superior performance of GM Double-RIS over 3-bit GM Double-RIS. Furthermore, it showcases the comparable performance of GM Double-RIS RT and 3-bit GM Double-RIS RT in the given system. This trend aligns with the anticipated outcome, where all algorithms experience performance enhancement with a rise in the number of antennas N.

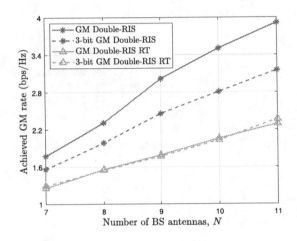

Fig. 4. Achieved GM rate versus the number of antennas N.

The GM rate is further analyzed across varying power budgets P and the number of RIS elements M, as depicted in Fig. 5 and Fig. 6. As anticipated, the GM rate exhibits an upward trend with the augmentation of the power budget, enabling greater power allocation for information transmission. Furthermore, it is notable that the GM rate experiences an upsurge as M increases. This effect can be attributed to the heightened power capabilities of the reflecting RISs, indicating a positive correlation between the number of RIS elements and the achieved GM rate.

Finally, Fig. 7 facilitates a comparison of the performance achieved by the b-bit solution across varying values of b. As anticipated, the b-bit GM Double-RIS algorithm demonstrates improved performance as b increases. Furthermore, Fig. 7 reveals that the b-bit GM Double-RIS RT algorithm does not exhibit significant improvements with increasing values of b. This finding underscores the limitations of the b-bit GM Double-RIS RT approach in benefiting from higher values of b.

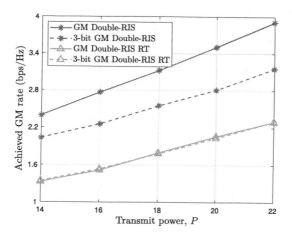

Fig. 5. Achieved GM rate versus the transmit power P.

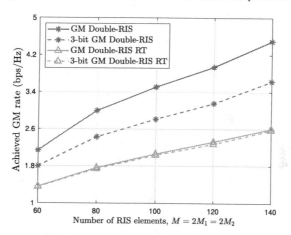

Fig. 6. Achieved GM rate versus the number of RISs elements $M = 2M_1 = 2M_2 = 100$.

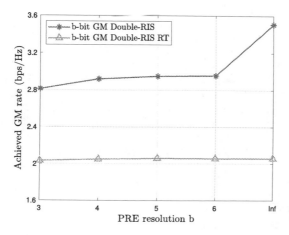

Fig. 7. Achieved GM rate vs the value of b.

5   Conclusions

We have investigated a communication network assisted by a double-RIS system, comprising a BS equipped with an antenna array to serve multiple users in the downlink direction. To enhance the system's performance, we have introduced effective alternating descent iteration algorithms. These algorithms aim to optimize the system by maximizing the GM of the users' rates. This optimization strategy contributes to a balanced distribution of rates among users while ensuring reasonable overall sum rates. Through comprehensive simulations, we have validated the effectiveness and practical applicability of the proposed algorithms.

References

1. Xu, C., et al.: Sixty years of coherent versus non-coherent tradeoffs and the road from 5g to wireless futures. IEEE Access **7**, 178246–178299 (2019). https://doi.org/10.1109/ACCESS.2019.2957706
2. Wu, Q., Zhang, S., Zheng, B., You, C., Zhang, R.: Intelligent reflecting surface-aided wireless communications: a tutorial. IEEE Trans. Commun. **69**(5), 3313–3351 (2021). https://doi.org/10.1109/TCOMM.2021.3051897
3. Liaskos, C., Nie, S., Tsioliaridou, A., Pitsillides, A., Ioannidis, S., Akyildiz, I.: A new wireless communication paradigm through software-controlled metasurfaces. IEEE Commun. Mag. **56**(9), 162–169 (2018). https://doi.org/10.1109/MCOM.2018.1700659
4. Dhok, S., Raut, P., Sharma, P.K., Singh, K., Li, C.P.: Non-linear energy harvesting in RIS-assisted URLLC networks for industry automation. IEEE Trans. Commun. **69**(11), 7761–7774 (2021). https://doi.org/10.1109/TCOMM.2021.3100611
5. You, C., Zheng, B., Zhang, R.: Channel estimation and passive beamforming for intelligent reflecting surface: discrete phase shift and progressive refinement. IEEE J. Sel. Areas Commun. **38**(11), 2604–2620 (2020). https://doi.org/10.1109/JSAC.2020.3007056
6. Hu, X., Zhong, C., Alouini, M.S., Zhang, Z.: Robust design for IRS-aided communication systems with user location uncertainty. IEEE Wirel. Commun. Lett. **10**(1), 63–67 (2021). https://doi.org/10.1109/LWC.2020.3020850
7. Zheng, B., Zhang, R.: IRS meets relaying: joint resource allocation and passive beamforming optimization. IEEE Wirel. Commun. Lett. **10**(9), 2080–2084 (2021). https://doi.org/10.1109/LWC.2021.3092222
8. Papazafeiropoulos, A., Kourtessis, P., Chatzinotas, S., Senior, J.M.: Coverage probability of double-IRS assisted communication systems. IEEE Wirel. Commun. Lett. **11**(1), 96–100 (2022). https://doi.org/10.1109/LWC.2021.3121209
9. Dong, L., Wang, H.M., Bai, J., Xiao, H.: Double intelligent reflecting surface for secure transmission with inter-surface signal reflection. IEEE Trans. Veh. Technol. **70**(3), 2912–2916 (2021). https://doi.org/10.1109/TVT.2021.3062059
10. Zheng, B., You, C., Zhang, R.: Double-IRS assisted multi-user MIMO: cooperative passive beamforming design. IEEE Trans. Wirel. Commun. **20**(7), 4513–4526 (2021). https://doi.org/10.1109/TWC.2021.3059945
11. Han, Y., Zhang, S., Duan, L., Zhang, R.: Double-IRS aided MIMO communication under LOS channels: capacity maximization and scaling. IEEE Trans. Commun. **70**(4), 2820–2837 (2022). https://doi.org/10.1109/TCOMM.2022.3151893

12. Han, Y., Zhang, S., Duan, L., Zhang, R.: Cooperative double-IRS aided communication: beamforming design and power scaling. IEEE Wirel. Commun. Lett. **9**(8), 1206–1210 (2020). https://doi.org/10.1109/LWC.2020.2986290

13. You, C., Zheng, B., Zhang, R.: Wireless communication via double IRS: channel estimation and passive beamforming designs. IEEE Wirel. Commun. Lett. **10**(2), 431–435 (2021). https://doi.org/10.1109/LWC.2020.3034388

14. Huang, C., Zappone, A., Alexandropoulos, G.C., Debbah, M., Yuen, C.: Reconfigurable intelligent surfaces for energy efficiency in wireless communication. IEEE Trans. Wirel. Commun. **18**(8), 4157–4170 (2019)

15. Wei, L., Huang, C., Alexandropoulos, G.C., Yuen, C., Zhang, Z., Debbah, M.: Channel estimation for RIS-empowered multi-user miso wireless communications. IEEE Trans. Commun. **69**(6), 4144–4157 (2021). https://doi.org/10.1109/TCOMM.2021.3063236

16. Torabzadeh, M., Ajib, W.: Proportional fairness packet scheduling with transmit beamforming for multi-user MIMO systems. In: 2009 IEEE Radio and Wireless Symposium, pp. 630–633 (2009). https://doi.org/10.1109/RWS.2009.4957430

17. Cirik, A.C.: Fairness considerations for full duplex multi-user MIMO systems. IEEE Wirel. Commun. Lett. **4**(4), 361–364 (2015). https://doi.org/10.1109/LWC.2015.2419672

18. Tam, H.H.M., Tuan, H.D., Ngo, D.T.: Successive convex quadratic programming for quality-of-service management in full-duplex MU-MIMO multicell networks. IEEE Trans. Commun. **64**(6), 2340–2353 (2016). https://doi.org/10.1109/TCOMM.2016.2550440

Hybrid Beamforming Design for Multi-user mmWave Sum Rate Maximization

Chunyang Wang[1], Guannan Tan[2], Yong Fang[1], Hao Wei[3], Zhichao Sheng[1], and Hongwen Yu[1(✉)]

[1] Shanghai University, Shanghai 200444, China
{chunyangwang,yfang,zcsheng,hw_yu}@shu.edu.cn
[2] Huizhou Speed Wireless Technology Company, Huizhou 516000, China
[3] ZTE Coperation, Shenzhen 518055, China
wei.hao@zte.com.cn

Abstract. This paper considers a multi-user multiple-input-single-output (MU-MISO) mmWave downlink communication system. The hybrid beamforming (HBF) is applied at the base station (BS). A joint analog beamforming (ABF) and digital beamforming (DBF) optimization problem is formulated to maximize the sum rate (SR) of the users, the problem is generally non-convex due to the log-determinant as well as unit modulus constraints (UMC) for ABF. Two efficient alternating descent iteration algorithms are developed to solve the intractable problem. Finally, simulation results are included to verify the efficiency of the proposed approaches, results also show that the proposed algorithms can accommodate discrete phase shifts for ABF.

Keywords: Millimeter wave downlink system · Sum rate maximization · Non-convex optimization algorithm

1 Introduction

The wavelength of millimeter-wave (mmWave) is between $1 - 10$ mm, and its frequency band ranges from 30 GHz to 300 GHz [1]. The mmWave communication has emerged as a key technology to meet the explosive growth in data rate and quality of service (QoS) requirements in beyond fifth-generation (B5G) networks [2]. Short wavelength and a large path loss are key characteristics of mmWave communication systems. Fortunately, the small wavelength of mmWave systems allows the use of a large number of antennas, and yet achieves high array gain for directional communications by exploiting precoding techniques [3,4].

However, in the case of mmWave communication, the use of conventional fully digital beamforming is impractical. Although the optimal performance can

This work was supported by Technology Key Project of Guangdong Province, China (HZJBGS-2021001).

N.-S. Vo and H.-A. Tran (Eds.): INISCOM 2023, LNICST 531, pp. 104–118, 2023.
https://doi.org/10.1007/978-3-031-47359-3_8

be achieved theoretically, it is faced with the problem of high implementation complexity, large power consumption of mmWave radio frequency (RF) chains, and hardware limitations [5,6]. To address this issue, hybrid beamforming (HBF) has been proposed as an efficient approach with near-optimal performance [7–10]. The key idea of HBF is to decompose the fully digital beamforming into a high-dimensional analog beamforming (ABF) to increase the antenna gain and a low-dimensional digital beamforming (DBF) to cancel interference [11]. However, the design of HBF is extremely challenging for the reason that HBF is a product of ABF and DBF, which are coupled together. Additionally, the entries of ABF matrix are subject to the unit modulus constraint (UMC). In the studies of mmWave HBF communication systems, HBF was formulated for single-user (SU) mmWave multiple-input multiple-output (MIMO) communication [12–14]. In [12], the authors studied the beamforming design of HBF in a mmWave system. The system adopted a fully adaptive beamforming structure, wherein a switch control connection was deployed between each antenna and the RF link. In order to maximize the energy efficiency, the joint optimization problem of switching control connection and hybrid precoders was formulated as a large-scale mixed-integer non-convex problem with high dimensional power constraints. In this paper, an alternating HBF algorithm was proposed to solve continuous HBF subproblem, and then a fully adaptive HBF algorithm with matching assistance was developed to solve discrete connection-state non-convex problems. The work [13] studied a mmWave large-scale MIMO communication system and proposed a HBF scheme based on model-driven deep learning and alternating minimization. The main idea of this scheme was to maximize spectral efficiency by solving ABF and DBF alternately. In this paper, ABF network was used to solve phase shifts, and Lagrange multiplier method was used to solve DBF. The work [14] studied a mmWave MIMO communication system in order to maximize user rate. The problem was formulated and then decoupled into a series of subproblems. A method of singular value decomposition was proposed to solve the problem. However, all the aforementioned research works [12–14], only consider the simple SU communication scenario, and fail to extend the multi-user complex communication scenario.

Researchers have also remained interest in HBF design for multi-user (MU) downlink communication. The authors of [15] studied the beamforming problem in the transmission scenarios of mmWave SU MIMO communication and MU communication systems. A heuristic hybrid beamforming algorithm was proposed to maximize the sum rate (SR), and the proposed algorithm was still applicable for the case of discrete resolution. The authors in [16] studied the multi-BS and MU downlink communication system, with the aim of maximizing energy efficiency. The authors used fractional programming theory, penalty dual decomposition method, and the relationship between user rate and mean square error to transform the initial problem into a tractable problem. This optimization problem was solved by alternating direction multiplier method and block successive upper-bound minimization method. The work [17] studied mmWave MU MIMO system in a single base station (BS), and proposed a penalized dual decomposition method to directly solve the non-convex HBF problem of the system in order to maximize spectral efficiency. The proposed algorithms can ensure convergence to Karush-Kuhn-Tucker (KKT) solution of HBF problem, which were also suitable for discrete resolution cases. However, these works [15–17] fail to provide an effective solution for UMC, which makes the calculation complexity very high.

This paper is organized as follows: In Sect. 2 and Sect. 3 respectively develop penalty optimization (PO) and alternating descent round (ADR) algorithms for the HBF design to maximize the SR. Section 4 evaluates the performance of all the algorithms. Section 5 concludes the paper.

The following inequality for all $\boldsymbol{x}$, $\bar{x}$, and positive definite $\mathbf{y}$ and $\bar{y}$ of appropriate dimension is frequently used in the paper:

$$\frac{|\boldsymbol{x}|^2}{\mathbf{y}} \geq -\frac{|\bar{x}|^4}{\bar{y}^2} + 2\frac{\bar{y} + |\bar{x}|^2}{\bar{y}^2}\Re\{\bar{x}^H \boldsymbol{x}\} - \frac{|\bar{x}|^2}{\bar{y}^2}(|\boldsymbol{x}|^2 + \mathbf{y}). \tag{1}$$

2   Penalty Optimization Approach

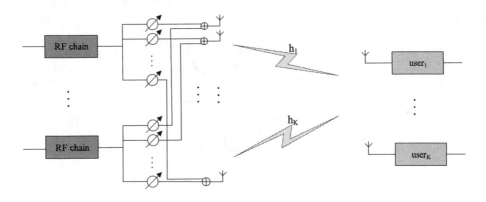

Fig. 1. MmWave MU-MISO downlink communication systems.

We consider a RIS-aided mmWave MU-MISO DL system as illustrated by Fig. 1, where the BS equips with N antennas and N_{RF} RF chains communicates with K single-antenna users, the BS is in the form of a uniform planar array (ULA) [18].

For $\mathcal{N} \triangleq \{1, \ldots, N\}$ and $\mathcal{N}_{RF} \triangleq \{1, \ldots, N_{RF}\}$, let $\boldsymbol{\theta} \triangleq [\boldsymbol{\theta}_{n,j}]_{(n,j)\in\mathcal{N}\times\mathcal{N}_{RF}} \in [0, 2\pi)^{N \times N_{RF}}$ be the phase shift matrix. Define the following one-to-one mapping from $[0, 2\pi)^{N \times N_{RF}}$ to $\mathbb{U}^{N \times N_{RF}} \triangleq \{\mathbf{U} = [\mathbf{u}(n,j)]_{(n,j)\in\mathcal{N}\times\mathcal{N}_{RF}} : |\mathbf{u}_{n,j}| = 1, (n,j) \in \mathcal{N} \times \mathcal{N}_{RF}\}$:

$$A(\boldsymbol{\theta}) \triangleq [A^1(\boldsymbol{\theta}) \ldots A^{N_{RF}}(\boldsymbol{\theta})]$$
$$= [e^{j\boldsymbol{\theta}_{n,j}}]_{(n,j)\in\mathcal{N}\times\mathcal{N}_{RF}} \in \mathbb{U}^{N \times N_{RF}}, \tag{2}$$

to represent the phase shift based ABF matrix. Due to hardware limitations, the phase shift can not take an arbitrary value, b-bit resolution is optimized, and we thus have

$$\boldsymbol{\theta}_{n,j} \in \mathcal{A} \triangleq \{0, \frac{2\pi}{2^b}, \ldots, \frac{2\pi(2^b - 1)}{2^b}\}, \tag{3}$$

and the special case of $b = \infty$ corresponds to the continuous phase shifts.

For $k \in \mathcal{K} \triangleq \{1, \ldots, K\}$, $\mathbf{s} \triangleq (s_1, s_2, \ldots, s_K)$, let $s_k \in \mathbb{C}$ with $\mathbb{E}(s_k s_k^H) = I$ be the transmitted signal for user k, which is beamformed by $\mathbf{D}_k \in \mathbb{C}^{N_{RF}}$, and DBF matrix is:

$$\mathbf{D} \triangleq [\mathbf{D}_1 \ldots \mathbf{D}_K] \in \mathbb{C}^{N_{RF} \times K}, \tag{4}$$

the baseband signal x is $x = \mathbf{Ds} = \sum_{k=1}^{K} \mathbf{D}_k s_k$. The mmWave channel between the BS and user $k \in \mathcal{K}$ by $H_k \in \mathbb{C}^{1 \times N}$, the signal received at user k is formulated as:

$$y_k = H_k A(\boldsymbol{\theta}) \sum_{k=1}^{K} \mathbf{D}_k s_k + n_k \tag{5}$$

$$= H_k(\boldsymbol{\theta}) \sum_{k=1}^{K} \mathbf{D}_k s_k + n_k. \tag{6}$$

The HBF is given by producting of ABF $A(\boldsymbol{\theta})$ and DBF $\mathbf{D}_k$, $k \in \mathcal{K}$:

$$\mathbf{w}_k \triangleq A(\boldsymbol{\theta})\mathbf{D}_k \in \mathbb{C}^N, \tag{7}$$

and accordingly,

$$\mathbf{w} \triangleq [\mathbf{w}_1 \ldots \mathbf{w}_K] \in \mathbb{C}^{N \times K}. \tag{8}$$

According to the equations (6), the signal-to-interference-plus-noise ratio (SINR) at user k is:

$$\rho_k(\boldsymbol{\theta}, \mathbf{D}) \triangleq \frac{|H_k(\boldsymbol{\theta})\mathbf{D}_k|^2}{\sum_{l \neq k}^{K} |H_k(\boldsymbol{\theta})\mathbf{D}_l|^2 + \sigma}, \tag{9}$$

thus, the rate at user k is:

$$\mathcal{R}_k(\boldsymbol{\theta}, \mathbf{D}) \triangleq \ln(1 + \rho_k(\boldsymbol{\theta}, \mathbf{D})). \tag{10}$$

Given the power budget P, the transmit power constraint at the BS can be expressed as:

$$\sum_{k=1}^{K} ||A(\boldsymbol{\theta})\mathbf{D}_k||^2 \leq P. \tag{11}$$

The HBF design problem of maximizing the SR of users is formulated as:

$$\max_{\boldsymbol{\theta}, \mathbf{D}} \sum_{k=1}^{K} \mathcal{R}_k(\boldsymbol{\theta}, \mathbf{D}) \triangleq \max_{\boldsymbol{\theta}, \mathbf{D}} \ln(\prod_{k=1}^{K}(1 + \rho_k(\boldsymbol{\theta}, \mathbf{D}))) \tag{12a}$$

$$\text{s.t.} \quad (3), (11). \tag{12b}$$

Defining the following equation:

$$\Lambda(1 + \rho_1(\boldsymbol{\theta}, \mathbf{D}), \ldots, 1 + \rho_K(\boldsymbol{\theta}, \mathbf{D})) \triangleq \prod_{k=1}^{K} (1 + \rho_k(\boldsymbol{\theta}, \mathbf{D})). \tag{13}$$

Let $(\theta^{(\kappa)}, D^{(\kappa)})$ be a feasible point for (13), we linearize $\Lambda(1 + \rho_1(\boldsymbol{\theta}, \mathbf{D}), \ldots, 1 + \rho_K(\boldsymbol{\theta}, \mathbf{D}))$ at $(1 + \rho_1(\theta^{(\kappa)}, D^{(\kappa)}), \ldots, 1 + \rho_K(\theta^{(\kappa)}, D^{(\kappa)}))$ is

$$(1 - K)\Lambda(1 + \rho_1(\theta^{(\kappa)}, D^{(\kappa)}), \ldots, 1 + \rho_K(\theta^{(\kappa)}, D^{(\kappa)}))$$
$$+ \sum_{k=1}^{K} \frac{\Lambda(1 + \rho_1(\theta^{(\kappa)}, D^{(\kappa)}), \ldots, 1 + \rho_K(\theta^{(\kappa)}, D^{(\kappa)}))}{1 + \rho_k(\theta^{(\kappa)}, D^{(\kappa)})} (1 + \rho_k(\boldsymbol{\theta}, \mathbf{D})). \tag{14}$$

It is plausible that this problem is equivalent to the following problem:

$$\max_{\boldsymbol{\theta}, \mathbf{D}} f(\boldsymbol{\theta}, \mathbf{D}) \triangleq \sum_{k=1}^{K} \gamma_k(1 + \rho_k(\boldsymbol{\theta}, \mathbf{D})) \tag{15a}$$

$$\text{s.t.} \quad (3), (11), \tag{15b}$$

for

$$\gamma_k^{(\kappa)} \triangleq \frac{\Lambda(1 + \rho_1(\theta^{(\kappa)}, D^{(\kappa)}), \ldots, 1 + \rho_K(\theta^{(\kappa)}, D^{(\kappa)}))}{1 + \rho_k(\theta^{(\kappa)}, D^{(\kappa)})}, k = 1, \ldots, K, \tag{16}$$

for computational stability, $\gamma_k^{(\kappa)}$ is scaled as

$$\gamma_k^{(\kappa)} \longrightarrow \frac{\gamma_k^{(\kappa)}}{\min_{j=1,\ldots,K} \gamma_j^{(\kappa)}}, k = 1, \ldots, K. \tag{17}$$

Recalling the definition (7) of HBF, the SINR of user k defined by (9) can be expressed as:

$$\rho_k(\mathbf{w}) \triangleq \frac{|H_k \mathbf{w}_k|^2}{\sum_{l \neq k}^{K} |H_k \mathbf{w}_l|^2 + \sigma}, \tag{18}$$

and rate is:

$$\mathcal{R}_k(\mathbf{w}) \triangleq \ln(1 + \rho_k(\mathbf{w})). \tag{19}$$

Thus, the optimization problem can be expressed as:

$$\max_{\mathbf{w}} \sum_{k=1}^{K} \mathcal{R}_k(\mathbf{w}) \triangleq \max_{\mathbf{w}} \ln(\prod_{k=1}^{K} (1 + \rho_k(\mathbf{w}))) \tag{20a}$$

$$\text{s.t.} \quad \sum_{k=1}^{K} ||\mathbf{w}_k||^2 \leq P, (3), (7), \tag{20b}$$

equivalence problem:

$$\max_{\mathbf{w}} f(\mathbf{w}) \triangleq \sum_{k=1}^{K} \gamma_k (1 + \rho_k(\mathbf{w})) \quad \text{s.t.} \quad (3), \tag{21a}$$

$$\sum_{k=1}^{K} |\mathbf{w}_k||^2 \leq P. \tag{21b}$$

We will address (21) PO optimization problem:

$$\max_{\boldsymbol{\theta}, \mathbf{D}, \mathbf{w}} F(\boldsymbol{\theta}, \mathbf{D}, \mathbf{w}) \triangleq f(\mathbf{w}) - c||\mathbf{w}_k - A(\boldsymbol{\theta})\mathbf{D}_k||^2 \tag{22a}$$

$$\text{s.t.} \quad (3), (21b). \tag{22b}$$

with the penalty parameter $c > 0$ to be updated.

2.1 Hybrid Beamforming Design

We seek HBF $w^{(\kappa+1)}$ ensuring that

$$F(\theta^{(\kappa)}, D^{(\kappa)}, w^{(\kappa+1)}) > F(\theta^{(\kappa)}, D^{(\kappa)}, w^{(\kappa)}), \tag{23}$$

by considering the following problem:

$$\max_{\mathbf{w}} F(\theta^{(\kappa)}, D^{(\kappa)}, \mathbf{w}) \tag{24a}$$

$$\text{s.t.} \quad (21b). \tag{24b}$$

The following tight concave quadratic minorant is obtained by (1):

$$1 + \rho_k(\mathbf{w}) \geq 1 + \rho_k^{(\kappa)}(\mathbf{w})$$

$$\triangleq a_k^{(\kappa)} + 2b_k^{(\kappa)} \Re\{\langle c_k^{(\kappa)} \mathbf{w}_k \rangle\} - d_k^{(\kappa)} \left(\sum_{l=1}^{K} |H_k \mathbf{w}_l|^2 \right), \tag{25}$$

with $a_k^{(\kappa)} \triangleq -\dfrac{|H_k w_k^{(\kappa)}|^4}{(\sum_{l \neq k}^{K} |H_k w_l^{(\kappa)}|^2 + \sigma)^2} - \sigma \dfrac{|H_k w_k^{(\kappa)}|^2}{(\sum_{l \neq k}^{K} |H_k w_l^{(\kappa)}|^2 + \sigma)^2} + 1$, $b_k^{(\kappa)} \triangleq \dfrac{\sum_{l=1}^{K} |H_k w_l^{(\kappa)}|^2 + \sigma}{(\sum_{l \neq k}^{K} |H_k w_l^{(\kappa)}|^2 + \sigma)^2}$, $c_k^{(\kappa)} \triangleq (H_k w_k^{(\kappa)})^H H_k$, $d_k^{(\kappa)} \triangleq \dfrac{|H_k w_k^{(\kappa)}|^2}{(\sum_{l \neq k}^{K} |H_k w_l^{(\kappa)}|^2 + \sigma)^2}$. Then we get:

$$\tilde{f}(\mathbf{w}) \triangleq \sum_{k=1}^{K} \gamma_k^{(\kappa)} (1 + \rho_k^{(\kappa)}(\mathbf{w})) - c||\mathbf{w} - A(\theta^{(\kappa)})D^{(\kappa)}||^2$$

$$\triangleq \tilde{a}^{(\kappa)} + 2 \sum_{k=1}^{K} \Re\{\langle \tilde{b}_k^{(\kappa)} \mathbf{w}_k \rangle\} - \sum_{l=1}^{K} \langle Q^{(\kappa)}, [\mathbf{w}_l]^2 \rangle, \tag{26}$$

with $\tilde{a}^{(\kappa)} \triangleq \sum_{k=1}^{K} \gamma_k^{(\kappa)} a_k^{(\kappa)} - c||A(\theta^{(\kappa)})D^{(\kappa)}||^2$, $\tilde{b}_k^{(\kappa)} \triangleq \gamma_k^{(\kappa)} b_k^{(\kappa)} c_k^{(\kappa)} + c(D_k^{(\kappa)})^H A^H(\theta^{(\kappa)})$, $Q^{(\kappa)} \triangleq \sum_{k=1}^{K} \gamma_k^{(\kappa)} d_k^{(\kappa)} H_k^H H_k + cI_N$. We get following optimization problem:

$$\max_{\mathbf{w}} \tilde{f}(\mathbf{w}) \tag{27a}$$

$$\text{s.t.} \quad (21b), \tag{27b}$$

we use Lagrangian gradient method:

$$w_k^{(\kappa+1)} = \begin{cases} (Q^{(\kappa)})^{-1}(\tilde{b}_k^{(\kappa)})^H & \text{if } \sum_{k=1}^{K} ||(Q^{(\kappa)})^{-1}(\tilde{b}_k^{(\kappa)})^H||^2 \le P \\ \left(Q^{(\kappa)} + \mu I_N\right)^{-1}(\tilde{b}_k^{(\kappa)})^H & \text{otherwise,} \end{cases} \tag{28}$$

where $\mu > 0$ is chosen such that

$$\sum_{k=1}^{K} ||\left(Q^{(\kappa)} + \mu I_N\right)^{-1}(\tilde{b}_k^{(\kappa)})^H||^2 = P. \tag{29}$$

According to [19], we have closed-form solution.

2.2 Analog Beamforming Design

We seek HBF $w^{(\kappa+1)}$ ensuring that

$$F(\theta^{(\kappa+1)}, D^{(\kappa)}, w^{(\kappa+1)}) > F(\theta^{(\kappa)}, D^{(\kappa)}, w^{(\kappa+1)}), \tag{30}$$

which is equivalent to

$$-||w^{(\kappa+1)} - A(\theta^{(\kappa+1)})D^{(\kappa)}||^2 > -||w^{(\kappa+1)} - A(\theta^{(\kappa)})D^{(\kappa)}||^2, \tag{31}$$

by considering the following problem:

$$\max_{\theta} \varphi^{(\kappa)}(\theta) \triangleq -||w_k^{(\kappa+1)} - A(\theta)D_k^{(\kappa)}||^2 \tag{32}$$

$$\text{s.t.} \quad (3). \tag{33}$$

We have

$$\begin{aligned} \varphi^{(\kappa)}(\boldsymbol{\theta}) &= -||w^{(\kappa+1)}||^2 + 2\Re\{\langle D^{(\kappa)}(w^{(\kappa+1)})^H A(\boldsymbol{\theta})\rangle\} \\ &\quad - \langle [D^{(\kappa)}]^2 A^H(\boldsymbol{\theta})A(\boldsymbol{\theta})\rangle \\ &= -||w^{(\kappa+1)}||^2 + 2\Re\{\langle D^{(\kappa)}(w^{(\kappa+1)})^H A(\boldsymbol{\theta})\rangle\} \\ &\quad - \lambda^{(\kappa)} N N_{RF} + \left[\lambda^{(\kappa)}||A(\boldsymbol{\theta})||^2 - \langle [D^{(\kappa)}]^2 A^H(\boldsymbol{\theta})A(\boldsymbol{\theta})\rangle\right] \\ &\ge -||w^{(\kappa+1)}||^2 - \lambda^{(\kappa)} N N_{RF} + 2\Re\{\langle D^{(\kappa)}(w^{(\kappa+1)})^H A(\boldsymbol{\theta})\rangle\} \\ &\quad + \left[2\Re\{\lambda^{(\kappa)}\langle A^H(\theta^{(\kappa)})A(\boldsymbol{\theta})\rangle\} - 2\Re\{\langle [D^{(\kappa)}]^2 A^H(\theta^{(\kappa)})A(\boldsymbol{\theta})\rangle\} \right. \\ &\quad \left. - \lambda^{(\kappa)} N N_{RF} + \langle [D^{(\kappa)}]^2 A^H(\theta^{(\kappa)})A(\theta^{(\kappa)})\rangle\right] \tag{34} \\ &= \hat{a}^{(\kappa)} + 2\Re\{\langle A^{(\kappa)}A(\boldsymbol{\theta})\rangle\}, \tag{35} \end{aligned}$$

with $\lambda^{(\kappa)} \triangleq \lambda_{\max}([D^{(\kappa)}]^2)$, $\hat{a}^{(\kappa)} \triangleq -||w^{(\kappa+1)}||^2 - 2\lambda^{(\kappa)}NN_{RF} + \langle[D^{(\kappa)}]^2 A^H(\theta^{(\kappa)})A(\theta^{(\kappa)})\rangle$, $A^{(\kappa)} \triangleq D^{(\kappa)}(w^{(\kappa+1)})^H + \lambda^{(\kappa)}A^H(\theta^{(\kappa)}) - [D^{(\kappa)}]^2 A^H(\theta^{(\kappa)})$, then we get:

$$\max_{\boldsymbol{\theta}} \varphi^{(\kappa)}(\boldsymbol{\theta}) \tag{36a}$$

$$\text{s.t.} \quad (3), \tag{36b}$$

and

$$\theta^{(\kappa+1)} = \left[2\pi - \lfloor \angle A^{(\kappa)}(j,n)\rceil_b\right]_{(n,j)\in\mathcal{N}\times\mathcal{N}_{RF}}. \tag{37}$$

According to [19], we have closed-form solution.

2.3 Digital Beamforming Design

DBF can be found by

$$\begin{aligned}
D^{(\kappa+1)} &= \arg\max_{\mathbf{D}} F(\theta^{(\kappa+1)}, \mathbf{D}, w^{(\kappa+1)}) \\
&= \arg\min_{\mathbf{D}} ||w^{(\kappa+1)} - A(\theta^{(\kappa+1)})\mathbf{D}||^2 \\
&= (A^H(\theta^{(\kappa+1)})A(\theta^{(\kappa+1)}))^{-1}A^H(\theta^{(\kappa+1)})w^{(\kappa+1)}.
\end{aligned} \tag{38}$$

Algorithm 1. PO Algorithm

1: **Initialization:** Initialize $\theta^{(0)}$, $D^{(0)}$, and $w^{(0)}$. Set $\kappa = 0$ and $c = c_0$.
2: **Repeat until** $||w^{(\kappa)} - A(\theta^{(\kappa)})D^{(\kappa)}||^2 \leq K10^{-3}$: Generate $w^{(\kappa+1)}$ by (28). Generate $\theta^{(\kappa+1)}$ by (37) , and $D^{(\kappa+1)}$ by (38). If $||w^{(\kappa+1)} - A(\theta^{(\kappa+1)})D^{(\kappa+1)}||^2 > 0.9||w^{(\kappa)} - A(\theta^{(\kappa)})D^{(\kappa)}||^2$, reset $c := 1.2c$. Reset $\kappa := \kappa + 1$.
3: **Output** $w^{(\kappa)}$, $\theta^{(\kappa)}$ and $D^{(\kappa)}$. Reset

$$D^{(\kappa)} \to t_0 D^{(\kappa)}, t_0 = \sqrt{P/||A(\theta^{(\kappa)})D^{(\kappa)}||^2}.$$

---

3 Alternating Descent Round Approach

Based on (9) defined by:

$$\rho_k(\boldsymbol{\theta}, \mathbf{D}) \triangleq \frac{|H_k A(\boldsymbol{\theta})\mathbf{D}_k|^2}{\sum_{l\neq k}^{K} |H_k A(\boldsymbol{\theta})\mathbf{D}_l|^2 + \sigma}, \tag{39}$$

the rate at user k is:

$$\mathcal{R}_k(\boldsymbol{\theta}, \mathbf{D}) \triangleq \ln(1 + \rho_k(\boldsymbol{\theta}, \mathbf{D})). \tag{40}$$

Thus, the optimization problem can be expressed as:

$$\max_{\boldsymbol{\theta},\mathbf{D}} \sum_{k=1}^{K} \mathcal{R}_k(\boldsymbol{\theta},\mathbf{D}) \triangleq \max_{\boldsymbol{\theta},\mathbf{D}} \ln(\prod_{k=1}^{K}(1+\rho_k(\boldsymbol{\theta},\mathbf{D})))\text{s.t.} \quad (3),(11), \quad (41a)$$

$$|\theta_{m,n}|^2 \leq 1, n=1,\ldots,N; m=1,\ldots,N_{RF}, \quad (41b)$$

accordingly, the rquivalence problem:

$$\max_{\boldsymbol{\theta},\mathbf{D}} \tilde{f}(\boldsymbol{\theta},\mathbf{D}) \triangleq \sum_{k=1}^{K} \gamma_k^{(\kappa)}(1+\rho_k(\boldsymbol{\theta},\mathbf{D})) \quad (42a)$$

$$\text{s.t.} \quad (3),(11),(41b). \quad (42b)$$

According to [20], we have the following penalized optimization problem:

$$\max_{\boldsymbol{\theta},\mathbf{D}} \hat{f}(\boldsymbol{\theta},\mathbf{D}) \triangleq \tilde{f}(\boldsymbol{\theta},\mathbf{D}) + \mu(\frac{1}{NN_{RF}} - \frac{1}{\sum_{m=1}^{N}\sum_{n=1}^{N_{RF}}|\theta_{m,n}|^2}) \quad (43a)$$

$$\text{s.t.} \quad (3),(11),(41b). \quad (43b)$$

3.1 Digital Beamforming Design

We seek $D^{(\kappa+1)}$ such that

$$\tilde{f}(\theta^{(\kappa)}, D^{(\kappa+1)}) > \tilde{f}(\theta^{(\kappa)}, D^{(\kappa)}), \quad (44)$$

using the inequality (1), then we get:

$$1 + \rho_k(\theta^{(\kappa)},\mathbf{D}) \geq 1 + \rho_k^{(\kappa)}(\mathbf{D})$$

$$\triangleq a_k^{(\kappa)} + 2b_k^{(\kappa)}\Re\{\langle c_k^{(\kappa)}\mathbf{D}_k\rangle\} - d_k^{(\kappa)}(\sum_{l=1}^{K}|H_k A(\theta^{(\kappa)})\mathbf{D}_l|^2), \quad (45)$$

with $a_k^{(\kappa)} \triangleq -\dfrac{|H_k A(\theta^{(\kappa)})D_k^{(\kappa)}|^4}{(\sum_{l\neq k}^{K}|H_k A(\theta^{(\kappa)})D_l^{(\kappa)}|^2+\sigma)^2} - \sigma\dfrac{|H_k A(\theta^{(\kappa)})D_k^{(\kappa)}|^2}{(\sum_{l\neq k}^{K}|H_k A(\theta^{(\kappa)})D_l^{(\kappa)}|^2+\sigma)^2} + 1, \, b_k^{(\kappa)} \triangleq$

$\dfrac{\sum_{l=1}^{K}|H_k A(\theta^{(\kappa)})D_l^{(\kappa)}|^2+\sigma}{(\sum_{l\neq k}^{K}|H_k A(\theta^{(\kappa)})D_l^{(\kappa)}|^2+\sigma)^2}, \quad c_k^{(\kappa)} \triangleq (H_k A(\theta^{(\kappa)})D_k^{(\kappa)})^H H_k A(\theta^{(\kappa)}), \, d_k^{(\kappa)} \triangleq$

$\dfrac{|H_k A(\theta^{(\kappa)})D_k^{(\kappa)}|^2}{(\sum_{l\neq k}^{K}|H_k A(\theta^{(\kappa)})D_l^{(\kappa)}|^2+\sigma)^2}.$ Then we get:

$$\hat{f}(\mathbf{D}) \triangleq \sum_{k=1}^{K} \gamma_k^{(\kappa)}(1+\rho_k^{(\kappa)}(\mathbf{D}))$$

$$\triangleq \sum_{k=1}^{K} \gamma_k^{(\kappa)}a_k^{(\kappa)} + 2\sum_{k=1}^{K}\gamma_k^{(\kappa)}b_k^{(\kappa)}\Re\{\langle c_k^{(\kappa)}\mathbf{D}_k\rangle\} - \sum_{l=1}^{K}\langle Q^{(\kappa)},[\mathbf{D}_l]^2\rangle, \quad (46)$$

with $Q^{(\kappa)} \triangleq \sum_{k=1}^{K}\gamma_k^{(\kappa)}A^H(\theta^{(\kappa)})H_k^H H_k A(\theta^{(\kappa)})$, We solve th following convex problem at κ-th iteration to generate $D_k^{(\kappa+1)}$:

$$\max_{\mathbf{D}} \hat{f}(\mathbf{D}) \quad (47a)$$

$$\text{s.t.} \quad (11). \quad (47b)$$

3.2   Analog Beamforming Design

Similarly, we seek $\theta^{(\kappa+1)}$ such that

$$\tilde{f}(\theta^{(\kappa+1)}, D^{(\kappa+1)}) > \tilde{f}(\theta^{(\kappa+1)}, D^{(\kappa+1)}), \tag{48}$$

using the inequality (1), then we get:

$$1 + \rho_k(\boldsymbol{\theta}, D^{(\kappa+1)}) \geq 1 + \tilde{\rho}_k^{(\kappa)}(\boldsymbol{\theta})$$

$$\triangleq \tilde{a}_k^{(\kappa)} + 2\tilde{b}_k^{(\kappa)}\Re\{\langle \tilde{c}_k^{(\kappa)} A(\boldsymbol{\theta})\rangle\} - \tilde{d}_k^{(\kappa)}(\sum_{l=1}^{K}|H_k A(\boldsymbol{\theta})D_l^{(\kappa+1)}|^2) \tag{49}$$

with $\tilde{a}_k^{(\kappa)} \triangleq -\dfrac{|H_k(\theta^{(\kappa)})D_k^{(\kappa+1)}|^4}{(\sum_{l\neq k}^{K}|H_k(\theta^{(\kappa)})D_l^{(\kappa+1)}|^2+\sigma)^2} - \sigma\dfrac{|H_k(\theta^{(\kappa)})D_k^{(\kappa+1)}|^2}{(\sum_{l\neq k}^{K}|H_k(\theta^{(\kappa)})D_l^{(\kappa+1)}|^2+\sigma)^2} + 1$, $\tilde{b}_k^{(\kappa)} \triangleq$

$\dfrac{\sum_{l=1}^{K}|H_k(\theta^{(\kappa)})D_l^{(\kappa+1)}|^2+\sigma}{(\sum_{l\neq k}^{K}|H_k(\theta^{(\kappa)})D_l^{(\kappa+1)}|^2+\sigma)^2}$, $\tilde{c}_k^{(\kappa)} \triangleq D_k^{(\kappa+1)}(H_k(\theta^{(\kappa)})D_k^{(\kappa+1)})^H H_k$, $\tilde{d}_k^{(\kappa)} \triangleq$

$\dfrac{|H_k(\theta^{(\kappa)})D_k^{(\kappa+1)}|^2}{(\sum_{l\neq k}^{K}|H_k(\theta^{(\kappa)})D_l^{(\kappa+1)}|^2+\sigma)^2}$. We thus have

$$\hat{f}(\boldsymbol{\theta}) \triangleq \sum_{k=1}^{K}\gamma_k(1 + \tilde{\rho}_k^{(\kappa)}(\boldsymbol{\theta}))$$

$$= \tilde{a} + 2\Re\{\tilde{A}^{(\kappa)} A(\boldsymbol{\theta})\} - \langle \tilde{B}^{(\kappa)}, A(\boldsymbol{\theta})\tilde{C}^{(\kappa)} A^H(\boldsymbol{\theta})\rangle, \tag{50}$$

with $\tilde{a}^{(\kappa)} \triangleq \sum_{k=1}^{K}\gamma_k^{(\kappa)}\tilde{a}_k^{(\kappa)}$, $\tilde{A}^{(\kappa)} \triangleq \sum_{k=1}^{K}\gamma_k^{(\kappa)}\tilde{b}_k^{(\kappa)}\tilde{c}_k^{(\kappa)}$, $\tilde{B}^{(\kappa)} \triangleq$ $\sum_{k=1}^{K}\gamma_k^{(\kappa)}\tilde{d}_k^{(\kappa)}H_k^H H_k$, $\tilde{C}^{(\kappa)} \triangleq \sum_{l=1}^{K}[D_l^{(\kappa+1)}]^2$.

and

$$\frac{1}{\sum_{m=1}^{N}\sum_{n=1}^{N_{RF}}|\theta_{m,n}|^2} \leq \phi(\boldsymbol{\theta}) \triangleq \frac{1}{\sum_{m=1}^{N}\sum_{n=1}^{N_{RF}}(2\Re\{(\theta_{m,n}^{(\kappa)})^*\theta_{m,n}\} - |\theta_{m,n}^{(\kappa)}|^2)} \tag{51}$$

over the trust region

$$\sum_{m=1}^{N}\sum_{n=1}^{N_{RF}}(2\Re\{(\theta_{m,n}^{(\kappa)})^*\theta_{m,n}\} - |\theta_{m,n}^{(\kappa)}|^2) > 0, \tag{52}$$

we solve the following optimization problem at the κ-th iteration to generate $\theta^{(\kappa+1)}$:

$$\max_{\boldsymbol{\theta}} g^{(\kappa)}(\boldsymbol{\theta}) \triangleq [\hat{f}(\boldsymbol{\theta}) + \mu(\frac{1}{NN_{RF}} - \phi(\boldsymbol{\theta}))] \tag{53a}$$

$$\text{s.t.} \quad (3), (41b), \sum_{m=1}^{N}\sum_{n=1}^{N_{RF}}(2\Re\{(\theta_{m,n}^{(\kappa)})^*\theta_{m,n}\} - |\theta_{m,n}^{(\kappa)}|^2) > 0, \tag{53b}$$

and determine μ by

$$\mu = \frac{\gamma^{(0)}}{\frac{1}{\sum_{m=1}^{N}\sum_{n=1}^{N_{RF}}|\theta_{m,n}^{(0)}|^2} - \frac{1}{NN_{RF}}}, \tag{54}$$

to make the values of the objective function and penalty term in (43) of similar magnitudes [21].

Algorithm 2. ADR Algorithm

1: **Initialization:** Initialize $(\theta^{(0)}, D^{(0)})$.
2: **Repeat until convergence of the objective function in (42):** Generate $\theta^{(\kappa+1)}$, $D^{(\kappa+1)}$, and μ by (47), (53) and (54). Reset $\kappa := \kappa + 1$.
3: **Output** $(\theta^{(opt)}, D^{(opt)}) = (\theta^{(\kappa)}, D^{(\kappa)})$.

---

4   Numerical Results

With the users randomly located within the cell radius of 200 meters. The path-loss of user k experienced at a distance d_k from the BS is set to $\rho_k = 36.72 + 35.3 \log 10(d_k)$dB taking into account a 16.5 dB gain due to multiple-antenna mmWave transmission [22,23]. The mmWave channel $H_k \in \mathbb{C}^{1 \times N}$ between the BS and UE k in (5) is modelled by [18]

$$H_k = \sqrt{10^{-\rho_k/10}} \sqrt{\frac{N}{N_c N_{sc}}} \sum_{c=1}^{N_c} \sum_{\ell=1}^{N_{sc}} \alpha_{k,c,\ell} a_r\left(\phi_{k,c,\ell}^r\right) a_t^H\left(\phi_{k,c,\ell}^t\right), \qquad (55)$$

where N_c is the number of scattering clusters, N_{sc} is the number of scatterers within each cluster, and $\alpha_{k,c,\ell} \sim \mathcal{CN}(0,1)$ is the complex gain of the ℓth path in the cth cluster between the BS and user k. Under the classic uniform linear array antenna configuration having half-wavelength antenna spacing, the steering vectors $a_t\left(\phi_{k,c,\ell}^t\right)$ and $a_r\left(\phi_{k,c,\ell}^r\right)$ are defined by

$$a_t(\phi_{k,c,\ell}^t) = \frac{1}{\sqrt{N}}\left[1, e^{j\pi \sin \phi_{k,c,\ell}^t}, \ldots, e^{j\pi(N-1)\sin \phi_{k,c,\ell}^t}\right]^T, \qquad (56)$$

and

$$a_r(\phi_{k,c,\ell}^r) = \frac{1}{\sqrt{N_R}}\left[1, e^{j\pi \sin \phi_{k,c,\ell}^r}, \ldots, e^{j\pi(N_R-1)\sin \phi_{k,c,\ell}^r}\right]^T, \qquad (57)$$

where $\phi_{k,c,\ell}^t$ ($\phi_{k,c,\ell}^r$, resp.) is the azimuth angle of departure (arrival, resp.) for the ℓth path in the cth cluster from the BS to UE k, which is generated according to the Laplacian distribution in conjunction with random mean cluster angles in the interval $[0, 2\pi)$ and spreads of 10 degrees within each cluster. As in [23], we set $N_c = 5$ and $N_{sc} = 10$. The carrier frequency is set to 28 GHz, the noise power density is set to -174 dBm/Hz, while the bandwidth is set to B $= 100$ MHz. Unless otherwise stated, $b = 3$, $P = 15$ dBm, $N_{RF} = 8$, $K = 8$ and $N = 64$ are used. The results are multiplied by $\log_2 e$ to convert the unit nats/sec into the unit bps/Hz. The convergence tolerance of the proposed algorithms is set to 10^{-3}.

- PO: This result simulates the performance of algorithm 1 with continuous phase at the θ.
- 3-bit PO: This result simulates the performance of algorithm 1 with 3-bit discrete phase at the θ.

- ADR: This result simulates the performance of algorithm 2 with continuous phase at the θ.
- 3-bit ADR: This result simulates the performance of algorithm 2 with 3-bit discrete phase at the θ.

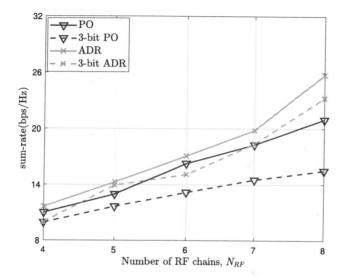

Fig. 2. SR vs the number of RF chains.

Figure 2 plots the SR under different number of RF chains for the proposed algorithms. From the point of view of the continuous phase shifts, ADR has the best SR, which outperforms PO all the time. From the point of view of the discrete phase shifts, their 3-bit resolution algorithms follow the same trend.

Figure 3, which plots the SR under different numbers of BS antennas N. PO better than ADR for $N = 16$, while ADR has the best performance for $N \geq 32$, and among 3-bit resolution algorithms 3-bit ADR has the best performance.

We also examine the SR under different BS transmit power P in Fig. 4. As expected, all the algorithms benefit from increasing the number of transmit power. And they have the same trend follow Fig. 2.

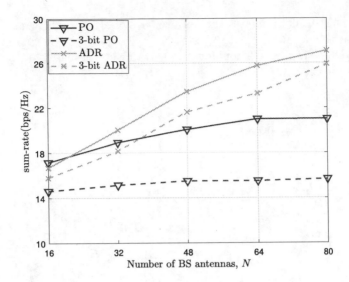

Fig. 3. SR vs the number of BS antennas.

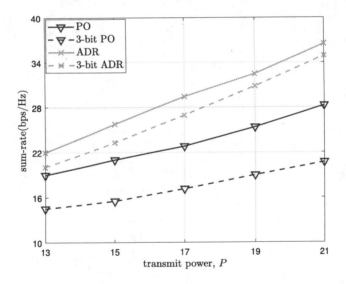

Fig. 4. SR vs the BS transmit power.

5   Conclusions

In this paper, we considered a mmWave MU-MISO downlink communication network, the objective is to maximize the SR by jointly optimizing ABF and DBF. The formulated non-convex optimization problem was solved by using the proposed alternating descent iteration algorithms. Simulation results were provided to demonstrate the superiority of our proposed algorithm.

References

1. Zhang, W., Xia, X., Fu, Y., Bao, X.: Hybrid and full-digital beamforming in mmWave massive MIMO systems: a comparison considering low-resolution ADCS. China Commun. **16**(6), 91–102 (2019)
2. Abdallah, A., Celik, A., Mansour, M.M., Eltawil, A.M.: Deep learning based frequency-selective channel estimation for hybrid mmWave MIMO systems. IEEE Trans. Wirel. Commun. **21**, 3804–3821 (2021)
3. Nguyen, N.T., Lee, K.: Coverage and cell-edge sum-rate analysis of mmWave massive MIMO systems with ORP schemes and MMSE receivers. IEEE Trans. Signal Process. **66**(20), 5349–5363 (2018)
4. Guo, R., Cai, Y., Zhao, M., Shi, Q., Champagne, B., Hanzo, L.: Joint design of beam selection and precoding matrices for mmWave mu-MIMO systems relying on lens antenna arrays. IEEE J. Select. Topics Signal Process. **12**(2), 313–325 (2018)
5. Pang, L., et al.: Joint power allocation and hybrid beamforming for downlink mmWave-NOMA systems. IEEE Trans. Veh. Tech. **70**(10), 10173–10184 (2021)
6. Li, H., Li, M., Liu, Q., Swindlehurst, A.L.: Dynamic hybrid beamforming with low-resolution PSS for wideband mmWave MIMO-OFDM systems. IEEE J. Select. Areas Commun. **38**(9), 2168–2181 (2020)
7. Heath, R.W., Gonzalez-Prelcic, N., Rangan, S., Roh, W., Sayeed, A.M.: An overview of signal processing techniques for millimeter wave MIMO systems. IEEE J. Select. Topics Signal Process. **10**(3), 436–453 (2016)
8. Busari, S.A., Huq, K.M.S., Mumtaz, S., Dai, L., Rodriguez, J.: Millimeter-wave massive MIMO communication for future wireless systems: a survey. IEEE Commun. Surv. Tut. **20**(2), 836–869 (2017)
9. Roh, W., et al.: Millimeter-wave beamforming as an enabling technology for 5g cellular communications: theoretical feasibility and prototype results. IEEE Commun. Mag. **52**(2), 106–113 (2014)
10. Li, M., Wang, Z., Li, H., Liu, Q., Zhou, L.: A hardware-efficient hybrid beamforming solution for mmWave MIMO systems. IEEE Wirel. Commun. **26**(1), 137–143 (2019)
11. Gao, X., Dai, L., Han, S., Chih-Lin, I., Heath, R.W.: Energy-efficient hybrid analog and digital precoding for mmWave MIMO systems with large antenna arrays. IEEE J. Sel. Areas Commun. **34**(4), 998–1009 (2016)
12. Xue, X., Wang, Y., Yang, L., Shi, J., Li, Z.: Energy-efficient hybrid precoding for massive mmWave MIMO systems with a fully-adaptive-connected structure. IEEE Trans. Commun. **68**(6), 3521–3535 (2020)
13. Luo, J., Fan, J., Zhang, J.: MDL-ALTMIN: A hybrid precoding scheme for mmWave systems with deep learning and alternate optimization. IEEE Wirel. Commun. Lett. **11**(9), 1925–1929 (2022)
14. Ni, W., Dong, X., Lu, W.-S.: Near-optimal hybrid processing for massive MIMO systems via matrix decomposition. IEEE Trans. Signal Process. **65**(15), 3922–3933 (2017)
15. Sohrabi, F., Yu, W.: Hybrid digital and analog beamforming design for large-scale antenna arrays. IEEE J. Select. Topics Signal Process. **10**(3), 501–513 (2016)
16. He, S., Wang, J., Huang, W., Huang, Y., Xiao, M., Zhang, Y.: Energy-efficient transceiver design for cache-enabled millimeter-wave systems. IEEE Trans. Commun. **68**(6), 3876–3889 (2020)
17. Shi, Q., Hong, M.: Spectral efficiency optimization for millimeter wave multiuser MIMO systems. IEEE J. Select. Topics Signal Process. **12**(3), 455–468 (2018)

18. El Ayach, O., Rajagopal, S., Abu-Surra, S., Pi, Z., Heath, R.W.: Spatially sparse precoding in millimeter wave MIMO systems. IEEE Trans. Wirel. Commun. **13**(3), 1499–1513 (2014)
19. Tuy, H.: Convex Analysis and Global Optimization, 2nd edn. Springer International, Cham (2017). https://doi.org/10.1007/978-3-319-31484-6
20. Yu, H., Tuan, H.D., Nasir, A.A., Duong, T.Q., Poor, H.V.: Joint design of reconfigurable intelligent surfaces and transmit beamforming under proper and improper gaussian signaling. IEEE J. Sel. Areas Commun. **38**(11), 2589–2603 (2020)
21. Shi, Y., Tuan, H.D., Tuy, H., Su, S.: Global optimization for optimal power flow over transmission networks. J. Glob. Optim. **69**(3), 745–760 (2017)
22. Rappaport, T.S., Xing, Y., MacCartney, G.R., Molisch, A.F., Mellios, E., Zhang, J.: Overview of millimeter wave communications for fifth-generation (5G) wireless networks with a focus on propagation models. IEEE Trans. Antenn. Propag. **65**(12), 6213–6230 (2017)
23. Akdeniz, M.R., et al.: Millimeter wave channel modeling and cellular capacity evaluation. IEEE J. Select. Areas Commun. **32**(6), 1164–1179 (2014)

Multiple Mobile Equipment Localization in Indoor Environment Based on Cell Sectoring

Viet Thuy Vu[1](✉)[iD], Yevhen Ivanenko[1][iD], Aman Batra[2][iD],
Mats I. Pettersson[1][iD], and Thomas Kaiser[2][iD]

[1] Blekinge Institute of Technology, Karlskrona, Sweden
{viet.thuy.vu,yevhen.ivanenko,mats.pettersson}@bth.se
[2] University of Duisburg-Essen, Duisburg, Germany
{aman.batra,thomas.kaiser}@uni-due.de

Abstract. Precise mobile equipment localization in indoor environment is possible for mobile equipment with an integrated radar system. Deploying an omni-directional antenna at a base station allows localizing a single mobile unit at a time slot and a frequency resource block. With cell sectoring, an approach to cope with increasing capacity in a cell of a mobile network, helps to localize multiple mobile units at a time slot and a frequency resource block. Most importantly, cell sectoring helps to avoid localization ambiguity caused by the backprojection process. The paper presents the precise multiple mobile equipment localization approach in indoor environment based on cell sectoring. The simulation illustrates the benefit of the approach. The practicality of the approach is also addressed in the paper.

Keywords: Localization · 6G · FMCW radar

1 Introduction

Several frequency ranges including D-band (110 to 175 GHz) and THz range (0.3 to 10 THz) are under consideration for 6G. Although these frequency ranges have been researched for long time they have mainly designated for astronomy and military, e.g., radar systems. Sharing the same radio frequency (RF) resources by mobile communication and radar opens the opportunity to integrate radar system on mobile equipment. Such system can be called a joint radar?communication (JRC) system [1,2]. Another name used for such systems

---

The authors would like to thank 2π-Labs GmbH, Germany, for providing the radar system for the research.

The research work presented in this paper was supported by the Crafoord Foundation, Sweden, ("Crafoordska stiftelsen") under Project 20230898 and by the German Research Foundation ("Deutsche Forschungsgemeinschaft") (DFG) under Project-ID 287022738 TRR 196 for Project S05.

N.-S. Vo and H.-A. Tran (Eds.): INISCOM 2023, LNICST 531, pp. 119–131, 2023.
https://doi.org/10.1007/978-3-031-47359-3_9

is a joint communication and sensing (JCAS) system. A large number of research on JRC systems has been done, focusing on the challenges of JRC front-end for 6G applications [3], waveform designa for JRC systems [4] and other technical problems [5–8].

The use cases of the next generation of mobile communication (6G) have been introduced recently by NGMN Alliance [9]. Localization at centimeter or better level, particularly in indoor environment, is listed in the class Enabling Services of the high-level grouping of use cases. A JRC system has shown the capability of precise localization in indoor environment [10–12]. In [13], different configuration to realize synthetic aperture radar (SAR) for localization on mobile equipment with integrated radar system are proposed. The movement of mobile users helps to synthesize an aperture that is much larger than the physical aperture of a radar system. In [14], a discussion about mobile user localization is presented. It is shown that a mobile unit can feasibly be localized by implementing backprojection at a base station. However, the localization ambiguity occurs as an inherit problem of a backprojection process. This can be avoided if we know the orientation of an antenna.

Cell sectoring is an approach to cope with increasing capacity in a cell of a mobile network [15]. A cell is divided into several sectors, typically three sectors, and each is with their own set of frequency resources. In common situation, omnidirectional antennas are deployed at base stations. To implement cell sectoring, an omni-directional antenna is replaced by a number of directional antennas, and each is oriented to a specified sector. This approach also helps to decrease the number of interfering co-channel cells and co-channel interference, leading to the small separation between co-channel cells.

Deploying several passive receivers at a base station and orienting the directional antenna of each receiver to a specified sector allow localizing multiple mobile units in a time slot and a frequency resource block. With this arrangement, the radar measurements are in the side-looking mode. The localization ambiguity, which is caused by the backprojection process, is therefore eliminated. This approach will be presented in this paper and the approach is called the precise multiple mobile equipment localization approach in indoor environment based on cell sectoring.

The rest of the paper is organized as follows: Sect. 2 gives a summary of the precise mobile equipment localization approach in indoor environment. The multiple mobile equipment localization version based on cell sectoring is proposed in Sect. 3. Sections 4 and 5 present the simulation results and the experimental results, respectively. Section 6 provides the conclusions.

2   Precise Mobile Equipment Localization Approach in Indoor Environment

Consider a scenario given in Fig. 1. A microcell (femto or pico) is served by a base station. There are several mobile users operating in the cell. The mobile equipment is integrated with radar systems. The mobile equipment has a clear

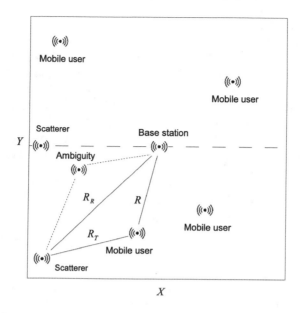

Fig. 1. Arrangement for mobile user localization and localization plane.

line of sight (LOS) to the base station. In the cell, several scatterers are also strategically positioned so that they have a clear LOS to both the base station and the mobile equipment.

Assume that the base station wants to localize a mobile unit of interest. A command is sent to that mobile equipment. The integrated radar system is activated and emits the radar signal. If the integrated radar system is a frequency-modulated continuous wave (FMCW), the passive receiver at the base station receives two delayed versions of the transmitted radar signal

$$S_1\left(\nu\right) = W\left(\nu - \kappa\frac{R}{c}\right)\exp\left\{\frac{j2\pi\nu_{min}R}{c} - j\pi\kappa\left(\frac{R}{c}\right)^2\right\} \tag{1}$$

and

$$S_2\left(\nu\right) = W\left(\nu - \kappa\frac{R_T + R_R}{c}\right)\exp\left\{\frac{j2\pi\nu_{min}\left(R_T + R_R\right)}{c} - j\pi\kappa\left(\frac{R_T + R_R}{c}\right)^2\right\} \tag{2}$$

where τ denotes range time and c is the speed of the wave propagation. If $w\left(\tau\right)$ is the envelope of the FMCW radar output, then $W\left(\nu\right)$ is the range compressed envelope in the ν domain. If $w\left(\tau\right)$ is a rectangular window, $W\left(\nu\right)$ will be a sinc function and if $w\left(\tau\right)$ is a tapered window, $W\left(\nu\right)$ will be a sinc-like function with lower sidelobe. The radar signal in the time-frequency analysis is a ramp signal with the start frequency ν_{min} and with the slope κ. The modulation time T results in a bandwidth of $B = \kappa T$. In (1) and (2), R, R_T and R_R denote the ranges (distances) between the base station and the mobile equipment of interest, between the mobile user and the scatterer, and between the scatterer and the base station, respectively.

The localization plane (X, Y) is defined by the ground-range plane. The center of the plane is selected by the position of the base station as shown in Fig. 1. The delayed versions of the radar signal $S_1(\nu)$ and $S_2(\nu)$ are backprojected into the localization plane [16]. The backprojection process results in two visible circles (or one circle and one ellipse) in the localization plane. One circle corresponds to the monostatic radar measurement (mobile equipment - base station) and it is the intersection of the sphere of radius $\hat{R}$ with the localization plane

$$
\begin{cases}
\Im(X, Y) = S_1\left(\hat{R}\right) \exp\left\{ -\frac{j2\pi\nu_{min}\hat{R}}{c} + j\pi\kappa \left(\frac{\hat{R}}{c}\right)^2 \right\} \\
\hat{R} = \sqrt{X^2 + Y^2 + \Delta Z^2}
\end{cases}
\tag{3}
$$

where ΔZ denotes the difference in height between the base station and the mobile equipment. The other corresponds to the bistatic radar measurement (mobile equipment - scatterer - base station) and it is the intersection of the sphere of radius $\hat{R}_T$ with the localization plane

$$
\begin{cases}
\Im(X, Y) = S_2\left(t, \hat{R}_T + R_R\right) \exp\left\{ -\frac{j2\pi\nu_{min}\left(\hat{R}_T + R_R\right)}{c} + j\pi\kappa \left(\frac{\hat{R}_T + R_R}{c}\right)^2 \right\} \\
\hat{R}_T = \sqrt{(X - X_S)^2 + (Y - Y_S)^2 + \Delta Z_S^2}
\end{cases}
\tag{4}
$$

where ΔZ_S is the difference in height between the scatterer and the mobile user, and (X_S, Y_S) indicates the position of the scatterer. The intersection of the two circles in the localization plane localizes the mobile equipment of interest.

3   Multiple Mobile Equipment Localization

There are several technical issues with the localization approach presented in the previous section, in which the localization ambiguity needs to be solved. The ambiguity can be avoided if the scatter is strategically positioned, and the cell is divided into a number of sectors.

Figure 1 considers the case where a cell is divided into two sectors $0°$–$180°$ and $180°$–$360°$, separated by the dashed line. There should be two directional antennas that are deployed and oriented to two sectors. The localization plane is also divided in to two parts $0°$–$180°$ and $180°$–$360°$. Assume that, there is one mobile equipment that is object to be localized in the sector $180°$–$360°$. According to the localization approach, the localization result is given by the intersection of two circles in the localization plane. This can give two localization results for the same mobile equipment of interest as the intersection of two circle can be two different points. One point corresponds to the true position of the mobile equipment, whereas the other is its image that is symmetrical to the true position of the mobile equipment with respect to R_R. In Fig. 1, this point is marked by the text "Ambiguity" in the part 180°–360° of the localization plane. Cell sectoring is therefore only the necessary condition to avoid the localization ambiguity. The sufficient condition is that the scatterer must be strategically positioned.

Figure 1 suggests how to position a scatterer to avoid the localization ambiguity. In the case where the cell is divided into two sectors, the scatterer should be placed in the border of two sectors (the dashed line). There will be a single intersection of two circles lying in the part 180°–360° of the localization plane. The part 0°–180° of the localization plane is excluded from the backprojection process. The localization result is therefore unique.

Similarly, if the mobile equipment of interest is in the sector 0°–180°, the localization result will be given by a single intersection and in the part 0°–180° of the localization plane. The part 180°–360° of the localization plane is excluded from the backprojection process. The localization result is therefore unique.

With such, two mobile units can be localized a time slot and a frequency resource block.

The considered cell can also be divided into four sectors, 0°–90°, 90°–180°, 180°–270° and 270°–360°. In this case, there should be four directional antennas and they are deployed and oriented to four sectors. The localization plane is divided correspondingly into four parts. With strategical positioning scatters, four mobile units can be localized a time slot and a frequency resource block.

4   Simulation Results

In this section, we present some simulation results to examine and evaluate the proposal introduced in Sect. 3. The same scenario given in Fig. 1 is considered in the simulations.

4.1   System Parameters

Several mobile units operate in a microcell and served by a base station. Each mobile unit is cquiped with a FMCW radar system. The parameters of the radar system are summarized in the first part Table 1. The radar system parameters are identical to the ones of 2πSENSE, a D-band FMCW radar [15]. The radar system can share the same antenna of the mobile equipment, giving omni-directional pattern.

The cell is divided into two sectors (0°–180°) and (180°–360°). Two passive receivers with two directional antennas are deployed at the base station. Each antenna is oriented to one sector. The simulation parameters for the base station are given in the second part of Table 1.

The scatterer is positioned at the border of two sectors. The radar cross section of the scatterer is normalized so that the signal attenuation is excluded. The simulation parameters for the scatterer are given in the third part of Table 1.

Table 1. Parameters FMCW radar system and scenario.

Parameter	Value
Mobile equipment	
Frequency span	126 GHz–182 GHz
Modulation time	$4.096 \cdot 10^{-3}$s
Duty cycle	$5 \cdot 10^{-3}$s
Antenna of mobile equipment	omni-directional
Mobile equipment antenna heights	1.8 m (0°–180°)
	1.2 m (180°–360°)
Scatterer	
Characteristics	point-like scatterers
Scatterer height	5 m
Radar cross sections	1 m^2
Scatterer - mobile eqipment range	12 m (0°–180°)
	10 m (180° − 360°)
Base station	
Number of passive receivers	2
Antennas	directional
Base station antenna height	5 m
Base station - scatterer range	5 m
Base station - mobile equipment range	8 m (0°–180°)
	10 m (180° − 360°)

Figures 2(a) and (b) provide the range-compressed radar signals, obtained with a Fourier transform of the outputs of the FMCW radar systems. In the plots, we convert the range time to the radar range by multiplying the time axis with the speed of propagation, i.e., with the speed of light in vacuum.

The range-compressed radar signal given in Fig. 2(a) corresponds to the radar measurement in the sector 0°–180° of the cell. Two peaks can be observed at the radar ranges about 8 m and 17 m. One peak is the LOS radar signal coming from the mobile equipment in the sector 0°–180° and the other is the multipath delayed version via the scatterer. The radar ranges are matched with the simulation parameters given in Table 1, found in base station - mobile equipment range, and the sum of scatterer - mobile equipment range and base station - scatterer range.

In Fig. 2(b), the given range-compressed radar signal corresponds to the radar measurement in the sector 180°–360° of the cell. We can also observe two peaks at the radar ranges about 10 m and 15 m. One peak is the LOS radar signal coming from the mobile equipment in the sector 180°–360° and the other is the multipath delayed version via the scatterer. The radar ranges are also matched with the simulation parameters given in Table 1.

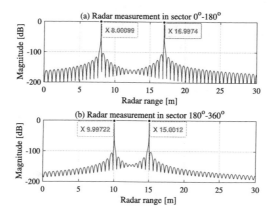

Fig. 2. Range-compressed radar signals.

4.2   Backprojection

As proved in [13], the accuracy of mobile user localization depends strongly on the assumptions on the differences in height between base station and mobile user ΔZ, and between scatterer and mobile user ΔZ_S. The heights of the base station and the scatterer are known, whereas the heights of mobile equipment are unknown and can vary in a wide range. They depend on the how tall the mobile users are and where the mobile equipment is placed, e.g., on a table and in the pocket of a mobile user. As suggested, in common cases, we can consider the range of $[1,2]$ m for the height of mobile equipment. If we select the height of 1.5 for the backprojection process, the differences in height will be $\Delta Z = \Delta Z_S = 3.5$ m.

The backprojection of the range-compressed radar signal given in Fig. 2(a) into the part $0°–180°$ of the localization plane results in two halves of circle that can be observed in the upper part of Fig. 3. The intensity of the image pixels plotting the circles are identical to the peaks value of the range-compressed radar signal. The intersection of two halves of circle localizes a mobile unit at the coordinate $(5.50147, 4.63343)$ m. Compared with the parameters used in the simulations, the errors are estimated by $|\Delta X| = 0.0016$ m and $|\Delta Y| = 0.2154$ m.

The range-compressed radar signal given in Fig. 2(b) is backprojected into the part $180°–360°$ of the localization plane, resulting in four halves of circle. This effect is caused by the small separation between the peaks. Actually, two peaks of the range-compressed radar signal are close together. The backprojection processes consider both two peaks and each gives two circles. However, there is only an unique intersection of two halves of circle, localizing another mobile unit at the coordinate $(-2.25199, -9.04399)$ m. The errors are estimated by $|\Delta X| = 0.2479$ m and $|\Delta Y| = 0.1383$ m.

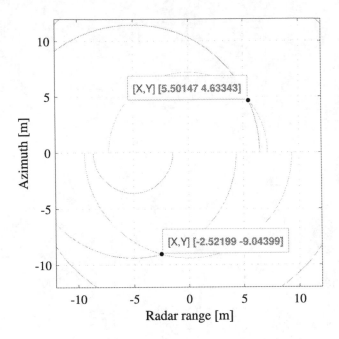

Fig. 3. Mobile user localization by implementing backprojection with unknown heights of mobile equipment. The value of 1.5 m is selected for the backprojection process.

4.3   Evaluation

To examine of the localization results, we can use the results to calculate the ranges based on (3) and (4). For the mobile equipment localized at the coordinate $(5.50147, 4.63343)$ m and with the height assumption of 1.5 m, (3) gives an estimation for the monostatic radar range (base station - mobile equipment range). A range of about 7.9991 m is retrieved. (4) gives an estimation for the bistatic radar range (mobile equipment - scatterer - base station range). A range of about $12 + 5 = 17$ m is retrieved. The estimations are almost identical to the parameters used in the simulation, verifying the localization results.

For the mobile equipment localized at the coordinate $(-2.25199, -9.04399)$ m and with the height assumption of 1.5 m, the estimated monostatic radar range is about 9.9557 m and the estimated bistatic radar range is about $10.0795 + 5 = 17.0795$ m. These vaues are also very close to the parameters used in the simulation.

The errors can be recognized in the localization results and can also be estimated. They are originated from the unknown heights of mobile equipment. In the simulations, we consider two mobile units with different heights (1.2 m and 1.8 m). An average height of 1.5 m is assumed and considered for all backprojection processes. This assumption leads to the different errors of the localization results. The maximum error is shown to be 0.25 m in the simulations and still meets the demand of the localization at centimeter level in indoor environment for 6G [9].

Reaching a better level of accuracy for localization is also possible with three-dimension (3D) localization. In this case, the heights of mobile equipment will be estimated directly from the radar measurements. Armed with the information about the heights of mobile equipment, the localization results obtained with the 2D approach will be much more accurate. However, 3D localization requires more scatterers to be deployed and more radar measurements are also required. The computation complexity will therefore be increased.

4.4   Cell Sectoring and Multiple Mobile User Localization

In the simulations, a cell is divided into two sectors, helping to localize two mobile units at a time slot and a frequency resource block. As presented in Sect. 3, a cell can also be divided in to four sectors. Localizing fours mobile units at a time slot and a frequency resource block is therefore possible. A cell can be further divided into narrower sectors, e.g., 8 sectors, facilitating multiple mobile user localization but this might be unnecessary. There are the scheduling approaches in time and/or frequency that can be used for multiple mobile user localization.

As shown in [14], time scheduling is possible due to the small modulation time and small duty cycle of the radar system. For the duty cycle of 5 ms, 200 mobile units can be localized in one second. In combination with the cell sectoring with four sectors, the number of mobile units that can be localized is up to 800 in one second.

5   Practicality

The radar system parameters considered in the simulations are identical to the parameters of 2π SENSE, a D-band FMCW radar system [17]. The lower right of Fig. 4 shows the dimension of the FMCW radar in practice. The dimension of the electronic circuit is only about 2×3 cm, allowing an integration into mobile equipment. The electronic components of mobile equipment can also be used to build a FMCW radar system. Basically, integrating a radar system into mobile equipment is feasible.

5.1   FMCW Radar Operation

For a FMCW radar, the phase of the transmitted complex linear frequency-modulated chirp signal in the radio frequency (RF) domain can be expressed by [18]

$$\phi_{TX}(\tau) = \exp\left\{ j2\pi\nu_{min}\tau + j\pi\kappa\tau^2 \right\}, \quad 0 \leq \tau \leq T. \tag{5}$$

The chirp signal is assumed to propagate through a homogeneous medium. If there is a target at the range R, a part of the emitted chirp signal will be reflected

Fig. 4. Experiment setup for localization with indoor monostatic radar measurement using FMCW radar system.

to the radar system. The reflection is recorded by the receiver. The expression for the received signal due to the reflection is given by

$$\phi_{RX}(t, \tau) = \exp\left\{ j2\pi\nu_{min}\left(\tau - \frac{2R}{c}\right) + j\pi\kappa\left(\tau - \frac{2R}{c}\right)^2 \right\}. \tag{6}$$

The received signal is in the RF domain and needs to be downconverted to the intermediate frequency (IF) domain by mixing the transmitted and received signals. The result of the down-conversion is expressed by

$$\phi_{IF}(t, \tau) = s_{TX}(\tau)\,\bar{s}_{RX}(t, \tau)$$

$$= \exp\left\{ j2\pi\left(\nu_{min} + \kappa\tau\right)\frac{2R}{c} - j\pi\kappa\left(\frac{2R}{c}\right)^2 \right\}, \tag{7}$$

where $\nu(\tau) = \nu_{min} + \kappa\tau$ denotes the linear modulated frequency of the chirp.

For range compression, the down-converted signal is transformed to the frequency domain using Fourier transform. The expression of the signal after Fourier transform is

$$S_{IF}(t, \nu) = W\left(\nu - \kappa\frac{2R}{c}\right)\exp\left\{ \frac{j4\pi\nu_{min}R}{c} - j\pi\kappa\left(\frac{2R}{c}\right)^2 \right\} \tag{8}$$

The frequency shift defines a beat at

$$\nu_b = \kappa \frac{2R}{c} \tag{9}$$

showing the relationship between the range R and the beat frequency ν_b. We can also rewrite (9) using the ramp duration T and the sweep bandwidth B as

$$\nu_b = \frac{B}{T}\frac{2R}{c} \Leftrightarrow R = \frac{cT}{2}\frac{\nu_b}{B} \tag{10}$$

Equation (8) is the standard equation for a FMCW radar system. Equations (1) and (2) have similar expressions but the range terms are different. In (1), since no reflection is considered, the factor 2 in (8) is excluded. In (2), the factor 2 in (8) is replaced by the sum of R_T and R_R.

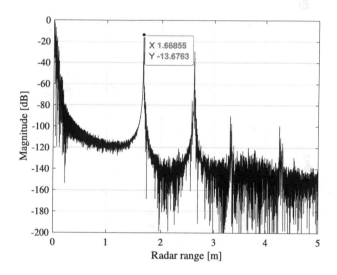

Fig. 5. Range-compressed radar signal provided by 2πSENSE.

5.2 Experiment

Figure 4 provides a simple measurement as a part of mobile user localization. The measurement is purely monostatic radar and carried out in the indoor environment. It is an office that is filled with furniture. The radar system is mounted at the height of about 2 m. A corner reflector is placed in front of the radar system with the range of about 1.6 m and at the height of about 1.5 m. Behind the corner reflector is the wall that is built with different materials including glass, wood and plastic. With this arrangement, the corner reflector plays the role of the mobile equipment with integrated radar system, whereas the radar system plays the role of passive receiver with respect to the arrangement for mobile user localization. The radar system uses a horn, a directional antenna.

Figure 5 shows the range-compressed radar signal, obtained by a Fourier transform of 2πSENSEs output. A peak of the radar signal can be easily observed at the radar range $R \approx 1.7$ m, indicating the location of the corner reflector.

With the radar system parameters given in Table 1, we can calculate the radar signal bandwidth and then retrieve the range resolution. For the bandwidth of 56 GHz, the theoretical range resolution is down to 2.7 mm that is extremely accurate for localization.

6   Conclusion and Future Work

The paper discusses about the localization ambiguity and the approach for the problem. Cell sectoring is the necessary condition to avoid the localization ambiguity, whereas the sufficient condition is that the scatterer must be strategically positioned. The simulations examine and evaluate the multiple mobile equipment localization in indoor environment based on cell sectoring approach. A simple monostatic radar measurement partially shows the practicality of the approach.

The study will be continued with different extensions, resulting into different research topics. For example, hyper-accurate 3D localization in indoor environment for mobile equipment should be investigated in the future study. An investigation into non-stationary mobile equipment localization can also be a necessary study.

References

1. Kaushik, A., Vlachos, E., Thompson, J., Nekovee, M., Coutts, F.: Towards 6G: spectrally efficient joint radar and communication with radio frequency selection, interference and hardware impairment. IET Signal Process. **16**, 851–863 (2022)
2. de Oliveira, L.G., Nuss, B., Alabd, M.B., Diewald, A., Pauli, M., Zwick, T.: Joint radar-communication systems: modulation schemes and system design. IEEE Trans. Microwave Theory Tech. **70**(3), 1521–1551 (2022)
3. Bozorgi, F., Sen, P., Barreto, A.N., Fettweis, G.: RF front-end challenges for joint communication and radar sensing. In: IEEE JC&S, Dresden, Germany, pp. 1–6 (2021)
4. Sturm, C., Wiesbeck, W.: Waveform design and signal processing aspects for fusion of wireless communications and radar sensing. Proc. IEEE **99**(7), 1236–1259 (2011)
5. Herschfelt, A., Bliss, D.W.: Joint radar-communications waveform multiple access and synthetic aperture radar receiver. In: Proceedings of IEEE ACSSC, Pacific Grove, CA, USA, pp. 69–74 (2017)
6. Herschfelt, A., Bliss, D.W.: Spectrum management and advanced receiver techniques (SMART): joint radar-communications network performance. In: Proceedings of IEEE RadarConf, Oklahoma City, OK, USA, pp. 1078–1083 (2018)
7. Basit, A., et al.: Adaptive main lobe/sidelobes controls selection in FDA based joint radar-communication design. In: Proceedings of IEEE ICECCE, Swat, Pakistan, pp. (3) (2019)

8. Chen, X., Wei, Z., Fang, Z., Ma, H., Feng, Z., Wu, H.: Performance of joint radar-communication enabled cooperative UAV network. In: Proceedings of IEEE ICSIDP, Chongqing, China, pp. 1–5 (2019)

9. NGMN, 6G use cases and analysis. https://www.ngmn.org/wp-content/uploads/NGMN-6G-Use-Cases-and-Analysis.pdf

10. Sakhnini, A., Guenach, M., Bourdoux, A., Pollin, S.: A Cramr-Rao lower bound for analyzing the localization performance of a multistatic joint radar-communication system. In: IEEE JC&S, Dresden, Germany, pp. 1–5 (2021)

11. Ellison, S., Nanzer, J.A.: High-accuracy localization in joint radar and communications systems using multi-tone waveform modulation. In: IEEE AP-S/URSI, Montral, Qubec, Canada, pp. 1635–1636 (2020)

12. Kim, Y.H., Choi, J., Nemati, M.: Toward joint radar, communication, computation, localization, and sensing in IoT. IEEE Access **10**, 11772–11788 (2022)

13. Vu, V.T., Ivanenko, Y., Sjgren, T.K., Pettersson, M.I.: Realizing SAR for localization on mobile equipment with integrated radar system. In: Proceedings of IEEE IAICT, Bali, Indonesia, pp. 1–7 (2023, accepted for publication)

14. Vu, V.T., Ivanenko, Y., Batra, A., Sjgren, T.K., Pettersson, M.I., Kaiser, T.: Implementing backprojection at base station for precise localization in indoor environment. In: Proceedings of IEEE RIVF, Hanoi, Vietnam, pp. 1–6 (2023, submitted for publication)

15. Beard, C., Stallings, W.: Wireless Communication Networks and Systems, 1st edn. Pearson, London, UK (2015)

16. Hellsten, H., Andersson, L.E.: An inverse method for the processing of synthetic aperture radar data. Inverse Probl. **3**(1), 111–124 (1987)

17. Kueppers, S., Jaeschke, T., Pohl, N., Barowski, J.: Versatile 126–182 GHz UWB D-band FMCW radar for industrial and scientific applications. IEEE Sens. Lett. **6**(1), 1–4 (2021)

18. Skolnik, M.I.: Radar Handbook, 2nd edn. McGraw-Hill, New York (1990). ch. 16

Information Processing and Data Analysis

Facial Skin Condition Detection Using Deep Learning-Building Skin Care System

Anh-Thu T. Chau, Duc-Man Nguyen[✉], Nghia-Khue Hoang, Minh-Phu Phan, Phuoc-An Dong, and Kim-Sanh Tran

International School, Duy Tan University, 550000 Da Nang, Vietnam
{chautanhthu,hoangnghiakhue,phanminhphu1,
dongphuocan}@dtu.edu.vn, {mannd,trankimsanh}@duytan.edu.vn

Abstract. The demand for skincare solutions has grown significantly in recent years, with individuals of all genders seeking ways to maintain healthy and beautiful facial skin. However, environmental pollutants, stress, and hormonal changes can negatively impact the skin, leading to issues like acne and dark spots. To address these concerns, we have developed FaSkare, an intelligent facial skin condition detection system. FaSkare utilizes advanced technologies, including FastAI and deep learning, to analyze and accurately predict users' facial skin conditions. By understanding the precise condition of their skin, users can receive personalized recommendations for suitable skincare services and cosmetics. The system is designed to be practical and effective, capable of being applied in various conditions. Experimental results demonstrate the practicality and effectiveness of FaSkare in analyzing facial skin conditions and providing tailored solutions. The system's user-friendly website platform ensures ease of use and accessibility for individuals seeking skincare advice. By leveraging the power of data and machine learning, FaSkare aims to bridge the gap between beauty awareness and accessible skincare solutions.

Keywords: FaSkare · Facial skin care · FastAI · Deep learning · facial detection

1 Introduction

In today's modern era, skincare has become a common concern for both women and men, as the desire for beauty is universal. Among all aspects of skincare, the condition of facial skin holds paramount importance. Our facial skin is exposed daily to environmental factors such as smoke, dust, and ultraviolet rays, along with the effects of life pressures, work stress, nutritional deficiencies, and hormonal changes. These factors can weaken the facial skin and lead to issues like acne, dark spots, and freckles.

To maintain the long-term beauty and health of the skin, it is essential to engage in daily skincare routines that nourish the skin from within and protect it from external agents. Consistent skin care practices can effectively prevent early skin problems and minimize aging and damage. However, not everyone has sufficient time or knowledge

N.-S. Vo and H.-A. Tran (Eds.): INISCOM 2023, LNICST 531, pp. 135–147, 2023.
https://doi.org/10.1007/978-3-031-47359-3_10

about proper facial skincare procedures. The demands of busy daily lives often make it challenging to visit beauty salons or allocate hours for skincare routines. Furthermore, the ongoing challenge of the Covid-19 pandemic has further complicated matters, making it difficult for individuals to access beauty salons or seek professional advice while adhering to social distancing measures.

Artificial Intelligence (AI) has emerged as a practical solution in various domains [4, 5], attracting considerable attention due to its potential to process vast amounts of data at an unprecedented speed. AI technology enables machines to perceive the world like humans, learn autonomously, and solve real-life problems effectively. Computer Vision, a subset of AI, has witnessed rapid expansion and has found application in diverse real-world scenarios [6]. In light of these considerations, we propose a solution that leverages FastAI [1, 2], a powerful deep-learning framework, for detecting facial skin conditions and determining skin types. Additionally, we utilize TFLearn [3], a transparent and modular deep learning library built on top of TensorFlow, to enhance the accuracy and effectiveness of our approach.

By employing AI technologies for facial skin detection and classification, we aim to address the challenges mentioned earlier and provide individuals with a comprehensive skincare system that can assess their skin conditions and recommend suitable skincare routines. This solution offers a convenient alternative for those who have limited time, lack knowledge of skincare, or face difficulties accessing traditional skincare services due to the constraints of daily life or external factors such as the Covid-19 pandemic.

The remainder of this paper is organized as follows: Sect. 2 introduces some approaches and projects related to our work; Sect. 3 presents the proposed solution, Sect. 4 presents the experimental results, and lastly, Sect. 5 gives a conclusion of what has been currently achieved and future work.

2 Related Work

In the modern era of information and communication systems, people have become reliant on online applications [7], which have become indispensable tools for addressing various life challenges [8].

FastAI [1] is a deep learning library that offers practitioners high-level components capable of delivering state-of-the-art results in standard deep learning domains. Additionally, it provides researchers with flexible low-level components that can be combined to create novel approaches.

Numerous studies have emphasized the significance of skincare, given the difficulty people face in determining their skin type and effectively caring for their skin to maintain its health. This system incorporates CNN and DNN to implement facial recognition functionalities and chatbots.

Several existing applications cater to skincare users and offer various features, as outlined in Table 1. For instance, TroveSkin [9] enables users to identify their skin triggers by monitoring skincare products, lifestyle choices, habits, and more. VietSkin [10] serves as a platform connecting patients with dermatologists for remote dermatology consultations. Skincare Routine [11] assists in creating personalized skincare routines, organizing beauty and makeup products, understanding their proper usage order, and tracking usage. FeelinMySkin Skincare Routine [12] provides users with a comprehensive skincare app that facilitates routine creation for consistent skincare, tracks product usage, and expiration dates, monitors changes in the skin, and offers skincare tips and information about ingredient purposes.

Table 1. Compare FaSkare with the app on the market.

Features	Trove-Skin	VietSkin	SkincareRoutine	FeelinMySkin	FaSkare
Recommend effective services				+	+
Track user's cosmetic			+		
Track & compare changes in skin	+			+	
Create a personalized routine for your skincare			+	+	
Facial skin condition analysis				+	+
Skincare advice	+				+
AI Chatbot					+
Spa booking					+
Connect with doctor		+			+
Find effective cosmetic	+	+			+
Chat real-time		+			+
Remind & notification	+		+		+

Facial skin detection and classification using deep learning has garnered significant attention in the field of computer vision, resulting in numerous research endeavors. Noteworthy contributions in this domain include the works of Deng et al. [13], which provide a comprehensive overview of recent advancements in deep learning-based face recognition techniques, covering face detection, alignment, feature extraction, and classification. Mellouk et al. [14] present the current state-of-the-art in Facial Expression Recognition (FER) utilizing deep learning, discussing crucial insights and challenges across datasets and preprocessing, model architecture, training and optimization, and evaluation metrics. Prasad [16] proposes a deep learning-based approach for face representation under various conditions, encompassing occlusions, misalignment, different head poses, changing illuminations, and flawed facial feature localization. This paper investigates two popular deep learning models, Lightened CNN and VGG-Face, for extracting face representations. Additionally, Jin et al. [15] introduce Deep facial diagnosis, a technique that employs transfer learning from face recognition to facilitate facial diagnosis. This approach involves fine-tuning a pre-trained CNN on a smaller labeled dataset of facial images tailored to the specific diagnosis task. Deep facial diagnosis demonstrates promising results in diverse medical applications, including skin cancer detection, predicting cardiovascular disease risk, and identifying genetic disorders. The utilization of deep learning techniques in medical diagnosis holds the potential to enhance accuracy and efficiency, ultimately leading to improved patient outcomes.

Despite the abundance of beauty care applications in the current market, there is a lack of applications capable of swiftly detecting facial skin conditions or identifying acne types while seamlessly integrating additional utilities for users, such as personalized cosmetic suggestions, direct consultation with doctors, and scheduling within the system.

To address this gap, we have developed FaSkare, a comprehensive system that not only detects acne on the skin but also integrates a multitude of utilities to deliver an exceptional user experience.

3 Proposed Solution

A high-level overview of the process that we propose for building a facial skin condition detection system using deep learning is as follows:

1. Data Collection: Gather a diverse dataset of facial images that cover different skin conditions, such as acne, wrinkles, dark spots, rosacea, etc. The images are labeled with the corresponding skin condition for training purposes.
2. Data Preprocessing: Clean and preprocess the collected dataset. This step involves resizing the images, normalizing pixel values, and applying any necessary image augmentation techniques to increase the robustness of the model.
3. Model Selection: FastAI model and Convolutional Neural Networks (CNNs) are used for facial skin detection and image classification tasks (detailed in the experiment section).
4. Model Training: Split the dataset into training and validation sets. Use the training set to train the selected model on the labeled facial images. During training, the model will learn to extract relevant features from the images and classify them into different skin conditions. Optimize the model using an appropriate loss function and update the model's parameters using backpropagation and gradient descent.
5. Model Evaluation: Evaluate the trained model's performance on the validation set to assess its accuracy, precision, recall, and F1 score. Fine-tune the model and hyperparameters, if necessary, to improve its performance.
6. Deployment: the model can be deployed as part of a skincare system. This system can take input images of faces, process them using the trained model, and provide predictions and recommendations based on the detected skin conditions. It will be deployed as a web-based application - FaSkare.
7. Ongoing Improvement: Continue to collect new data and periodically retrain the model to improve its accuracy and keep it up to date with emerging skin conditions and trends. Incorporate user feedback and iterate on the system based on user experiences and requirements.

The process of facial skin condition detection and classification using a CNN model and Fastai can be carried out using five steps, as depicted in Fig. 1. The experimental section of this paper provides detailed information about each of these steps. In addition to facial skin condition recognition and classification, our approach involves the development of an intelligent chatbot using the TFLearn model, which offers automated skin care advice.

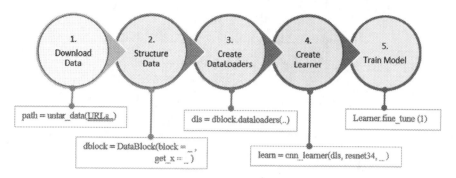

Fig. 1. FastAI model workflow utilizing our proposed solution.

The overall architecture of our proposed solution, along with its components and related elements, is illustrated in Fig. 2.

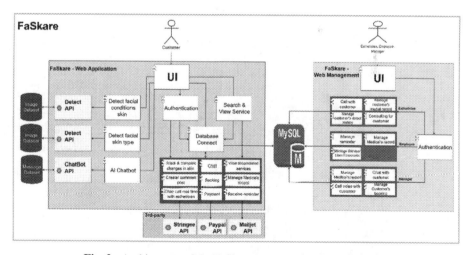

Fig. 2. Architecture of the FaSkare system using Deep Learning

This architecture consists of two subsystems: the customer subsystem and the management subsystem. Within the customer subsystem, there are implemented models for facial recognition, skin classification, and chatbot AI. Additionally, the customer subsystem includes components/features that support users, such as recommendations for skincare services and medical products, consultation services, scheduling appointments, and online payment. The management subsystem, on the other hand, comprises components that manage the post-service interactions related to skincare consultation for users who have utilized the online services. It also handles the management of interactions among relevant parties within the system. Table 2 describes the roles and responsibilities of each component in the architecture of the FaSKare system shown in Fig. 1.

Table 2. Component and Connector Element & Responsibility Description

Element	Responsibilities
Web Application	Web Client is an application for end-user
Web Management	Web Management is an application for managing, admin
Payment service	The payment service is Paypal API (third-party) for user payment service
AI Chatbot service	AI chatbot service is a bot to an assistant for customer
Detect service	Detect services help the user identify their facial skin condition and type
Database	A database is a component that contains data of the system
Call video Service	Call video service is Stringee API (third-party) for use to call video together
Send reminder Service	Send reminder service is Mailjet API (third-party) for use to send mail

The system FaSkare has been developed based on the business need illustrated in Fig. 3 below:

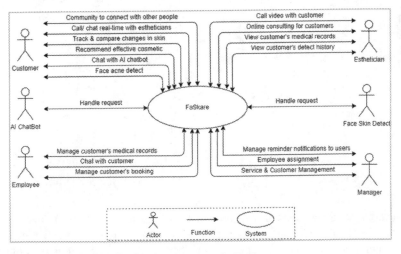

Fig. 3. Context diagram of a FaSKare system

Face Skin Detect: This component receives images from customers and predicts their facial skin condition and type.

Manager: Also known as the system administrator, this role involves managing the services, viewing statistics and reports, overseeing center employees, and handling user notifications regarding their schedules.

Doctor: The doctor directly examines customers' skin and provides face-to-face or online consultations, including real-time chat and calls.

Employee: Employees can manage customer bookings, including accepting or denying appointments, scheduling bookings, maintaining customer records, engaging in chat conversations to address inquiries, and providing advice.

Customers: Customers have various capabilities, such as booking appointments and making online payments, engaging with a chatbot for automated assistance and answers to questions, communicating with doctors for advice and additional inquiries, using a camera or selecting a picture from their gallery to detect their facial skin condition, managing their medical records, and connecting with other individuals within the system's community.

AI Chatbot: This intelligent chatbot is responsible for answering customer questions and performing automated tasks on their behalf.

4 Experiment Results

FaSkare is deployed according to the business requirements and system architecture depicted in Fig. 4. The system is deployed within a website environment, where it interacts with the server through APIs to access and modify data in the MySQL database. Additionally, the system utilizes APIs to provide results back to customers.

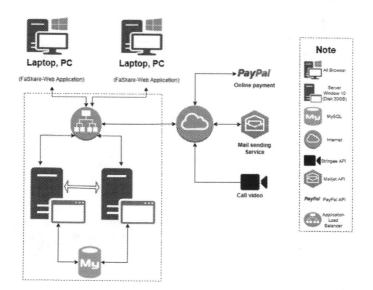

Fig. 4. Deployment Architecture of FaSkare

The implementation of facial skin condition recognition and classification, based on the FastAI model, is carried out through the following five steps in the experimental phase.

Step 1: Download data or prepare data set and label for them. Figure 5 shows the example of preparing and labeling dataset and data training for each skin.

We have built datasets for 20 different facial skin types shown in Table 3.

Table 3. The dataset for training and testing of 20 facial skin types

N.O	Facial skin condition type	Training	Test
1	Acne fulminans	63	7
2	Tinea facialis	64	7
3	Blackhead	63	7
4	Dermatitis perioral	63	7
5	Eksim	63	7
6	Flek hitam	66	7
7	Folikulitis	62	7
8	Fungal acne	63	7
9	Herpes	63	10
10	Karsinoma	63	7
11	Kutil filiform	63	7
12	Melanoma	63	7
13	Milia	77	7
14	Panu	63	7
15	Papula	63	7
16	Psoriasis	63	7
17	Pustula	63	7
18	Rosacea	76	7
19	Tinea facialis	63	7
20	Whitehead	63	7
SUM		1290	

STEP 2: Structure Data has restructured the datasets before training them.

```
skin_condition = DataBlock(
    blocks = (ImageBlock, CategoryBlock),
    get_items = get_image_files,
    splitter = RandomSplitter(valid_pct = 0.2),
    get_y = parent_label,
    item_tfms = Resize(224),
    batch_tfms = aug_transforms())
```

FastAI has an extremely flexible system called the **data block API.** With this API you can fully customize every stage in the creation of your DataLoaders. Here is what we need to create DataLoaders for the dataset that we just prepared.

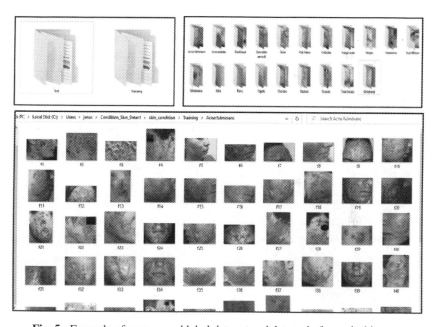

Fig. 5. Example of prepare and label data set and data train for each skin type

We provide a tuple where we specify what types we want for the independent and dependent variables: blocks= (ImageBlock, CategoryBlock).

- The independent variable is the thing we are using to make predictions (image) - is often referred to as x.
- The dependent variable is our target (label - type of facial skin condition) for each image. - is often referred to as y.

The get_image_files function takes a path and returns a list of all of the images in that path. We simply want to split our training and validation sets randomly.

- Validation: 20%
- Training: 80%

- **parent_label** is a function provided by FastAI that simply gets the name of the folder a file is in.
- To group them in a big array (usually called a tensor) that is going to go through our model, they all need to be of the same size (224-pixel square). We use 224 pixels because this is the standard size for historical reasons. If you increase the size, you'll often get a model with better results (since it will be able to focus on more details), but at the price of speed and memory consumption; the opposite is true if you decrease the size.
- **Data augmentation** refers to creating random variations of our input data, such that they appear different, but do not actually change the meaning of the data. Examples of common data augmentation techniques for images are rotation, flipping, perspective warping, brightness changes, and contrast changes.

Step 3: Create DataLoaders.

```
dls = skin_condition.dataloaders('./skin_condition')
```

- DataLoaders: A class provided by FastAI that allows the storage of multiple DataLoader objects. Typically, it includes a training DataLoader and a validation DataLoader.
- For these DataLoaders, the underlying items are file paths. It is necessary to instruct FastAI on how to obtain a list of these file paths.

Step 4: Create Learner:

```
Learn = cnn_learner(dls, resnet34, metrics = error_rate)
```

FastAI is utilized to create a convolutional neural network (CNN) by specifying the desired architecture, training data, and metric selection. Here are the key points:

- CNNs are the cutting-edge approach for developing computer vision models, drawing inspiration from the human visual system's functioning.
- Specifically, we will employ the ResNet34 architecture, which is a state-of-the-art model widely used in solving various computer vision tasks. The "34" in ResNet34 denotes the number of layers in this variant (other options include 18, 50, 101, and 152).
- Models with more layers require longer training time and are susceptible to overfitting. However, with larger datasets, they can yield higher accuracy.
- A metric is a function that assesses the model's predictions using the validation set and is displayed at the end of each training epoch.
- The error_rate metric, provided by FastAI, determines the percentage of misclassified images in the validation set.
- The accuracy metric can be calculated as 1.0 minus the error_rate, providing the proportion of correctly classified images.

Step 5: Train model:

- Fine-tuning: Fine-tuning is a transfer learning technique where a pre-trained model's parameters are utilized, and these parameters are updated by training for additional epochs using a different dataset.

- When employing the fine-tuning method, FastAI automates several techniques for you. There are a few adjustable parameters, and the process consists of two steps:

  - The first step involves fitting only the necessary parts of the model for the new random head to function with your dataset. This is accomplished during a single epoch.
  - The second step involves fitting the entire model using the predefined number of epochs specified when calling the method. During this step, the weights of the later layers, particularly the head, are updated at a faster rate compared to the earlier layers. Typically, the earlier layers do not require significant modifications from the pre-trained weights, as we will explore further (Fig. 6 and Table 4).

```
learn = cnn_learner(dls, resnet34, metrics=error_rate)
learn.fine_tune(10)
```

epoch	train_loss	valid_loss	error_rate	time
0	3.749378	2.005819	0.590909	01:20

epoch	train_loss	valid_loss	error_rate	time
0	2.561823	1.673017	0.525253	01:45
1	2.236070	1.441373	0.459596	01:33
2	1.893474	1.201677	0.343434	01:31
3	1.565830	1.067930	0.318182	01:30
4	1.317157	1.065876	0.313131	01:31
5	1.118879	0.948428	0.262626	01:30
6	0.940833	0.983236	0.277778	01:30
7	0.804211	0.971482	0.257576	01:32
8	0.708475	0.964892	0.252525	01:33
9	0.625439	0.959079	0.252525	01:33

Fig. 6. Train model

Result of the Experiment:

Discussion:
The experimental results demonstrate the practicality and effectiveness of FaSkare. The average time per detection attempt is approximately 0.2 s on a 200 x 200px frame, with slight variations for larger frames. The overall accuracy of FaSkare is reported to be 75%, with over 85% accuracy on facial skin with a filled background and average size.

Table 4. The experiment results.

Average time per detection attempt	Approx. 0.2 s on a 200 x 200px frame (region), varies slightly up to 960 x 1080 frame
Average accuracy	75% overall
Facial skin condition accuracy	75% overall Approx. Over 85% on the facial skin with filled background, average size Below 65% when the facial skin is greater than 60% of the image

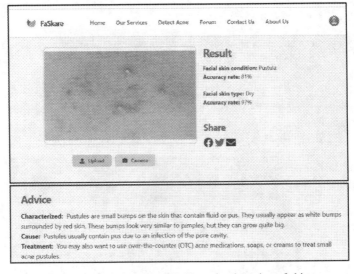

Fig.7. Example screenshot of FaSkare for detection of skin type

However, the accuracy drops below 65% when the facial skin occupies more than 60% of the image.

We acknowledge the limitations encountered during the research, such as the need for a larger and more diverse dataset for certain facial skin conditions. Additionally, this study highlights the potential for future improvements, such as incorporating more advanced image augmentation techniques and exploring other deep learning models for enhanced accuracy. Figure 7 demonstrates an instance of skin type detection.

5   Conclusion

The study presents FaSkare as a comprehensive system that addresses the lack of applications capable of swiftly detecting facial skin conditions while seamlessly integrating additional utilities for users. By utilizing the FastAI model and Convolutional Neural

Networks (CNNs), FaSkare demonstrates its effectiveness in detecting and classifying various skin conditions, including acne, wrinkles, dark spots, and rosacea.

The result highlights the importance of data collection and preprocessing in building an accurate and robust facial skin condition detection system. By gathering a diverse dataset of labeled facial images and applying necessary preprocessing techniques, FaSkare ensures the reliability of its model.

The limitation of the study is the need for a larger and more diverse dataset for certain skin conditions that will improve in the future. We also explore advanced image augmentation techniques and consider alternative deep learning models to further enhance the accuracy and performance of FaSkare.

Overall, the study result demonstrates the effectiveness of FaSkare in providing an exceptional user experience by offering personalized cosmetic suggestions, direct consultation with doctors, and scheduling within the system. FaSkare fills the existing gap in the market for comprehensive beauty care applications and showcases the potential of AI-based solutions in the beauty industry.

References

1. Howard, J., Gugger, S.: Deep Learning for Coders with fastai and PyTorch. O'Reilly Media.) (2020)
2. Hameed, N., Shabut, A.M., Hossain, M.A.. Multi-class skin diseases classification using deep convolutional neural network and support vector machine. In: 2018 12th International Conference on Software, Knowledge, Information Management & Applications (SKIMA), pp. 1–7. IEEE (2018)
3. http://tflearn.org/#tflearn-deep-learning-library-featuring-a-higher-level-api-for-tensorflow
4. Pothen, A.S.: Artificial intelligence and its increasing importance. Learning outcomes of classroom research. L ORDINE NUOVO PUBLICATION, India (2021)
5. Makridakis, S.: The forthcoming artificial intelligence (AI) revolution: its impact on society and firms. Futures **90**, 46–60 (2017)
6. Su, N.M.., Crandall, D.J.: The affective growth of computer vision. Proceedings of the IEEE/CVF Conference on Computer Vision and Pattern Recognition (2021)
7. Rashedul, I., Islam, R., Mazumder, T.: Mobile application and its global impact. International Journal of Engineering & Technology (IJEST) **10**(6), 72–78 (2010)
8. Kaur, M.A., Dhawan, S.: Mobile applications: a boon to human. Asian Journal of Manage. **8**(3), 607–613 (2017)
9. TroveSkin. https://www.troveskin.com. Accessed 18 May 2022
10. VietSkin. https://www.vietskin.vn/. Accessed 18 May 2022
11. Skincrare Routine. https://apps.apple.com/us/app/skincare-routine/id1428570992/. Accessed 18 May 2022
12. FeelinMySkin Skincare Routine. https://play.google.com/store/apps/details?id=com.feelin myskin.app. Accessed 18 May 2022
13. Wang, M., Deng, W.: Deep face recognition: a survey. Neurocomputing **429**, 215–244 (2021)
14. Mellouk, W., Handouzi, W.: Facial emotion recognition using deep learning: review and insights. Procedia Computer Sci. **175**, 689–694 (2020)
15. Jin, B., Cruz, L., Gonçalves, N.: Deep facial diagnosis: deep transfer learning from face recognition to facial diagnosis. IEEE Access **8**, 123649–123661 (2020)
16. Prasad, P.S., Pathak, R., Gunjan, V.K., Ramana Rao, H.V.: Deep learning based representation for face recognition. In: ICCCE 2019: Proceedings of the 2nd International Conference on Communications and Cyber Physical Engineering, pp. 419–424). Springer Singapore (2020)

Multi-modal Speech Emotion Recognition: Improving Accuracy Through Fusion of VGGish and BERT Features with Multi-head Attention

Phuong-Nam Tran[1], Thuy-Duong Thi Vu[1], Duc Ngoc Minh Dang[1(✉)],
Nhat Truong Pham[2], and Anh-Khoa Tran[3]

[1] Computing Fundamental Department, FPT University, Ho Chi Minh City,
Vietnam
namtpse150004@fpt.edu.vn, {duongvtt9,ducdnm2}@fe.edu.vn
[2] Department of Integrative Biotechnology, Sungkyunkwan University, Suwon,
Republic of Korea
truongpham96@skku.edu
[3] Modeling Evolutionary Algorithms Simulation and Artificial Intelligence, Faculty of
Electrical and Electronics Engineering, Ton Duc Thang University, Ho Chi Minh
City, Vietnam
trananhkhoa@tdtu.edu.vn

Abstract. Recent research has shown that multi-modal learning is a successful method for enhancing classification performance by mixing several forms of input, notably in speech-emotion recognition (SER) tasks. However, the difference between the modalities may affect SER performance. To overcome this problem, a novel approach for multi-modal SER called 3M-SER is proposed in this paper. The 3M-SER leverages multi-head attention to fuse information from multiple feature embeddings, including audio and text features. The 3M-SER approach is based on the SERVER approach but includes an additional fusion module that improves the integration of text and audio features, leading to improved classification performance. To further enhance the correlation between the modalities, a LayerNorm is applied to audio features prior to fusion. Our approach achieved an unweighted accuracy (UA) and weighted accuracy (WA) of 79.96% and 80.66%, respectively, on the IEMOCAP benchmark dataset. This indicates that the proposed approach is better than SERVER and recent methods with similar approaches. In addition, it highlights the effectiveness of incorporating an extra fusion module in multi-modal learning.

Keywords: 3M-SER · Multi-modal analysis · Speech Emotion Recognition · Multi-head Attention · Multi-feature Embeddings

1 Introduction

Speech emotion recognition (SER) is a rapidly growing field of research that focuses on the development of algorithms and systems capable of automati-

N.-S. Vo and H.-A. Tran (Eds.): INISCOM 2023, LNICST 531, pp. 148–158, 2023.
https://doi.org/10.1007/978-3-031-47359-3_11

cally detecting, analyzing, and interpreting emotions conveyed through speech. The capacity to detect emotional states from speech offers a broad scope of potential benefits and useful applications, encompassing healthcare, education, entertainment, and human-computer interaction. Traditionally SER focused on analyzing only the audio component of speech to detect and interpret emotions. Feature extraction from speech signals has been the mainstay of SER, where various acoustic features such as pitch, loudness, spectral [1], spectrograms [2] are extracted from the speech signal and used to recognize emotions. Deep learning (DL) models are often used as end-to-end models that can learn to extract relevant features from the audio and directly predict the emotion label. Pham *et al.* [2] developed a DL approach for speech emotion recognition that involved modifying an existing DL model and incorporating a novel loss function specifically designed for recognizing emotional states from speech signals. Bao *et al.* [3] took a different approach by proposing a DL-based model as a data augmentation method to improve the performance of SER systems. Specifically, they developed a generative adversarial network with emotional style transfer that can generate emotional data samples, thereby increasing the amount and diversity of training data and enhancing the performance of the SER system.

As stated in [4], most previous methods only focus on a single modality, either audio or text input, to recognize emotional states. In recent years, researchers have recognized that using multiple modalities, such as audio combined with text, can improve the accuracy of emotion recognition. A multi-modal SER system can capture complementary information from different modalities and combine them to provide a more complete understanding of the emotional state of the speaker. SERVER [5] is a recent example of a multi-modal SER system that combines information from both audio and text modalities. In the SERVER [5] system, audio features are extracted from the speech signal using Mel frequency cepstral coefficients (MFCCs) and are fed into the pre-trained VGGish [6]. To obtain the embedding of text input, the pre-trained BERT [7] model is utilized for text embedding. The embeddings are then combined using concatenation and fed to a fully connected layer for emotional state classification.

The SERVER [5] has shown an increase in performance in the system by using multi-modal. However, the difference between the emotions represented in text and in audio may affect the performance of the model. SERVER [5] only uses the concatenation of the feature of text and audio which may create a huge impact on the classifier head if the model relies on the text feature too much to classify the emotion rather than rely on the audio feature. For instance, if the text contains the word "cry", but the audio does not reflect sadness, the system may bias to recognize the emotions of the audio as sadness rather than neutral or the label emotion.

To overcome the aforementioned problem, we propose a novel method that fusion the feature embeddings of text and audio through an attention [8] mechanism. Our approach uses multi-head attention, which is a type of attention mechanism that allows the model to attend to different parts of the input simultaneously and learn which parts are most relevant for predicting the emotion.

Experimental results of our method IEMOCAP [9] have shown improved performance by integrating the attention fusion module into the SERVER model. Our method achieved a new highest score on IEMOCAP [9] with a UA of 79.96% and a WA of 80.66%, respectively.

The structure of this paper is organized as follows. Section 1 provides an introduction to the study. Section 2 presents a summary of the literature review and related studies. In Sect. 3, we elaborate on the motivation behind the proposed methodology and provide a detailed explanation of the methodology itself. The employed dataset, experimental setup, preliminary results, and discussions are presented in Sect. 4. Finally, Sect. 5 concludes the study and outlines potential future work.

2   Related Work

The emotions in human speech are complicated and are not easy to recognize even if the listener is a human. Numerous research efforts have focused on analyzing speech features and accurately classifying them to enhance speech emotion recognition.

Particularly, Google researchers [6] have recently proposed a method that applies CNN architectures to convert audio into a latent space dimension known as audio embedding. A feature extraction model, namely VGGish is applied to the log Mel-Spectrogram, which is transformed from the audio input, to retrieve an audio embedding. The design of VGGish is influenced by the popular VGG networks used in image classification and can function either as a feature extractor or as a downstream classification model. VGGish has shown a high performance on a large-scale audio dataset (AudioSet) [10].

BERT (Bidirectional Encoder Representations from Transformers) [7] is a powerful language model that has been widely used in natural language processing (NLP) tasks such as sentiment analysis and emotion detection. In addition to its applications in sentiment analysis and emotion detection, BERT has also been combined with other modalities such as text and audio to create multimodal models. Multimodal models combine different types of data to gain a more comprehensive understanding of the input and improve the accuracy of the models.

For instance, Lee *et al.* [11] took multimodal modeling further by combining BERT with heterogeneous features extracted from multi-modal inputs, including textual, visual, and acoustic information, to enhance the ability of the BERT model to recognize emotional states. By incorporating these additional features, the model achieved improved accuracy and outperformed previous state-of-the-art models on several benchmark datasets. This demonstrates the potential of combining BERT with other modalities to create more effective multimodal models for emotion recognition.

Recent studies have investigated the use of both audio and text inputs in DL models for SER. Lee *et al.* [12] proposed a cross-attention network that aligns audio and text embeddings for multimodal SER. By employing bidirectional

LSTM, the audio embedding was created by processing the Mel-frequency cepstral coefficients (MFCCs) that were extracted from the audio waveform. Similarly, the text embedding was generated by using bidirectional LSTM to process
the extracted GloVe embeddings. These embeddings were then fed into the cross-
attention network for final emotion classification. Yoon *et al.* [13] proposed an
audio recurrent encoder and a text recurrent encoder for multi-modal SER based
on MFCC features and word embedding that was extracted from audio and text,
respectively. Pham *et al.* [5] proposed a multi-modal speech emotion recognition
using BERT and VGGish (SERVER). SERVER is very competitive and better
than most of the latest and state-of-the-art methods using multi-modal analysis
for SER. It achieves 63.10% unweighted accuracy and 63.00% weighted accuracy
on the IEMOCAP [9] dataset.

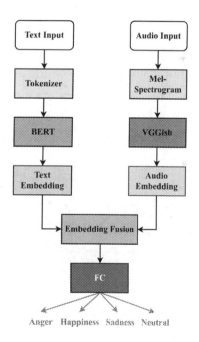

Fig. 1. The flowchart of the SERVER [5].

3   Methodology

3M-SER is an improved version of SERVER [5] by extending the architecture with the addition of multi-head attention over the fusion module and the
text module. As shown in Fig. 1, the audio input is transformed to log Mel-
Spectrogram of 96 × 64 bins and fed into the pre-train VGGish [6] model to
extract audio features. The text features are extracted using the pre-trained

BERT [7] model. Both audio and text are transformed to the latent spaces dimension which can represent their features in a fixed size. These features can be called text-embedding $v_t \in \mathcal{R}^{d_t}$ and audio-embedding $v_a \in \mathcal{R}^{d_a}$ The different sizes of the latent spaces in each feature require designing a module to combine these features. SERVER [5] proposes to transform the text-embedding v_t spaces to the v_a by simply adding a linear layer after the output of the BERT [7] model. After obtaining the text and audio embeddings, they are combined through concatenation to create a fusion feature, which is employed in the classification of emotional states. This method shows an improvement in the performance model, however, we can further improve this result by designing an attention fusion module rather than the simple linear. The details of our method are shown in Fig. 2.

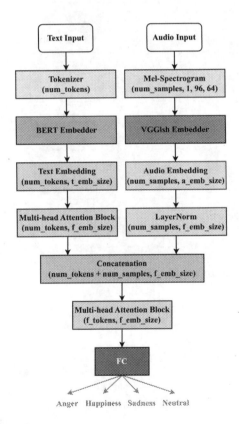

Fig. 2. The flowchart of the proposed 3M-SER.

A multi-head attention [8] block is applied to the text embeddings to figure out which feature is useful to the classification process. This block also converts the text embeddings from v_t spaces to the v_a by using a linear and Layer-Norm [14] after the multi-head attention.

Although the dimension of the audio embeddings stays the same, the combination of the audio embeddings with the text embeddings feature creates a significant disparity in the feature values of v_t and v_a that are derived from their corresponding pre-trained feature extraction model. The BERT model tries to transform a text to $v_t \in \mathcal{R}^{d_t}$ which R^{d_t} mostly in $[-2.0, 2.0]$ while the VGGish [6] transforms the log Mel-Spectrogram to $v_a \in \mathcal{R}^{d_a}$ which R^{d_a} mostly in $[0.0, 255.0]$. This imbalance may lead to audio-based judgment much more than the text feature and may overwhelm the text feature if we simply concatenate two features without performing any linear layer. To make the fairness between each feature, we apply the LayerNorm [14] to both the audio embedding and text embedding. LayerNorm [14] will make both the v_a and v_t have a closer value which makes the 3M-SER slightly study better.

In the concatenate layer, rather than the fusion of two features based on the dimension space like SERVER [5], our 3M-SER fuses two features based on the tokens and samples axis of text embeddings and audio embedding, respectively. This technique will help 3M-SER view the entire sentence and Mel-Spectrogram samples to assess the emotion in the sound through another multi-head attention [8] block.

4 Preliminary Results and Discussion

4.1 Dataset

In our experiments, we use the same dataset which is used to evaluate the SERVER [5] and other single-modal approaches. The Interactive Emotional Dyadic Motion Capture (IEMOCAP) dataset, as described in [9], is a multimodal and multi-speaker database containing the acted audiovisual data. The dataset comprises around 12 h of content, including video, speech, motion capture of facial expressions, and text transcriptions. To validate the effectiveness of the 3M-SER along with SERVER [5], the same text, audio, and number of samples are investigated in this study. The same dataset contains only four major classes such as anger (1,103 samples), happiness (1,635 samples), sadness (1,084 samples), and neutral (1,708 samples). The distribution of each class used in this study is shown in Fig. 3.

4.2 Experimental Setup

The 3M-SER is implemented using the PyTorch [15] DL framework and trained on a Linux machine (Debian Bookworm) with Intel(R) Core(TM) i9-12900K, 64 GB RAM, and 1 Nvidia GeForce RTX 3090 Graphics Card. We follow the settings in SERVER [5] to set our optimizer, the learning rate decay, and the dataset. The multi-head attention component, which is composed of 8 heads, is succeeded by a linear layer and a LayerNorm layer [14]. The multi-head attention block after the text embedding has the linear layer with 768 in-feature and 128 out-feature to convert text latent space dimension from $v_t \in \mathcal{R}^{768}$ to $v_t \in \mathcal{R}^{128}$

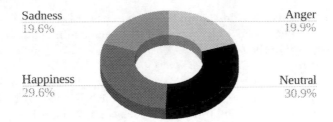

Fig. 3. The distribution of the employed emotions in the IEMOCAP dataset used for training 3M-SER.

for the concatenating process in fusion module. The same multi-head attention block is applied after the fusion module, however, the in-feature and out-feature in the linear layer are set to 128. Two linear layers with 64 and 4 units in the fully connected (FC) layers are added after embedding fusion. The 4 units are the classification head with softmax activation which is used to calculate the category cross-entropy loss.

4.3   Results and Discussion

Figures 4a, 4b, and 5 display the confusion matrices of the models using only text embedding, only audio embedding, and both embeddings, respectively, which were reported in SERVER [5]. Figures 6a and 6b display our 3M-SER confusion matrices which show the impact of the fusion module on the SERVER [5] model and the effect of LayerNorm [14]. It is observed that adding an attention mechanism can improve the performance of the model through the meaning of text and audio. The accuracy of 3M-SER helps improve the model recognition of "anger", "happiness", and "sadness", however, the model is still confused about "neutral" emotion and seems to fail to recognize it.

Table 1. Performance comparison of the different multi-modal SER methods on the IEMOCAP dataset.

Method	Accuracy (%)	
	UA	WA
Ref. [16]	51.70	–
Ref. [17]	56.00	61.20
Ref. [12]	48.70	57.90
SERVER [5]	63.00	63.10
3M-SER	**75.35**	**76.81**
3M-SER with LayerNorm	**79.96**	**80.66**

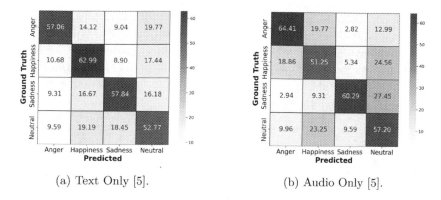

(a) Text Only [5].   (b) Audio Only [5].

Fig. 4. The confusion matrix of the SERVER [5] using single data.

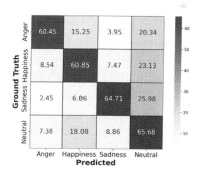

Fig. 5. The confusion matrix of the SERVER [5] using both text and audio embeddings.

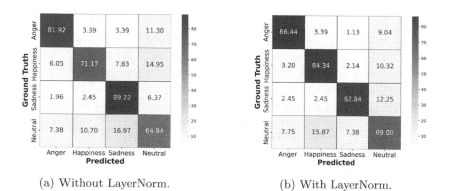

(a) Without LayerNorm.   (b) With LayerNorm.

Fig. 6. The confusion matrix of the proposed 3M-SER using both text and audio embeddings with attention fusion module.

As shown in Table 1, the proposed method has the best accuracy in terms of unweighted accuracy and weighted accuracy. Table 1 demonstrates that the proposed method outperforms other methods in both unweighted accuracy and weighted accuracy. Compared to notable references such as [12, 16, 17] and [5], the proposed method achieves the improvements of 10.88%, 15.18%, 18.18% and 3.88%, respectively, in terms of UA. Similarly, the proposed method surpasses [12, 17], and [5] by 6.01%, 9.31% and 4.11%, respectively, in terms of WA. Moreover, Table 2 presents a comparison of different methods in terms of model complexity and performance, including the number of parameters (Params), FLoating point OPerations (FLOPs), and accuracy. Based on Tables 1 and 2, although the proposed 3M-SER method has the highest complexity, its performance shows a significant improvement.

Table 2. Comparison of model complexity and performance for different multi-modal SER methods on the IEMOCAP dataset.

Method	Params	FLOPs	Accuracy (%)	
			UA	WA
Text Only	109M	0.00683G	57.67	57.77
Audio Only	72M	1.73G	57.56	58.41
SERVER [5]	181M	1.74 G	63.00	63.10
Ours	**203M**	**1.74 G**	**79.96**	**80.66**

5   Conclusion and Future Work

In this paper, a novel multi-head attention fusion mechanism has been proposed to improve the accuracy of multi-modal speech emotion recognition. Learning from the text embeddings and audio embeddings which are extracted from the BERT and VGGish respectively using the attention mechanism helps model learning better on understanding the meaning of text along with the audio. The experimental results have shown that our proposed method improved the performance of the previous multi-modal. The proposed method achieves the highest UA of 79.96% and WA of 80.66%, respectively, on the IEMOCAP dataset.

In future work, we plan to investigate multi-lingual and multi-task learning approaches to further extend this study. This extension aims to enhance the generalization and robustness of multi-modal speech emotion recognition (SER) systems. Additionally, the exploration of new architectures, along with the utilization of data collection and augmentation techniques such as hybrid data augmentation (HDA) [18], will be considered. These efforts aim to further improve the model performance, reduce the bias among features, and generate additional data for the task of speech emotion recognition. Moreover, in this preliminary study, we have observed the significance of correlation or similarity between different modalities. Therefore, in the extended version of this study, we will place significant emphasis on exploring the similarity/correlation between text embeddings and audio embeddings to improve the overall performance of the multi-modal SER system.

References

1. Liu, D., Chen, L., Wang, Z., Diao, G.: Speech expression multimodal emotion recognition based on deep belief network. J. Grid Comput. **19**(2), 22 (2021)
2. Pham, N.T., Dang, D.N.M., Nguyen, S.D.: A method upon deep learning for speech emotion recognition. J. Adv. Eng. Comput. **4**(4), 273–285 (2020)
3. Bao, F., Neumann, M., Vu, N.T.: Cyclegan-based emotion style transfer as data augmentation for speech emotion recognition. In: Kubin, G., Kacic, Z. (eds.) Interspeech 2019, 20th Annual Conference of the International Speech Communication Association, Graz, Austria, 15–19 September 2019, pp. 2828–2832. ISCA (2019)
4. Pham, N.T., et al.: Speech emotion recognition: a brief review of multi-modal multi-task learning approaches. In: AETA 2022-Recent Advances in Electrical Engineering and Related Sciences: Theory and Application. Springer, Cham (2022)
5. Pham, N.T., Dang, D.N.M., Pham, B.N.H., Nguyen, S.D.: SERVER: multi-modal speech emotion recognition using transformer-based and vision-based embeddings. In: ICIIT 2023: 8th International Conference on Intelligent Information Technology, Da Nang, Vietnam, 24–26 February 2023. ACM (2023)
6. Hershey, S., et al.: CNN architectures for large-scale audio classification. In: 2017 IEEE International Conference on Acoustics, Speech and Signal Processing, ICASSP 2017, New Orleans, LA, USA, 5–9 March 2017, pp. 131–135. IEEE (2017)
7. Devlin, J., Chang, M.-W., Lee, K., Toutanova, K.: BERT: pre-training of deep bidirectional transformers for language understanding. In: Burstein, J., Doran, C., Solorio, T. (eds.) Proceedings of the 2019 Conference of the North American Chapter of the Association for Computational Linguistics: Human Language Technologies, NAACL-HLT 2019, Minneapolis, MN, USA, 2–7 June 2019, Volume 1 (Long and Short Papers), pp. 4171–4186. Association for Computational Linguistics (2019)
8. Vaswani, A., et al.: Attention is all you need. In: Proceedings of the 31st International Conference on Neural Information Processing Systems, NIPS 2017, Red Hook, NY, USA, pp. 6000–6010. Curran Associates Inc. (2017)
9. Busso, C., et al.: IEMOCAP: interactive emotional dyadic motion capture database. Lang. Resour. Eval. **42**(4), 335–359 (2008)
10. Gemmeke, J.F., et al.: Audio set: an ontology and human-labeled dataset for audio events. In: 2017 IEEE International Conference on Acoustics, Speech and Signal Processing, ICASSP 2017, New Orleans, LA, USA, 5–9 March 2017, pp. 776–780. IEEE (2017)
11. Lee, S., Han, D.K., Ko, H.: Multimodal emotion recognition fusion analysis adapting BERT with heterogeneous feature unification. IEEE Access **9**, 94557–94572 (2021)
12. Lee, Y., Yoon, S., Jung, K.: Multimodal speech emotion recognition using cross attention with aligned audio and text. In: Meng, H., Xu, B., Zheng, T.F. (eds.) Interspeech 2020, 21st Annual Conference of the International Speech Communication Association, Virtual Event, Shanghai, China, 25–29 October 2020, pp. 2717–2721. ISCA (2020)

13. Yoon, S., Byun, S., Jung, K.: Multimodal speech emotion recognition using audio and text. In: 2018 IEEE Spoken Language Technology Workshop, SLT 2018, Athens, Greece, 18–21 December 2018, pp. 112–118. IEEE (2018)
14. Ba, J.L., Kiros, J.R., Hinton, G.E.: Layer normalization. arXiv preprint arXiv:1607.06450 (2016)
15. Paszke, A., et al.: Pytorch: an imperative style, high-performance deep learning library (2019). https://pytorch.org/
16. Tseng, S.-Y., Narayanan, S., Georgiou, P.G.: Multimodal embeddings from language models for emotion recognition in the wild. IEEE Signal Process. Lett. **28**, 608–612 (2021)
17. Sun, L., Liu, B., Tao, J., Lian, Z.: Multimodal cross- and self-attention network for speech emotion recognition. In: IEEE International Conference on Acoustics, Speech and Signal Processing, ICASSP 2021, Toronto, ON, Canada, 6–11 June 2021, pp. 4275–4279. IEEE (2021)
18. Pham, N.T., et al.: Hybrid data augmentation and deep attention-based dilated convolutional-recurrent neural networks for speech emotion recognition. Expert Syst. Appl. 120608 (2023)

Performance Analysis of Distributed Learning in Edge Computing on Handwritten Digits Dataset

Tinh Phuc Vo[1] , Viet Anh Nguyen[2] , Xuyen Bao Le Nguyen[2] ,
Duc Ngoc Minh Dang[2(✉)] , and Anh Khoa Tran[1]

[1] Modeling Evolutionary Algorithms Simulation and Artificial Intelligence,
Faculty of Electrical and Electronics Engineering,
Ton Duc Thang University, Ho Chi Minh City, Vietnam
`41702149@student.tdtu.edu.vn, trananhkhoa@tdtu.edu.vn`
[2] Computing Fundamental Department,
FPT University, Ho Chi Minh City, Vietnam
`{anhnvse170371,xuyennlbse170455}@fpt.edu.vn, ducdnm2@fe.edu.vn`

Abstract. Deep learning models often consist of millions or even billions of parameters, making it challenging to deploy them on devices with limited resources. Therefore, this study presents scenarios to assess the computational capability of edge devices to provide an evaluation of the learning performance of distributed learning methods. It focuses on using Deep Neural Network and the handwritten digit dataset (MNIST) in edge computing to evaluate the performance of distributed learning methods (no-offloading, full-offloading, split computing, and federated computing) in both ideal and realistic conditions. The performance evaluations are based on Precision, Recall, Accuracy, F1-score, and Estimated time complexity. The findings indicate that the full-offloading method achieved the highest performance in ideal conditions. However, in realistic situations, the split computing and federated computing methods performed better than the others.

Keywords: Edge Computing · Split Computing · Deep Neural Networks · computation offloading

1 Introduction

Deep Neural Networks (DNNs) have become increasingly popular in recent years due to their ability to learn and represent complex features in data. It consists of multiple layers of interconnected nodes used to process and transform input data and generate output predictions. By utilizing DNNs in mobile devices, we can develop predictive models that analyze user behavior and learning patterns, then generate personalized recommendations for individual users. However, the processing power and memory requirements of DNNs are significant, which is a challenge for resource-constrained mobile devices. Mobile Edge Computing

N.-S. Vo and H.-A. Tran (Eds.): INISCOM 2023, LNICST 531, pp. 159–169, 2023.
https://doi.org/10.1007/978-3-031-47359-3_12

(MEC) was first proposed in 2014 to reduce latency and improve the performance of mobile applications by processing data closer to the end user rather than in a centralized data center. MEC can help to offload some of the processing requirements of DNNs from mobile devices to the edge cloud that allows faster and more efficient processing of user data and enables new and innovative applications for self-studying systems in mobile devices. The current approach would focus on the "Machine learning" branch. MEC is predicted to promote self-learning approaches in the "Distributed computing methodologies" branch with less human intervention in processing input data. This research represents the performance analysis of 4 methods.

The rest of the paper is organized as follows. Section 2 provides an overview of related works. The main model used in this research is outlined in Sect. 3, and Sect. 4 presents evaluations of different approaches based on the selected standards derived from the experiments. Finally, Sect. 5 offers a conclusion.

2   Related Works

There are continuous new technologies and a list of updated research studies to optimize the user's experiment with higher speed and lower latency, increased capabilities and coverage, enhanced network reliability, efficient spectrum utilization, etc. This section focuses on recent research studies to overview the ways human beings reduce the computational complexity of DNNs. Some lightweight models such as MobileNets [1–3] are specially designed with very small, low latency models to easily match with resource-constrained devices. A different approach to building a small DNNs model is compressing a large model [4] has been proposed in the literature. The compression model changes the initial structure of DNNs by trying to remove parameters that are not crucial to model performance. Another approach, called Early Existing (EE) [5,6], adds early exit points after hidden layers of DNNs to give the chance for inputs to be classified early before reaching the final model's exit point. EE provides a "sub-branch" into the DNNs models so that full computation of the model can be halted, and the prediction result can be returned earlier than traditional ones - if the back is not necessary and it is highly confident about the prediction. Besides, there are numerous papers on distributed learning methods [6–10].

3   System Model

Figure 1 presents 4 approaches that this paper focuses on. With no-offloading (Fig. 1a), the entire DNN runs on the mobile device itself, using its local resources. This can be beneficial in situations where there is limited connectivity or where the privacy of the data is a concern. However, running the DNNs locally can be slow and resource-intensive, leading to increased power consumption and reduced battery life. Full-offloading (Fig. 1b) refers to transferring some of the computational tasks from the mobile device to a more powerful resource, such as a cloud or a remote server. This approach can be used to speed up the computation of DNNs and reduce the energy consumption of mobile devices. There are also hybrid offloading approaches, where some parts of the DNN are run on the mobile device, and others are offloaded to the MEC server: Split Computing (Fig. 1c) and Federated Computing (Fig. 1d). This can balance the benefits and drawbacks of both no-offloading and full-offloading, resulting in improved performance and reduced power consumption.

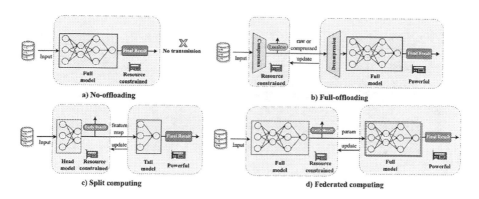

Fig. 1. Diagram of different learning approaches.

Full-Offloading. The entire DNN is offloaded to the MEC server, which runs the DNNs on its resources. This can significantly speed up the DNN, as the MEC server typically has more computing power and memory than the mobile device. However, full offloading requires a stable and reliable network connection, which may not always be available.

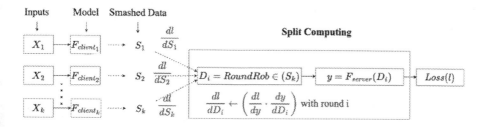

Fig. 2. Diagram of Split Computing.

Split Computing. Each head model network is a model that is cut in half as $F = F_{client} + F_{server}$ with the same output and derivative $\frac{dl}{dS}$ to make the data broken and then passed to train a deep server network. A DNN can be defined as a function F (Fig. 2), where the device is the head model and the edge server is the tail model, which can be described as a sequence of D_i at each time point i is a S_k (partial aggregation method) of the values after the head model's calculation and reduction of the necessary parameters and smaller than the input X_k. Then, calculate the loss $Loss(l)$ at the tail model (F_{server}). Split learning has the potential to reduce the computational and energy requirements of the local applications as they only need to perform a partial computation.

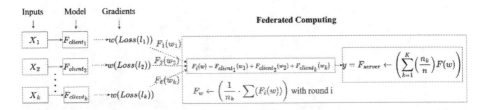

Fig. 3. Diagram of Federated Computing.

Federated Computing. Federated Computing (FC) enables multiple devices to collaborate on a shared computation task without requiring them to share raw data. FC is based on the "FedAvg" federated averaging method (Fig. 3). Let $n = 1, 2, 3, ..K$ denote end devices while F(w) shows the loss in device k. The goal of each round of $FedAvg$ is to reduce the global model's objective w, which is just the total of the weighted average of the local device loss. A random device is chosen. Each device receives the model and executes the SGD on its loss function. After that, it transmits the learned model to the F_{server} for model aggregation. The server then uses the average of these local models to update its global model. The above process of local training-global aggregation is repeated for multiple rounds until achieving a certain level of accuracy. Each device performs local computation on its data and shares only the parameter with a central server.

4 Performance Evaluation

We have established an edge server environment consisting of a central server and ten end devices. The server is configured for training using the Linux operating system, Python 3.7, and TensorFlow 2.10 with the CuDNN library for GPU utilization during training. Full channel conditions are assumed, and available bandwidth between the devices and the server is ignored during simulation. The experiments are conducted in a loop environment similar to that of real testing devices. This project is building a 6-layer MLP model for the classification task at hand. The input data shape and the number of layers are passed as arguments to the nodes. The loss function is *sparse_categorical_crossentropy*. The

Multilayer Perceptron (MLP) model with 60,970 computational parameters is used to train the MNIST dataset, which includes 50,000 training samples, 10,000 validation samples, and 10,000 test samples. The training samples are uniformly divided among the ten devices without overlapping. The entire test dataset is available on the server. The SGD function is used as the optimization tool with an initial learning rate of 0.01, which gradually decreases over the course of the task's iterations. For faster experimentation and development, this project uses a High-Performance Computing (HPC) platform built on the Google Cloud Workspace platform, using the Colab Notebook to compile with a partner GPU for computation. This research runs both device and server on the same HPC platform provided. Devices and server scenarios change from no-offloading, full-offloading, and split computing, with data transfer being reduced in the number of times compared to full transfer. Finally, the federated learning principle is that only the MLP model parameters are shared.

Our research is evaluated based on the correlation between model predictions and actual results. The overall result of the system is evaluated using the following metrics: Precision, Recall, Accuracy, F1-score, and Estimated Training Time. The research initially evaluated the use of scenario-based and random models for devices using the Round Robin Scheduling Algorithm to ensure equal participation of all 10 members at each parameter model time point. The choice of using the MNIST dataset for training is popular and well-suited for DNN models, therefore, the training process consisted of approximately 100 iterations. In addition, our research performed training on the main purpose MNIST dataset and consulted the Fashion MNIST dataset, which is a dataset of 60,000 28×28 grayscale images belonging to 10 fashion and clothing categories, for example. such as shoes, t-shirts, and skirts, ... Mapped data of all integers 0–9 corresponding to MNIST-like class labels (top, trouser, pullover, dress, coat, sandal, shirt, sneaker, bag, boot) were used up in all 10 classes for the task of training in Figs. 4, 5, 6, and 7. The experiment consists of 10,000 images equally divided into 1,000 images for each class to compare the final prediction performance at the server (Figs. 8 and 9). This dataset can be used as an optional alternative to MNIST for evaluating machine learning algorithms, as it has the same 28×28 image size, 2D data format training, validation, and testing split.

Considering the results of Fig. 4 and with positive criteria, device performance differs significantly between scenarios and there is no overfitting. In the theoretical condition (no noise), no-offloading only gives 92% validation data compared to the case of full-offloading, split computing, and federated computing achieved 100%, 98%, and 98%, respectively. Specifically, no-offloading with no edge server involvement for more learning (edge device data is independent) makes the performance curve grow slower by only 90% at the 10th round of communication. For Fashion data MNIST (Fig. 5) without input noise, within 100 communication rounds the training to find the best accuracy takes longer than with the MNIST data, and there is a clear difference between the scenarios. In general, the lowest no-offloading and full-offloading work best when a complete model is learned with all data free of noise.

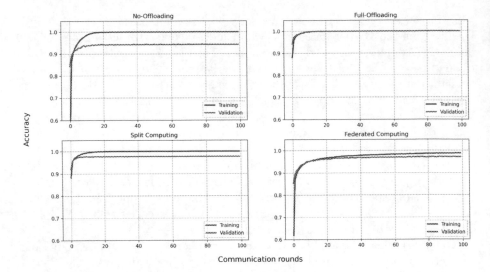

Fig. 4. The average accuracy with 10 devices during the MNIST data training process in a theoretical condition (without noise).

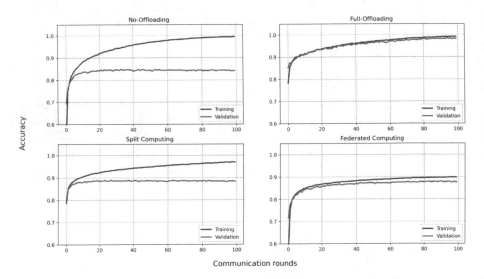

Fig. 5. The average accuracy with 10 devices during the Fashion MNIST data training process in a theoretical condition (without noise).

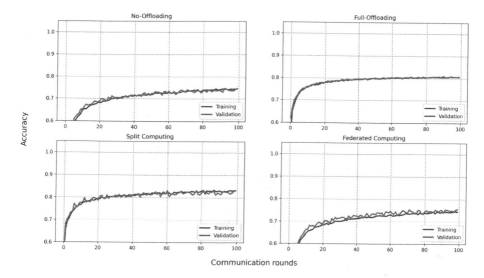

Fig. 6. The average accuracy with 10 devices during the MNIST data training process in realistic conditions (with Gaussian noise).

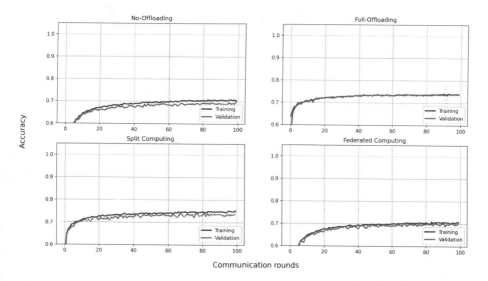

Fig. 7. The average accuracy with 10 devices during the Fashion MNIST data training process in realistic conditions (with Gaussian noise).

However, considering the actual conditions (Figs. 6 and 7), we assume that the input data has random Gaussian noise in the 2D image, just as in the real case the data will be lost through the transmission channel, the result will be lower than 15% on the same test conditions, within 100 rounds of communication. Split computing shows the greatest advantage when the validation data reaches 82% with MNIST data and Fashion MNIST data is about 75%. In the remaining cases of no-offloading, federated computing is not higher than 75% because there are many sub-model parameters on personal data, then full-offloading reaches 80% with MNIST data, and Fashion MNIST data is about 75 % because all data is learned on the same unified model structure.

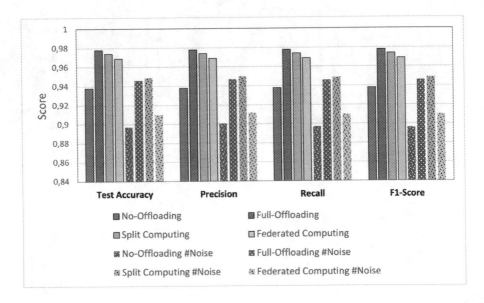

Fig. 8. The performance of the edge server during the MNIST data training process in ideal and realistic conditions.

In comparing the performance of each scenario at each communication round and the final test with the test data set located at the edge server, we choose the frequency of the performance evaluation test to be 50 times out of a total of 100 rounds. Because of some resource optimization requirements, testing does not take place continuously. In Fig. 8, the full-offloading scenario gives the highest Fig. 97.8% and when there is noise, split computing gives the final result 95% higher than the remaining scenarios due to taking advantage of device performance and reducing resources transferred to the edge server. Second is full-offloading 94.6% but not feasible if privacy is required. Federated computing is the 3rd choice 91.3% in the condition that it makes sure the cloud device meets the recommended configuration. The performance tests are still stable above 90% and negligible compared to no-offloading 89.4% of the training plan training on the device and ignoring the edge server, the performance is not higher than the

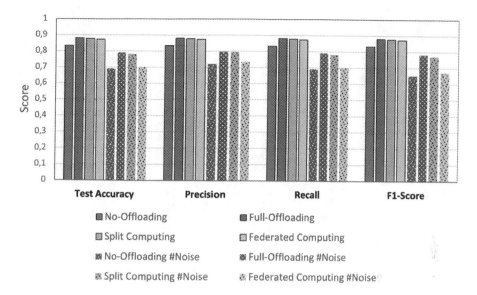

Fig. 9. The performance of the edge server during the Fashion MNIST data training process in ideal and realistic conditions.

link configuration, which separates the training process. It is possible to understand that partial loss recovery from interference per device by serial training at the server helps to maintain accuracy in split computing, regardless of edge devices, and interference from many devices. In Fig. 9, Fashion MNIST data also have no major difference in order and tasks compared to MNIST except the test results will be lower than MNIST due to slower convergence at the round 100th communication. The full-offloading, split computing and federated computing scenarios reached 89.8% in the condition without noise. When there was noise the full-offloading and split computing scenarios reach 79%, higher than the maintaining scenarios.

In Fig. 10, the average training time for the entire process on both the local device and the edge server is shown in detail. Split computing has the lowest total training time at 8.84 s in the Sequential simulation, and the on-device training time is lower than the local training cases by about 9.7 s for the setup. SC has the shortest one-round communication time in Sequential comparison with local cases for two main reasons. In the local comparison, split computing focuses only on providing smashed data without considering the calculation of metrics (accuracy, precision, recall, F1-score). In global comparison, split computing trains with a model that is half the size of 10 devices are sent to the server (full-offloading) in 6.49 s. Full-offloading takes about 14.01 s. In the case of parallel simulation, federated computing transmits the model parameters that have the shortest communication time of 1.2 s/round.

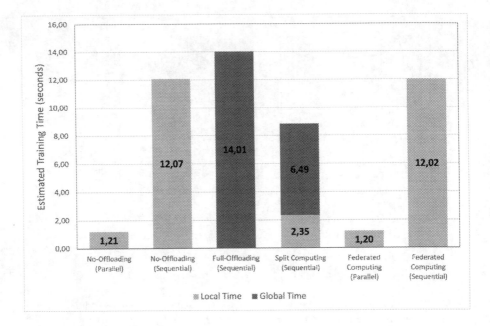

Fig. 10. Comparison chart of training time across learning scenarios.

5   Conclusion

This research paper investigated and analyzed the learning performance of distributed learning in the MEC environment. We have explored several methods such as split computing, federated computing, full-offloading, and no-offloading to improve the learning speed of DNNs in the mobile environment. These results can be applied to practical applications in the future, improving user experience and optimizing computing resources.

References

1. Howard, A.G., et al.: MobileNets: efficient convolutional neural networks for mobile vision applications (2017). https://arxiv.org/abs/1704.04861v1
2. Sandler, M., Howard, A., Zhu, M., Zhmoginov, A., Chen, L.C.: MobileNetV2: inverted residuals and linear bottlenecks. In: Proceedings of the IEEE Computer Society Conference on Computer Vision and Pattern Recognition, pp. 4510–4520 (2018). https://arxiv.org/abs/1801.04381v4
3. Howard, A., et al.: Searching for MobileNetV3. In: Proceedings of the IEEE International Conference on Computer Vision, vol. 2019-October, pp. 1314–1324 (2019)
4. Cheng, Y., Wang, D., Zhou, P., Zhang, T.: Model compression and acceleration for deep neural networks: the principles, progress, and challenges. IEEE Signal Process. Mag. **35**(1), 126–136 (2018)
5. Scardapane, S., Scarpiniti, M., Baccarelli, E., Uncini, A.: Why should we add early exits to neural networks? Cogn. Comput. **12**(5), 954–966 (2020)

6. Matsubara, Y., Levorato, M., Restuccia, F.: Split computing and early exiting for deep learning applications: survey and research challenges. ACM Comput. Surv. **55**, 1–30 (2022). https://doi.org/10.1145/3527155
7. Jeong, H.J., Jeong, I., Lee, H.J., Moon, S.M.: Computation offloading for machine learning web apps in the edge server environment. In: Proceedings - International Conference on Distributed Computing Systems, vol. 2018-July, pp. 1492–1499 (2018)
8. Wang, X., Han, Y., Leung, V.C., Niyato, D., Yan, X., Chen, X.: Convergence of edge computing and deep learning: a comprehensive survey. IEEE Commun. Surv. Tutor. **22**, 869–904 (2020)
9. Duan, Q., Hu, S., Deng, R., Lu, Z.: Combined federated and split learning in edge computing for ubiquitous intelligence in internet of things: state-of-the-art and future directions. Sensors **22**(16), 5983 (2022)
10. Ceballos, I., et al.: SplitNN-driven vertical partitioning (2020). https://arxiv.org/abs/2008.04137v1

FLASH: Facial Landmark Detection Using Active Shape Model and Heatmap Regression

Nguyen Van Nam[1,2(✉)] and Ngo Thi Ngoc Quyen[3]

[1] Viettel Information Technology, Viettel Group, 7 Alley, TonThatThuyet Street, CauGiay, Hanoi, Vietnam
namnv78@viettel.com.vn
[2] Thuyloi University, 175 Tayson, DongDa, Hanoi, Vietnam
nvnam@tlu.edu.vn
[3] Viettel Cyberspace Center, Viettel Group, 7 Alley, TonThatThuyet Street, CauGiay, Hanoi, Vietnam
quyenntn3@viettel.com.vn

Abstract. Detection of facial landmarks is a critical task for human face identification, emotion recognition in autopilot and real-time visual monitoring applications. This is really challenging due to the high number of discrete landmarks spreading over the face which is of different shapes and may be occluded or obscured. Many methods have been proposed over the years including ASMNet and AnchorFace. However, their performance is still limited in terms of both accuracy and efficiency. In this paper, we propose a novel method for facial landmark detection based on active shape model and heatmap called FLASH. The heatmap aims to highlight the important landmarks. Meanwhile, the shape model helps to conform the distribution of such landmarks. FLASH has been evaluated on two public datasets 300W-Challenging, WFLW and achieved a normalized mean square error (NME) of 6.67%, 7.34% correspondingly, which outperforms most existing methods. Specifically, this is much better than the recent ASMNet method with a NME of 8.20%, 10.77% on the two datasets, respectively. This is also comparable to the state of the art AnchorFace with a NME of 6.19%, 4.62%, correspondingly. The source code of FLASH is also publicly available.

Keywords: facial landmarks · heatmap regression · shape fitting · coordination regression

1 Introduction

In many real-time driver monitoring systems (DMS), facial emotion recognition from images captured by camera is an essential task. In fact, this helps to minimize potential accidents caused by attentionless drivers by detecting if there exists any sleepy, drunk or tired expressions in their face and notifying

N.-S. Vo and H.-A. Tran (Eds.): INISCOM 2023, LNICST 531, pp. 170–182, 2023.
https://doi.org/10.1007/978-3-031-47359-3_13

Fig. 1. Description of 68 points of facial landmark.

Fig. 2. Demonstration of the detection of 68 points of facial landmark on a given image: The left one is of a bus driver. The middle one denotes his angry face associated with 68 points detected. The right one describes the resulted locations of the landmarks on an angry face.

them accordingly. Existing methods for facial emotion recognition usually take as input either the hidden features or the transparent landmarks of the facial images. However, the latter ones are preferable thanks to its explainability.

Facial landmarks include certain principal points locating around the eyes, the nose, the mouth and the boundary of a human face as shown in Fig. 1. The task of facial landmark detection is to locate these points in a given face image as depicted in Fig. 2[1]. This problem is very challenging due to the high number

---

[1] The original image is referred from https://www.dreamstime.com/photos-images/bus-driver.html.

of discrete points distributed in various shapes of face which can be captured from different angles of view.

Earlier efficient approaches for facial landmark detection are of shape fitting models including Active Shape Model (ASM) [6], Active Appearance Models (AAM) [5], Constrained Local Model (CLM) [7], Discriminative Response Map Fitting (DRMF) [1] as well as DeFA [20]. However, their efficiency is only limited on individual datasets due to the fact that their final prediction depends mainly on the initial shape. In fact, such methods are fast converged but not well generalized.

Recent deep learning models usually consist of a convolutional neural networks (CNN) backbone and a regression head. The direct regression methods like take as input the last flattened feature map of the CNN backbone. Meanwhile, in heatmap regression models such as Style Aggregation Network (SAN) [9] and MobileFAN [33] certain de-convolutional layers are added to the CNN backbone to form a fully CNN (called FCN). Its outputted set of 2D heatmaps with the same width and height to the original image are then used for locating position of the landmarks. These models are well generalized thanks to their non-linearity but hardly converged due to high number of dispersal landmarks.

In this paper, we propose a novel model for **F**acial **L**andmark detection combining the **A**ctive **S**hape model and the **H**eatmap regression called FLASH. Our main contributions are therefore three-fold. Firstly, we designed a FCN backbone based on Resnet to produce a set of high quality heatmaps. Secondly, we added a softmax-argmax layer to our backbone for locating the position of the landmarks on the corresponding heatmap. Then, we combined the active shape model loss and the heatmap regression loss in an efficient manner. Thirdly, we trained and evaluated FLASH on two public datasets 300W-Challenging and WFLW achieved a normalized mean square error (NMSE) of 6.67% and 7.34%, respectively. These results are much better than DeFA (9.38%), MobileFAN (6.87%) and SAN (6.60%) on the 300W-Challenging dataset. These also overcome the coarse-to-fine face shape searching CFSS [4](9.07%) and the ASM-Net [11] (10.77%) which is a combination of active shape models and a direct regression network on WFLW dataset.

The rest of the paper is organized as follows. In Sect. 2, we study recent approaches for facial landmark detection relating to our work. Then, our proposed model FLASH is presented in detail in Sect. 3. We summarize and analyze the experimental results of FLASH on two public datasets in Sect. 4. Open issues about the work are discussed in Sect. 4.5. Finally, Sect. 5 concludes our works.

2   Related Works

Over decades, lots of methods for facial landmark detection have been proposed. In this paper, we concerns mainly on the visual landmark regression and the facial shape fitting.

2.1 Shape Fitting

Traditional template matching approaches such as ASM [6], AAM [5], CLM [7] and DeFA [20] detect the facial landmarks by learning their common distribution and from a mean shape, computed from certain active samples, regressing them. ASM is based on the dimension reduction method Principle Component Analysis (PCA) [16] for shape fitting. AAM improved the performance of ASM by combining both the shape and appearance models in iterative manner. CLM introduced another appearance sampling technique in which the pixel values in the texture patches are normalized with zero mean and unit variance. Using CNN, DeFA models the facial shape in 3D to not only aligns facial landmarks but also matches SIFT (Scale-Invariant Feature Transform) points as well as the facial contours. However, due to limited feature engineering, the performance of such approaches are limited especially in case of occluded face images.

2.2 Landmark Regression

As introduced, the neural networks for facial landmark detection usually include a CNN backbone and a regression head which is fed with a feature vector. The networks can be categorized as coordinate and heatmap regression according to the way such vector is built from the backbone.

Coordinate Regression. In case of coordinate regression networks, any CNN encoder can be used as their backbone. The regression head is directly fed with the flattened feature embedding of the backbone. Mnemonic Descent Method (MDM) [26] is a combined convolutional recurrent neural network which aims to cooperate the regressors of facial landmarks. DeepReg [21] is a deep regressor for gradual detection of facial landmarks with two-stage initialisation. In Wing [12], the wing regression loss was proposed for landmark localization rather than the L1 and L2 losses thanks to its ability to help the regression networks not only deal with large localization errors as L1 and L2, but treat also well the medium and small localization ones. Wing has been experimented with Resnet-50 [13] backbone. However, such average loss for regression of a high number of positions on the whole face is unable to assure small prediction errors for individual landmarks.

Heatmap Regression. The heatmap regression networks such as AWing [27], MobileFAN [33], Gaussian Vector (GV) [31] and AdNet [15] are autoencoder backbone which is composed of a CNN encoder and a decoder to produce probability distributions in form of heatmaps corresponding to the facial landmarks. In each heatmap, the position with the highest probability is chosen for the respective landmark.

AWing proposed an adaptive Wing loss function for coordinate regression from facial boundary map for better conforming the heatmap pixels to the facial shape. Gaussian Vector (GV) converts heatmap in to a pair of vector for each landmark to preserve spacial information and simplify the post-processing. AdNet introduced anisotropic direction loss and anisotropic attention module for better learning the facial structure as well as the texture details and mitigating the error-bias of facial landmarks.

2.3   Joint Shape Fitting and Regression Networks

There are also few methods which combine the shape fitting approach and the regression network such as LAB [28], ASMNet [11] and AnchorFace [32]. LAB is a combination of the boundary fitting and the coordinate regression. Using a stacked Hourglass network [24] as an autoencoder backbone to produce facial boundary map, LAB then regresses the coordination of facial landmarks from the boundary in order to avoid the ambiguities of such key-points. ASMNet leveraged the light-weight MobileNetV2 [25] as backbone and presented a multi-task loss which is the sum of the mean square error and the active shape model loss. This enables ASMNet to learn both the shape and the coordination of the facial landmarks with less parameters than LAB.

In AnchorFace, the authors introduced certain anchor templates and regress the offsets on each template. They then aggregates the predictions on every templates to produce the final results. AnchorFace utilized ShuffleNetV2 [22] as its backbone. AnchorFace can deal with face poses of large variations thanks to its anchor templates. Nevertheless, the anchor templates need to be carefully selected and the inference time must be improved. AnchorFace is also known as anchor-based method.

Such joint approaches are usually more performant than the separate ones. However, existing joint methods are only between coordinate regression and the shape fitting. In this paper, we propose FLASH, a facial landmark detection method based on shape fitting and heatmap regression to fill the gap as well as to leverage the robustness of such combination.

3   FLASH: The Proposed Method

Our proposed method FLASH consists of a heatmap regression network a training loss function including both the coordination and the shape matching errors. Two principal components of the heatmap regression network are the heatmap-generated backbone and the heatmap regression head.

3.1   The Heatmap-Generated Backbone

As depicted in Fig. 3, the backbone is an autoencoder which takes as input the face image of size 224×224 and produces a set of heatmaps. The encoder is composed of five multi-filter convolutional layers which are activated by ReLU function and dimensionally reduced by Max-Pooling. Meanwhile, the decoder is based on three deconvolutional layers to produce a set of heatmaps of the same size with the input image, each of which corresponds to a facial landmark.

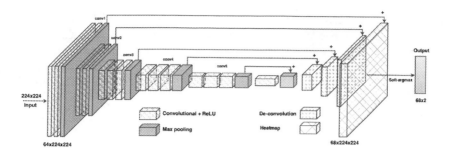

Fig. 3. The network architecture of FLASH.

3.2 The Heatmap Regression Head

Given a set of n heatmaps $H = \{H^i\}, i = \overline{1, n}$, each of size K × K (in this case K is qual to 224) and flattened to a vector of K^2 dimensions $h^i = (h^i_1, h^i_2, .., h^i_{K^2})$, the regression head of FLASH can predict the coordination for the respective facial landmarks using a soft arg-max function as follows:

$$\{\hat{x}_i, \hat{y}_i\} = softargmax_j(j \cdot f(j)) \tag{1}$$

where $f(j), j = \overline{1, K^2}$ is a probability distribution function defined as follows

$$f(j) = \frac{e^{\alpha \cdot h^i_j}}{\sum_{k=1}^{K^2} e^{\alpha \cdot h^i_k}} \tag{2}$$

in which $\alpha \geq 1$ is the temperature parameter. For the ith heatmap H^i, the function $softargmax$ returns an index j^* where $f(j^*)$ is the maximal value of $\{f(j), \forall j = \overline{1, K^2}\}$. From j^*, we can calculate the coordination $(\hat{x}_i, \hat{y}_i)$ for the corresponding i^{th} facial landmark. This function can be differentiated that can be used in FLASH instead of the traditional $argmax$ and $softmax$ functions.

3.3 The Multitask Loss Function

As we aim to integrate the facial landmarks in to a given shape, we designed a multitask loss function for training our proposed network.

The Coordination Loss. The mean square error is used as the coordination loss as follows:

$$\mathcal{L}_{coord} = \frac{1}{n} \sum_{i=1}^{n} [(x_i - \hat{x}_i)^2 + (y_i - \hat{y}_j)^2] \tag{3}$$

where n is the number of facial landmarks, $(x_i, y_i), (\hat{x}_i, \hat{x}_j), i = \overline{1, n}$ is the ground truth and predicted coordination of the ith facial landmark, respectively.

The Shape Loss. Given a training set with m samples in which the $i^{th}, i = \overline{1, m}$ is represented as a vector of $2n$ dimensions $s^i = (x_1^i, y_1^i, x_2^i, y_2^i, ..x_n^i, y_n^i)$, using PCA (Principal Component Analysis) [6], this can be approximated by $\tilde{s}^i$ as follows:

$$\tilde{s}^i = \overline{s} + P \cdot b^i \tag{4}$$

where $\overline{s}$ is the mean shape

$$\overline{s} = \frac{1}{m} \sum_{j=1}^{m} s^j \tag{5}$$

and $P = (p_1|p_2|..|p_t)$ is a matrix constituted from t eigenvectors with the highest corresponding eigenvalues $\lambda_1, \lambda_1, .., \lambda_t$ of the following co-variance matrix:

$$S = \frac{1}{m-1} \sum_{j=1}^{m} (s^j - \overline{s})(s^j - \overline{s})^T \tag{6}$$

and b^i is a t-dimensional vector containing a set of parameters for a deformable model:

$$b^i = P^T(s^i - \overline{s}) \tag{7}$$

The shape loss is then calculated as follows

$$\mathcal{L}_{shape} = \frac{1}{2 \cdot n} \sum_{j=1}^{2n} (s_j^i - \tilde{s}_j^i)^2 \tag{8}$$

The Multitask Loss. For every training samples, the overall loss is the combination of the coordinate and the shape ones as the following

$$\mathcal{L} = \mathcal{L}_{coord} + \beta \cdot \mathcal{L}_{shape} \tag{9}$$

where β is the shape fitting rate which varies in reverse proportionally to the number of the training epochs for FLASH. This is because as many other convolutional neural networks, FLASH learns the shape before featuring the pixel-wise image. The ratio can then be defined as the following discrete function:

$$\beta = \begin{cases} 2 & \text{if } e \leq \frac{N_e}{5} \\ 1 & \text{if } e \leq 2 \cdot \frac{N_e}{5} \\ 0.5 & \text{if } e \leq 3 \cdot \frac{N_e}{5} \\ 0 & \text{if } e > 3 \cdot \frac{N_e}{5} \end{cases} \tag{10}$$

where e, N_e is the current and total number of training epochs, respectively. At the initial steps of FLASH training where the shape features are important, the shape fitting rate β is also high enough. Reversely, at the final steps, β is set to zero since there exists mainly pixel featuring in the network.

4   Experiments

4.1   Datasets

Our proposed FLASH method is evaluated on two famous facial landmark datasets including 300W and WFLW.

300W. The 300W dataset totally consists of 3837 facial images with 68 landmarks annotated. The training set includes 3148 images in which 2000 are from HELEN [19], 811 from LFPW [2] and 337 from AFW [17]. The full testing set is composed of 689 images which is divided in to a common set of 554 combining those from HELEN and LFPW and a challenging set with 135 images.

WFLW. The WFLW dataset [28] includes 10000 facial images which are annotated by 98 landmarks. Three fourths of the dataset are used for training and the rest for testing. This latter is composed of six subsets with different difficulties including 314 for expression, 326 for large pose, 206 for make-up, 736 for occlusion, 698 for illumination and 773 for blurring.

4.2   Evaluation Metrics

As commonly used for benchmarking of facial landmark detection methods, we also based on the **normalized mean error (NME)** to evaluate the accuracy of our proposed FLASH as follows:

$$NME = \frac{1}{n} \sum_{i=1}^{n} \frac{\sqrt{(x_i - \hat{x}_i)^2 + (y_i - \hat{y}_i)^2}}{d} \tag{11}$$

where d is the distance between the two outer eye corners (inter-ocular) specifically for each dataset. This is also the normalized factor used in the 300W and WFLW datasets.

The **failure rate (FR)** is also involved in this case to evaluate the robustness of the methods in term of NME. This indicates the rate of failed recognition in which NME is less than 10%. The smaller FR is, the more powerful the model is.

4.3   Model Training

The input images are all resized to 224×224 before training. FLASH used Resnet 50 as its backbone for better heatmap featuring and is implemented in Pytorch. The model is trained by 50 epochs using Adam optimizer with the learning rate of 10e-5, the decay of 10e-5 and batch size of 64 on a K80 GPU of Google Colaboratory.

4.4   Results

Evaluation Results on 300W Dataset. The results of FLASH on 300W dataset can be seen on the Table 1. Our model FLASH achieved a NME of 3.79%, 6.67% and 4.35% on the Common, Challenging and Full subset of 300W, respectively. These outperform most of the recent methods of coordinate regression, heatmap regression as well as shape fitting such as DeFA, MobileFAN, PCD-CNN, CPM, ASMNet especially on the Challenging subset. FLASH is a bit less accurate than the state-of-the-art AnchorFace but it runs faster at the rate of 43 frames per second (FPS) on NVIDIA Tesla K80 GPU than Anchor-Face with 45 FPS on much more powerful NVIDIA GTX Titan Xp GPU. These results prove the efficiency of the combination between the heatmap regression and the shape fitting in our FLASH method.

Table 1. Accuracy of FLASH and other comparative methods on 300W dataset.

Model	Category	Common	Challenging	Full
CFSS [34]	Shape Fitting	4.73	9.98	5.76
DSRN [23]	Coordinate Regression	4.12	9.68	5.21
DeFA	Shape Fitting	5.37	9.38	6.10
RDR [29]	Coordinate Regression and Shape Fitting	5.37	9.38	6.10
RCN [14]	Coordinate Regression	4.67	8.44	5.41
ASMNet	Coordinate regression and Shape Fitting	4.82	8.20	5.50
CPM [10]	Coordinate Regression	3.39	8.14	4.36
PCD-CNN [18]	Heatmap Regression	3.67	7.62	4.44
CPM+SBR [10]	Coordinate Regression	3.28	7.78	4.10
MobileFAN	Heatmap Regression	4.22	6.87	4.74
ODN [8]	Coordinate Regression	3.56	6.67	4.17
SAN	Coordinate Regression	3.34	6.60	3.98
AnchorFace	Anchor-based Regression	**3.12**	**6.19**	**3.72**
FLASH (ours)	Heatmap Regression and Shape Fitting	*3.79*	*6.67*	*4.35*

Evaluation Results on WFLW Dataset. FLASH is also evaluated on the WFLW dataset using both NME and FR metrics as in Table 2. FLASH achieved the best performance and robustness with a NME of 7.34% and a FR of 17.08% in comparison with recent advanced methods such as ESR (with NME of 11.13%, FR of 35.24%), SDM (with NME of 10.29%, FR of 29.40%), CFSS (with NME of 9.07%, FR of 20.56%) and ASMNet (with NME of 10.77%, FR of 39.12%) on the full WFLW dataset. However, these results are far from those of AnchoFace with NME of 4.62% and FR of 4.2% on the full dataset. This is because FLASH is not efficient for the large pose, occlusion and blur subsets with a NME of 14.81%, 9.10%, 8.15% and a FR of 64.11%, 25.95% and 19.40%, respectively. In fact, AnchorFace is fine-tuned according to various shapes while our FLASH is relied on only one for a given dataset.

Table 2. Accuracy of FLASH and other comparative methods on WFLW dataset.

Data	Metric	ESR [3]	SDM [30]	CFSS	ASMNet	AnchorFace	FLASH (ours)
Full	NME	11.13	10.29	9.07	10.77	**4.62**	*7.34*
	FR	35.24	29.40	20.56	39.12	**4.2**	*17.08*
Large Pose	NME	25.88	24.10	21.36	21.11	–	**14.81**
	FR	90.18	84.36	66.22	98.41	–	**64.11**
Expression	NME	11.47	11.45	10.09	12.02	–	**7.74**
	FR	42.04	33.44	23.25	59.87	–	**14.33**
Illumination	NME	10.49	9.32	8.30	9.93	–	**6.92**
	FR	30.80	26.22	17.34	33.38	–	**12.75**
Makeup	NME	11.05	9.38	8.74	10.55	–	**7.16**
	FR	38.84	27.67	21.84	38.34	–	**16.50**
Occlusion	NME	13.75	13.03	11.76	12.34	–	**9.10**
	FR	47.28	41.85	32.88	48.64	–	**25.95**
Blur	NME	12.20	11.28	9.96	11.62	–	**8.15**
	FR	41.40	35.32	23.67	46.31	–	**19.40**

4.5 Discussion

Facial landmark detection is an active research topic over many years because this can be more efficiently used to recognize the human facial emotion than relying on the whole human face. However, most recent methods focus more on the feature engineering of the individual facial landmarks but less on their distribution meaning the shape of the face. Although, the power of deep learning backbone networks has been thoroughly leveraged, the performance of such coordination and heatmap regression methods remains limited. ASMNet was the first to take in to account the shape fitting in to its coordination regression and initially gained positive results. However, the coordination regression approach aims to extract features at the cell level while the heatmap regression targets to the pixel level of the image which is closer to the facial landmarks in this case. Our proposed method FLASH is a combination of heatmap regression and shape fitting achieved a much better performance and robustness than ASMNet in both 300W and WFLW datasets which proved our judgments.

5 Conclusion

As discussed, the facial landmark detection is necessary for recognition of human emotion which can be applied in advanced driver assistance systems. This task is really hard due to the dispersion of high number of landmarks on the human face. Efficient methods such as ASMNet and AnchorFace all take in to account their distribution meaning the facial shape. However, these coordination regression methods extract the feature at the cell level which is less accurate than at the pixel level as in case of heatmap regression. In this paper, we proposed a novel facial landmark detection method called FLASH which is the first combination between heatmap regression and shape fitting. The evaluation on 300W and WFLW datasets showed that FLASH outperforms many existing methods including ASMNet. FLASH can not be compared to AnchorFace due to using less number of anchor shapes. These results proved that such combination is reasonable and the FLASH can also be better improved with more performant backbone and more facial priors.

References

1. Asthana, A., Zafeiriou, S., Cheng, S., Pantic, M.: Robust discriminative response map fitting with constrained local models. In: Proceedings of the 2013 IEEE Conference on Computer Vision and Pattern Recognition, pp. 3444–3451. CVPR 2013, IEEE Computer Society, USA (2013). https://doi.org/10.1109/CVPR.2013.442
2. Belhumeur, P.N., Jacobs, D.W., Kriegman, D.J., Kumar, N.: Localizing parts of faces using a consensus of exemplars. IEEE Trans. Pattern Anal. Mach. Intell. **35**(12), 2930–2940 (2013). https://doi.org/10.1109/TPAMI.2013.23
3. Cao, X., Wei, Y., Wen, F., Sun, J.: Face alignment by explicit shape regression. In: 2012 IEEE Conference on Computer Vision and Pattern Recognition, pp. 2887–2894 (2012). https://doi.org/10.1109/CVPR.2012.6248015
4. Cao, X., Wei, Y., Wen, F., Sun, J.: Face alignment by explicit shape regression. Int. J. Comput. Vision **107**(2), 177–190 (2014)
5. Cootes, T.F., Edwards, G.J., Taylor, C.J.: Active appearance models. In: Burkhardt, H., Neumann, B. (eds.) Computer Vision – ECCV 1998, pp. 484–498. Springer, Berlin Heidelberg, Berlin, Heidelberg (1998)
6. Cootes, T., Baldock, E., Graham, J.: An introduction to active shape models. Image Process. Anal. **328**, 223–248 (2000)
7. Cristinacce, D., Cootes, T.: Feature detection and tracking with constrained local models, vol. 41, pp. 929–938 (2006). https://doi.org/10.5244/C.20.95
8. Ding, H., Zhou, P., Chellappa, R.: Occlusion-adaptive deep network for robust facial expression recognition. In: 2020 IEEE International Joint Conference on Biometrics (IJCB), pp. 1–9. IEEE Press (2020). https://doi.org/10.1109/IJCB48548.2020.9304923
9. Dong, X., Yan, Y., Ouyang, W., Yang, Y.: Style aggregated network for facial landmark detection. In: Proceedings of the IEEE Conference on Computer Vision and Pattern Recognition, pp. 379–388 (2018)
10. Dong, X., Yu, S.I., Weng, X., Wei, S.E., Yang, Y., Sheikh, Y.: Supervision-by-Registration: an unsupervised approach to improve the precision of facial landmark detectors. In: Proceedings of the IEEE Conference on Computer Vision and Pattern Recognition (CVPR), pp. 360–368 (2018)

11. Fard, A.P., Abdollahi, H., Mahoor, M.H.: ASMNet: a lightweight deep neural network for face alignment and pose estimation. In: IEEE Conference on Computer Vision and Pattern Recognition Workshops, CVPR Workshops 2021, virtual, June 19–25, 2021, pp. 1521–1530. Computer Vision Foundation / IEEE (2021). https://doi.org/10.1109/CVPRW53098.2021.00168

12. Feng, Z., Kittler, J., Awais, M., Huber, P., Wu, X.: Wing loss for robust facial landmark localisation with convolutional neural networks. In: 2018 IEEE/CVF Conference on Computer Vision and Pattern Recognition (CVPR), pp. 2235–2245. IEEE Computer Society, Los Alamitos, CA, USA (2018). https://doi.org/10.1109/CVPR.2018.00238, https://doi.ieeecomputersociety.org/10.1109/CVPR.2018.00238

13. He, K., Zhang, X., Ren, S., Sun, J.: Deep residual learning for image recognition. In: Proceedings of 2016 IEEE Conference on Computer Vision and Pattern Recognition, pp. 770–778. CVPR 2016, IEEE (2016). https://doi.org/10.1109/CVPR.2016.90, http://ieeexplore.ieee.org/document/7780459

14. Honari, S., Yosinski, J., Vincent, P., Pal, C.: Recombinator networks: learning coarse-to-fine feature aggregation. In: Computer Vision and Pattern Recognition (CVPR), 2016 IEEE Conference on. IEEE (2016)

15. Huang, Y., Yang, H., Li, C., Kim, J., Wei, F.: ADNet: leveraging error-bias towards normal direction in face alignment. In: 2021 IEEE/CVF International Conference on Computer Vision (ICCV), pp. 3060–3070 (2021)

16. Jolliffe, I.T., Cadima, J.: Principal component analysis: a review and recent developments. Philos. Trans. Royal Soc. A Math. Phys. Eng. Sci. **374**(2065), 20150202 (2016)

17. Köstinger, M., Wohlhart, P., Roth, P.M., Bischof, H.: Annotated facial landmarks in the wild: a large-scale, real-world database for facial landmark localization. In: 2011 IEEE International Conference on Computer Vision Workshops (ICCV Workshops), pp. 2144–2151 (2011). https://doi.org/10.1109/ICCVW.2011.6130513

18. Kumar, A., Chellappa, R.: Disentangling 3D pose in a dendritic CNN for unconstrained 2D face alignment. In: 2018 IEEE/CVF Conference on Computer Vision and Pattern Recognition (CVPR), pp. 430–439. IEEE Computer Society, Los Alamitos, CA, USA (2018). https://doi.org/10.1109/CVPR.2018.00052, https://doi.ieeecomputersociety.org/10.1109/CVPR.2018.00052

19. Le, V., Brandt, J., Lin, Z., Bourdev, L., Huang, T.S.: Interactive facial feature localization. In: Fitzgibbon, A., Lazebnik, S., Perona, P., Sato, Y., Schmid, C. (eds.) Computer Vision - ECCV 2012, pp. 679–692. Springer, Berlin Heidelberg, Berlin, Heidelberg (2012)

20. Liu, Y., Jourabloo, A., Ren, W., Liu, X.: Dense face alignment. In: Proceedings of the IEEE International Conference on Computer Vision Workshops, pp. 1619–1628 (2017)

21. Lv, J., Shao, X., Xing, J., Cheng, C., Zhou, X.: A deep regression architecture with two-stage re-initialization for high performance facial landmark detection. In: 2017 IEEE Conference on Computer Vision and Pattern Recognition (CVPR), pp. 3691–3700 (2017). https://doi.org/10.1109/CVPR.2017.393

22. Ma, N., Zhang, X., Zheng, H.T., Sun, J.: ShuffleNet V2: practical guidelines for efficient CNN architecture design. In: Ferrari, V., Hebert, M., Sminchisescu, C., Weiss, Y. (eds.) Computer Vision - ECCV 2018, pp. 122–138. Springer International Publishing, Cham (2018)

23. Miao, X., Zhen, X., Liu, X., Deng, C., Athitsos, V., Huang, H.: Direct shape regression networks for end-to-end face alignment. In: Proceedings of the IEEE Conference on Computer Vision and Pattern Recognition (CVPR) (2018)

24. Newell, A., Yang, K., Deng, J.: Stacked hourglass networks for human pose estimation. In: Leibe, B., Matas, J., Sebe, N., Welling, M. (eds.) Computer Vision - ECCV 2016, pp. 483–499. Springer International Publishing, Cham (2016)
25. Sandler, M., Howard, A.G., Zhu, M., Zhmoginov, A., Chen, L.: MobileNetV2: inverted residuals and linear bottlenecks. In: 2018 IEEE Conference on Computer Vision and Pattern Recognition, CVPR 2018, Salt Lake City, UT, USA, June 18–22, 2018, pp. 4510–4520. Computer Vision Foundation / IEEE Computer Society (2018). https://doi.org/10.1109/CVPR.2018.00474
26. Trigeorgis, G., Snape, P., Nicolaou, M.A., Antonakos, E., Zafeiriou, S.: Mnemonic descent method: a recurrent process applied for end-to-end face alignment. In: 2016 IEEE Conference on Computer Vision and Pattern Recognition (CVPR), pp. 4177–4187. IEEE Computer Society, Los Alamitos, CA, USA (2016). https://doi.org/10.1109/CVPR.2016.453, https://doi.ieeecomputersociety.org/10.1109/CVPR.2016.453
27. Wang, X., Bo, L., Fuxin, L.: Adaptive wing loss for robust face alignment via heatmap regression. In: The IEEE International Conference on Computer Vision (ICCV) (2019)
28. Wu, W., Qian, C., Yang, S., Wang, Q., Cai, Y., Zhou, Q.: Look at boundary: a boundary-aware face alignment algorithm. In: CVPR (2018)
29. Xiao, S., et al.: Recurrent 3D–2D dual learning for large-pose facial landmark detection. In: 2017 IEEE International Conference on Computer Vision (ICCV), pp. 1642–1651 (2017). https://doi.org/10.1109/ICCV.2017.181
30. Xiong, X., De la Torre, F.: Supervised descent method and its applications to face alignment. In: 2013 IEEE Conference on Computer Vision and Pattern Recognition, pp. 532–539 (2013). https://doi.org/10.1109/CVPR.2013.75
31. Xiong, Y., Zhou, Z., Dou, Y., Su, Z.: Gaussian vector: an efficient solution for facial landmark detection. In: Ishikawa, H., Liu, C.-L., Pajdla, T., Shi, J. (eds.) ACCV 2020. LNCS, vol. 12626, pp. 70–87. Springer, Cham (2021). https://doi.org/10.1007/978-3-030-69541-5_5
32. Xu, Z., Li, B., Yuan, Y., Geng, M.: AnchorFace: an anchor-based facial landmark detector across large poses. In: Proceedings of the AAAI Conference on Artificial Intelligence, vol. 35, pp. 3092–3100 (2021)
33. Zhao, Y., Liu, Y., Shen, C., Gao, Y., Xiong, S.: MobileFAN: transferring deep hidden representation for face alignment. Pattern Recognit. **100**, 107114 (2019). https://doi.org/10.1016/j.patcog.2019.107114
34. Zhu, S., Li, C., Loy, C.C., Tang, X.: Face alignment by coarse-to-fine shape searching. In: 2015 IEEE Conference on Computer Vision and Pattern Recognition (CVPR), pp. 4998–5006 (2015). https://doi.org/10.1109/CVPR.2015.7299134

Industrial Networks and Intelligent Systems

Adaptive Backstepping Sliding Mode Control for Speed of PMSM and DC-Link Voltage in Bidirectional Quasi Z-Source Inverter

Cong-Thanh Pham$^{(\boxtimes)}$, Chan Thanh Nguyen Huu, Quoc-Khai Tran, Tran Van Thien, and Duc Tam-Hong Nguyen

Faculty of Electrical and Electronic, Vietnam Aviation Academy,
Ho Chi Minh City 700000, Vietnam
{thanhpc,thanhnhc,khaitq,thientv,ducnth}@vaa.edu.vn

Abstract. Researching and designing the controller for speed of permanent magnet synchronous motor (PMSM) and the DC-link voltage controller (DCV) in bidirectional quasi z-source inverter (BQ-ZSI) have a strong influence on the efficiency of electric vehicle applications. This paper presents two control strategies: Firstly, the speed of PMSM is controlled via sliding mode control (SMC) and adaptive backstepping which are called SA; Secondly, the peak of DCV in BQ-ZSI is regulated by controlling the total of the two capacitor voltages of BQ-ZSI. When the system operates, limitations of inverter current and voltage level on the motor output power have been reduced. With these strategies, DCV and speed of PMSM are stabilized, which improve the system efficiency. To demonstrate the effectiveness of the proposed method, the PMSM drive model and the controllers are simulated using MATLAB software.

Keywords: Z-source inverter · PMSM · Quasi-Z-source inverter · Backstepping Control · Sliding Mode Control

1 Introduction

Permanent magnet synchronous motor (PMSM) is a type of AC motor commonly used in industrial rotating systems, especially in the electric vehicles (EVs) [1]. Research on controller design with the aim of reducing errors, reduces costs and improving performance is increasingly interested by many researchers [2–5]. In recent years, the main method for controlling the speed of the PMSM is the field oriented control (FOC) scheme, where one speed and two current loops are decoupled on dq-axis [6]. The speed controller of motor is designed to track reference speed and it also generates a reference current signal on q-axis, two current controllers are used to stabilize the voltage on d and q-axis [7].

In PMSM drive systems, the speed controller is designed to satisfy the requirements of the control systems such as: a wide adjustable speed range, adaptation to high instantaneous torque response, load disturbances and parameter

© ICST Institute for Computer Sciences, Social Informatics and Telecommunications Engineering 2023
Published by Springer Nature Switzerland AG 2023. All Rights Reserved
N.-S. Vo and H.-A. Tran (Eds.): INISCOM 2023, LNICST 531, pp. 185–202, 2023.
https://doi.org/10.1007/978-3-031-47359-3_14

variations, low error ripple speed, low ripple torque, reliability, high efficiency and robustness. Therefore, the fixed coefficients K_p, K_i and K_d of traditional PID controller are not inconsonant with the high performance requirements of systems. Many artificial intelligence techniques were used to adjust the gains of the PID controllers as: genetic algorithms (GA) and particle swarm optimization (PSO) [8]. However, in order to achieve online gain tuning of the PI controllers, the speed of the microcontroller and the convergence speed of the GA and PSO must be fast, leading to a high computational burden [9]. Therefore, the study of an adaptive back-stepping controller is applied for controlling the speed motor which it is given in this paper.

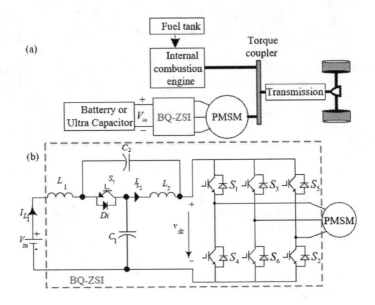

Fig. 1. The bidirectional quasi-Z-source inverter topology.

When applying the PMSM for electric vehicles, voltage source inverters with direct current (DC) voltage are used as battery. At high current, when the battery discharges, the voltage of battery decreases greatly and when the battery charges the voltage of battery increases greatly [10]. The voltage drop will impact the output power, speed motor, load torque and performance of PMSM drives system. The bidirectional DC to DC converter topology is applied to convert energy back and forth in the system between DC source supply and inverter. It can correct the mismatch between the DC power source and the DC-link voltage (DCV) of inverter and also ensures that the DCV is always kept stable.

In 2003, F.Z.Peng proposed Z-source inverter (ZSI) which is a boost/buck converter, it solves many of the disadvantages of traditional voltage source converters. [11]. The DCV is adjusted by changing duty in ZSI so that it increases the reliability of ZSI. Comparing with ZSI, QZSI has the advantages as low stress on the voltage and continuous current, the power transfers on directional flow from the DC source to the AC side [12]. The bidirectional quasi-Z-source inverter (BQ-ZSI) as response requirements of EV that is able to reverse the direction of power transmission when the motor is decelerating or braking, the energy from PMSM can be transferred back to the source with an additional seventh switch. The current of the inductor is always continuous and small inductance in BQ-ZSI topology have a better effective which it is suitable for electric vehicle applications as Fig. 1 on page 2 a) and b).

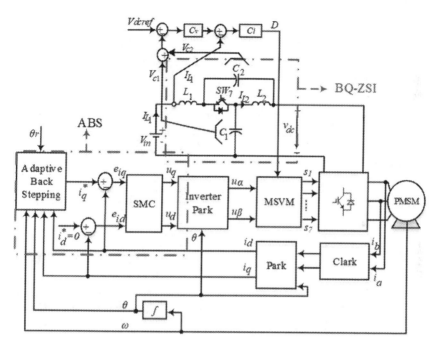

Fig. 2. The adaptive Backstepping Speed Control in PMSM Fed by a BQ-ZSI topology.

This paper studies the application of BQ-ZSI scheme for the PMSM drive for electric vehicle. Moreover, two control algorithms between the DC source and the AC side of the PMSM drive for electric vehicle are presented: the first one is the speed control motor (AC side controller) based on adaptive backstepping and sliding mode control; the second one is to control the peak DCV in BQ-ZSI (DC side controller) based on the regulation of the two capacitors voltages when the input DC voltage (battery or super capacitor) of BQ-ZSI is dropped durring EV operation (the load torque and the speed of the motor change continuously). As a result, the efficiency of the electric vehicle system is enhanced.

The organization of this paper include as: Sect. 2 introduces the description of PMSM drive system and the BQ-ZSI scheme. Section 3 presents the two proposed controllers for the speed motor and the BQ-ZSI. Section 4 discusses the simulation results on MATLAB software and Sect. 5 concludes the effectiveness of the proposed methods.

2   Description PMSM and BQ-ZSI Scheme

2.1   Description PMSM Drive System

The mathematical model of the PMSM drive system is derived in the $d - q$ axis as:

$$\begin{cases} \dot{\omega} = -\frac{B}{J}.\omega - \frac{T_L}{J} + \frac{1.5n_p\Psi_f}{J}i_q \\ \dot{i}_d = \frac{R_s}{L_d}i_d + n_p\omega i_q + \frac{1}{L_d}u_d \\ \dot{i}_q = -n_p\omega i_d - \frac{R_s}{L_d}i_q - n_p\frac{\Psi_f}{L_q}\omega + \frac{1}{L_q}u_q \\ \dot{\theta} = \omega \end{cases} \tag{1}$$

In which ω is the rotor speed. u_d, u_q, i_d, i_q are the voltages and stator currents, respectively, in the dq-axes frame. The limited voltage is λ on dq-axis, which $|u_d| \leq \lambda$ and $|u_q| \leq \lambda, (\lambda < 1)$. The stator inductance are L_d, L_q and without any loss of generality, the asumption $L_d = L_q$ is valid [6]. Ψ_f, R_s, J, T_L, B, and n_p are respectively the permanent magnet flux linkage, the stator resistance, the moment of inertia, the load torque, the viscous friction coefficient, and the number of pole pairs.

2.2   Analysis of the BQ-ZSI Network Modeling

The structure diagram of the BQ-ZSI is presented in Fig. 1 which is called DC-side model. There are two operating as belows: 1) the bidirectional quasi z-source network (BQ-ZSN), which is comprised of C_1, C_2, L_1, L_2, and switch S_7 with a parallel diode D_i. 2) the three-phase inverter. With these two switches, the power flow can be controlled bidirectionally. The three-phase bridge include six switch and the motor is replaced by R_l and L_l.

The BQ-ZSI has three common operating states: the non shoot-through state (NST), the zero state, and the shoot-through state (ST) [13]. In the ST, the DCV (V_{dc}) is boosted by conducting the lower and upper switches of the three-phase inverter at the same time.

From Fig. 1b), it also shows that the BQ-ZSI allows the inductor current to flow continuously in both two directions. When the three-phase inverter is in the ST with S_i close circuit as Fig. 3a), the diode D_i is reversely blocked, the switch S_7 is open circuit, the current and the voltage on capacitors and inductors are shown as Fig. 3a). When the three-phase inverter is in the NST as Fig. 3b), the switch S_7 is close circuit and the power back to the DC source input through switch S_7, this is in the generatoring mode of BQ-ZSI. Instead, the power through diode transfer inverter [12]. Therefore, at all operating conditions, the continuous conduction mode of the BQ-ZSI is maintained and the performance of the three phases inverter is enhanced. This property is very good for EV applications.

The state variables $x(t)$ of this BQ-ZSI model are shown as Fig. 3. The inductor currents through L_1, L_2 as $(i_{L_1}(t))$ and $(i_{L_2}(t))$. The capacitor voltages C_1, C_2 are $v_{C_1}(t)$ and $v_{C_2}(t)$. The load current is $i_{lo}(t)$. The variables is $c(t)$, $c(t) = v_{in}(t)$.

$$
\text{Set } x(t) = \begin{bmatrix} i_{L_1}(t) \\ i_{L_2}(t) \\ v_{C_1}(t) \\ v_{C_2}(t) \\ i_{lo}(t) \end{bmatrix}
$$

– In the ST, the switch S_7 and diode D_i are closed circut, S_i is close circuit, the circuit as Fig. 3a). In the state space form, the equation group can be written: $A.\dot{x}(t) = B_1.x(t) + C_1.c(t)$, where

$$
A = \begin{bmatrix} L_1 & 0 & 0 & 0 & 0 \\ 0 & L_2 & 0 & 0 & 0 \\ 0 & 0 & C_1 & 0 & 0 \\ 0 & 0 & 0 & C_2 & 0 \\ 0 & 0 & 0 & 0 & L_l \end{bmatrix}; B_1 = \begin{bmatrix} 0 & 0 & 0 & 1 & 0 \\ 0 & 0 & 1 & 0 & 0 \\ 0 & -1 & 0 & 0 & 0 \\ -1 & 0 & 0 & 0 & 0 \\ 0 & 0 & 0 & 0 & -R_l \end{bmatrix}; C_1 = \begin{bmatrix} 1 \\ 0 \\ 0 \\ 0 \\ 0 \end{bmatrix}
$$

– In the NST, the switch S_7 and diode D_i are close circuit, the switch uper and lo S_i is open circuit, the circuit as Fig. 3b). Similar, in the state space form, the equation group can be obtained as $A.\dot{x}(t) = B_2.x(t) + C_2.c(t)$, where

$$
B_2 = \begin{bmatrix} 0 & 0 & -1 & 0 & 0 \\ 0 & 0 & 0 & -1 & 0 \\ 1 & 0 & 0 & 0 & -1 \\ 0 & 1 & 0 & 0 & -1 \\ 0 & 0 & 1 & 1 & -R_l \end{bmatrix}; C_2 = \begin{bmatrix} 1 \\ 0 \\ 0 \\ 0 \\ 0 \end{bmatrix}
$$

Where the D_u is shoot-through duty. The D'_u is non shoot-through duty, in one of switching period (T_{sf}). Total duty is calculated in one of switching period as: $D_u + D'_u = 1$.

With the switching period T_{sf} of the space vector modulation, the BQ-ZSI state-average of each state matrix is processed as below:

$$
A\dot{\bar{x}} = [D_u B_1 + (1 - D_u) B_2] \bar{x} + [D_u C_1 + (1 - D_u) C_2] \bar{c} \tag{2}
$$

In which $\bar{x}$ and X are state variable period average and balance operation point. Farther, in the operation points, state variable has a small signal disturbances with low frequency which are presented as: $\bar{x} = X + \hat{x}$; $\bar{d}'_u = 1 - \bar{d}_u$; $\bar{c} = C + \hat{c}$; $\bar{d}_u = D_u + \hat{d}_u$;

In space vector modulation method, the switching frequency of S_i in three-phases inverter is fast. Hence, around the operation points of the BQ-ZSI system which is linearized and the steady-state of this system has Eq. (2) as belows:

$$
0 = [D_u.B_1 + (1 - D_u).B_2]X + (D_u.C_1 + (1 - D_u).C_2] C \tag{3}
$$

The steady-state of system has $X = \begin{bmatrix} I_{L_1} I_{L_2} & V_{C_1} V_{C_2} & I_{lo} \end{bmatrix}^T$ and $C = V_{in}$. Solving Eq. (3), the steady-state values of the capacitor voltages on C_1, C_2 and the inductor current through L_1, L_2 can be calculated as:

$$
\begin{cases}
V_{C_1} = \left(\frac{D'_u}{D'_u - D_u}\right).V_{in} = \left(\frac{1-D_u}{1-2D_u}\right).V_{in} \\
V_{C_2} = \left(\frac{D_u}{1-2D_u}\right).V_{in} \\
I_{L_1} = I_{L_2} = \left(\frac{D'_u}{D'_u - D_u}\right)^2.\frac{V_{in}}{R_l} = \left(\frac{1-D_u}{1-2D_u}\right)^2.\frac{V_{in}}{R_{lo}} \\
I_{lo} = \left(\frac{D'_u}{D'_u - D_u}\right).\frac{V_{in}}{R_{lo}} = \left(\frac{1-D_u}{1-2D_u}\right).\frac{V_{in}}{R_{lo}}
\end{cases}
\tag{4}
$$

In NST, the relationship between DC-link voltage and input voltage is:

$$
V_{dc} = V_{C_1} + V_{C_2} = \left(\frac{1}{1-2D_u}\right).V_{in}
\tag{5}
$$

From Eq. (4) and (5) the equation can be obtained as

$$
\begin{cases}
\frac{V_{C_1}}{V_{dc}} = 1 - D_u \\
\frac{V_{C_2}}{V_{dc}} = D_u
\end{cases}
\tag{6}
$$

Refer in [12], the small signal state space equation can be written as

$$
A.\dot{\hat{x}} = [D_u B_1 + (1-D_u) B_2].\hat{x} + [D_u C_1 + (1-D_u).C_2].\hat{c} \\
[(B_1 - B_2).X + (C_1 - C_2) C].\hat{c}(t)
\tag{7}
$$

Based on equation of (7) and refer Eq. (12) to (15) in paper [12]. Transfer function of the capacitor voltage on C_1 with the shoot-through duty D_u is calculated as:

$$
G_{v2d}(s) = \frac{(I_{lo} - I_{L_1} - I_{L_2}).L_{lo}.L.s^2 +}{L_{lo}.L.C.s^3 + R_{lo}.L.C.s^2 + [L_{lo}.(1-2.D_u)^2 + 2(1-D_u)^2.L]s}
$$
$$
\frac{[L_{lo}.V_{in} + (1-D_u).L.(V_{C_1} + V_{C_2}) + R_{lo}.L.(I_{lo} - I_{L_1} - I_{L_2}).s] + V_{in}.R_{lo}}{+(1-2.D_u)^2.R_{lo}}
\tag{8}
$$

And then, transfer function of the inductor current through L_1 with DC input voltage is calculated as:

$$
G_{v2in}(s) = \frac{(1-D_u).L_{lo}.L.C.s^3 + (1-D_u).R_{lo}LC.s^2 + \{[(1-D_u)^2 - (1-D_u).D_u].L_{lo} + (1-D_u)^2.L\}.s+}{(L.C.s^2 + 1)\times}
$$
$$
\frac{[(1-D_u)^2 - (1-D_u).D_u].R_{lo}}{\{L_{lo}LC.s^3 + R_{lo}.L.C.s^2 + [L_{lo}.(1-2D_u)^2 + 2(1-D_u)^2.L].s + (1-2D_u)^2.R_{lo}\}}
\tag{9}
$$

Transfer function of the inductor current L_1 with the shoot-through duty cycle is obtained as

$$
G_{i2d}(s) = \frac{(V_{C_1} + V_{C_2} - R_{lo}.I_{lo}).C.s + (2.D_u - 1)(I_{lo} - I_{L_1} - I_{L_2}) + V_{in}.R_{lo}}{L.C.s^2 + R_{lo}.L.C.s^2 + [L_{lo}.(1-2.D_u)^2 + 2(1-D_u)^2.L].s + (1-2.D_u)^2.R_{lo}}
\tag{10}
$$

$$
G_{inv}(s) = \frac{1}{T_{sf}s + 1}
\tag{11}
$$

Table 1. Nominal Parameters of BQ-ZSI.

Parameters ($Units$)	Symbols	Values
Load current (A)	I_l	0.8
Inductor current on $L_1(H)$	I_{L_1}	0.7
Inductor current on $L_2(H)$	I_{L_2}	0.7
Switching frequency (kHz)	f_{sf}	5
Input voltage (V)	V_{in}	40
Load inductor (H)	L_l	17
Load resistor (Ω)	R_l	2.7
Shoot-through duty	$D_u = 1 - D'_u$	0.45
The proportional gain of current controller	K_{pi}	0.44
The integral gain of current controller	K_{ii}	4.4
The proportional gain of current controller	K_{pv}	0.0176
The integral gain of current controller	K_{iv}	0.264
Inductors of the BQ-ZSI (H)	$L_1 = L_2 = L$	$0.6 * 10^{-4}$
Capacitors of the BQ-ZSI (F)	$C_1 = C_2 = C$	$47 * 10^{-5}$

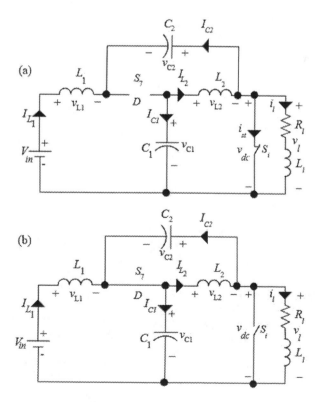

Fig. 3. Operation states of the BQ-ZSI.

3   Design of Controller for AC Side and DC Side

3.1   Adaptive Backstepping and Sliding Mode Controller (SA) for Speed Motor (AC Side)

In the functions of BQ-ZSI motor drive system, it is motor speed control (AC side control), which is designed to adapt to the torque motor and the tracking reference speed.

Adaptive Backstepping Controller is Presented in Fig. 1: The structure of adaptive backstepping controller for speed of PMSM, based on FOC and is shown in [6]. The position control of rotor according to tracking the reference position with the least error is the first priority of the controller. In the backstepping technique, it is transformed from the position tracking problem to the problem of tracking error. The position error is defined $e_\theta = \theta - \theta_r$, hence, its derivative is shown

$$\dot{e}_\theta = \dot{\theta} - \dot{\theta}_r = \omega - \dot{\theta}_r \tag{12}$$

The speed rotor reference is chosen as below

$$\omega_r = \dot{\theta}_r - k_1 e_\theta \tag{13}$$

where, $k_1 > 0$ and k_1 is a constant. Replacing equation of (13) into the (12), Eq. (12) is written as:

$$\dot{e}_\theta = -k_1 e_\theta \tag{14}$$

Based on Lyapunov theory, The function is chosen as

$$L_1 = \frac{1}{2} e_\theta^2 \tag{15}$$

And take the derivative Eq. (15) as

$$\dot{L}_1 = \dot{e}_\theta . e_\theta = -k_1 e_\theta^2 \leq 0 \tag{16}$$

The speed error is defined as $e_\omega = \omega - \omega_r$, speed error derivative $\dot{e}_\omega = \dot{\omega} - \dot{\omega}_r$ is and look at the Eq. (1), replacing $\dot{\omega}$ into its derivative which it is written as

$$\dot{e}_\omega = -\frac{B}{J}.\omega - \frac{T_L}{J} + \frac{1,5.n_p.\Psi_f}{J}.i_q - \dot{\omega}_r \tag{17}$$

The Lyapunov function can be chosen as $L_2 = \frac{1}{2} e_\omega^2$, take the derivative to get

$$\dot{L}_2 = e_\omega . \left(-\frac{B}{J}.\omega - \frac{T_L}{J} + \frac{1.5 n_p \Psi_f}{J} i_q - \dot{\omega}_r \right) \tag{18}$$

In FOC scheme, assuming that the virtual control variables are i_d and i_q currents. In order to get $\dot{L}_2 \leq 0$, from (18), it should be written as

$$-k_2 e_\omega = -\frac{B}{J}.\omega - \frac{T_L}{J} + \frac{1.5 n_p \Psi_f}{J} i_q - \dot{\omega}_r \tag{19}$$

where, k_2 is a constant and $k_2 > 0$. Hence, the virtual control current variable on q-axis is chosen as

$$i_q^* = \frac{J}{1.5 n_p \Psi_f} \left(-k_2.e_\omega + \frac{T_L}{J} + \frac{B}{J}.\omega + \dot{\omega}_r \right) \tag{20}$$

Due to the PMSM drive of the EV systems, the torque of the load often changes, and it has to be estimated so that it is possible to derive. Consequenstly, these i_d and i_q currents controllers is written as

$$\begin{cases} i_d^* = 0 \\ i_q^* = \frac{J}{1.5 n_p \Psi_f} \left(-k_2 e_\omega + \frac{\hat{T}_L}{J} + \frac{B}{J}.\omega + \dot{\omega}_r \right) \end{cases} \tag{21}$$

Substituting (21) into (18), it is derived

$$\dot{L}_2 = -k_2 e_\omega^2 \le 0 \tag{22}$$

where, $k_2 > 0$, k_2 is a constant. Replacing (21) into (17), $\dot{e}_\omega$ is written as

$$\dot{e}_\omega = -k_2.e_\omega - \frac{\Delta T_L}{J} \tag{23}$$

Based on Lyapunov theory, the function of Lyapunov is designed to obtain a with the ability to attenuate the disturbance torque of the load. This Lyapunov fuction is chosen as belows equation:

$$L_3 = L_1 + L_2 + \frac{1}{2a} \left(T_L - \hat{T}_L \right)^2 \tag{24}$$

where a is the adaptive coefficient, $a > 0$. The Eq. (24) is derived as belows

$$\dot{L}_3 = -k_1 e_\theta^2 - k_2 e_\omega^2 + \Delta T_L \left(-\frac{e_\omega}{J} - \frac{\dot{\hat{T}}_L}{a} \right) \tag{25}$$

From (25), if $\dot{L}_3 \le 0$ then $\Delta T_L \left(-\frac{e_\omega}{J} - \frac{\dot{\hat{T}}_L}{a} \right) = 0 \implies -\frac{e_\omega}{J} - \frac{\dot{\hat{T}}_L}{a} = 0$
Therefore, the load torque is estimated as

$$\dot{\hat{T}}_L = -\frac{a.e_\omega}{J} \tag{26}$$

Sliding Mode Controller: The problem that is always exists in SMC is chattering problem. In order to reduce chattering, the surface of SMC and the reaching law have to be chosen a suitable. In this paper, the reaching law is chosen as the exponential reaching law (EL), as a result, the dynamic response of system moves quickly to the switching surface. This exponential reaching law is designed as

$$\dot{s} = - \left(1 - \frac{1}{e^{\lambda s} + 1} \right) - \delta s \tag{27}$$

The currents error on the dq−axis are defined as $\tilde{i}_d = i_d - i_d^*, \tilde{i}_q = i_q - i_q^*$. The Base on the currents error on dq−axis, the surfaces of SMC s_1 and s_2 are designed, respectively

$$s_1 = \gamma_1 \tilde{i}_q = \gamma_1 \left(i_q - i_q^* \right) \tag{28}$$

$$s_2 = \gamma_2 \tilde{i}_d = \gamma_2 \left(i_d - i_d^* \right) \tag{29}$$

where, γ_1 and γ_2 are constant, and $\gamma_1 > 0$, $\gamma_2 > 0$. The ELs are written as

$$\dot{s}_1 = - \left(1 - \frac{1}{e^{\lambda_1 s_1} + 1} \right) - \delta_1 s_1 \tag{30}$$

$$\dot{s}_2 = - \left(1 - \frac{1}{e^{\lambda_2 s_2} + 1} \right) - \delta_2 s_2 \tag{31}$$

where, $\lambda_1, \lambda_2, \delta_1, \delta_2$ are constant, $\gamma_1, \gamma_2 > 0$; and $\delta_1, \delta_2 > 0$.

From (1) and the derivative of (28), it is written as

$$\dot{s}_1 = \gamma_1 \left(\dot{i}_q - \dot{i}_q^* \right) = \gamma_1 \left(-n_p \omega i_d - \frac{R_s}{L_d} i_q - n_p \frac{\Psi_f}{L_q} \omega + \frac{1}{L_q} u_q - \dot{i}_q^* \right) \tag{32}$$

Based on the derivative of (28) equal (30),

$$\dot{s}_1 = - \left(1 - \frac{1}{e^{\lambda_1 s_1} + 1} \right) - \delta_1 s_1 = \gamma_1 \left(\dot{i}_q - \dot{i}_q^* \right)$$

$$\Longleftrightarrow \dot{i}_q = \frac{- \left(1 - \frac{1}{e^{\lambda_1 s_1} + 1} \right) - \delta_1 s_1}{\gamma_1} + \dot{i}_q^* \tag{33}$$

Similarly, the current on q-axis is also obtained

$$\dot{i}_d = \frac{- \left(1 - \frac{1}{e^{\lambda_2 s_2} + 1} \right) - \delta_2 s_2}{\gamma_2} + \dot{i}_d^* \tag{34}$$

Replacing (33) into (1), the control input u_q is achieved

$$u_q = L_q \left(\frac{- \left(1 - \frac{1}{e^{\lambda_1 s_1} + 1} \right) - \delta_1 s_1}{\gamma_1} + \dot{i}_q^* \right) + n_p \omega i_d L_q + R_s i_q + n_p \Psi_f \omega \tag{35}$$

And the control input u_d is achieved as

$$u_d = L_d \left(\frac{- \left(1 - \frac{1}{e^{\lambda_2 s_2} + 1} \right) - \delta_2 s_2}{\gamma_2} + \dot{i}_d^* \right) - \frac{R_s}{L_d} i_d - n_p \omega i_q \tag{36}$$

System Stability Analysis: Lyapunov function is defined (1) below

$$L = \frac{1}{2}s^T I s + \frac{1}{2}e_\theta^2 + \frac{1}{2}e_\omega^2 + \frac{1}{2a}\left(T_L - \hat{T}_L\right)^2 \tag{37}$$

The derivative of (37), it is obtained

$$\dot{L} = -\left(1 - \frac{1}{e^{\lambda_1 s_1} + 1}\right)s_1 - \delta_1 s_1^2 - \left(1 - \frac{1}{e^{\lambda_2 s_2} + 1}\right)s_2 - \delta_2 s_2^2 - k_2 e_\theta^2 - k_1 e_\omega^2 \tag{38}$$

with $\left(1 - \frac{1}{e^{\lambda_i s_i} + 1}\right)s_i \geq 0$, if the system is a steady-state, then there are $e_\theta = e_\omega = 0$, $s_1 = s_2 = 0$, $\dot{L} = 0$. Therefore, $L \leq 0$. Due to L is positive definite (38), and the PMSM drives system is a stable base on Lyapunov theory.

3.2   Design Controller for the DCV (DC Side Controller Design)

In the PMSM drive system, it contains DC-link voltage (DCV) control (DC side). When the DC input battery pack voltage (DIV) and the load torque of electric vehicle will be change continously depends on time, then the DCV (V_{dc}) can be controlled to stabilize the system. Although the DIV changes but the DCV is still kept stable when the DCV controller supplying the inverter is not short-circuited and the PMSM drive system works well.

In the BQ-ZSI system, there are two phases call ST and NST, with the DCV of BQ-ZSI is a square waveform [13]. During the NST, the DCV equals peak value of DCV $\left(\hat{V}_{dc}\right)$ and it equals zero in ST. Hence, the DCV can not be controlled directly but it has to be controlled by regulating total of two capacitors voltages [14]. From (4) and (5)the peak of DCV equals the capacitor voltage C_1 plus the capacitor voltage C_2 in BQZSI, it is uesd as the signal feedback of DCV in drive motor system Fig. 2 on page 3. Therefore, in this paper, the DCV voltage is controlled by controlling the total voltage across the two capacitors of the BQZSI as shown in Fig. 4 on page 12.

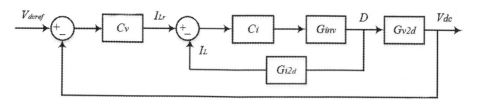

Fig. 4. Control block diagram of DC-link voltage loop.

In order to control the peak DCV voltage, transfer function of $G_{i2d}(s)$, $G_{inv}(s)$, $G_{v2d}(s)$are calculated base on (8), (9),(10), (11) where the parameters are used in 1. Using sisotool of Matlab, the first, PI controllers C_i is designed with frequency-response approach so that I_{L_r} tracking I_L. After that, C_v is also designed with frequency-response as Fig. 5 on page 13. As result, these k_{p_i}, k_{i_i} of C_i and k_{p_v}, k_{i_v} of C_v are identified and updated into the system PMSM and simulated on Matlab software.

$$\begin{cases} C_i\left(s\right) = K_{p_i} + \frac{K_{i_i}}{s} \\ C_v\left(s\right) = K_{p_v} + \frac{K_{i_v}}{s} \end{cases} \tag{39}$$

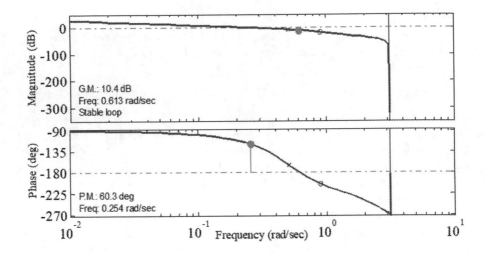

Fig. 5. Bode after designing PI controller for DCV.

4   Simulation

4.1   Simulation Result of PMSM

This simulation shows the motor speed response tracking reference motor speed under variations of the load torque and the DIV when applying backstepping control (SA) strategy with the parameters as in Table 2 [15].

Figure 6 page 14 presents the electromagnetic torque (T_e) which it tracks to the load torque (T_L). The SA strategy have a less ripple of the electromagnetic torque in comparision with the PI method. It also shows that the torque of load is continuous change at times t = 2 s, 4 s, the speed response of PMSM SA (red-line) are presented in Fig. 7 page 14 is able to achieve a better result than the motor speed response of PI controller (blue-line). In the simulation, the PMSM is started in unload operating mode, it shows that the speed of the PMSM is able to track the reference speed in a quickly manner.

At times t = 2 s, the nominal load torque suddenly increases from zero to 1.27 N.m as given in Fig. 6 on page 14, the speed response strategies as: SA

Table 2. Nominal Parameters of PMSM drives.

Parameters ($Units$)	Symbols	Values
Rated Power (W)	P_n	400
Rated Voltage (V)	U_n	200
Rated Speed (rpm)	c	3000
Rate Torque ($N.m$)	T_L	1.27
Permanent Magnet Flux (Wb)	Ψ_f	0.0615
Nominal Stator Resistance (Ω)	R_s	2.7
Nominal Stator Inductance (mH)	L_d, L_q	8.5
Moment of Inertia ($kg.m^2$)	J	$31.69 \times 10 - 6$
Viscous Friction Coefficient ($N.m.srad$)	B	$52.79 \times 10 - 6$
Pole Pair ($pair$)	n_p	4
The coefficient of adaptive backstepping	K_1	0.5
The coefficient of adaptive backstepping	K_2	40
The adaptive gain	a	0.001
The coefficient of SMC	γ_1	50
The coefficient of SMC	γ_2	50
The coefficient of SMC	λ_1	5
The coefficient of SMC	λ_2	5
The coefficient of SMC	δ_1	3000
The coefficient of SMC	δ_2	2000

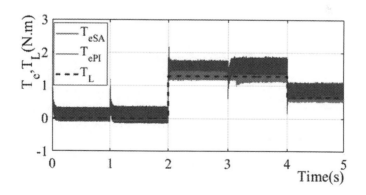

Fig. 6. Electromagnetic torque T_e and load torque T_L with PI, SA.

and PI that drops to 693 rmp and 638 rpm then are corrected back to speed reference value ($\approx$700 rmp) after 0.2 s. Results showed that the SA has the lower than speed reduction compared to the PI controller and tracking error of the SA is also lower than the PI controller as Fig. 8 on page 15. Similar analysis, at times t = 4 s, the nominal load torque suddenly decreases from 1.27 to 1.27/2 N.m, as

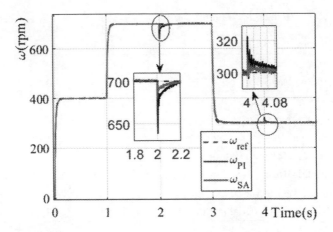

Fig. 7. Speed response with PI, SA.

given in Fig. 6 on page 14, the motor speed response with the different strategies as: SA and PI that rises up to 302 rmp, 311 rmp and 323 rpm then it comes back to speed reference value ($\approx$300 rmp) after 4.1 s. Results also shows that the SA has the speed rise of the motor lower than the speed rise of the motor under PI controller as Fig. 8 on page 15.

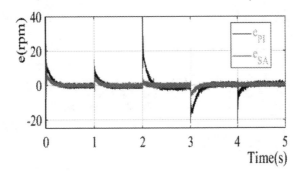

Fig. 8. Tracking errors using PI and SA controllers.

In the period, from t = 0 s to t = 1 s, the normal load torque is 0 N.m, the control voltage on d−axis, $u_d \approx 0$, i_d tracking zeros as shown in Fig. 9 on page 16. The control voltage on q−axis ($0 < u_q < 1$) also changes to variation of the load torque and the motor speed in the PMSM drive system. Simulation results show that under normal operating modes as: the load torque and speed control variation, using the SA method gives smaller tracking error as compared to the PI controller Fig. 9 on page 16.

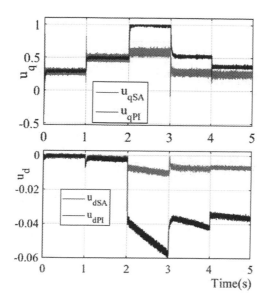

Fig. 9. The voltage control u_d, u_q with SA, PI controllers.

4.2   Simulation Result of BQ-ZSI

The DC-input voltage DIV (V_{in}) can be used for fuel cells or batteries. These sources are used as the supply voltage source for the BQ-ZSI and the PMSM applications for electric vehicles. Therefore, the purpose of DCV control is: to boost the DCV and keep it stable when the V_{in}, load torque and speed motor changes, to avoid overmodulation in the BQ-ZSI, thereby reducing harmonic of voltage and current, which ultimately improve the system performance.

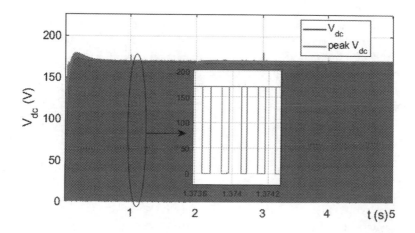

Fig. 10. a) The DC-link voltage V_{dc}. (Color figure online)

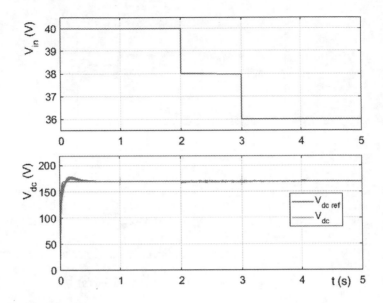

Fig. 11. a) V_{in} decreases by 5% after 1 s and continuously decreases by 5% after 2 s b) The response of the peakV_{dc} tracking V_{dcref} when the V_{in} and load torque change. (Color figure online)

Because the DCV is a square waveform is shown Fig. 10 on page 16, the DCV can not be controlled directly It must be controlled by regulating two capacitors voltages. Zoon "+" this waveform in Fig. 10 on page 16, from 1.3738 s to 1.3742, the DCV (blue line) is square waveform and the peak DCV equals total capacitor voltage on C_1 and C_2 of BQ-ZSI. That result is correct to Eq. (5).

From t = 0 s to t = 2 s, V_{in} has a value (40 V), at t = 2 s to 3 s, the V_{in} suddenly drops 5% (38 V). Continuously at t = 3 s to 5 s, the V_{in} also decreases by 5% (36 V) as shown in Fig. 11 on page 17 a). The DCV's required voltage is 170V as shown in Fig. 11 on page 17b) (red line), the BQ-ZSI unit is the booster, the voltage is raised from 40 V to 17 0V and stabilized at 170 V as shown Fig. 11 on page 17b) (blue line). If the input voltage changes, the DCV voltage remains stable at 170 V by the DCV controller. With this controller, the DCV track to the reference very well under the input voltage changes. And, this voltage is raised more than four times and is kept stable with variation of the input voltage, the speed motor and the load torque of the PMSM drive system.

5   Conclusion

In summary, this paper presents a comparison and evaluations of the different control strategies such as SA and PI for the speed control of PMSM. The SA enhances control quality of PMSM drive system, by compensating for the errors of the PI motor speed controller. Under normal operating conditions as load torque, speed control and input voltage variation, applying the SA tracking method resulted in smaller errors compared to PI controllers. Besides, this study proposes a control method to stabilize the voltage of DCV in BQ-ZSI by controlling total two capacitor voltages in BQ-ZSI which yields an improvement to the system performance. These results have been verified carefully in simulation on the Matlab software.

Acknowledgment. The authors would like to thank the Vietnam Aviation Academy for Science and Technology Development for the support in 2022/2023.

References

1. Laoufi, C., Sadoune, Z., Abbou, A., Akherraz, M.: New model of electric traction drive based sliding mode controller in field oriented control of induction motor fed by multilevel inverter. Int. J. Power Electron. Drive Syst. (IJPEDS) **11**(1), 242–250 (2020)
2. Aghili, F.: Optimal feedback linearization control of interior PM synchronous motors subject to timevarying operation conditions minimizing power loss. IEEE Trans. Ind. Electron. **65**(7), 5414–5421 (2018)
3. Qu, L., Qiao, W., Qu, L.: An enhanced linear active disturbance rejection rotor position sensorless control for permanent magnet synchronous motors. IEEE Trans. Power Electron. **35**(6), 6175–6184 (2020)
4. Sun, Y., Preindl, M., Sirouspour, S., Emadi, A.: Unified wide-speed sensorless scheme using nonlinear optimization for IP-MSM drives. IEEE Trans. Power Electron. **32**(8), 6308–6322 (2017)
5. Massaq, Z., Abounada, A., Ramzi, M.: Robust non-linear control of a hybrid water pumping system based on in-duction motor. Int. J. Power Electron. Drive Syst. (IJPEDS) **11**(4), 1995–2006 (2020)
6. Tan, L.N., Pham, T.C.: Optimal tracking control for PMSM With partially unknown dynamics, saturation voltages, torque, and voltage disturbances. IEEE Trans. Ind. Electron. **69**(4), 3481–3491 (2022). https://doi.org/10.1109/TIE.2021.3075892
7. Bose, B.K.: Modern Power Electronics and AC Drives. Prentice-Hall, Upper Saddle River (2002)
8. Shen, A.W., Pham, C.T., Dzung, P.Q., Anh, N.B., Viet, L.H.: Using fuzzy logic self-tuning pi controller in z-source inverter for hybrid electric vehicles. In: 2012 World Conference on Science and Engineering, Hong Kong, China (2012)
9. Nguyen, T.N.A., Pham, D.C., Pham, C.T., Thanh, N.H.C.: D-axis stator current control methods applied to PMSG-based wind energy systems: a comparative study. WSEAS Trans. Syst. Control **14**, 239–239 (2019)
10. Wang, R., Jia, X., Dong, S., Zhang, Q.: PMSM driving system design for electric vehicle applications based on bi-directional quasi-Z-source inverter. In: 2018 13th IEEE Conference on Industrial Electronics and Applications (ICIEA) (2018)
11. Peng, F.Z.: Z-source inverter. IEEE Trans. Ind. Appl. **39**(2), 504–510 (2003)
12. Guo, F., Fu, L., Lin, C.H., et al.: Development of an 85-kW bidirectional quasi-Z-source inverter with DC-link feed-forward compensation for electric vehicle applications. IEEE Trans. Power Electron. **28**(12), 5477–5488 (2013)

13. Cong-Thanh, P., Anwen, S., Phan Quoc, D., Nguyen Bao, A., Nguyen Xuan, P.: A comparison of control methods for Z-source inverter. J. Energy Power Eng. **04**(04), 187–195 (2012)
14. Thanh, P.C., Wen, S.A.: A comparative study of control methods for induction motor and high performance Z-source inverter. TELKOMNIKA Ind. J. Electr. Eng. **11**(6), 2912–2925 (2013)
15. Tan, L.N., Cong, T.P., Cong, D.P.: Neural network observers and sensorless robust optimal control for partially unknown PMSM with disturbances and saturating voltages. IEEE Trans. Power Electron. **36**(10), 12045–12056 (2021)

Neural Networks with Variational Quantum Circuits

Syed Muhammad Abuzar Rizvi, Muhammad Shohibul Ulum, Naema Asif,
and Hyundong Shin[✉]

Department of Electronics and Information Convergence Engineering,
Kyung Hee University, Yongin 17104, Republic of Korea
hshin@khu.ac.kr

Abstract. The field of machine learning is an interdisciplinary area
that aims to extract useful information from data through mathematical
means. Integrating quantum computing with machine learning has led to
exciting new avenues of research, where quantum mechanics principles
are applied to enhance and optimize classical machine learning algorithms. In this study, we explore hybrid quantum-classical neural networks with an approach that combines both classical and quantum computing. We achieve this by implementing a variational quantum circuit
as the output layer of a classical convolutional neural network. We use
this hybrid neural network to classify images of digits from the MNIST
dataset. Using this approach, we were able to classify images with high
accuracy. Furthermore, due to its flexibility, this hybrid algorithm can
be adapted to explore the potential of quantum computing especially in
the era of noisy intermediate-scale quantum devices.

Keywords: Quantum Computing · Variational Quantum Circuits ·
Neural Networks · Image Classification

1 Introduction

Machine learning (ML) has become a fundamental aspect of modern computing,
enabling computers to learn from data and make predictions or decisions based
on that knowledge. ML algorithms have applications in various fields, including
computer vision, natural language processing, speech recognition, recommenda-
tion systems, and quantum science, among others [11,23]. However, the growing
complexity of modern data sets has made it increasingly challenging to develop

This work was supported by the National Research Foundation of Korea (NRF)
grant funded by the Korea government (MSIT) (NRF-2019R1A2C2007037, NRF-
2022R1A4A3033401) and by the MSIT (Ministry of Science and ICT), Korea, under
the ITRC (Information Technology Research Center) support program (IITP-2023-
2021-0-02046) supervised by the IITP (Institute for Information & Communications
Technology Planning & Evaluation). This research is partially funded by the BK21
FOUR program of National Research Foundation of Korea.

© ICST Institute for Computer Sciences, Social Informatics and Telecommunications Engineering 2023
Published by Springer Nature Switzerland AG 2023. All Rights Reserved
N.-S. Vo and H.-A. Tran (Eds.): INISCOM 2023, LNICST 531, pp. 203–214, 2023.
https://doi.org/10.1007/978-3-031-47359-3_15

accurate and efficient ML models using classical computing techniques. Quantum machine learning (QML) is a rapidly emerging field that seeks to address some of the limitations of classical ML by harnessing the power of quantum computing. [6,7,25]. Quantum computing is a paradigm of computing that exploits the principles of quantum mechanics to perform certain calculations much faster than classical computers [8,17]. By combining the two fields, quantum-enhanced ML promises to develop more accurate and efficient ML models that can process larger data sets and solve more complex problems [10]. Moreover, quantum computers have the ability to extract intricate features from datasets that might not be possible to do with classical computers [9]. This makes QML a promising tool for drug discovery, optimization, and other areas of science and engineering [2].

Despite its potential, QML is still in its infancy, and many challenges must be overcome to develop practical QML algorithms and hardware. One of the most significant challenges is developing a fault-tolerant quantum computer. The current hardware of quantum computers falls under the category of noisy intermediate-scale quantum (NISQ), where we have a few hundred noisy qubits. As a result, running complex quantum algorithms on NISQ devices can be challenging [20]. Another challenge is developing efficient algorithms that can take advantage of the limited qubit resources of current quantum computers. Hence, researchers are trying to figure out algorithms suitable for NISQ devices [3].

In this paper, we implement a hybrid ML model that combines the classical ML model and variational quantum circuit (VQC). VQCs are parameterized quantum circuits that can learn parameters based on optimization methods and are helpful for many applications, including ML [16]. We applied this model to the MNIST dataset, which consists of numerical digits from 0 to 9. The model consists of a classical convolutional neural network (CNN) model combined with a VQC in the final layer that will be used for the prediction. The parameters of the quantum circuit are trained in a similar way to the weights in a classical model. This approach enabled us to effectively train the model as well as classify images with high accuracy. Furthermore, this hybrid model requires only a few qubits and shallow circuit depths, making it suitable for NISQ hardware. This hybrid model can serve as a basis for future QML applications and research.

2   Preliminary

2.1   Quantum Computing

In traditional classical computing, information is processed and stored as bits, which are either 0 or 1. These bits are used to represent information in the form of digital signals that are processed by classical computers. However, in quantum computing, the basic unit of information is the qubit (quantum bit), which is a two-state quantum-mechanical system that can exist in a superposition of both 0 and 1 states simultaneously [17]. A qubit can be represented by a vector in two-dimensional complex Hilbert space $\mathbf{C}^2$, and its superposition form can be written as

$$|\psi\rangle = \alpha|0\rangle + \beta|1\rangle, \tag{1}$$

where $|0\rangle = [1 \ 0]^T$ and $|1\rangle = [0 \ 1]^T$ which represents the orthonormal basis for $\mathbf{C}^2$ known as the computational basis and $\alpha, \beta \in \mathbf{C}$ are the probability amplitudes obeying $|\alpha|^2 + |\beta|^2 = 1$.

A quantum gate is a fundamental operation that can be performed on a quantum system, such as a qubit, in quantum computing. These gates are denoted by a unitary operator $\mathbf{U}$ in the Hilbert space. They serve as the quantum equivalent of classical logic gates in traditional computing and enable manipulation of the qubit's state. The Pauli gates (X, Y, and Z) and the Hadamard gate are examples of single qubit quantum gates. A Hadamard gate transforms the qubit to a superposition state that is equally likely to be either 0 or 1. The Hadamard operation can be represented with matrix notation as

$$\mathbf{H} = \frac{1}{\sqrt{2}} \begin{bmatrix} 1 & 1 \\ 1 & -1 \end{bmatrix}. \tag{2}$$

Another type of single qubit quantum gates are the quantum rotation gates, which rotates the qubit state around the X, Y, and Z axes. These gates are typically represented by unitary matrices and are defined by a rotation angle. There are three common type of rotation gates namely $\mathbf{R_x}(\theta)$, $\mathbf{R_y}(\theta)$, and $\mathbf{R_z}(\theta)$ that are given in computational basis by

$$\mathbf{R_x}(\theta) = \begin{bmatrix} \cos\frac{\theta}{2} & -\iota\sin\frac{\theta}{2} \\ -\iota\sin\frac{\theta}{2} & \cos\frac{\theta}{2} \end{bmatrix}, \ \mathbf{R_y}(\theta) = \begin{bmatrix} \cos\frac{\theta}{2} & -\sin\frac{\theta}{2} \\ \sin\frac{\theta}{2} & \cos\frac{\theta}{2} \end{bmatrix}, \ \mathbf{R_z}(\theta) = \begin{bmatrix} e^{-\iota\frac{\theta}{2}} & 0 \\ 0 & e^{\iota\frac{\theta}{2}} \end{bmatrix}. \tag{3}$$

To achieve a comprehensive set of gates for quantum computation, it is essential to include two-qubit gates. The Controlled NOT (CNOT) gate is one of the most commonly used two-qubit gates, which flips the state of the target qubit if the control qubit is in the state $|1\rangle$ and leaves it unchanged if the control qubit is in the state $|0\rangle$. The CNOT gate is represented in the computational basis as follows

$$\mathbf{C_x} = \begin{bmatrix} 1 & 0 & 0 & 0 \\ 0 & 1 & 0 & 0 \\ 0 & 0 & 0 & 1 \\ 0 & 0 & 1 & 0 \end{bmatrix}. \tag{4}$$

Once the information in the qubits has been processed by quantum gates, the result of the computation must be obtained through quantum measurement. Quantum measurement is achieved by projecting the quantum state onto the basis of the Hilbert space. In the case of a single qubit using the computational basis, the measurement operators $\mathbf{M_0} = |0\rangle\langle 0|$ and $\mathbf{M_1} = |1\rangle\langle 1|$ correspond to measurement outcomes 0 and 1 respectively.

2.2 Variational Quantum Circuits (VQCs)

There are many quantum circuits that can implement various quantum algorithms. One class is the VQCs that are used for optimizing the parameters of a quantum algorithm to obtain a specific output [4]. In a VQC, the quantum gates used in the circuit are parameterized, meaning that the values of the gate parameters can be adjusted to obtain a desired output. The circuit is initialized in a specific quantum state, and the parameters of the circuit are iteratively updated using a classical optimization algorithm until the desired output is obtained. An example of VQC is shown in Fig. 1. VQCs are particularly useful in situations where the exact solution to a problem is difficult to obtain using classical methods. By optimizing the parameters of the quantum circuit, the output of the circuit can be used as an approximation to the exact solution. VQCs have been demonstrated to be capable of solving problems in quantum chemistry, optimization, and ML with a level of accuracy that surpasses classical methods in certain cases [5, 16, 26].

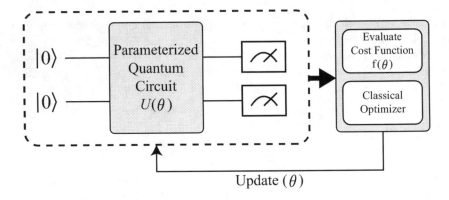

Fig. 1. A variational quantum circuit.

2.3   Neural Networks

A neural network is a type of ML technique that employs layers of interconnected nodes or neurons to process data [29]. Each neuron has an associated weight and threshold and is connected to other neurons. When the output of any neuron exceeds the specified threshold, the neuron is activated by an activation function, and the data is passed to the next layer. Otherwise, no data is transmitted to the next layer of the network. Through a kind of machine perception, the neural network can label or cluster raw input data. These networks learn similarly to the human brain by analyzing labeled or unlabeled training examples [1].

During the training process of a neural network, the weights are initialized randomly. Following this, forward propagation takes place where the input data is fed into the neural network, and the activation of neurons in each layer is computed using the current weights and biases. The neural network's loss is then determined by measuring the error between the predicted and actual labels. To update the weights and biases in the neural network, we employ backward propagation to compute the gradient of the loss function. The gradient is then used to adjust the weights and biases in the opposite direction, aiming to minimize the loss function. Finally, the weights and biases in the neural network are updated using an optimization algorithm such as Adam or gradient descent in the parameter update rule. This process is repeated until the neural network has converged and the loss function has reached its minimum. Once the neural network is trained, its performance on unseen data is evaluated through a test set. With the advent of deep learning, neural networks have emerged as a powerful technology in recent years, finding numerous applications across different domains. For instance, they are used in image and speech recognition, as well as natural language processing (NLP) [18, 22, 27].

In image processing, CNNs are very popular [14]. They use specialized layers such as convolutional, pooling, activation, batch normalization, dropout, and fully connected layers. The convolutional layer performs convolution operations on the input image to extract features. The pooling layer reduces the spatial dimensions of the input by downsampling, typically using max or average pooling. The activation layer applies a non-linear activation function such as ReLU to introduce non-linearity into the network. The batch normalization layer normalizes the input data to speed up training and improve model stability. The dropout layer randomly drops out units from the network during training to reduce overfitting. The fully connected layer performs classification or regression on the output of the preceding layers. By stacking these layers together, CNNs can learn hierarchical representations of the input data and make predictions based on them.

3   Methods

We used a hybrid quantum-classical model which enables the use of quantum computers along with classical computers. This approach allows us to use a small number of qubits and circuit depth by outsourcing some computation to classical computers. On the classical side, we used CNN to process the input image and provide meaningful features [12, 13]. On the quantum side, we used VQC to process the extracted features and classify the given image into the correct label [15]. We used Hadamard, parameterized rotation, and CNOT gates for our VQC. After the VQC computation, we measured the quantum state and used the measurement outcomes to predict the input images. From the loss function, we used the backward propagation algorithm to update the parameters in the VQC as well as the weights in CNN. To process classical data with a quantum circuit, we need to first encode the data from a classical one into a quantum domain. This encoding enables the mapping of the classical data into high-dimensional Hilbert space with a nonlinear mapping. In this high-dimensional Hilbert space, the quantum operation is performed to move the data position, enabling easier classification compared to lower dimensional space. There are several ways to realize this encoding process, such as basis encoding, Hamiltonian encoding, and angle encoding [24]. We used angle encoding as the classical data can be easily used as angles in rotation gates.

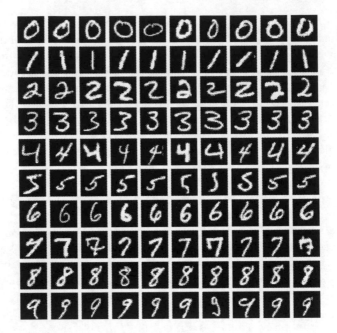

Fig. 2. Images from MNIST dataset.

We used MNIST handwritten digits dataset to train and test our hybrid model shown in Fig. 2. The dataset has images of digits from 0–9, resulting in a 10-classes classification problem. We used 5000 images from MNIST dataset where the images are divided with a ratio of 8:2 into training and testing datasets. The training dataset is divided again with the same ratio into training and validation datasets. The size of the input image is 28 × 28 pixels with a single channel. These input images are fed into the CNN that act as a feature extractor which is followed by the VQC as the predictor. Block diagram of the hybrid model is shown in Fig. 3.

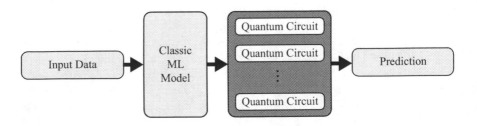

Fig. 3. Hybrid quantum-classical ML model.

For the hybrid model, we first used a convolutional layer with 5 × 5 kernel size and 16 filters followed by a max-pooling layer with strides of 2 on its output.

Then, we used a convolutional layer with the same kernel size and 32 filters. The next convolutional layer used 3×3 kernel size with 64 filters and followed by a max-pooling layer with strides of 2. Then, a two-dimensional dropout layer is applied. The output is flattened and fed to the fully connected layer having 128 neurons. The convolutional and fully connected layers used the ReLU activation function. The CNN model architecture is summarized in Fig. 4. Then, we again used a fully connected layer with $10 \times n_p$ where n_p is the number of parameters used in the quantum circuit. This output of the fully connected layers is fed to the quantum circuit.

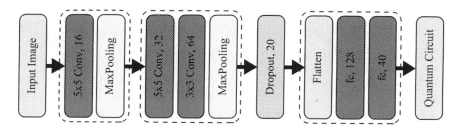

Fig. 4. CNN model architecture.

For our VQC, we used a 3 qubits quantum circuit and 4 parameters. We initialized the circuit with an equal superposition state by means of Hadamard gates. This Hadamard operation can be represented with matrix notation as,

$$(\mathbf{H}|0\rangle)^{\otimes n} = \frac{1}{\sqrt{2^n}} \sum_{i=0}^{2^n-1} |i\rangle, \tag{5}$$

where n is the number of qubits. Then, a parameterized rotation around Z axis is applied to every qubit which can be represented as,

$$\bigotimes_{i=1}^{n} \mathbf{R_z}(\phi_i), \tag{6}$$

where n is the number of qubits. We applied an entangling gate, CNOT gate, between qubit 3 and 2. The circuit is followed by a parameterized rotation around the Z axis on qubit 2 and a CNOT gate between qubit 2 and 1. We then applied Hadamard gate to qubit 1. Our final unitary gate can be represented as

$$\mathbf{U}(\phi) = (\mathbf{H} \otimes \mathbf{I} \otimes \mathbf{I})(\mathbf{C_x}^{(2)} \otimes \mathbf{I})(\mathbf{I} \otimes \mathbf{R_z}(\phi_4) \otimes \mathbf{I})(\mathbf{I} \otimes \mathbf{C_x}^{(3)}) \bigotimes_{i=1}^{3} \mathbf{R_z}(\phi_i)\mathbf{H}, \tag{7}$$

where we used $\mathbf{C_x}^{(k)}$ to denote the CNOT gate with qubit k as the control qubit and $\mathbf{I}$ denotes the identity matrix. Finally, we measured the first qubit using the computational basis, which can result in outcomes 0 and 1 with probability,

$$p(i) = \langle \psi(\phi)|\mathbf{M}_i \otimes \mathbf{I} \otimes \mathbf{I}|\psi(\phi)\rangle, \tag{8}$$

where $|\psi(\phi)\rangle = \mathbf{U}(\phi)|0\rangle^{\otimes 3}$ and $i = \{0, 1\}$. We then classified the input image based on the measurement outcome. Our VQC is shown in Fig. 5.

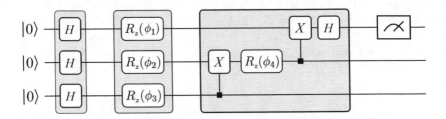

Fig. 5. VQC of our hybrid quantum-classical neural network.

We used 10 such quantum circuits where each quantum circuit corresponds to each class. In general, quantum circuits have the ability to learn complex features which might not be possible classically [9]. We took the probability of getting outcome 0 for each quantum circuit and predicted that the input image is in class p if the p-th quantum circuit has the maximum probability among all the circuits. The quantum circuit is trained using gradient that is computed using the parameter-shift rule [28]. For each parameter in the quantum circuit, we can calculate the gradient as,

$$\partial_{\phi_i} \mathbf{U}(\phi) = \mathbf{U}(\phi + \epsilon \cdot \mathbf{e_i}) - \mathbf{U}(\phi - \epsilon \cdot \mathbf{e_i}), \tag{9}$$

where ϵ is the shift of the parameter and $\mathbf{e_i}$ is the i-th column of $n_p \times n_p$ identity matrix.

We implemented the quantum circuit using Qiskit 0.38.0 with 'qasm simulator'. Qiskit is an open-source software development kit for quantum computers [21]. We used PyTorch 1.12.1 to apply the CNN model. We trained the model for 20 epochs and using cross-entropy as the loss function. The optimizer was set as Adam with a learning rate of 0.001. We used 1000 shots for the quantum measurement and set $\epsilon = \pi/2$ for the parameter-shift rule.

4   Results

To evaluate the performance of the hybrid model, we calculated the precision, recall, F1-score, and accuracy of the model, which are the commonly used performance metrics [19]. These performance metrics are defined as

$$\text{precision} = \frac{t_p}{t_p + f_p}, \tag{10}$$

$$\text{recall} = \frac{t_p}{t_p + f_n}, \tag{11}$$

$$\text{F1} - \text{score} = 2\frac{\text{precision} \cdot \text{recall}}{\text{precision} + \text{recall}}, \tag{12}$$

$$\text{accuracy} = \frac{t_p + t_n}{t_p + t_n + f_p + f_n}, \tag{13}$$

where t_p, t_n, f_p, and f_n are the number of true positive, true negative, false positive, and false negative cases, respectively. The results are shown in Table 1. We can see that the model performed well in all the categories with an average accuracy of 97%. The validation loss and accuracy plot can be seen in Fig. 6, where the model converges as the number of epochs increase.

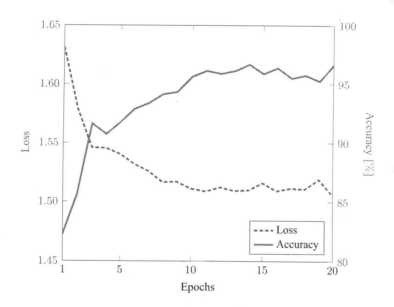

Fig. 6. The validation loss and accuracy of the model are plotted as a function of epochs.

We also provided the confusion matrix on the test dataset in Fig. 7 where we can see that the hybrid model can predict the actual digits of the test dataset images with at least 95% correct prediction. These results showed that quantum and classical computers could be trained together to perform machine learning tasks. Specifically, the VQC can play a role as a predictor in image classification task with good performance with the help of CNN as the feature extractor.

Table 1. Classification report of our hybrid model on MNIST dataset.

Digit	Precision	Recall	F1-score
0	0.99	0.98	0.98
1	0.99	0.98	0.99
2	0.97	0.96	0.96
3	0.98	0.95	0.97
4	0.96	0.96	0.96
5	0.99	0.99	0.99
6	0.99	1.00	0.99
7	0.98	0.98	0.98
8	0.98	0.98	0.98
9	0.91	0.95	0.93
Accuracy	N/A	N/A	0.97
Macro Avg	0.97	0.97	0.97

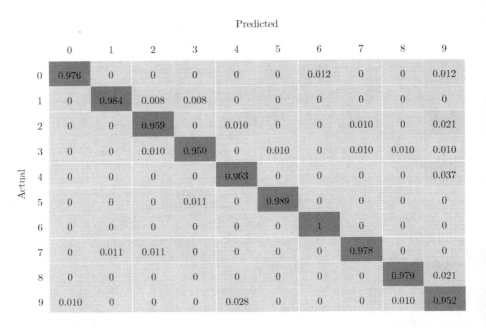

Fig. 7. Confusion matrix of hybrid model on test dataset.

5   Conclusion

QML is an interdisciplinary field that combines quantum physics and machine learning algorithms to solve complex problems more efficiently. In this study, we demonstrated a hybrid approach that utilizes a conventional CNN model with a VQC for image classification with good accuracy. This approach paves the way for quantum-enhanced machine learning, which aims to leverage quantum mechanical effects to enhance machine learning performance. Additionally, this hybrid VQC and QML algorithm can be adapted to the limitations of NISQ devices by adjusting circuit parameters, such as depth and number of qubits. This flexibility allows researchers to explore the potential of hybrid algorithms, even in the face of hardware limitations.

References

1. Abiodun, O.I., Jantan, A., Omolara, A.E., Dada, K.V., Mohamed, N.A., Arshad, H.: State-of-the-art in artificial neural network applications: a survey. Heliyon **4**(11), e00938 (2018)
2. Biamonte, J., Wittek, P., Pancotti, N., Rebentrost, P., Wiebe, N., Lloyd, S.: Quantum machine learning. Nature **549**(7671), 195–202 (2017)
3. Boixo, S., et al.: Characterizing quantum supremacy in near-term devices. Nat. Phys. **14**(6), 595–600 (2018)
4. Cerezo, M., et al.: Variational quantum algorithms. Nat. Rev. Phys. **3**(9), 625–644 (2021)
5. Chen, S.Y.C., Yang, C.H.H., Qi, J., Chen, P.Y., Ma, X., Goan, H.S.: Variational quantum circuits for deep reinforcement learning. IEEE Access **8**, 141007–141024 (2020)
6. Dunjko, V., Briegel, H.J.: Machine learning & artificial intelligence in the quantum domain: a review of recent progress. Rep. Prog. Phys. **81**(7), 074001 (2018)
7. Duong, T.Q., Ansere, J.A., Narottama, B., Sharma, V., Dobre, O.A., Shin, H.: Quantum-inspired machine learning for 6G: fundamentals, security, resource allocations, challenges, and future research directions. IEEE Open J. Veh. Technol. **3**, 375–387 (2022)
8. Duong, T.Q., Nguyen, L.D., Narottama, B., Ansere, J.A., Huynh, D.V., Shin, H.: Quantum-inspired real-time optimization for 6g networks: opportunities, challenges, and the road ahead. IEEE Open J. Commun. Soc. **3**, 1347–1359 (2022)
9. Havlíček, V., et al.: Supervised learning with quantum-enhanced feature spaces. Nature **567**(7747), 209–212 (2019)
10. Huang, H.Y., et al.: Power of data in quantum machine learning. Nat. Commun. **12**(1), 2631 (2021)
11. Jordan, M.I., Mitchell, T.M.: Machine learning: trends, perspectives, and prospects. Science **349**(6245), 255–260 (2015)
12. Krizhevsky, A., Sutskever, I., Hinton, G.E.: ImageNet classification with deep convolutional neural networks. In: Proceedings of the 25th International Conference on Neural Information Processing Systems, NIPS 2012, vol. 1, pp. 1097–1105. Curran Associates Inc., Red Hook (2012)
13. Lecun, Y., Bottou, L., Bengio, Y., Haffner, P.: Gradient-based learning applied to document recognition. Proc. IEEE **86**(11), 2278–2324 (1998)

14. Li, Z., Liu, F., Yang, W., Peng, S., Zhou, J.: A survey of convolutional neural networks: analysis, applications, and prospects. IEEE Trans. Neural Netw. Learn. Syst. **33**, 6999–7019 (2021)
15. McClean, J.R., Romero, J., Babbush, R., Aspuru-Guzik, A.: The theory of variational hybrid quantum-classical algorithms. New J. Phys. **18**(2), 023023 (2016)
16. Mitarai, K., Negoro, M., Kitagawa, M., Fujii, K.: Quantum circuit learning. Phys. Rev. A **98**(3), 032309 (2018)
17. Nielsen, M.A., Chuang, I.: Quantum computation and quantum information. Am. J. Phys. **70**(5), 558–559 (2002)
18. Palaz, D., Magimai-Doss, M., Collobert, R.: End-to-end acoustic modeling using convolutional neural networks for HMM-based automatic speech recognition. Speech Commun. **108**, 15–32 (2019)
19. Powers, D.M.W.: Evaluation: from precision, recall and F-measure to ROC, informedness, markedness and correlation. arXiv arXiv:2010.16061 (2018)
20. Preskill, J.: Quantum computing in the NISQ era and beyond. Quantum **2**, 79 (2018)
21. Qiskit contributors: Qiskit: an open-source framework for quantum computing (2023)
22. Qiu, X., Sun, T., Xu, Y., Shao, Y., Dai, N., Huang, X.: Pre-trained models for natural language processing: a survey. Sci. Chin. Technol. Sci. **63**(10), 1872–1897 (2020)
23. Rizvi, S.M.A., Asif, N., Ulum, M.S., Duong, T.Q., Shin, H.: Multiclass classification of metrologically resourceful tripartite quantum states with deep neural networks. Sensors **22**(18), 6767 (2022)
24. Schuld, M., Killoran, N.: Quantum machine learning in feature Hilbert spaces. Phys. Rev. Lett. **122**(6), 040504 (2019)
25. Schuld, M., Sinayskiy, I., Petruccione, F.: An introduction to quantum machine learning. Contemp. Phys. **56**(2), 172–185 (2014)
26. Tilly, J., et al.: The variational quantum eigensolver: a review of methods and best practices. Phys. Rep. **986**, 1–128 (2022)
27. Traore, B.B., Kamsu-Foguem, B., Tangara, F.: Deep convolution neural network for image recognition. Ecol. Inform. **48**, 257–268 (2018)
28. Wierichs, D., Izaac, J., Wang, C., Lin, C.Y.Y.: General parameter-shift rules for quantum gradients. Quantum **6**, 677 (2022)
29. Zou, J., Han, Y., So, S.S.: Overview of artificial neural networks. Artif. Neural Netw. Meth. Appl. **458**, 14–22 (2009)

Sudden Cardiac Arrest Detection Using Deep Learning and Principal Component Analysis

Van-Su Pham[1(✉)], Hang Duy Thi Nguyen[2], Hai-Chau Le[2], and Minh Tuan Nguyen[2]

[1] Faculty of Electronics Engineering, Posts and Telecommunications Institute of Technology, Hanoi, Vietnam
supv@ptit.edu.vn
[2] Faculty of Telecommunication, Posts and Telecommunications Institute of Technology, Hanoi, Vietnam
{duynth,chaulh,nmtuan}@ptit.edu.vn

Abstract. Sudden cardiac arrest (SCA) is mainly caused by ventricular fibrillation and ventricular tachycardia, which are known as shockable rhythms and can be effectively treated with automated external defibrillators (AED). In this study, we propose a novel algorithm with high performance for detecting SCA on electrocardiogram (ECG) signals for use in the shock advice algorithm (SAA) applied in the AED. The algorithm utilizes a combination of principal component analysis (PCA) and convolutional neural network (CNN) model, using 5-fold cross-validation (CV). The PCA algorithm transforms 20 features extracted from ECG signals into 20 component features in different spaces where they are uncorrelated. Our proposed SAA algorithm achieves an accuracy of 99.0 %, a sensitivity of 94.7%, a specificity of 99.4%, and a balanced error rate of 2.9%.

Keywords: Sudden cardiac arrest (SCA) · Principal component analysis (PCA) · Deep learning (DL) · Automated External Defibrillators (AED) · Electrocardiogram (ECG)

1 Introduction

One of the serious health concerns in the world is sudden cardiac arrest (SCA), which also is considered a vital and life-threatening condition. The event appears when the heart experiences sudden, unpredictable electrical disturbances, resulting in the interruption of the pumping of blood. The source of this disease is shockable rhythms including ventricular fibrillation (VF) and ventricular tachycardia (VT), known as the abnormal waveforms of electrocardiogram (ECG) signals [1]. The ECG signals during SCA also include other abnormalities such as a widening of the QRS complex, a decrease in the amplitude of the QRS complex, and changes in the ST segment, for which correct diagnosis is implemented

© ICST Institute for Computer Sciences, Social Informatics and Telecommunications Engineering 2023
Published by Springer Nature Switzerland AG 2023. All Rights Reserved
N.-S. Vo and H.-A. Tran (Eds.): INISCOM 2023, LNICST 531, pp. 215–224, 2023.
https://doi.org/10.1007/978-3-031-47359-3_16

for decision support related to relevant treatments. Moreover, patients, who are under the SCA without basic life-support or emergency services in minutes, certainly have a relatively high mortality. Therefore, early prediction of SCA based on ECG signals is crucial for timely intervention, such as immediate treatment with cardiopulmonary resuscitation (CPR) and defibrillation by delivering an electric shock to the heart, which results in survival improvement [2]. In addition, prompt access to emergency medical services and treatment increases the chances of survival and reduces the risk of long-term complications. Currently, automated external defibrillators (AED) are effective portable medical device, which is used for SCA diagnosis and treatment with coutershocks to restore the electrical heart system. The center of the AED is a shock advice algorithm (SAA), which is responsible for quick SCA diagnosis for further decision-making [3].

In recent years, SCA detection has been paid intensive attention from scientists, especially, performance improvement of SAA using intelligent technologies. Correct detection of the shockable or non-shockable rhythm is crucial in providing effective treatment for patients with SCA. Recent advancements in machine learning (ML) [4–6] and deep learning (DL) [7–10] techniques have exposed promising results in ECG signal processing and SCA detection. Indeed, ML and DL techniques have been proposed to improve the performance of the AEDs for the SCA diagnosis with better performance in comparison to conventional methods including thresholds according to American Heart Association (AHA) recommendations [11]. DL-based SAAs have several advantages over ML-based SAAs, such as no feature extraction, better feature selection, and complexity reduction [8]. In addition, the main advantages of DL are automatic feature learning from data and no requirement for feature engineering. This is particularly useful due to complex ECG signals, which demand high-quality signal preprocessing and feature extraction techniques. Furthermore, a large amount of data is necessary for DL training, which allows this method to learn more complex relationships between input features and target outputs. This is particularly important in the case of SCA detection, where access to large and diverse datasets is crucial for achieving optimal performance.

Principal Component Analysis (PCA) is widely used for feature reduction extracted from non-stationary ECG signals containing the rapid changes of the waveform. Therefore, PCA is a useful tool in the development of accurate and efficient SCA detection systems. A key factor of informative feature selection is the correlation between input features, which is simply solved by the PCA. Indeed, this powerful method provides a robust feature estimation by the correlation degrees among the input features [12]. The transformation of the input feature space into a new space is implemented to generate ordered principal components based on their corresponding correlation degrees. As a result, the featured representative comprising a subset of highly uncorrelated input features is highlighted through the PCA transformation for further stages.

In our work, a novel SAA design is proposed using a convolution neural network (CNN) and principal components transformed from the original features by PCA, which contribute to the performance improvement of the proposed SAA for SCA diagnosis based on the ECG signals. Furthermore, the performance of the DL model using feature transformation is estimated through the 5-fold CV method on the validation set.

The main contribution of this work is the utilization of the PCA algorithm for feature transformation. The original features extracted from ECG signals, which are highly correlated with each other, are transformed into a new space including differently uncorrelated component features. Additionally, the utility of the CNN model with the 5-fold cross-validation method improves the SCA classification performance in the healthcare system, which leads to significantly reliable performance results for practical use in clinic environments.

The rest of the paper is organized as follows: Sect. 2 presents the data used for our method. Section 3 includes a description of the methodology of the proposed technique using feature extraction with conventional techniques, PCA algorithm to transform features, and DL models to diagnose SCA. The performance comparisons of the proposed algorithm with other existing methods are discussed in Sect. 4, followed by a discussion of the results. Finally, The conclusions are presented in Sect. 5.

2   Data

Creighton University Ventricular Tachyarrhythmia Database (CUDB) [13] and the MIT-BIH Malignant Ventricular Arrhythmia Database (VFDB) [14] are used for this work due to its widely spread use in previous studies, which makes it easily compared. The ECG signals in these databases consist of shockable signals containing VF, VT, and ventricular flutter. Other rhythms in the above databases are the non-shockable signals. The CUDB contains 35 single-channel records with a length of 8 min for each record. The VFDB consists of 22 double-channel records of 35 min. For performance improvement purposes, the first channel of the individual is employed. The total of all records is 57, which are then separated into non-overlapping 8-s ECG segments. Therefore, there are 1135 shockable and 5185 non-shockable segments of these databases, which are considered for sampling at a frequency of 250 Hz. We grouped the entire ECG segments into training and testing data corresponding to 70% and 30%, respectively. As a result, 4303 segments of 40 records were used for training and 2017 segments of 17 records were for testing. Here, each record corresponds to a separate patient in the databases. Figure 1 shows the shockable and non-shockable 8 s ECG segments. The ECG signals are preprocessed as following steps:

(i) Implementation of the five-order moving average filtering to achieve signal smooth.
(ii) Removal of the baseline wander by the use of high-pass filtering with 1 Hz cutoff frequency.
(iii) Elimination of high-frequency noise by the 30 Hz low-pass Butterworth filtering.

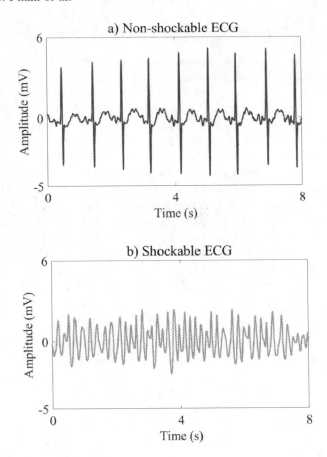

Fig. 1. Waveforms of non-shockable and shockable ECG signals.

3   Method

The are three steps shown in Fig. 2 for the construction of the proposed SAA. In the first step, the ECG databases are segmented and preprocessed for feature extraction in time and frequency domains. Then, two datasets are generated for training and testing corresponding to 70% and 30% of the total. In the second step, PCA is implemented for the transformation of the extracted features into the component space. Finally, two DL models, which are Long-short term memory (LSTM), and CNN are trained and validated by a 5-fold CV procedure.

3.1   Feature Extraction

The feature extraction is implemented by various conventional techniques. The three main categories of features are extracted temporal, spectral, and complexity features. Table 1 shows a set of 20 features extracted from the 8 s ECG segments [6].

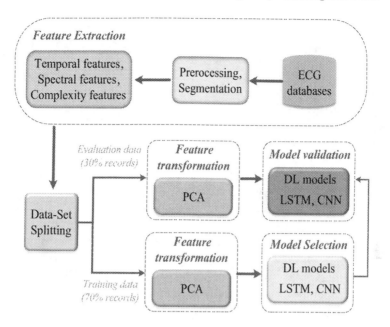

Fig. 2. Steps of method development.

Table 1. Extracted features.

Feature Type	Feature Name
Temporal features	bCP, threshold crossing sample count (TCSC), threshold crossing interval (TCI), modified exponential algorithm (MEA), Count1, Count2, and Count3
Spectral features	spectral analysis (S2), Li, bWT, bW, VF-filter leakage measure (Lk)
Complexity features	phase space reconstruction (PSR), frequency calculation (FB), Kurtosis (Kurt), complexity measure (CM), fuzzy entropy (FE), sample entropy (SE), energy (EN), Renyi entropy (RE)

3.2 Feature Transformation

The feature set is transformed into component space by the PCA technique. More precisely, all of the 20 features, known as observed variable Z_k, are transformed into a new space of 20 principal components F_k, which are independent and uncorrelated variables as follows [12]:

$$Z_k = l_{k1}F_1 + l_{k2}F_2 + ... + l_{kl}F_l + ... + l_{k20}F_{20} \qquad (1)$$

Conversely, the components F_j can also be expressed as a linear combination of the original variables as follows:

$$F_j = a_{1j}Z_1 + a_{2j}Z_2 + ... + a_{20j}Z_{20} \qquad (2)$$

The component F_j are uncorrelated with each other and ordered by the sample variance λ, that is, the largest sample variance represents F_1, the second largest sample variance is F_2, and so on. The sample variances corresponding to different components are known as eigenvalues, which show the share proportion in the total variance. Particularly, a constituent that holds a greater portion of the overall variation, denoted by a higher eigenvalue, within the initial features, holds more significance compared to those with smaller eigenvalues. The covariance matrix R of the original feature Z is as follows:

$$R = \begin{bmatrix} 1 & r_{12} & \cdots & r_{1,20} \\ r_{21} & 1 & \cdots & r_{2,20} \\ . & . & \cdots & . \\ r_{20,1} & r_{20,2} & \cdots & 1 \end{bmatrix} \tag{3}$$

where r_{12} represents the correlation between Z_1 and Z_2. The coefficients a_{1j} for component F_j, where j ranges from 1 to 20, encompass the eigenvector associated with the jth largest eigenvalue λ_j. As a result of standardization, the sum of variances across all features is equal to the number of features, demonstrated as follows:

$$\lambda_1 + \lambda_2 + \ldots + \lambda_{20} = 20 \tag{4}$$

Hence, $\lambda_j/20$ represents the ratio of the entire variation attributed to the jth component.

3.3 Model Selection

LSTM and CNN [15] are optimized models with parameter structures on the training set. Hyper-parameter tuning is crucial to identify optimal models and prevent over-fitting. Additionally, the classification performance of the selected model is estimated on the validation set. To determine the optimal parameter values for the model, we employ a combination of grid search and the 5-fold CV method in this work.

Convolutional Neural Networks: The most important element of the CNN is the neurons, which construct the layers within the CNN. The neurons are organized with three dimensions such as spatial dimensionality of the input including height width, and depth. There are three main layers of the CNN structure, which are the convolutional, pooling, and fully connected layers.

Convolutional Layer: This layer computes the output of neurons connected to local regions of the input by calculating the scalar product between their weights and the corresponding region within the input volume. The rectified linear unit (ReLu) is employed to introduce a wise activation function, such as the sigmoid, to the output generated by the preceding layer.

Pooling Layer: The layer simply performs downsampling along the spatial dimensionality of the given input, further reducing the number of parameters within that activation.

Fully-Connected Layer: This attempts to produce class scores from the activations, which are used for classification. The ReLu can be placed between the fully connected layers for performance improvement.

Long Short Term Memory: Vanishing gradients, which arise when learning long-term dependencies, even when the minimal time lags are very long, are serious problems. The LSTM model is one of the effective methods to overcome such problems. In general, a constant error carousel is used to prevent such a problem, which remains the error signal inside each cell of the unit. The LSTM architecture consists of a set of recurrently connected sub-networks, also known as memory blocks. The block functions to preserve the state across time and control the passage of information through nonlinear gate elements. The output of the block is cyclically linked back to its input and all of the gating components.

3.4   Model Validation

The 5-fold CV procedure is employed by the division of the ECG dataset into 5 parts. Each part is considered as testing data, while the remaining parts are arranged for training data. Hence, the procedure includes 5 run to complete an entire process. Moreover, the models are trained and tested repeatedly five times so that each subset serves as the testing data in the latter iterations to increase reliability. The mean and standard deviation of the classification performance are calculated for further estimation. Additionally, LSTM and CNN are optimized with parameter structures on the training set. Hyper-parameter tuning is crucial to identify an optimal model and prevent over-fitting. Then, the classification performance of the optimal model is estimated on the validation set. To determine the optimal parameter values of the model, we employ a combination of grid search and the 5-fold CV procedure in this work. The optimal model with the highest detection accuracy among others is selected as the final model for practical AED applications.

4   Results and Discussion

4.1   Results

The measured parameters are used in this work to estimate to diagnostic performance of the DL models. They are accuracy (Acc), sensitivity (Se), specificity (Sp), and Balanced Error Rate (BER). The Acc shows the proportion of ECG segments identified correctly. The accuracy of correctly identifying shockable and non-shockable ECG segments is represented by Se and Sp, respectively. The BER is calculated as $1 - 0.5.(Se + Sp)$.

Model Selection: The 20 features extracted from the ECG segments are transformed into a different space using the PCA transformation technique. They are used as the input features of DL models for searching for optimal structures.

Model Validation: The performance of two optimal DL classifiers is presented in Table 2. Generally, the CNN model is marginally more efficient than the LSTM model, achieving Acc of 99.03 %, Se of 94.74%, Sp of 99.37% and BER of 2.94%. On the other hand, the LSTM model has Acc of 98.50 %, Se of 88.74%, Sp of 99.07%, and BER of 6.09%. Therefore, in this work, we chose the CNN model for proposing the SAA algorithm.

Table 2. The detection performance of the model on the evaluation data.

Model	Acc (%)	Se (%)	Sp (%)	BER (%)
CNN	99.03 ± 0.19	94.74 ± 2.03	99.37 ± 0.23	2.94 ± 1.12
LSTM	98.50 ± 0.17	88.74 ± 4.43	99.07 ± 0.37	6.09 ± 2.04

Proposed Algorithm of SAA for SCA Detection. The SAA design, which is proposed for the AED in this study, includes a CNN model and 20 extracted features from the 8 s segment length of the ECG signals.

4.2 Discussion

Currently, the most effective way to treat cardiac arrest is using an affordable, reliable electronic device called an AED. The AHA recommends relatively high sensitivity and specificity for designing the SAA, but improving the detection performance is crucial to avoid incorrect diagnoses and increase the chance of survival.

The degree of correlation between features is important for determining their quality in classifying shockable and non-shockable rhythms on ECG signals. Feature correlation measures how much information is shared between features. Therefore, each feature should contain distinct information that can accurately distinguish between shockable and non-shockable ECG segments. The generation of the feature correlation is implemented by the PCA transformation. Indeed, the transformed features resulting from the PCA technique are highly uncorrelated and referred to as principal components, as shown in Eq. 2.

LSTM models are well-suited for modeling sequential data, which have a time-varying nature. They can capture long-term dependencies in the signal and can remember information from previous time steps, making them effective at predicting future events based on past events. Besides, CNN models are good at identifying patterns in time-series data, which is important for ECG analysis. They can identify important features in the ECG signal, such as the QRS complex or the ST segment, which are used to diagnose heart conditions. Therefore, LSTM and CNN models have been widely used for analyzing ECG data. They can capture temporal patterns, identify important features in the signal, and achieve high accuracy in predicting cardiac events. Indeed, Table 2 shows

Table 3. Performance comparison of the proposed algorithm to existing methods.

Ref	Database	Methods	Acc (%)	Se (%)	Sp (%)
This work	**CUDB, VFDB**	**PCA, CNN**	**99.03**	**94.74**	**99.37**
[16]	CUDB, VFDB	KNN, fuzzy C-mean clustering	99.01	99.14	98.97
[4]	MITDB, CUDB, VFDB	SVM, adBoost, Differential Evolution	98.2	98.25	98.10
[17]	CUDB, SDBB	CNN, LSTM	NA	92.71	97.6

the high performance of the DL models. The performance of the CNN model is higher than that of the LSTM.

In our work, a novel SCA detection algorithm based on PCA transformation and CNN technique is proposed that can be applied to the AED. To avoid overfitting problems caused by the small size of the public CUDB and VFDB databases, which are used in the training and validation data of the proposed SAA, the 5-fold CV method is applied to compute statistical performance results in both training and validation phases. The performance of proposed SCA detection in this work meets the AHA's requirement for accuracy Acc ($\geq$90%), sensitive Se ($\geq$90%), and specificity Sp ($\geq$95%) [6].

Table 3 presents a comparison of our proposed SCA detection performance among recent publications using different methods. The results demonstrate that our proposed algorithm outperforms existing methods, making it suitable for use in the SAA algorithm for AED applications.

5   Conclusion

The timely and accurate detection of SCA plays a critical role in increasing the chances of survival. Therefore, the development of an SAA algorithm for SCA diagnosis that can achieve highly reliable detection performance is paramount to ensuring safe and effective diagnosis in AED applications. In our work, we proposed an effective SAA algorithm for AED that utilizes the PCA technique to transform the features into a different space where they are uncorrelated and independent variables. Additionally, we utilized a CNN model for diagnosis. The CNN model is carefully optimized using the 5-fold CV approach to increase the model's reliability and accuracy, making it suitable for practical healthcare systems. The combination of PCA with CNN achieves the high performance of SCA detection. Indeed, the proposed SAA demonstrates high performance on the evaluation data, with Acc of 99.03 %, Se of 94.74%, Sp of 99.37% and BER of 2.94%, which are higher than that existing using others DL and ML algorithms.

References

1. Amann, A., Tratnig, R., Unterkofler, K.: Reliability of old and new ventricular fibrillation detection algorithms for automated external defibrillators. Biomed. Eng. Online **4**, 60 (2005). https://doi.org/10.1186/1475-925X-4-60

2. De Gauna, S.R., Irusta, U., Ruiz, J., Ayala, U., Aramendi, E., Eftestøl, T.: Rhythm Analysis during cardiopulmonary resuscitation: past, present, and future. Biomed. Res. Int. **2014**, e386010 (2014)
3. Nguyen, M.T., Nguyen, B.V., Kim, K.: Diagnosis of shockable rhythms for automated external defibrillators using a reliable support vector machine classifier. Biomed. Sig. Process. Control **44**, 258–269 (2018). https://doi.org/10.1016/j.bspc. 2018.03.014
4. Panigrahy, D., Sahu, P.K., Albu, F.: Detection of ventricular fibrillation rhythm by using boosted support vector machine with an optimal variable combination. Comput. Electr. Eng. **91**, 1–14 (2021). https://doi.org/10.1016/j.compeleceng.2021. 107035
5. Mohanty, M., Dash, M., Biswal, P., Sabut, S.: Classification of ventricular arrhythmias using empirical mode decomposition and machine learning algorithms. Prog. Artif. Intell. **10**, 489–504 (2021). https://doi.org/10.1007/s13748-021-00250-6
6. Nguyen, M.T., Nguyen, T.T., Le, H.C.: A review of progress and an advanced method for shock advice algorithms in automated external defibrillators. Biomed. Eng. Online **21**, 1–33 (2022). https://doi.org/10.1186/s12938-022-00993-w
7. Acharya, U.R., et al.: Automated identification of shockable and non-shockable life-threatening ventricular arrhythmias using convolutional neural network. Fut. Gener. Comput. Syst. **79**, 952–959 (2018). https://doi.org/10.1016/j.future.2017. 08.039
8. Nguyen, M.T., Nguyen, B.V., Kim, K.: Deep feature learning for sudden cardiac arrest detection in automated external defibrillators. Sci. Rep. **8**, 1–12 (2018). https://doi.org/10.1038/s41598-018-33424-9
9. Panda, R., Jain, S., Tripathy, R.K., Acharya, U.R.: Detection of shockable ventricular cardiac arrhythmias from ECG signals using FFREWT filter-bank and deep convolutional neural network. Comput. Biol. Med. **124**, 1–9 (2020). https://doi. org/10.1016/j.compbiomed.2020.103939
10. Jaureguibeitia, X., et al.: Shock decision algorithms for automated external defibrillators based on convolutional networks. IEEE Access **8**, 154746–154758 (2020). https://doi.org/10.1109/ACCESS.2020.3018704
11. Kerber, R.E., et al.: Automatic external defibrillators for public access defibrillation: recommendations for specifying and reporting arrhythmia analysis algorithm performance, incorporating new waveforms, and enhancing safety. Circulation **95**, 1677–1682 (1997). https://doi.org/10.1161/01.CIR.95.6.1677
12. Castells, F., Laguna, P., Sornmo, L., Bollmann, A., Roig, J.M.: Principal component analysis in ECG signal processing. EURASIP J. Adv. Sig. Process. **2007**, 1–21 (2007). https://doi.org/10.1155/2007/74580
13. Nolle F.M., Bowser, R.W.: Creighton University Ventricular Tachyarrhythmia Database. Physionet.org (1992). https://physionet.org/content/cudb/1.0.0/
14. Greenwald, S.D.: The MIT-BIH Malignant Ventricular Arrhythmia Database. Physionet.org (1992). https://physionet.org/content/vfdb/1.0.0/
15. Alpaydın, E.: Introduction to Machine Learning, 2nd edn. The MIT Press (2014)
16. Nguyen, M.T., Nguyen, H.-T., Le, H.-C.: Feature reinforcement in intelligent automated external defibrillators for sudden cardiac arrest detection. In: 2022 IEEE Ninth International Conference on Communications and Electronics (ICCE), Nha Trang, Vietnam, pp. 165–169 (2022). https://doi.org/10.1109/ICCE55644.2022. 9852093
17. Shirin, H., Alicia, C., Matt, V., Chon, K.H.: Deep neural network approach for continuous ECG-based automated external defibrillator shock advisory system during cardiopulmonary resuscitation. J. Am. Heart Assoc. **10**, e019065 (2021)

Experimental Study on Fuzzy PD Control for Logistics Transportation Mobile Robot

Quoc-Khai Tran[(⊠)], Chan Thanh Nguyen Huu, and Cong-Thanh Pham

Faculty of Electrical-Electronic Engineering, VAA University,
Ho Chi Minh City 700000, Vietnam
{khaitq,thanhnhc,thanhpc}@vaa.edu.vn

Abstract. This paper presents the method of designing a line following Fuzzy-PD controller for a differential-driven logistics transport mobile robot (LTMR). The line following controller is in charge of assisting the robot in moving along a predetermined path that has been installed or painted on the ground. The experimental results in this study demonstrate that the Fuzzy-PD controller can adjust the control parameters to better adapt to a rapid change in direction of the reference line when compared to using the PD controller. Furthermore, this paper provides an innovative approach to designing the control algorithm for differential-driven LTMR to enable a simple transition from manual to line following mode or vice versa.

Keywords: PD controller · Fuzzy-PD controller · Differential-driven logistics transportation mobile robots · manual mode · line following mode

1 Introduction

In general, regardless of sensor type, the line following control method uses position sensor information installed on the robot body to drive the robot such that the sensor's midpoint is as close to the reference line as possible [1–10]. The research results in these studies [7–10] have shown the effectiveness and ease of implementation of conventional Proportional-Integral-Derivative (PID) control technique for line following robot. Balaji et al. [7] also presented the roles of proportional, integral and derivative terms of PID controller in line following control. For example, with a large value of proportional gain - K_p, the robot is able to response quickly when the reference line changes its direction but oscillates strongly in the straight lines. With a small value of K_p, in contrast, the robot runs very stably on the straight lines but its ability to change the direction is much worse. Next, the derivative term of PID controller is known for its overshoot reduction function and transient response improvement related to the sudden change in direction of the path. However, given the large value of the derivative gain - K_d, the system can become quite sensitive to disturbing signals related to the quality of the sensor or of the reference line. The system also becomes unstable if the K_d is too large.

© ICST Institute for Computer Sciences, Social Informatics and Telecommunications Engineering 2023
Published by Springer Nature Switzerland AG 2023. All Rights Reserved
N.-S. Vo and H.-A. Tran (Eds.): INISCOM 2023, LNICST 531, pp. 225–235, 2023.
https://doi.org/10.1007/978-3-031-47359-3_17

In basic PID-controlled systems the integral term is used to eliminate steady error provided that the reference value is fixed or little changed. However, in line following control system, the characteristic of the predefined line often changes, thus the reference value for the line following controller is not fixed. With the presence of the integral term in PID controller the robot's performance can become unstable because of the instability of reference value for whole system. So that, to increase the stability of the control system, the integral term should be removed. The PD controller should be implemented with the K_p that can be adjusted, while the K_d should be selected appropriately and unchanged.

As an intelligent controller, fuzzy logic controller (FLC) is known with its ability to supervise the nonlinear systems and to be used to adjust the PID parameters to help the system achieve optimal state [11–13] . For the above reasons, this paper proposes a fuzzy PD controller with the ability to change K_p parameter by itself for line following robots to accommodate the variation of characteristics of the entire system.

In this study, the line following control mode can conventionally be called automatic control mode (ACM). Although the robot is built for the ACM, it may not always work in this manner. When the sensor system or magnetic line is damaged, or the robot has to operate in locations where there is no install line, the operator must control the robot directly. Manual control mode (MCM) refers to the control mode in which the robot is directly instructed by the operator. As a result, for research, an easy technique to transition from MCM to ACM or vice versa is required. There are commonly two techniques in the MCM for controlling the robot moving forward or backward, turning left or right using reference linear and angular velocity values. The first technique converts its reference values into two distinct signals, each of which is utilized to individually regulate the velocity of each wheel using its own PID controller with proper settings [14]. In the second technique, the robot velocities are directly controlled by two PID controllers, linear and angular PID controllers, without any reference value conversion [15]. Because the first technique makes the transition between MCM and ACM more difficult. Therefore, the second technique is used in this study to make programming and control easier. The second technique enables the system to go from MCM to ACM by simply replacing the angular velocity PID controller with the following PID controller, resulting in a control structure that is not significantly different from the original.

The rest of this paper is organized as follows. The MCM is built in Sect. 2. The method of designing the ACM is explained in Sect. 3. The experimental results and discussion are given in Sect. 4. Finally, the conclusion is presented in Sect. 5.

2   Manual Control Mode

2.1   Model of Logistics Transportation Mobile Robot

To prevent the wheels from rolling onto the magnetic line during the line following test as well as the actual run in the case when the magnetic line is not

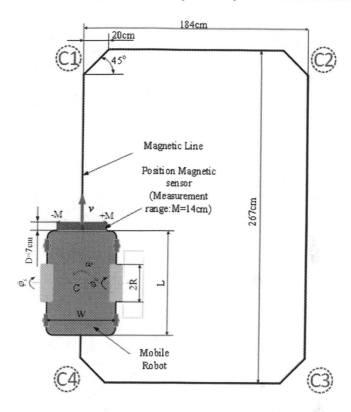

Fig. 1. Model of LTMR and magnetic line.

buried deep in the ground, the robot model with differential drive, as shown in Fig. 1, is used.

Two separate coaxial driving wheels with a 2R diameter are used to move the W×L-sized robot. Each of these wheels will be propelled by a BLDC motor that is managed by a motor drive. The velocities at which the left and right wheels rotate are $\dot{\varphi}_R$ and $\dot{\varphi}_L$, respectively. The placement of four castor wheels close to the rear of the robot body aids in improved robot balance and prevents the robot from rolling on the magnetic line and destroying it since the two driving wheels are positioned directly on the robot body's horizontal axis of symmetry. A magnetic sensor is attached at the head of the robot body for use while carrying out the line following function.

2.2 Velocity Control

Typically, the rotating velocities $\dot{\varphi}_R$ and $\dot{\varphi}_L$ are calculated based on signals returned from the encoder mounted directly on the motor shaft. The robot's

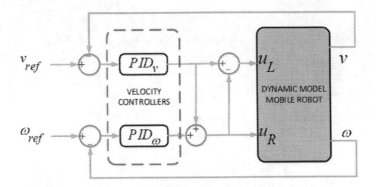

Fig. 2. Velocity control of LTMR.

angular and linear velocities may be calculated as

$$\begin{cases} v = \frac{v_R + v_L}{2} = \frac{R}{2}(\dot{\varphi}_R + \dot{\varphi}_L) \\ \omega = \frac{v_R - v_L}{2L} = \frac{R}{2L}(\dot{\varphi}_R - \dot{\varphi}_L) \end{cases}. \tag{1}$$

In the field of cargo transportation, it is not necessary to control a mobile robot at the highest speed but the robot needs to run at an appropriate and constant velocity even when the load of the freight is changed. The PID controller of linear velocity, denoted as PID_v, and the PID controller of angular velocity, denoted as PID_ω, can both regulate the robot's speeds. It is possible to acquire the output control signals u_v of PID_v and u_ω of PID_ω by

$$\begin{bmatrix} u_v \\ u_\omega \end{bmatrix} = \begin{bmatrix} K_{pv}e_v + K_{iv}\int_0^t e_v d\tau + K_{dv}\frac{d}{dt}e_v \\ K_{p\omega}e_\omega + K_{i\omega}\int_0^t e_\omega d\tau + K_{d\omega}\frac{d}{dt}e_\omega \end{bmatrix}, \tag{2}$$

Here, $[K_{pv}, K_{iv}, K_{dv}]$ and $[K_{p\omega}, K_{i\omega}, K_{d\omega}]$ are, respectively, parameters of PID_v and PID_ω.

The left and right motor drivers receive control voltage signals directly, which can be computed as

$$\begin{bmatrix} u_L \\ u_R \end{bmatrix} = \begin{bmatrix} u_v - u_\omega \\ u_v + u_\omega \end{bmatrix}. \tag{3}$$

Based on Eqs. (1) and (2), the velocity control scheme illustrated in Fig. 2.

3   Automatic Control Mode

In the ACM, the line following PD controller replaces the PID controller of angular velocity. Thus, Eq. (2) can be written as

$$\begin{bmatrix} u_v \\ u_\varepsilon \end{bmatrix} = \begin{bmatrix} K_{pv}e_v + K_{iv}\int_0^t e_v d\tau + K_{dv}\frac{d}{dt}e_v \\ K_{p\varepsilon}e_\varepsilon + K_{d\varepsilon}\frac{d}{dt}e_\varepsilon \end{bmatrix}, \tag{4}$$

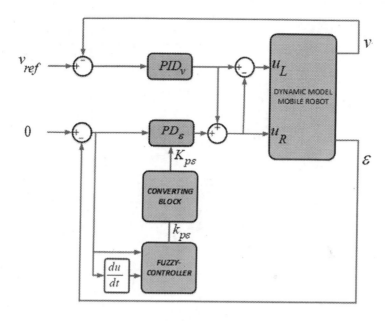

Fig. 3. Automatic control mode.

Here, $K_{p\varepsilon}$ and $K_{d\varepsilon}$ are parameters of the line following PD controllers. The line position and position error are represented by ε and $e_\varepsilon = -\varepsilon$, respectively.

Therefore, Eq. (3) can be written as

$$\begin{bmatrix} u_L \\ u_R \end{bmatrix} = \begin{bmatrix} u_v - u_\varepsilon \\ u_v + u_\varepsilon \end{bmatrix}, \tag{5}$$

As mentioned above, to adapt to the changes of the system, the Sugeno fuzzy controller known with its efficiency in computational processing [16] is used for adjusting the $K_{p\varepsilon}$ parameter, as shown in Fig. (3).

The fuzzy controller has two inputs: position error ε and position error change de_ε. The fuzzy controller's output signal $k_{p\varepsilon} \in [0, 1]$ is used to calculate $K_{p\varepsilon} \in [K_{p\varepsilon Min}, K_{p\varepsilon Max}]$ according to the following conversion formula.

$$K_{p\varepsilon} = (K_{p\varepsilon Max} - K_{p\varepsilon Min})k_{p\varepsilon} + K_{p\varepsilon Min}, \tag{6}$$

Here, $K_{p\varepsilon Min}$ and $K_{p\varepsilon Max}$ can be found by experimental testing explained in Sect. 4.

The fuzzy table rule is composed of nine rules, as stated in Table 1, in which **E** = {NE, ZE, PE}, **DE** = {NDE, ZDE, PDE}, and **KP** = {Z, M, B} represent the sets of linguistic variables of fuzzy inputs and output. Each rule is built as following:

Rule$_n$: if e_ε is $e_{\varepsilon i}$ and de_ε is $de_{\varepsilon j}$ then $k_{p\varepsilon}$ is $C_{i,j}$,

Where, $n = 9$ denotes the number of fuzzy control rules, and $C_{i,j}$ denotes the value of the cell corresponding to i^{th} row and j^{th} column in Table 1.

The membership functions of fuzzy inputs can be seen as in Figs. 4 and 5.

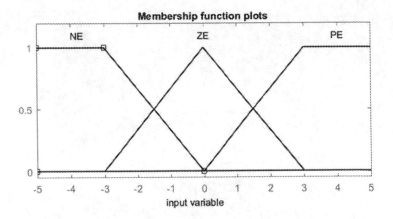

Fig. 4. Membership of position error.

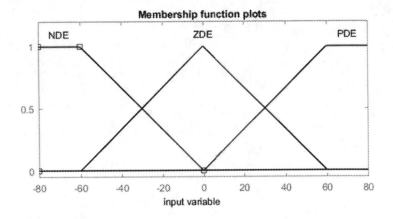

Fig. 5. Membership of change in error.

4   Experimental Results and Discussion

The LTMR created in our laboratory is shown in Fig. 6. The robot body's W and length L are 0.56 m and 0.84 m, respectively. Each wheel has a 2R diameter of 0.3 m. While not carrying things, the robot weighs 125 kg. For the robot's ACM, a magnetic position sensor with a measuring range M of 14 cm and a measurement resolution of 0.01 cm is utilized.

The velocities of the left and right wheel are measured based on digital signals generated by Hall effect sensors mounted inside two brushless DC motors (BLDC motor), and satisfy the constraint max $(v_L, v_R) \leq 0.94$ m (the maximum corresponding speed of the wheels is 60 rpm).

The robot's velocities are controlled by two PID controllers, which was programmed directly on the main control board of the robot. In our experimental

Table 1. Fuzzy rule table.

$k_{p\varepsilon}$	de_ε		
e_ε	NDE	ZDE	PDE
NE	B	B	M
ZE	M	Z	M
PE	M	B	B

Fig. 6. Logistics transportation mobile robot.

research, the parameters of PID_v and PID_ω were set with [0.2, 0.4, 0.15] and [1.0, 0.4, 0.15], respectively.

The PID controller for angular velocity was replaced in the ACM by the line following Fuzzy-PD controller. The $K_{p\varepsilon Min}$, $K_{p\varepsilon Max}$ and $K_{d\varepsilon}$ can be determined based on the test method when the robot ran on closed magnetic line as shown in Fig. 1 as follows.

1. Increase $K_{p\varepsilon}$ gradually until a value considered as $K_{p\varepsilon Min}$ so that the robot can flow the straight line. However, the robot is still unable to follow the line when the direction of the line changes at an angle of 45° from the original direction.
2. Increase $K_{d\varepsilon}$ until the robot can follow the closed line entirely. $K_{d\varepsilon}$ can be chosen larger but just enough so the robot can change direction faster.

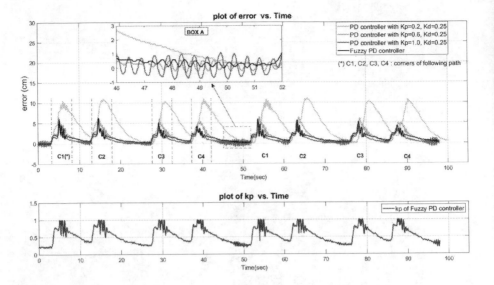

Fig. 7. Position errors of different PD controllers at 0.157 m/s.

3. Keep $K_{d\varepsilon}$ value unchanged, increase $K_{p\varepsilon}$ until the value considered as $K_{p\varepsilon Max}$ so that the robot oscillates quite strongly on the straight lines but still ensure the robot can follow the closed line.

With the values of $K_{p\varepsilon}$ and $K_{d\varepsilon}$ found, we can create a table with three following PD controllers as shown in Table 2. In fuzzy controller, the values of variables of fuzzy inputs and output were chosen as **E** = {NDE, ZDE, PDE} = {−3, 0, 3}, **DE** = {NE, ZE, PE}={−60 , 0, 60} and **KP** = {Z, M, B} = {0, 0.5, 1}.

Table 2. Following PD controllers.

PD controller	$K_{p\varepsilon}$	$K_{d\varepsilon}$
PD1 $(K_{p\varepsilon Min},\ K_{d\varepsilon})$	0.2	0.25
PD2 $((K_{p\varepsilon Min} + K_{p\varepsilon Max})/2,\ K_{d\varepsilon})$	0.6	0.25
PD3 $(K_{p\varepsilon Max},\ K_{d\varepsilon})$	1.0	0.25

The robots with different PD controllers were tested by running two rounds (8 corners) at a speed of 0.157 m/s (corresponding to wheel speed of 10 rpm). Figure 7 shows the position errors ε of each PD controller and the change in $K_{p\varepsilon}$ when using fuzzy PD. Figure 8 shows the stability of linear velocity and the change over time of angular velocity when the robot changes its direction.

From the results presented in Fig. 7, we can draw conclusions as shown in Table 3. Based on the results of the maximum position errors and root-mean-square errors (RMSEs) in Table 3, it can be clearly seen that the larger $K_{p\varepsilon}$, the

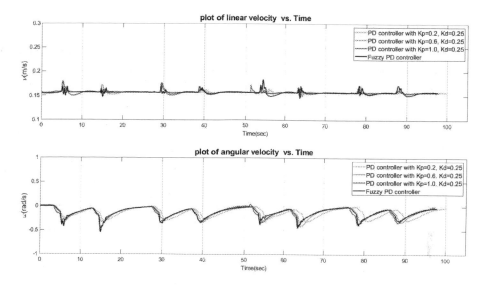

Fig. 8. Linear and angular velocities of the LTMR at 0.157 m/s.

better the robot follows the line. However, it has a disadvantage of making the system oscillate strongly on straight lines (maximal peak-to-peak error ripple is greatest when $K_{p\varepsilon} = K_{p\varepsilon Max}$). While with the smallest value of $K_{p\varepsilon}$, the system will become most stable, but the ability to follow the line becomes worse at the corners.

By comparing with the three PD controllers given above, the Fuzzy-PD controller has advantages such as not only in reducing ripple error but also in helping the robot to change direction quickly. With the low RMSE, comparing the Fuzzy-PD controller with the PD1 and PD2 controllers, it also shows that the use of Fuzzy-PD controller is a great good solution for line following.

Table 3. Experimental results at 0.157 m/s.

PD controller	MPPER in box A	MPE	AMCPE	RMSE	CT
PD1	0.1 cm	11.1 cm at 65.76 s	10.7 cm	5.70 cm	99.85 s
PD2	0.8 cm	6.6 cm at 54.08 s	6.08 cm	2.18 cm	98.07 s
PD3	1.8 cm	5.6 cm at 14.62 s	4.72 cm	1.39 cm	97.33 s
Fuzzy-PD	0.5 cm	6.3 cm at 14.66 s	5.39 cm	1.72 cm	97.77 s
MPPER: Maximal peak-to-peak error ripple					
MPE: Maximal position error					
AMCPE: Average of maximal corner position error					
CT: Completion time					

5   Conclusion

In this paper, a velocity and line following controllers were successfully built for the line following mobile robot. Switching from manual control mode to following control mode (automatic control mode) is also easy but still helps the robot keep the appropriate linear velocity even when the load changes. The use of PD controllers with fixed parameters shows that the following system cannot fully meet the operating requirements when environmental conditions change. The Fuzzy-PD following controller has the ability to change its own parameters, making the robot stable when running on straight lines but still ensuring good line following when there is a sudden change in the trajectory of predefined reference line.

Acknowledgement. The authors would like to thank the Vietnam Aviation Academy for Science and Technology Development for the support in 2022/2023.

References

1. Oltean, S.-E.: Mobile robot platform with arduino uno and raspberry PI for autonomous navigation. Proc. Manufact. **32**, 572–577 (2019)
2. Serrano Pèrez, E., Juàrez Lòpez, F., F.: An ultra-low cost line follower robot as educational tool for teaching programming and circuit's foundations. Comput. Appl. Eng. Educ. **27**(2), 288–302 (2019)
3. Pisarov, J.: Experience with mBot-wheeled mobile robot. Proc. XXXV. Jubileumi Kandó Konferencia 2019 (JKK2019), 47–51 (2019)
4. Saadatmand, S., Azizi, S., Kavousi, M., Wunsch, D.: Autonomous control of a line follower robot using a q-learning controller. In: 10th Annual Computing and Communication Workshop and Conference (CCWC), pp. 0556–0561, IEEE (2020)
5. Eleftheriou, G., Doitsidis, L., Zinonos, Z., Chatzichristofis, S.A.: A fuzzy rule-based control system for fast line-following robots. In: 2020 16th International Conference on Distributed Computing in Sensor Systems (DCOSS), pp. 388–395, IEEE (2020)
6. Oswal, S., Saravanakumar, D.: Line following robots on factory floors: significance and simulation study using coppeliasim. In: IOP Conference Series: Materials Science and Engineering, vol. 1012, no. 1. IOP Publishing, 2021, p. 012008 (2021)
7. Balaji, V., Balaji, M., Chandrasekaran, M., Elamvazuthi, I., et al.: Optimization of PID control for high speed line tracking robots. Proc. Comput. Sci. **76**, 147–154 (2015)
8. Kader, M.A., Islam, M.Z., Al Rafi, J., Islam, M.R., Hossain, F.S.: Line following autonomous office assistant robot with PID algorithm. In: 2018 International Conference on Innovations in Science, Engineering and Technology (ICISET), pp. 109–114, IEEE (2018)
9. Maàrif, A., Nuryono, A.A.: Vision-based line following robot in webots. In: 2020 FORTEI-International Conference on Electrical Engineering (FORTEI-ICEE), pp. 24–28, IEEE (2020)
10. Farkh, R., Aljaloud, K.: Vision navigation based PID control for line tracking robot. Intell. Autom. Soft Comput. **35**(1), 901–911 (2023)
11. Eltag, K., Aslamx, M.S., Ullah, R.: Dynamic stability enhancement using fuzzy PID control technology for power system. Int. J. Control Autom. Syst. **17**, 234–242 (2019)

12. Somwanshi, D., Bundele, M., Kumar, G., Parashar, G.: Comparison of fuzzy-PID and PID controller for speed control of dc motor using labview. Proc. Comput. Sci. **152**, 252–260 (2019)
13. Chao, C.-T., Sutarna, N., Chiou, J.-S., Wang, C.-J.: An optimal fuzzy PID controller design based on conventional PID control and nonlinear factors. Appl. Sci. **9**(6), 1224 (2019)
14. Saleh, A.L., Mohammed, M.J., Kadhim, A.S., Raadthy, H.M., Mohammed, H.J.: Design fuzzy neural petri net controller for trajectory tracking control of mobile robot. Int. J. Eng. Technol. **7**(4), 2256–2262 (2018)
15. Khai, T.Q., Ryoo, Y.-J., Gill, W.-R., Im, D.-Y.: Design of kinematic controller based on parameter tuning by fuzzy inference system for trajectory tracking of differential-drive mobile robot. Int. J. Fuzzy Syst. **22**, 1972–1978 (2020)
16. Topaloğlu, F., Pehlıvan, H.: Comparison of mamdani type and sugeno type fuzzy inference systems in wind power plant installations. In: 6th International Symposium on Digital Forensic and Security (ISDFS), pp. 1–4, IEEE (2018)

MQTT-CB: Cloud Based Intelligent MQTT Protocol

Muhammed Raşit Erol[1]([✉]) [iD], Tuğçe Bilen[2] [iD], Mehmet Özdem[2],
and Berk Canberk[1,3] [iD]

[1] Department of Computer Engineering, Istanbul Technical University, Istanbul,
Turkey
{erolm15,b.canberk}@itu.edu.tr
[2] Innovation and Product and Service Development Directorate, Türk Telekom,
Istanbul, Turkey
{tugce.bilen,mehmet.ozdem}@turktelekom.com.tr
[3] School of Computing, Engineering and the Build Environment,
Edinburgh Napier University, Edinburgh, UK
b.canberk@napier.ac.uk

Abstract. The MQTT protocol, which stands for Message Queuing
Telemetry Transport, is widely recognized within the IoT community as
one of the most frequently utilized communication protocols. Conventional MQTT protocols described in the literature could improve their
capacity to support distributed environments and scalability. In this manner, MQTT-ST is an advanced MQTT protocol that provides bridging
capabilities within a distributed environment, making it a preferred option
for IoT systems. In this study, we introduce a new, intelligent, scalable, and
distributed MQTT-ST-based protocol named MQTT-CB. Our approach
leverages containers to improve portability, and our protocol is designed
with a cloud-based architecture that streamlines deployment. The primary
contribution of our research is the integration of intelligent capabilities
into the MQTT-ST protocol, utilizing an LSTM (Long Short-Term Memory) network, which is the leading deep learning model. Specifically, our
protocol employs predictive algorithms to foresee retransmitted packets,
dynamically adjusts the number of brokers in real-time, and reduces the
number of brokers when clients are inactive. Our experiments demonstrate
that our protocol significantly outperforms conventional MQTT-ST protocol regarding latency between subscribers and publishers. Furthermore,
our protocol adapts seamlessly to changes in the publication rate. In summary, we present a cloud-based intelligent MQTT protocol that offers significant advantages over traditional MQTT-ST protocol.

Keywords: MQTT · MQTT-ST · IoT · LSTM · Cloud · Container ·
AI

1 Introduction

The MQTT protocol is commonly utilized within the IoT (Internet of
Things) ecosystem, as noted in [1]. MQTT utilizes a publish/subscribe-based

N.-S. Vo and H.-A. Tran (Eds.): INISCOM 2023, LNICST 531, pp. 236–254, 2023.
https://doi.org/10.1007/978-3-031-47359-3_18

communication model, which enables efficient message transfer between clients and servers. This lightweight and efficient protocol is especially suitable for IoT devices with limited resources. The publish/subscribe model eliminates the need for direct communication between devices, which reduces the burden on individual devices and enables effective communication with a broker [2]. Due to its dependability and adaptability, MQTT is extensively employed in IoT implementations like smart cities, intelligent devices, and transportation systems, as referenced in [3].

MQTT is well-suited for devices with limited resources; however, it experiences a single point of failure with its brokers, as mentioned in [4]. If the broker becomes unavailable, the entire network may become disconnected, and devices may not be able to exchange messages. Therefore, the centralized broker is a significant drawback for MQTT. Additionally, managing the number of devices and messages can present difficulties in terms of scaling the quantity of brokers, as stated in [5]. Careful consideration of these and other factors is vital to ensure the success of a large-scale MQTT deployment.

Several MQTT protocols [6–8] support distributed brokers and use multiple brokers to provide redundancy. However, even with multiple brokers, the network may still have a fault issue, depending on the configuration and deployment strategy. Clustering or load balancing technologies [9] can be used further to reduce the danger of a single point of failure, but this may add additional complexity to the system.

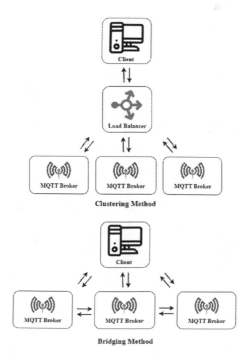

Fig. 1. Clustering and bridging methods.

The MQTT-ST project, an open-source MQTT protocol based on the widely used Mosquito implementation [10], supports distribution, as noted in [11]. Unlike several other MQTT protocols, such as [12–14], MQTT-ST does not sustain broker clustering but uses bridging to connect multiple brokers. Clustering refers to the collaboration of several brokers to establish a unified broker, whereas bridging enables the interchange of messages between brokers. Figure 1 illustrates the clustering and bridging approaches. According to [15], the bridging method is more effective than clustering regarding network traffic and broker resource usage. Consequently, MQTT-ST is well-suited for utilization in resource-limited and cost-conscious IoT settings.

The MQTT-ST protocol is a tree-based, distributed protocol that replicates messages across all brokers and can react to failures. It is an upgraded version of the Mosquitto source code and is designed for efficient message distribution, making it suitable for scaling the number of brokers. However, MQTT-ST is not a dynamic protocol, which means that it cannot increase or decrease the number of brokers in real-time, leading to resource consumption when IoT publishers are idle. Our proposed MQTT-CB protocol offers a dynamic, intelligent, cloud-based solution built on MQTT-ST to address this limitation.

MQTT-CB protocol can adapt to environmental conditions and operate optimally regarding resource consumption and network traffic overhead. It utilizes the LSTM model to predict retransmitted packets and adjusts the number of brokers accordingly. This makes the MQTT-CB protocol dynamic and intelligent, unlike other MQTT protocols. Additionally, MQTT-CB runs on Docker containers, making it cloud-based and highly portable compared to MQTT-ST and other MQTT protocols. Overall, the proposed MQTT-CB protocol offers a more efficient, adaptable, and portable solution for message distribution in IoT environments.

In summary, this paper's primary contributions are as follows:

- We propose a new MQTT-ST-based protocol that is intelligent and scalable in terms of broker numbers. While MQTT-ST is an open-source MQTT protocol, it lacks dynamic scalability by default. However, the proposed MQTT-CB protocol provides this feature by predicting the following retransmitted packets and adjusting the number of brokers in the future.
- The MQTT-CB protocol is a cloud-based MQTT protocol that can be easily deployed to the cloud without any burden. This makes it more flexible and portable in terms of deployment.
- We design the MQTT-CB protocol to run on Docker containers and orchestrate other container-based brokers using Docker CLI. This makes it more environment dependent and reusable in terms of development and simulation.
- We create a new system model with four modules to monitor MQTT packets and predict future retransmitted packets. This model is a layered architecture, making it a robust structure.
- We can improve the proposed system model in the future with more complicated deep learning methods to predict with higher accuracy and speed.

The remaining sections of this paper are organized as follows: Sect. 2 covers the related works. Section 3 describes the network architecture, while Sect. 4 outlines the system model. The simulation environment is detailed in Sect. 5, and we present our proposed model's performance evaluation in Sect. 6. Lastly, Sect. 7 concludes our work by summarizing its accomplishments.

2   Related Work

In literature, several works on distributed MQTT protocols employ bridging techniques [16,17]. The Mosquitto MQTT protocol has a Java-based implementation called D-MQTT, as cited in [16]. D-MQTT utilizes bridging and provides a distributed MQTT protocol that outperforms the Mosquito MQTT protocol regarding publication traffic exchanged between the brokers. Another MQTT bridge-based protocol, EMMA [17], is a QoS-aware MQTT protocol that enables edge computing. This work shows that communication between closely located devices has low latency and offers low-cost message transferring.

Additionally, there are several container-based MQTT implementations in the literature [18–20]. The work in [18] presents a microservice-based MQTT protocol in an edge computing environment with containers, where multiple brokers perform better in terms of throughput and multiple nodes work better than a single broker. Another work on container-based MQTT protocols, [19], provides dynamic MQTT deployment with containers, increasing resource utilization in CPU and memory. Moreover, [20] is a container-based MQTT protocol implements fog service as multiple containers. Their experimental results show that migrating container-based fog services performs better than no migration in terms of QoS.

Cloud-based MQTT protocols are also present in the literature [21,22]. FogMQ [21] provides a cloud-based MQTT protocol that uses bridging and offers self-deployment auto-migration in the cloud, achieving low latency in their work. Another cloud-based MQTT approach, [22], reduces processing message time in burst mode compared to the default algorithm in MQTT brokers.

Several works have also been on prediction using RNN models [23,24]. In [23], the authors forecast QoS in terms of loss rate, speed of the link, throughput, and RTT concerning user locations using several deep learning models with RNNs, achieving prediction accuracy above 90% in QoS status. Another work, [24], predicts network traffic in the future using time series network data. In terms of precision, their suggested model surpasses conventional RNN models.

However, these works do not provide an intelligent MQTT broker to adjust broker numbers in real-time. Our proposed model can be deployed in a cloud environment, making it more reachable and robust in terms of connectivity. Furthermore, our container-based model makes our work more portable. Additionally, adjusting broker numbers reduces resource consumption in terms of CPU power and memory.

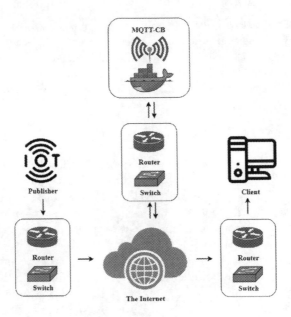

Fig. 2. Network Architecture.

3 Network Architecture

Our network architecture is founded on MQTT protocol and comprises three primary components: publishers and subscribers, serving as clients, and brokers. The brokers are responsible for collecting data from the publishers in the form of topics and subsequently delivering them to the subscribers. As a result, the brokers facilitate the data transfer between publishers and subscribers, starting from publishers to subscribers.

Each component, including brokers, publishers, and subscribers, situate on a local network that consists of a switch and a router. Therefore, our network topology encompasses three local networks, namely LN1, LN2, and LN3. LN1 comprises publishers, while LN2 consists of subscribers. The brokers are placed in LN3. The data flow between LN1 and LN3 is unidirectional, starting from LN1 to LN3. Conversely, the data flow between LN2 and LN3 is bidirectional. Additionally, we parameterize the delay between the local networks.

Each local network connects to the Internet through its router. Furthermore, each switch in the local network distributes packets among its connected devices. We also parameterize the number of publishers and subscribers. Furthermore, our model dynamically decides the number of brokers in real-time. We illustrate our network topology in Fig. 2.

4   System Model

The system model presented in this study illustrates our proposed MQTT-CB protocol, a virtual and software-based protocol implemented on the broker's side. Clients perceive the brokers as a single MQTT-CB broker, while the existing system may consist of multiple brokers orchestrated using Docker CLI.

The proposed system model comprises four primary modules, namely the Monitoring Module, Classification Module, AI Module, and MQTT-CB Controller Module, each of which performs a unique task independently of the other modules. This design approach results in a more robust system. The layered system model is depicted in Fig. 3.

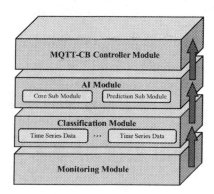

Fig. 3. The layered system model.

4.1   Monitoring Module

The Monitoring Module monitors each client and stores the resulting network traffic data in a database. This module ensures that monitoring is performed for each broker and that time-series data is persisted in a database. To achieve this, we employ the Tshark tool [25], a Linux-based command-line version of Wireshark, which enables us to monitor and analyze network traffic in a software-based manner. This approach provides us with the required capabilities for network monitoring while ensuring the system's scalability and flexibility. Furthermore, we utilize SQLite [26] as the database engine to store the monitored data. SQLite is a lightweight, fast, and stable database engine that is well-suited for our model's requirements.

4.2   Classification Module

The Classification Module of our proposed MQTT-CB protocol is tasked with classifying the monitored data that is stored in the database. This module is implemented using Python 3 programming language and reads the database that contains the monitored data. Upon reading the database, the module reduces the network data every five minutes into a single time series data. The time series data consists of the average delay, the average retransmitted packets and the total packet number. Once the classification process is complete, the classified data is transformed into a shape compatible with the AI module's requirements.

4.3   AI Module

The AI Module is designed to learn from the classified time series data and generate predictions about future network traffic patterns. An LSTM model is employed within the module to forecast the number of retransmitted packets within the upcoming five-minute periods. Deep learning techniques are utilized in this module to provide a more intelligent and scalable MQTT protocol for the IoT domain. By leveraging the power of artificial neural networks, the proposed model can identify complex patterns and make accurate predictions about network traffic, resulting in a more efficient and reliable communication system for IoT devices.

We have a scalable MQTT protocol in terms of broker numbers. To do that, we have to predict upcoming retransmitted packets in the future. The problem is that the number of retransmitted packets are dependent sequences, complicating the prediction. However, Recurrent Neural Network (RNN) solves this problem according to [27]. In that work, they define RNN as an artificial neural network (ANN) that uses time series to make predictions. Hence, the RNN model can predict retransmitted packets in the future. However, it is hard to train RNNs to solve issues that need learning long-term time series because the gradient of the loss function decreases fast when time passes, according to [28]. Thus, we prefer to use a more sophisticated RNN implementation called LSTM in terms of memory usage in our AI Module.

The LSTM is also suitable for time series data, and its main advantage over the RNN is that it can maintain information in its memory for a more extended period, as explained in [29]. LSTM models work like RNNs in that they can remember previous information and use it to process current inputs. However, due to the vanishing gradient situation, RNNs need to retain long-term dependencies. On the other hand, the LSTM model is explicitly designed to avoid long-term dependence problems. As noted in [30], LSTM networks construct on the capabilities of RNNs to expand memory and can serve as the core blocks for an RNN's layers. Therefore, the LSTM model is more suitable for making predictions regarding memory usage and performance, as indicated by [29,30].

In our LSTM model, we employ an autoregressive approach similar to that described in [31]. An autoregressive network is a neural network that generates the value of one sample by relying on previously generated samples. This approach involves making one prediction at a time and feeding the output back into the model. The mechanics of the autoregressive LSTM are illustrated in Fig. 4.

In summary, the AI Module incorporates an LSTM model to make predictions about retransmitted packets in the future, treating them as time series data. The

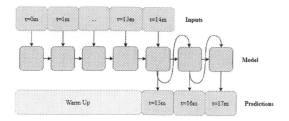

Fig. 4. Auto Regressive LSTM Model.

module comprises two sub-modules: the Core and Prediction Sub Modules, which facilitate these operations together.

Core Sub Module. The Core Sub Module plays a crucial role in our system by compiling and re-generating the LSTM model at pre-defined periods. However, since there is no input for the number of retransmitted packets when the model is run for the first time, it operates at a reduced capacity during the warm-up phase, which lasts for the first three hours after the module is booted up. During this time, the Monitoring Module collects the required network data while a single MQTT-CB broker is used. After the warm-up phase, the Core Sub Module generates the first LSTM model and makes its initial prediction.

After the first prediction, the Core Sub Module compiles and fits the LSTM model with new time series data every five minutes. The user can modify the period configuration as needed, initially set to five minutes in the default settings. The module performs this recompilation operation on the first day at five-minute intervals. After the first day, the periods are changed to one day, and the module recompiles the LSTM model daily.

The Core Sub Module of the AI Module generates predictions of the number of retransmitted packets for three-time steps ahead, which corresponds to fifteen minutes into the future. The predicted average retransmission number is then forwarded to the Prediction Sub Module for further processing.

Prediction Sub Module. The Prediction Sub Module predicts the following retransmitted packet number fifteen minutes later. We choose this value to give time to MQTT-CB Controller to run new brokers or stop the existing ones. The Prediction Sub Module makes its decisions as follows. If the percentage of predicted retransmitted packets fifteen minutes later is higher than ten percent, then the LSTM model decides that create a new broker. We calculate the retransmission percentage RP_t as in the Eq. 1.

$$R_t/P_t = RP_t(\%) \tag{1}$$

where, R_t refers to the number of retransmitted packets in a specific time slot t, while P_t denotes the total number of packets transmitted in the same time slot.

The Prediction Sub Module also checks the percentage of retransmitted packets in periods. Suppose the retransmitted packets are below one percent of the total number of packets in that period, which happens three times. In that case, the module passes the decision of shutting down a broker to the MQTT-CB Controller.

4.4   MQTT-CB Controller Module

The MQTT-CB Controller Module serves as an orchestrator for all MQTT-ST brokers. It is a Python 3-based software that manages the creation and deletion of brokers in response to predictions made by the AI Module. The MQTT-CB Controller leverages the Docker CLI to perform these operations. This module is a master, with all brokers operating as its slaves. The MQTT-CB Controller monitors the brokers' health and automatically creates new brokers if any go down. In summary, the MQTT-CB Controller Module is responsible for creating, deleting, and managing the brokers in order to maintain the overall health of the MQTT-ST system.

5   Simulation Environment

To simulate our MQTT-CB and MQTT-ST models in our experiments, we utilized the BORDER framework [15]. This framework places each client and broker in separate Docker containers, providing an isolated environment for each container using Docker Engine, container-based technology that provides a command line interface (CLI) to control or interact with each Docker container. The framework also relies on the Containernet network emulator, developed on Mininet, providing a variety of network components in the Docker containers for simulation. This emulator is container-based, providing an isolated environment in terms of computer resources and enabling a resource-independent test environment. Additionally, the Timing Compensated High-Speed Optical Link (TCLink) was used between each local network, which provides adjustable link configurations in terms of delay and bandwidth, thus providing a configurable network environment with Docker containers.

We have two simulation environments for our evaluations, one for MQTT-ST and one for our model MQTT-CB, inspired by the BORDER framework. In contrast to the BORDER framework, we provide a test environment where the number of brokers is dynamically changeable. We simulate MQTT-ST without changing the number of clients and brokers because it is not a dynamic MQTT protocol adapting to changing environmental conditions. We conduct these tests in the first simulation environment. The second test environment simulates our model MQTT-CB, a software-based upper layer on all brokers, as shown in Fig. 2. MQTT-CB has developed using Python 3, orchestrating the brokers using Docker CLI.

In our experiments, the MQTT-CB controller module is responsible for deciding whether a new broker is required. Based on the decision made by the controller, a new broker is created and launched using Docker CLI. In addition,

Table 1. Simulation Parameters.

Parameter	Value
MQTT-ST broker number	2
MQTT-CB broker number	starts with 2
RAM limit of brokers	2 GB
Number of CPU for each broker	1
Delay between router	10 ms
Delay between router and switch	0 ms
Delay between switch and client	0 ms
Subscriber number	200
Publisher number	10
Packet rate	5 msg/s
Packet size	20 bytes
Quality of Service (QoS)	1

the MQTT-CB controller can delete existing brokers, as determined by the prediction model. As a result, unlike MQTT-ST, the simulation environment for MQTT-CB is dynamic, with varying numbers of clients and brokers. The QoS (Quality of Service) level of the MQTT protocol is set to one, which is referred to at least once. This QoS level ensures that a packet is delivered to the receiver at least once, with the sender storing the message until it gets an ACK packet from the recipient. A packet can be sent or delivered multiple times, resulting in packet retransmission in the MQTT protocol. We provide a detailed overview of the simulation parameters in Table 1, which are the default values we adjust during the experiments to evaluate the protocol's behavior. Performance evaluation section contains additional information regarding these adjustments.

6   Performance Evaluation

In this study, we employ three types of evaluation strategies. Firstly, we conduct a real-time comparison of MQTT-ST and MQTT-CB to observe the running mechanism of our model and the delay between the subscribers and publishers. Secondly, we calculate the percentage of retransmitted packets in real-time to evaluate the prediction accuracy of our model. Lastly, we compare the overall delay of the two protocols over a certain amount of time.

We use a pre-trained model warmed up for three hours for all evaluations to collect necessary network data. As a result, all-time representations in the evaluation figures start after the initial three-hour running period. In all figures, we define the delay as the passing time between the publishers and subscribers.

We conduct three experiments with different publication rates using the evaluation mentioned earlier strategies. In the first experiment, we keep the publication rate constant for MQTT-ST and MQTT-CB, as specified in Table 1. In the second experiment, we increase the publication rate after a while and observe the behavior of our model. Lastly, in the third experiment, we evaluate the performance of our model as the publication rate decreased in real-time.

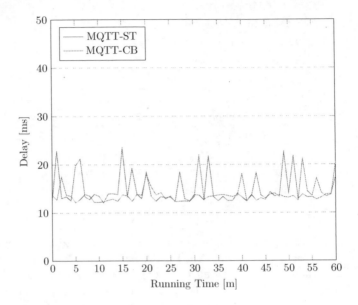

Fig. 5. Ex-1: The average delay of packets by constant 5 msg/s publication rate.

In the first experiment, we simulate MQTT-ST and MQTT-CB protocols with the same set of parameters listed in Table 1. We maintain constant values for all parameters to observe how our AI model performs in real-time. We introduced a burst of packets at a publication rate of 5 messages per second into the network. As shown in Fig. 5, both MQTT-ST and MQTT-CB behave similarly, as MQTT-CB is built on MQTT-ST and operates in the same way in a stable environment. The performance of our model can be seen in the prediction plot in Fig. 6. Moreover, the overall average delay of both protocols is approximately the same, as depicted in the plot in Fig. 7.

In the second experiment, we conduct simulations using the same parameters as in Table 1. All parameters were kept constant, except for the publication rate, which is varied. We initially fed the network with packets at a rate of 5 msg/s in bursting mode. After ten minutes, we increase the publication rate to 50 msg/s. In Zone-2, we observe that the delay for both protocols increased. Figure 8 depicts this increase in delay. At the end of Zone-2, the Prediction Module determines that the number of brokers needed to be increased by one. The reason for this can be seen in Fig. 9, which shows that the prediction percentage of retransmitted packets at the end of Zone-3 is higher than 10%. Thus, the MQTT-CB Controller creates a new broker at the end of Zone-2 because the model predicted according to values 15 min later, corresponding to the end of

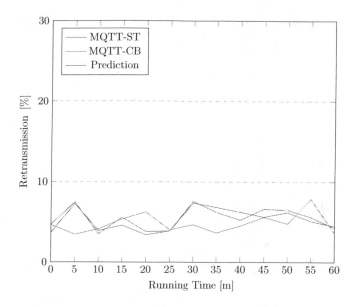

Fig. 6. Ex-1: The retransmission percentage by constant 5 msg/s publication rate.

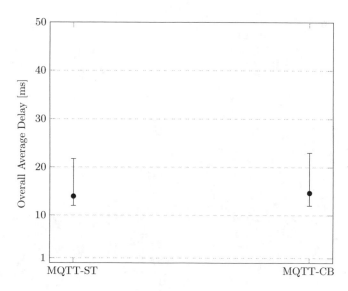

Fig. 7. Ex-1: The overall average delay of packets by constant 5 msg/s publication rate.

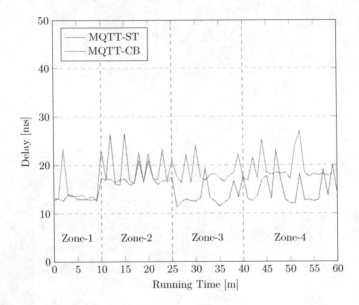

Fig. 8. Ex-2: The average delay of packets by increasing publication rate.

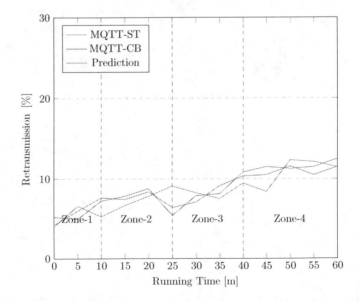

Fig. 9. Ex-2: The retransmission percentage by increasing publication rate.

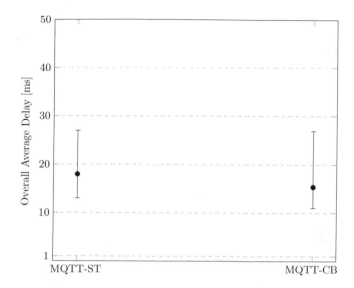

Fig. 10. Ex-2: The overall average delay of packets by increasing publication rate.

Zone-3. As a result, the delay for MQTT-CB decreases by approximately 3ms due to the increased number of brokers in Fig. 8. However, the retransmission rate for MQTT-ST and MQTT-CB is similar after Zone-2. Nevertheless, we focus on the delay for performance evaluation; hence, we use Fig. 9 for prediction. Moreover, the overall average delay of MQTT-CB is less than MQTT-ST, as illustrated in Fig. 10, although it has an extensive range.

In the third experiment, we conduct the simulation with the same parameters listed in Table 1. We decrease the publication rate in this experiment, feeding the network with packets in bursting mode at a rate of 5 msg/s until ten minutes have elapsed, after which we decrease the publication rate to 2 msg/s. In Zone-2, we observe that the delay for both protocols decreased. As shown in Fig. 11, at the end of Zone-3, the Prediction Module decides to decrease the number of brokers by one. This decision is based on the percentage of retransmitted packets predicted by the model, which was less than one percent at the end of Zone-2, and remained low until the end of Zone-3 in Fig. 12. This results in the MQTT-CB Controller deleting a broker at the end of Zone-3, which increases the delay of the MQTT-CB by about 3ms. Additionally, we can see in Fig. 13 that the overall average delay of MQTT-CB is higher than MQTT-ST. This is because we decrease the number of brokers, which impacts the delay. However, this approach helps decrease the resource consumption of brokers and clients without compromising performance in terms of delay. Here we assume the main reason for power consumption is the number of brokers, not the retransmission rate.

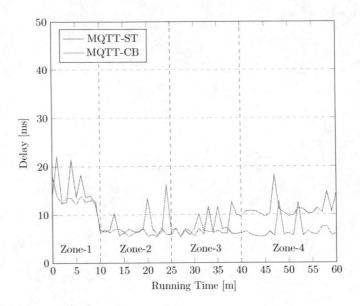

Fig. 11. Ex-3: The average delay of packets by decreasing publication rate.

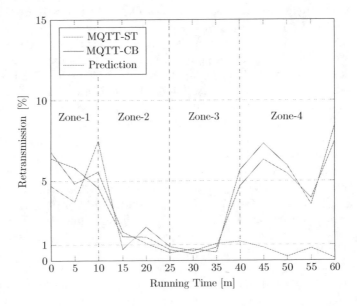

Fig. 12. Ex-3: The retransmission percentage by decreasing publication rate.

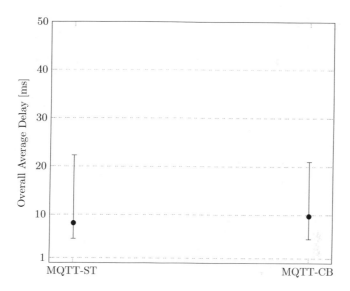

Fig. 13. Ex-3: The overall average delay of packets decreasing publication rate.

7   Conclusion

The MQTT protocol is widely used in the IoT industry. However, traditional MQTT protocols in literature are not designed for distributed environments and lack scalability. In this study, we propose a new MQTT-ST-based protocol that is intelligent, scalable, and distributed. To enhance the portability of our protocol, we utilize containers, and our cloud-based architecture facilitates easy deployment. Our primary contribution is adding intelligence to the MQTT-ST protocol. Our protocol can predict retransmitted packets in the future and dynamically adjust the number of brokers in real-time. Furthermore, it can decrease the number of brokers when clients are idle. Our experiments demonstrate that our protocol outperforms the MQTT-ST protocol regarding the delay between subscribers and publishers. Additionally, our protocol adapts well to changing environments regarding publication rates. Thus, we present an intelligent cloud-based MQTT protocol.

In future work, we aim to improve the accuracy of our prediction model and eliminate the warm-up time without affecting predictions. Also, we can evaluate our model with more brokers for all experiments, especially for resource consumption evaluation. Additionally, we can apply this intelligent model to other IoT protocols.

Acknowledgements. Muhammed Raşit Erol has received support from The Scientific and Technical Research Council of Turkey (TUBITAK) 2210A-National Scholarship Programme for MSc Students for this paper.

References

1. Mishra, B., Kertesz, A.: The use of MQTT in M2M and IoT systems: a survey. IEEE Access **8**, 201071–201086 (2020). https://doi.org/10.1109/ACCESS.2020. 3035849
2. Naik, N.: Choice of effective messaging protocols for IoT systems: MQTT, CoAP, AMQP and HTTP. In: IEEE International Systems Engineering Symposium (ISSE), Vienna, Austria 2017, pp. 1–7 (2017). https://doi.org/10.1109/SysEng. 2017.8088251
3. Al-Fuqaha, A., Guizani, M., Mohammadi, M., Aledhari, M., Ayyash, M.: Internet of Things: a survey on enabling technologies, protocols, and applications. IEEE Commun. Surv. Tutorials **17**(4), 2347–2376 (2015). https://doi.org/10.1109/ COMST.2015.2444095
4. Johnsen, F.T., Landmark, L., Hauge, M., Larsen, E., Kure, Ø.: Publish/subscribe versus a content-based approach for information dissemination. In: MILCOM 2018–2018 IEEE Military Communications Conference (MILCOM), Los Angeles, CA, USA, pp. 1–9 (2018). https://doi.org/10.1109/MILCOM.2018.8599786
5. Ronzani, D., Palazzi, C.E., Manzoni, P.: Bringing MQTT brokers to the edge: a preliminary evaluation. In: IEEE 19th Annual Consumer Communications and Networking Conference (CCNC), Las Vegas, NV, USA 2022, pp. 695–698 (2022). https://doi.org/10.1109/CCNC49033.2022.9700526
6. Koziolek, H., Grüner, S., Rückert, J.: A comparison of MQTT brokers for distributed IoT edge computing. In: Jansen, A., Malavolta, I., Muccini, H., Ozkaya, I., Zimmermann, O. (eds.) ECSA 2020. LNCS, vol. 12292, pp. 352–368. Springer, Cham (2020). https://doi.org/10.1007/978-3-030-58923-3_23
7. Banno, R., Sun, J., Fujita, M., Takeuchi, S., Shudo, K.: Dissemination of edge-heavy data on heterogeneous MQTT brokers. In: 2017 IEEE 6th International Conference on Cloud Networking (CloudNet), Prague, Czech Republic, pp. 1–7 (2017). https://doi.org/10.1109/CloudNet.2017.8071523
8. Banno, R., Ohsawa, K., Kitagawa, Y., Takada, T., Yoshizawa, T.: Measuring performance of MQTT v5.0 brokers with MQTTLoader. In: 2021 IEEE 18th Annual Consumer Communications and Networking Conference (CCNC), pp. 1–2 (2021)
9. Jutadhamakorn, P., Pillavas, T., Visoottiviseth, V., Takano, R., Haga, J., Kobayashi, D.: A scalable and low-cost MQTT broker clustering system. In: 2017 2nd International Conference on Information Technology (INCIT), Nakhonpathom, Thailand, 2017, pp. 1–5 (2017). https://doi.org/10.1109/INCIT.2017. 8257870
10. Bender, M., Kirdan, E., Pahl, M.-O., Carle, G.: Open-Source MQTT Evaluation. In: IEEE 18th Annual Consumer Communications & Networking Conference (CCNC), Las Vegas, NV, USA 2021, pp. 1–4 (2021). https://doi.org/10.1109/ CCNC49032.2021.9369499
11. Longo, E., Redondi, A.E., Cesana, M., Arcia-Moret, A., Manzoni, P.: MQTT-ST: a spanning tree protocol for distributed MQTT brokers. In: ICC 2020–2020 IEEE International Conference on Communications (ICC), Dublin, Ireland, pp. 1–6 (2020). https://doi.org/10.1109/ICC40277.2020.9149046
12. Emitter: Distributed Publish-Subscribe Platform. https://github.com/emitter-io/ emitter. Accessed 12 Aug 2022
13. Downloading and Installing RabbitMQ. https://www.rabbitmq.com/download. html. Accessed 14 Aug 2022

14. VerneMQ: A Distributed MQTT Broker. https://github.com/vernemq/vernemq. Accessed 14 Aug 2022

15. Longo, E., Redondi, A.E.C., Cesana, M., Manzoni, P.: BORDER: a benchmarking framework for distributed MQTT brokers. IEEE Internet Things J. **9**(18), 17728–17740 (2022). https://doi.org/10.1109/JIOT.2022.3155872

16. Staglianò, L., Longo, E., Redondi, A.E.: D-MQTT: design and implementation of a pub/sub broker for distributed environments. In: 2021 IEEE International Conference on Omni-Layer Intelligent Systems (COINS), Barcelona, Spain, pp. 1–6 (2021). https://doi.org/10.1109/COINS51742.2021.9524110

17. Rausch, T., Nastic, S., Dustdar, S.: EMMA: distributed QoS-aware MQTT middleware for edge computing applications. In: 2018 IEEE International Conference on Cloud Engineering (IC2E), Orlando, FL, USA, 2018, pp. 191–197 (2018). https://doi.org/10.1109/IC2E.2018.00043

18. Thean, Z.Y., Voon Yap, V., Teh, P.C.: Container-based MQTT broker cluster for edge computing. In: 4th International Conference and Workshops on Recent Advances and Innovations in Engineering (ICRAIE). Kedah, Malaysia, pp. 1–6 (2019). https://doi.org/10.1109/ICRAIE47735.2019.9037775

19. Bellavista, P., Foschini, L., Ghiselli, N., Reale, A.: MQTT-based middleware for container support in fog computing environments. In: IEEE Symposium on Computers and Communications (ISCC). Barcelona, Spain, pp. 1–7 (2019). https://doi.org/10.1109/ISCC47284.2019.8969615

20. Puliafito, C., Virdis, A., Mingozzi, E.: The impact of container migration on fog services as perceived by mobile things. In: 2020 IEEE International Conference on Smart Computing (SMARTCOMP), Bologna, Italy, pp. 9–16 (2020). https://doi.org/10.1109/SMARTCOMP50058.2020.00022

21. Abdelwahab, S., Hamdaoui, B.: FogMQ: A Message Broker System for Enabling Distributed, Internet-Scale IoT Applications over Heterogeneous Cloud Platforms (2016). ArXiv:1610.00620

22. Matic, M., Antic, M., Istvan, P.A.P.P., Ivanovic, S.: Optimization of MQTT communication between microservices in the IoT cloud. In: 2021 IEEE International Conference on Consumer Electronics (ICCE), Las Vegas, NV, USA, 2021, pp. 1–3 (2021). https://doi.org/10.1109/ICCE50685.2021.9427602

23. Ak, E., Canberk, B.: Forecasting quality of service for next-generation data-driven WiFi6 campus networks. IEEE Trans. Netw. Serv. Manage. **18**(4), 4744–4755 (2021). https://doi.org/10.1109/TNSM.2021.3108766

24. Madan, R., Mangipudi, P.S.: Predicting computer network traffic: a time series forecasting approach using DWT, ARIMA and RNN. In: 2018 Eleventh International Conference on Contemporary Computing (IC3), Noida, India, pp. 1–5 (2018). https://doi.org/10.1109/IC3.2018.8530608

25. tshark(1). (n.d.). https://www.wireshark.org/docs/man-pages/tshark.html Accessed 17 Jan 2022

26. SQLite Home Page. (n.d.). https://sqlite.org/index.html Accessed 15 Jan 2022

27. Mou, L., Ghamisi, P., Zhu, X.X.: Deep recurrent neural networks for hyperspectral image classification. IEEE Trans. Geosci. Remote Sens. **55**(7), 3639–3655 (2017). https://doi.org/10.1109/TGRS.2016.2636241

28. Chung, J., Gulcehre, C., Cho, K., Bengio, Y.: Empirical evaluation of gated recurrent neural networks on sequence modeling. In: NIPS 2014 Workshop on Deep Learning (2014)

29. Hochreiter, S., Schmidhuber, J.: Long short-term memory. Neural Comput. **9**(8), 1735–1780 (1997). https://doi.org/10.1162/neco.1997.9.8.1735

30. Karim, F., Majumdar, S., Darabi, H., Chen, S.: LSTM fully convolutional networks for time series classification. IEEE Access **6**, 1662–1669 (2018). https://doi.org/10.1109/ACCESS.2017.2779939

31. Fu, R., Zhang, Z., Li, L.: Using LSTM and GRU neural network methods for traffic flow prediction. In: 31st Youth Academic Annual Conference of Chinese Association of Automation (YAC), Wuhan, China 2016, pp. 324–328 (2016). https://doi.org/10.1109/YAC.2016.7804912

Security and Privacy

Enhancing Load Balancing in Cloud Computing Through Deadlock Prediction

Hieu Le Ngoc[1]([⊠]) [iD] and Hung Tran Cong[2]

[1] Ho Chi Minh City Open University, Ho Chi Minh City, Vietnam
hieu.ln@ou.edu.vn
[2] Posts and Telecommunication Institute of Technology, Ho Chi Minh City, Vietnam
conghung@ptithcm.edu.vn

Abstract. Cloud computing has become a crucial aspect of Information Technology, offering solutions to many of the challenges faced by internet users. However, the increasing number of users worldwide has led to congestion at certain nodes, resulting in unbalanced loads or hanging systems, commonly known as deadlock. This paper proposes an algorithm using deadlock prediction to enhance the load balancer in Cloud environment. This algorithm leverages Machine Learning and prediction techniques, specifically the Linear Regression Model, to forecast the possibility of deadlock in VMs. By predicting deadlock, the available resources can be allocated to satisfy all requests. The algorithm was deployed in the CloudSim simulation environment, which was integrated with Weka library for the Machine Learning techniques. The results were compared to well-known algorithms such as FCFS, RoundRobin, MaxMin, and MinMin. The evaluation revealed that the proposed algorithm outperformed these popular algorithms, demonstrating its effectiveness in enhancing Cloud computing's load balancing capabilities.

Keywords: Cloud Computing · Load Balancing · Deadlock Prediction

1 Introduction

Cloud computing, according to [1] and [2], is a rapidly growing field in information technology that has the potential to revolutionize the industry. IT developers can now create innovative internet services without needing significant investments in hardware or human resources to operate them. Through applications such as web browsers, mobile apps, and personal computers, many people can access and use cloud services.

Load balancing is crucial for maximizing the benefits of cloud computing. It helps to maintain a balanced state in the cloud and improve services for clients by evenly distributing resources and reducing deadlock. Load balancing algorithms typically focus on performance and economic metrics, scheduling and allocating algorithms, and heuristic or optimization-based enhanced balancers. However, internal factors are not the only ones that affect load balancing in the cloud. External factors, such as the network, users, and geography, can also impact its performance. Deadlock on the cloud can also occur due to user behavior.

© ICST Institute for Computer Sciences, Social Informatics and Telecommunications Engineering 2023
Published by Springer Nature Switzerland AG 2023. All Rights Reserved
N.-S. Vo and H.-A. Tran (Eds.): INISCOM 2023, LNICST 531, pp. 257–274, 2023.
https://doi.org/10.1007/978-3-031-47359-3_19

This paper takes an external perspective on load balancing in the cloud and focuses on the issue of deadlock. The authors propose a new approach for predicting deadlock, with the aim of reducing congestion and hanging status when distributing resources among virtual machines (VMs). To model deadlock, they use linear regression based on historical usage data of the VMs, taking into account both request properties and cloudlet features. Using this approach, the authors aim to allocate requests to the appropriate VM, based on the predicted usage data and the current status of all VMs, in order to avoid deadlock. The propose using thresholds for CPU, RAM, and storage usage to detect when a VM is likely to cause a deadlock and to allocate the request to a different VM. This approach has the potential to improve load balancing in cloud computing.

This article makes several key contributions. Firstly, it approaches load balancing in cloud computing from an external perspective, specifically examining the occurrence of deadlock in VMs. Secondly, it proposes a novel approach for predicting deadlock using Linear Regression Model and applying thresholds. Finally, it presents an experimental evaluation of the proposed algorithm, Deadlock Prediction Algorithm, which outperforms existing algorithms in load balancing.

To make our proposal more accessible, we have structured the paper into 5 sections. The first section, which is the current section, serves as the introduction. The following section reviews and examines related studies. Section 3 presents and explains our proposed algorithm, Deadlock Prediction Algorithm (DPA). In Sect. 4, we discuss the simulation and experiment outcomes, as well as the evaluations. Finally, in Sect. 5, we summarize the main findings of the paper and suggest possible future research.

2 Related Work

Based on references [3] and [4], Cloud Computing is a computing model that utilizes computer technologies and internet-based development. It is also known as virtual server with pay-per-use. Under this model, all resources, software, and information are shared and provided as services to computers, devices, and users over a public network, typically the internet, on an infrastructure platform. Figure 1 gives us an easy imagination about how computing is structured.

Load Balancing [5, 6] is a crucial technique in cloud computing that improves server performance by effectively distributing resources and avoiding deadlocks. It has several key functions, including blocking network traffic to prevent overloading on a single server, distributing loads to servers for processing, handling, and returning results. Load Balancing can also offer redundancy by using multiple failover scenarios.Subsequent paragraphs, however, are indented. Figure 2 illustrates the role of cloud load balancing in the internet.

Deadlock is a computer problem, and it is also a system problem [8–18]. Deadlock is a situation where a group of processes becomes stuck in an infinite waiting state, and this can occur in various computing systems, including cloud, distributed, and grid computing. The advancement of machine learning and data analysis techniques has made it possible to predict the occurrence of deadlock in cloud environments. This prediction can be useful in efficiently allocating resources, particularly virtual machines, on the cloud. Figure 3 shows the unsafe state and safe state and the possibilities of deadlock in allocating resources.

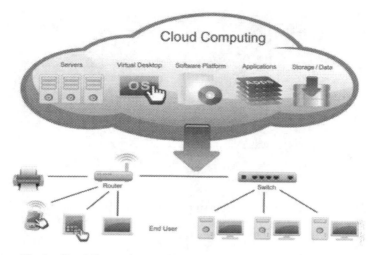

Fig. 1. Cloud Computing model (source: https://informationq.com/)

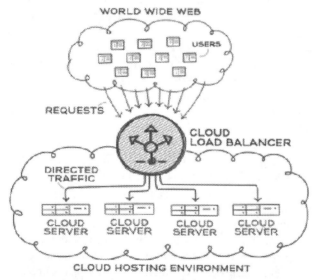

Fig. 2. An example of Cloud load balancer [7]

This article introduces a novel approach in cloud computing, which is predicting the usage of resources for a request. While there have been studies on using ML in distributed systems to predict resource usage, this approach is relatively new. Various ML methods can be used to predict resource usage, each with its own accuracy level [20, 21]. Linear Regression [22], Regression Trees [23], Bagging using Regression Trees [24], and Artificial Neural Networks [25] are some popular ML techniques for resource usage prediction. After evaluating these methods, this paper focuses on using Linear

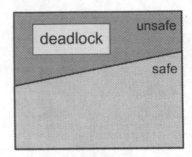

Fig. 3. Safe, unsafe, and deadlock state spaces [19]

Regression on historical data of processing requests from VMs to predict the resource usage of future requests, for the purpose of runtime response.

In 2012, Rashmi K.S and their team [8] from India proposed an algorithm to avoid deadlock in cloud computing, recognizing that a deadlock is possible due to decentralization and virtualization. Their algorithm aimed to increase the amount of processing work in the cloud for better service and to avoid deadlock, analyzing the capabilities and availability of virtual machines and updating the data structure. Although the proposed algorithm was a good approach at the time, it may need to be improved to fit more complicated and scalable cloud systems. In 2013, J.Lim et al. from Korea [9] proposed a scalable and fault-tolerant deadlock detection algorithm for cloud computing using gossip protocol. Their proposed algorithm considered circular wait and violations of safety and liveness properties. They used O(n) to evaluate the algorithm and the Peer-Sim simulator for the experiment, which showed significant improvement over existing algorithms in solving scalability and fault-tolerance issues. Mahitha.O et al. [10] proposed an efficient load balancing technique in their 2013 article "Deadlock Avoidance through Efficient Load Balancing to Control Disaster in Cloud Environment", to control deadlock issues in Cloud. The authors focused on the deadlock occurring due to a loop inside a VM where a job waits for another resource, and this resource also waits for that job. The proposed tuning algorithm uses CloudAnalyst tool to compare cloud performance with and without a load balancer, resulting in better resource management and improved response time. Figure 4 is the approach of the research by Mahitha.O et al.

In 2015, Cuong Nguyen and his co-author [11] improved the detection and avoidance of deadlock in heterogeneous distributed platforms. The authors highlighted that the main problem in this type of platform is task distribution among different processors. They proposed an algorithm [12] for resource allocation to improve the detection and avoidance of deadlock in heterogeneous platforms. The authors experimented with Resource Allocation Graph (RAG) and CloudSim, reducing the matrix complexity of the RAG for better efficiency in distributed systems like the cloud.

The article "Deadlock Avoidance in Sequential Resource Allocation Systems with Potential Resource Outages" by Spyros Reveliotis and his colleagues [13], published in 2016, aimed to extend the Sequential Resource Allocation Systems (RASs) by addressing potential resource outages. They used the Switched Discrete Event Systems (s-DES) to systematically treat the complicated version of the RAS deadlock avoidance problem. They decomposed the RAS operation and corresponding policy into operational modes

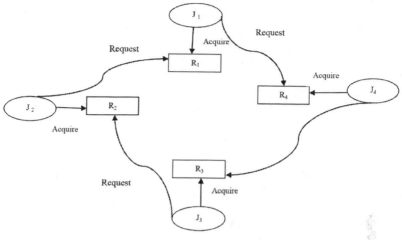

Fig. 4. Deadlock in Cloud [10].

and developed localized predicates to enable the formal characterization and effective computation of the sought supervisor, which leads to a distributed representation for the supervisor suitable for real-time implementation.

Deepti Malhotra [14] developed an efficient control scheme in 2016 to prevent deadlock in grid computing, which is difficult to avoid or detect. The objective of the study was to maximize resource availability and utilization to prevent deadlock and preserve data consistency. Using the C programming language, the proposed algorithm was tested and shown to detect deadlock and unstable states in virtual machines. In 2018, Emeka E. Ugwuanyi [15] proposed a resource provisioning algorithm using banker's deadlock avoidance technique for Industrial IoT devices in Multi-Access Edge Computing (MEC), which reduces communication overhead by incorporating SDN. The simulation results of the paper showed that applying the proposed algorithm prevents system deadlock and leads to a more reliable network interaction between mobile stations and MEC platforms (Table 1).

Table 1. Deadlock strategies [15]

Detection Algorithms	Lamport's algorithm
	Chandy-Misra-Haas algorithm
	Parallel Deadlock Detection Algorithm
	Detection in heterogeneous systems
	Unstructured deadlock detection
Prevention Algorithms	Load balancing methods
	Deadlock Prevention Algorithm in Grid Environment
Avoidance Algorithms	Banker's algorithm

In 2019, Cuong Nguyen and colleagues [16] introduced a novel model for resource allocation, called Avoid Deadlock Resource Allocation (ADRA). The authors aimed to improve resource allocation strategies for cloud computing, which inherited the concept of grid computing. The ADRA algorithm uses Wait-For-Graph (WFG) to prevent deadlock by allocating multiple resources to competing services running on heterogeneous distributed platforms. The algorithm was evaluated in a simulation environment using CloudSim, and its complexity was analyzed, revealing an improvement in time complexity compared to previous approaches. The experimental results showed that the ADRA algorithm is efficient and effective in managing resources and preventing deadlock.

In 2019, Sonam Sherpa et al. [17] presented a new approach to understanding and detecting deadlocks in software development. They focused on the perspective of developers and programmers who create the algorithms that can lead to deadlock. The authors argued that it is difficult to diagnose and reproduce deadlock bugs during the algorithm development process, resulting in high runtime overhead. To address this problem, they proposed the use of resource consumption footprints to identify concurrency bugs. This approach is based on the idea that the patterns of resource access and consumption are critical indicators of the behavior of concurrent software and can be used to guide the software debugging process. The authors demonstrated that monitoring resource footprints at runtime can effectively help detect software bugs, and for MPI programs, a simple SVM classifier can detect deadlocks with high accuracy using only the CPU usage patterns. The paper provides a different perspective on the problem of deadlock and suggests the use of machine learning techniques to detect and avoid it. Figure 5 is the testing result of Sonam Sherpa et al. which shows that the CPU usage can be reached to 100%.

In 2021, Yu V Bondarenko and colleagues [18] published a study on an algorithm and model to enhance the avoidance of deadlock in cloud environments. The objective was to improve the efficiency of resource allocation for the dynamic scaling of services and virtualized resources. As resource constraints can lead to deadlock, the authors designed an algorithm that leverages the execution time attribute of the process and a checking system to ensure a safe state and avoid deadlock. The improved algorithm builds on the banker algorithm by incorporating four arrays: MaxV for maximum available resources in VM, AlocV for allocation process in the initial state, AvelV for available resources in the initial state, and TQ for a temporary Queue to save the ID of waiting job requests. The paper provides a mathematical model and shows results obtained from the modeling.

After reviewing past research on deadlock in cloud environments, we have identified a gap in the field and propose a new prediction method to address it. Our method uses data on the virtual machines (VMs) and their resources to predict the likelihood of a deadlock occurring. This prediction is then integrated into the load balancing process, allowing requests to be allocated to the most appropriate VM for optimal performance. Importantly, our approach is fully automated and does not require input from expert analysts.

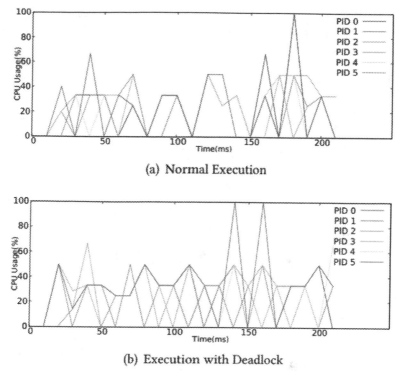

(a) Normal Execution

(b) Execution with Deadlock

Fig. 5. Resource Consumption Traces [17]

3 Proposal

Our proposal focuses on ensuring good responsiveness and avoiding deadlock in the cloud environment through the use of algorithms for deadlock prediction and probabilities. We aim to improve service for users by ensuring a safe state. Our approach specifically targets virtualization in the cloud, utilizing virtual machines (VMs) and VM pools on physical hosts and datacenters. We believe it is necessary to focus on potential deadlocks in VMs, as they are responsible for processing and handling all user requests.

3.1 Research Model

The resource allocation algorithm is not suitable for systems that have multiple instances for each resource type. However, the proposed algorithm for avoiding deadlock can be implemented in load balancing for cloud environments. The algorithm aims to predict and detect deadlock occurrences by identifying busy and active areas and reallocating requests to more available resources. The algorithm is called DPA, which stands for Deadlock Prediction Algorithm. The algorithm utilizes Linear Regression prediction to forecast the unsafe state of VMs and the possibility of deadlock. Based on this prediction, the algorithm allocates requests to available resources to prevent deadlock from occurring. Figure 6 illustrates our research model which is less simple than the real cloud environment model.

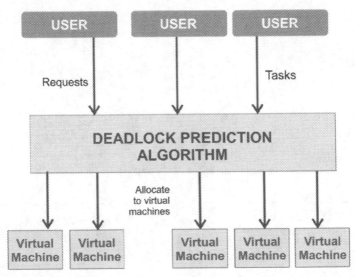

Fig. 6. The proposed DPA algorithm is developed and tested within the context of a research model for the cloud environment.

The Deadlock Prediction Algorithm (DPA) is developed based on the characteristics of deadlock in the Cloud research model. Deadlock is caused by tasks or requests that have processing times that are too long, leading to timeouts and disconnections. It can also occur when cloud resources are in conflict, where numerous requests or tasks are accessing the same resource at the same time, creating an endless loop that results in system crashes. The most common resources that are vulnerable to deadlock are the MEMORY (RAM), CPU, and STORAGE.

3.2 Proposed Algorithm

When a new request, or "cloudlet," is added to the Cloud, it comes with parameters such as size, number of files, return type, and more, which require a corresponding amount of resources to handle it. These resources are the virtual machines' resources and must not exceed the total available resources in the Cloud system. The system must first determine if allocating these resources will leave it in a safe state before proceeding with allocation. If it's safe, the resources are allocated, but if not, the process will have to wait until sufficient resources are released or be assigned to another virtual machine's resources.

To maintain a safe state and prevent deadlock, a prediction method is proposed based on calculating the probability of an unsafe state. This is achieved by using linear regression on historical data of past requests to build a prediction model. The input data includes request size, output size, file size, and the number of processors required, while the output data includes the usage of CPU, MEMORY, and STORAGE as percentages. If the predicted output values meet certain conditions, such as being less than the allowable thresholds, the request will be allocated to a virtual machine with suitable resource usage.

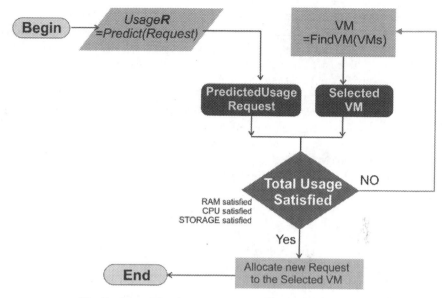

Fig. 7. Operating Diagram of the proposed algorithm DPA.

Figure 7 illustrates the proposed DPA, which comprises three main functions: 1) resource usage prediction function, which utilizes historical dataset and Linear Regression to predict resource usage; 2) select available VM function, which selects the VM with the minimum resource usage status among available VMs; and 3) allocation function, which allocates the request to the selected VM.

Pseudocode of DPA

---

1. **For each** Request **in** CloudRequests
2.   isLocated = false;
3.   PredictedUsage= {RAM, CPU, STORAGE}$_{predicted}$ = Predict(Request);
            ← Function 1: regression on historical dataset
4.   VM = FindVM(VMList);
            ← Function 2: select the VM with least resources usage
5.   **If** isSatisfied(PredictedUsage, VM)
6.   AllocateRequestToVM(VM, Request);
                ← Function 3: allocate the Request to the VM
7.   isLocated = true;
8.   **End If**
9.   **If**(!isLocated)
10.   VM = VMList.getSelectedVM();
11.   AllocateRequestToVM(VM, Request);
12.   **End If**
13. **End For**

This pseudocode outlines the steps of the proposed algorithm (DPA) for allocating resources to cloud requests in order to avoid deadlock. For each request in the list of CloudRequests, the algorithm first predicts the required resources (RAM, CPU, and

STORAGE) using historical data and a regression model. It then selects a virtual machine (VM) with the least resource usage that can satisfy the predicted resource requirements. If such a VM is found, the request is allocated to it. If not, the algorithm selects a VM based on a pre-defined selection criteria and allocates the request to it. The algorithm continues this process until all requests have been allocated to VMs. The proposed algorithm can be described in the following steps:

Step 1: The Deadlock Prediction Algorithm (DPA) maintains and updates information about the resource usage status of all virtual machines (VM) in real-time for load balancing. This information is stored in the Load Balancer (LB), which tracks the usage levels of each VM for MEMORY (RAM), CPU, and STORAGE, calculated as a percentage. Initially, all VMs are listed in the "VMUsageList" table with usage figures set to 0.

$$Usage = \{RAM, CPU, STORAGE\} \tag{1}$$

Step 2: When the load balancer receives a new request, it needs to process the task using appropriate resources. To predict which resources to use for the current request, the algorithm employs a Linear Regression Model that is built on the data of previous requests. If the algorithm is being initialized, the original dataset selected from the natural load balancing in Cloud is used for this purpose.

$$Predicted\ Usage = \{RAM, CPU, STORAGE\}_{predicted} = Predict(Request) \tag{2}$$

Step 3: The DPA load balancer is queried by the Central Command Control (CCC) for the next allocation. The corresponding resource usage for the current request is determined to allocate it to the virtual machine (VM) only if three conditions are met simultaneously. The RAM threshold is set between 90% and 95% of total RAM usage in the VM, depending on its power and configuration. The CPU threshold is set at a slightly higher level than the RAM threshold, within the range of 97% to 98%. The STORAGE threshold is set between 96% to 99%. If any of these three conditions is not met, the LB will reject the VM and try to find another suitable VM for allocation.

$$PredRAM\_UsageRequest + RAMUsageVM < ThresholdRAM \tag{3}$$

$$PredCPU\_UsageRequest + CPUUsageVM < ThresholdCPU \tag{4}$$

$$PredSTOR\_UsageRequest + STORUsageVM < ThresholdSTOR \tag{5}$$

Step 4: DPA load balancer selects the VM with the smallest usage and sends its ID to the Central Command Controller (CCC) to process the request. The load balancer updates the VM ID and waits for new requests. If no VMs are initialized, the load balancer returns -1 to the CCC and queues the request for the next allocation.

Step 5: After processing the request on the virtual machine (VM), the response is sent to the central controller (CCC), which will then notify the DPA load balancer. The load balancer will update the *"vmUsageList"* table and the Usage list of the VMs. If there are multiple requests, the central controller will perform Step 3 repeatedly until all the requests are processed properly.

Evaluation Criteria

In the experiment, the cloud was simulated with the given parameters, and CloudSim's load balancing algorithms including Round Robin, MaxMin, MinMin, and FCFS were executed with the same inputs. The outputs were compared, especially the Response Time parameters such as average, maximum, and minimum, as well as the total processing time (Makespan). The effectiveness of the evaluated algorithm is better if the predicted response time of the virtual machines and the predictive response time of the cloud have less error, which can lead to lower costs. The accuracy of the Linear Regression Model was evaluated using the RAE (Relative Absolute Error).

4 Simulation

This paper utilizes the CloudSim [26] library, written in the JAVA programming language, to simulate a Cloud environment. Additionally, the Weka library [27] is integrated into the simulation environment using JAVA, which allows for the use of the built-in LinearRegression function.

4.1 Simulation Environment

The Cloud environment used for the experiment consists of one Datacenter that has five hosts running five virtual machines. To test the effectiveness of the proposed Predicting Deadlock Occurrence Algorithm (DPA), random requests with different resource requirements are created (Tables 2 and 3).

Table 2. Configuration of Cloud Environment.

Datacenter configuration	Host and VM
- Number of hosts in datacenter: 5 - arch: x86 - OS: Linux - VMM: Xen - Time Zone: + 7 GMT - Cost: 3.0 - Cost per Memory: 0.05 - Cost per Storage: 0.1 - Cost per Bandwidth: 0.1	Each host in Datacenter has the following configuration: - CPU with 4 cores, each core is 1000 mips - Ram: 16384 (MB) - Storage: 1000000 Megabytes - Bandwidth: 10000 Mbps Each VM has the following configuration: - Size: 10000 MB - Ram: 512MB - Mips: 250 - Bandwith: 1000 Mbps - Pes no. 1 - VMM: Xen

Table 3. Request variant.

Length (MB)	File Size (Byte)	Output Size (Byte)	PEs
3000–1700	5000–45000	450–750	1

The proposed algorithm has been implemented in CloudSim's open source code by creating a class called *DPASchedulingAlgorithm* that inherits from the *BaseSchedulingAlgorithm* object. Several methods and properties have been updated to calculate virtual machine usage, and built-in functions have been adjusted to align with the proposed algorithm. The *predictRequestUsage* function has been added to forecast the resource usage of the request. Moreover, the *getMostSuitableVM* function is utilized to select a virtual machine that satisfies the three threshold conditions for request allocation.

4.2 Simulation Results

We performed simulation experiments using three different sets of input data, with 24, 100, and 997 requests. The request data was generated using *Epigenomics*, a tool proposed by https://github.com/WorkflowSim/WorkflowSim-1.0 [28].

Please note that the first paragraph of a section or subsection is not indented. The first paragraphs that follows a table, figure, equation etc. does not have an indent, either.

The first experiment, called *Case 1* (Epigenomics_24), involved simulating 24 requests in the Cloud environment using the proposed DPA algorithm and other load balancing algorithms. Table 4 and Fig. 8 display the results. Although the DPA algorithm seems to perform slightly better in terms of having the lowest average processing time, the difference between the algorithms is not significant due to the small number of requests. The FCFS algorithm, which processes requests in the order they are received, performed the worst with consistently higher processing times.

Table 4. Comparing the response times of algorithms in case 1.

Case 1	Overall response time		
	Avg (ms)	Min (ms)	Max (ms)
FCCS	1993.833	*0.18*	20363.49
MaxMin	1632.78	0.11	12825.62
Round Robin	1474.61	0.10	9487.84
MinMin	930.43	0.10	6027.47
DPA	**915.34**	0.11	**4582.72**

For *Case 2* (Epigenomics_100), a total of 100 requests were tested, and the outcome is illustrated in Table 5 and Fig. 9. The experiment revealed that the DPA algorithm

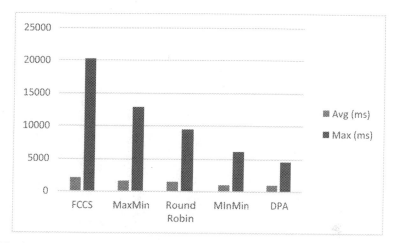

Fig. 8. Comparing the total response times of algorithms in case 1 with 24 requests.

outperforms other algorithms in terms of average processing time, while MaxMin has the lowest maximum processing time. Nonetheless, because of the limited number of requests, the variance between the algorithms is not significant. Additionally, the FCFS algorithm exhibits a natural pattern, with the processing time consistently the highest.

Table 5. Comparing the response times of algorithms in case 2.

Case 2	Overall response time		
	Avg (ms)	Min (ms)	Max (ms)
FCFS	6352.1466	0.11	139362.03
MaxMin	7,312.98	0.10	76,327.82
Round Robin	9,766.91	0.25	99,698.84
MinMin	10,158.29	0.11	407,527.17
DPA	6,659.82	0.12	76,659.82

In *Case 3*, which involves 997 available requests in CloudSim, the results are presented in "Fig. 10" and "Table 6". The DPA algorithm performs best with the lowest average processing time and the lowest maximum processing time. As the number of requests increases, the predictive power and processing ability of the algorithm become more evident. The FCFS algorithm consistently shows the highest processing time.

The simulation experiments showed that the DPA algorithm performed slightly better than conventional algorithms in certain input data cases. In terms of response time and total processing time, it was not inferior to the existing algorithms and consistently performed better than them (Table 7).

From Fig. 11, we can see that in all three cases, the FCFS algorithm has the highest total execution time among all the algorithms. This means that FCFS takes the longest

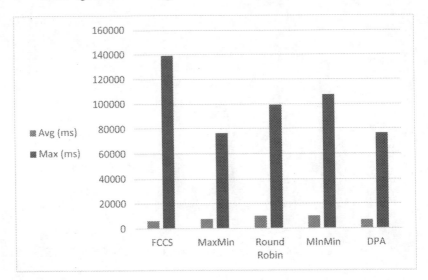

Fig. 9. Comparing the total response times of algorithms in case 2 with 100 requests.

Table 6. Comparing the response times of algorithms in case 3.

Case 3	Overall response time		
	Avg (ms)	Min (ms)	Max (ms)
FCFS	12927.32	0.13	380441.42
MaxMin	6,087.25	0.10	74,719.00
Round Robin	6,476.19	0.10	200,066.70
MinMin	6,455.54	0.11	204,196.72
DPA	5,940.80	0.11	57,559.75

time to process the requests in each case. In case 1, we can see that the MinMin algorithm has the lowest total execution time, followed by Round Robin, MaxMin, DPA, and FCFS, respectively. This suggests that in a scenario with a smaller number of requests, MinMin is the most efficient algorithm to use. In case 2, we can see that DPA has the lowest total execution time, followed by MinMin, Round Robin, MaxMin, and FCFS, respectively. This indicates that for a larger number of requests, DPA is the most efficient algorithm to use. In case 3, we can see that DPA again has the lowest total execution time, followed by MaxMin, MinMin, Round Robin, and FCFS, respectively. This suggests that as the number of requests increases further, DPA is still the most efficient algorithm to use. Overall, the chart indicates that the proposed DPA algorithm consistently outperforms

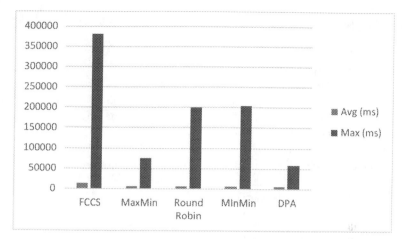

Fig. 10. Comparing the total response times of algorithms in case 3 with 997 requests.

Table 7. Comparing the Makespan of algorithms in all 3 cases

	Makespan (ms)		
	Epigenomics 24	Epigenomics 100	Epigenomics 997
FCFS	23,155	146,129	2,719,720
MaxMin	14,546	170,876	1,236,725
Round Robin	11,055	157,786	692,308
MinMin	7,593	414,381	1,303,421
DPA	6,297	152,507	1,206,652

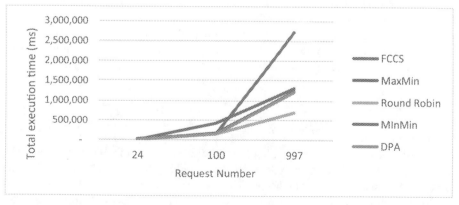

Fig. 11. Comparing the total execution time (makespan) of 5 algorithms in 3 cases.

the other algorithms in terms of total execution time, especially in scenarios with a larger number of requests.

Evaluation Linear Regression Model in DPA

In order to assess the performance of the Linear Regression Model used in the DPA algorithm, the Relative Absolute Error (RAE) metric was used to determine how accurately the model was able to predict the load balancer's values. The results are shown in Table 8, which indicates that the worst RAE value was obtained in predicting CPU usage in case 1, while the best value was obtained for Storage Usage prediction in the same case. Overall, the RAE values obtained in this experiment were deemed acceptable, although they varied depending on the request. However, the model's performance was not good in all cases due to the variability in requests.

Table 8. Comparing the RAE of DPA in 3 cases

	RAE metrics		
	Case 1 (24 requests)	Case 2 (100 requests)	Case 3 (997 requests)
CPU	0.565217	0.489868	0.324261
MEMORY (RAM)	0.148717	0.286780	0.310741
STORAGE	0.002531	0.006759	0.495361

From the RAE table, we can interpret that the prediction model performs better for CPU resource usage compared to Memory and Storage resources in all three cases. The RAE value for CPU decreases as the number of requests increases, indicating that the accuracy of the prediction model increases with more data. However, the RAE value for Memory increases in case 2, indicating a decrease in accuracy, while the RAE value for Storage is significantly higher in case 3, indicating poor accuracy in predicting Storage resource usage. Therefore, the prediction model needs improvement for predicting Memory and Storage resource usage accurately, especially in large-scale Cloud environments with a higher number of requests.

5   Conclusion

The main focus of this paper is to investigate deadlock and its avoidance in cloud computing using prediction algorithms, to ensure the safety of the cloud environment. The goal is to prevent deadlock occurrence so that the load balancer can allocate tasks to the appropriate virtual machine without encountering any deadlock issues. Through analyzing existing algorithms and previous studies, the researchers were able to gain a better understanding of the deadlock problem and identify the pros and cons of each algorithm. This led to the proposal of a new algorithm, the DPA algorithm, which improves load balancing in the cloud by improving response time, using limited resources, and providing more powerful virtual machines to handle requests more efficiently. The simulation experiments showed that the DPA algorithm outperformed the Round Robin, MaxMin, MinMin, and FCFS algorithms. This paper achieved the objectives of reviewing the key issues and problems of deadlock and deadlock avoidance in cloud environments, and proposing a promising approach to improve load balancing efficiency in practical cloud environments.

The paper has some limitations which include that the proposed algorithm has not been applied in a physical cloud yet. Additionally, the improvements in response time and processing time are minor. To address these limitations, future research could explore the use of additional prediction techniques and optimization methods for the proposed algorithm. It would also be beneficial to apply the proposed algorithm in practical applications instead of just in a simulation environment.

Acknowledgment. We would like to express our big appreciation to institutions: Posts and Telecommunication Institute of Technology Ho Chi Minh City, Vietnam and Ho Chi Minh City Open University, Ho Chi Minh City, Vietnam.

References

1. Wen, Y.-F., Chang, C.-L.: Load balancing job assignment for cluster-based cloud computing. In: 2014 Sixth International Conference on Ubiquitous and Future Networks -ICUFN (2014)
2. Shao, G., Chen, J.: A load balancing strategy based on data correlation in cloud computing. In: Proceedings of the 9th International Conference on Utility and Cloud Computing (2016)
3. Mishra, S.K., Sahoo, B., Parida, P.P.: Load balancing in cloud computing: a big picture. J. King Saud University – Computer and Information Sci. (2018)
4. Shahid, M.A., Islam, N., Alam, M.M., Su'ud, M.M., Musa, S.: A comprehensive study of load balancing approaches in the cloud computing environment and a novel fault tolerance approach. IEEE Access **8**, 130500–130526 (2020)
5. Iqbal, S., Kiah, M.L.M., Anuar, N.B., Daghighi, B., Wahab, A.W.A., Khan, S.: Service delivery models of cloud computing: security issues and open challenges: cloud computing security. Security and Communication Networks **9**(17), 4726–4750 (2016)
6. Tekale, S., Britto, J.G.M., Gousia Banu, A.S.: Load balancing in cloud computing. International J. Engineering and Advanced Technology **8**(6S3), 2164–2166 (2019)
7. Shah, N., Farik, M.: Static load balancing algorithms in cloud computing: challenges & solutions. International Journal of Scientific & Technol. Res. **4**(10), 365–367 (2015)
8. Rashmi, K.S., Suma, V., Vaidehi, M.: Enhanced Load Balancing Approach to Avoid Deadlocks in Cloud (2012)
9. Lim, J., Suh, T., Yu, H.: A deadlock detection algorithm using gossip in cloud computing environments. In: Lecture Notes in Electrical Engineering, Springer Netherlands, Dordrecht, pp. 781–789 (2013)
10. Mahitha, O., Suma, V.: Deadlock avoidance through efficient load balancing to control disaster in cloud environment. In: 2013 Fourth International Conference on Computing, Communications and Networking Technologies – ICCCNT (2013)
11. Ha Huy Cuong Nguyen, V.S.L.: Detection and avoidance deadlock for resource allocation in heterogeneous distributed platforms. International Journal of Computer Science and Telecommunications **6**(2) (2015)
12. Nguyen, H.H.C., Dang, H.V., Pham, N.M.N., Le, V.S., Nguyen, T.T.: Deadlock detection for resource allocation in heterogeneous distributed platforms. In: Advances in Intelligent Systems and Computing, Springer International Publishing, Cham, pp. 285–295 (2015)

13. Reveliotis, S., Fei, Z.: Robust deadlock avoidance for sequential resource allocation systems with resource outages. In: 2016 IEEE International Conference on Automation Science and Engineering - CASE (2016)
14. Malhotra, D.: Deadlock prevention algorithm in grid environment. MATEC Web Conference **57**, 02-013 (2016)
15. Ugwuanyi, E.E., Ghosh, S., Iqbal, M., Dagiuklas, T.: Reliable resource provisioning using bankers' deadlock avoidance algorithm in MEC for industrial IoT. IEEE Access **6**, 43327–43335 (2018)
16. Nguyen, H.H.C., Doan, V.T.: Avoid deadlock resource allocation (ADRA) model V VM-out-of-N PM. International Journal of Innovative Technology and Interdisciplinary Sciences **2**(1), 98–107 (2019)
17. Sherpa, S., Vicenciodelmoral, A., Zhao, X..: Deadlock detection for concurrent programs using resource footprints. In: Proceedings of the 12th IEEE/ACM International Conference on Utility and Cloud Computing Companion - UCC'19 Companion (2019)
18. Bondarenko, Y.V., Azeez, A.E.: Algorithm and model for improve the avoiding of deadlock with increasing efficiency of resource allocation in cloud environment. J. Physics - Conference Series **1902**(1), 012–054 (2021)
19. Almhanna, M.S., Almuttairi, R.M.: Chapter 6 methods for handling deadlocks. In: Operation System, University of Babylon (2019)
20. da Silva, R.F., Juve, G., Rynge, M., Deelman, E., Livny, M.: Online task resource consumption prediction for scientific workflows. Parallel Processing Letters **25**(03), 15–41 (2015)
21. Matsunaga, A., Fortes, J.A.B.: On the use of machine learning to predict the time and resources consumed by applications. In: 2010 10th IEEE/ACM International Conference on Cluster, Cloud and Grid Computing (2010)
22. Witten, I.H., Frank, E., Hall, M.A.: Data Mining.: Practical Machine Learning Tools and Techniques, 3rd ed. Morgan Kaufmann Publishers Inc., San Francisco, CA, USA (2011)
23. Salzberg, S.L.: C4.5: Programs for machine learning, J. ross Quinlan. Morgan Kaufmann publishers, inc., 1993, Machine learning **16**(3), 235–240 (1994)
24. Monge, D.A., Holec, M., Železný, F., Garino, C.G.: Ensemble learning of runtime prediction models for gene-expression analysis workflows. Cluster Computing **18**(4), 1317–1329 (2015)
25. Walczak, S., Cerpa, N.: Artificial neural networks. In: Encyclopedia of Physical Science and Technology, Elsevier, pp. 631–645 (2003)
26. Abdulkareem, D., Noor, Z.J., Abdullah, A.: CloudSim 3.0.3 Simulator Step by Step. Unpublished (2021)
27. Weka 3 - data mining with open source machine learning software in java. https://www.cs.waikato.ac.nz/ml/weka/. Accessed 27 Apr 2022
28. WorkflowSim-1.0: Wiki pages. https://github.com/WorkflowSim/WorkflowSim-1.0. Accessed 27 Apr 2022

A Secrecy Offloading in Radio Frequency Energy Harvesting NOMA Heterogeneous Mobile Edge Computing Network

Van-Truong Truong[1,2]($\boxtimes$), Dac-Binh Ha[1,2], and Minh-Thong Vo[1,2]

[1] Faculty of Electrical-Electronic Engineering, Duy Tan University, Da Nang 550000,
Vietnam
{truongvantruong,vominhthong}@dtu.edu.vn, hadacbinh@duytan.edu.vn
[2] Institute of Research and Development, Duy Tan University, Da Nang 550000,
Vietnam

Abstract. This paper studies a security offloading scheme in radio frequency energy harvesting (RF EH) non-orthogonal multiple access (NOMA) enabled heterogeneous mobile edge computing (Het-MEC) network over Rayleigh fading channel. Specifically, we investigate the model of a single mobile user (MU) offloading tasks to Het-MEC servers located at neighboring access points (APs) in the presence of a passive eavesdropper. In addition, the MU collects radio energy from a power station to ensure power throughout the offloading process. Accordingly, a four-phase energy-secrecy-offloading scheme is proposed under latency constraint, namely NOLES. We derive the exact close-form secrecy successful computation probability (SSCP) to evaluate the system performance. Numerical results under the Monte-Carlo simulation demonstrate the effective performance of our proposed framework.

Keywords: mobile edge computing · non-orthogonal multiple access · secrecy successful computation probability · security offloading · radio frequency energy harvesting

1 Introduction

The rapid development of applications in next-generation networks, such as virtual/augmented reality (VR/AR), autonomous driving, and tactile Internet of Things, has increased the demand for mobile data traffic explosively [1]. Additionally, each application is deployed with a massive user, requiring a large amount of computation, low latency, and some other security or power requirements. However, the path to effectively deploy such applications is still far, given that mobile terminals (MDs) have minimal computing capability and power for

© ICST Institute for Computer Sciences, Social Informatics and Telecommunications Engineering 2023
Published by Springer Nature Switzerland AG 2023. All Rights Reserved
N.-S. Vo and H.-A. Tran (Eds.): INISCOM 2023, LNICST 531, pp. 275–286, 2023.
https://doi.org/10.1007/978-3-031-47359-3_20

operation [2]. Furthermore, the valuable resources in a wireless network can be heterogeneous, leading to challenges in implementing operational protocols [3].

In order to effectively solve the above challenges, non-orthogonal multiple access (NOMA) and mobile edge computing (MEC) are proposed to be applied in 5G and 6G telecommunications networks. In the MEC-architectured system, MEC servers (MES) are set up at the network edge, which is close to the MDs to support them in computing services. In other words, MEC is the next generation of cloud computing, allowing it to support real-time applications more efficiently [4]. Meanwhile, NOMA uses advanced techniques in modulation and decoding to support better MDs in terms of spectrum efficiency, data rate, and user fairness. Thus, many studies have been carried out to clarify the NOMA-MEC system performance [5–7]. For instance, Ha *et al.* [6] examined a downlink NOMA MEC network under a Rayleigh channel, where one MD offloads the task to two neighboring APs under a tolerance constraint. The results demonstrate the effectiveness of the combination of NOMA and MEC and open up many exciting research directions for this model. However, the energy problem of MD has not been entirely solved by these studies.

Different from these prior works that only focus on investigating the time performance of the NOMA MEC system, many studies have proposed frameworks to solve the energy problem for MD [8,9]. One solution that has proven effective in solving the above problem is to deploy radio energy harvesting techniques. It is a technique that allows MDs to use specialized hardware to collect power from hybrid access points [10] or power stations [11,12]. One example is the wirelessly powered NOMA MEC IoT system proposed by Do *et al.* [12]. The study clarified the system performance regarding spectrum efficiency and significantly improved the MD lifetime.

However, NOMA-MEC-based networks still have an inherent risk because of the broadcast nature of wireless communication, which is the risk of information leakage [13]. Offloaded tasks from MD to MES can be eavesdropped by active or passive eavesdroppers, leading to an urgent need to pay attention to security issues for the success of the NOMA-MEC system. Accordingly, physical layer security (PLS) has been widely studied as a very effective wireless information security technique [14,15]. In the study [14], the authors investigated PLS-based MEC system with hybrid successive interference cancellation (SIC) technique deployed. The results show that the system performance outperforms the traditional OMA models.

According to the above discussion, the remaining problems in the RF EH NOMA Het-MEC network include eavesdropping devices that still need to be studied in depth to clarify. Therefore, in this study, we propose and investigate a secrecy task offloading model in RF EH NOMA Het-MEC networks. The main contributions of our paper are summarized as follows:

- We propose the downlink RF EH NOMA Het-MEC system model over Rayleigh fading channel. We correspondingly propose the energy-secrecy 4-phase offloading protocols based on NOMA.

- We derive the exact close-form expression of the secure successful completion probability (SSCP).
- We evaluate SSCP with essential system parameters, including time switching ratio, power allocation coefficient, task length, bandwidth, secure data rate threshold, and CPU operating frequency, to thoroughly comprehend the system's behavior.

The structure of the paper is presented as follows: Section 2 presents the system model and communication protocol. Section 3 presents the performance analysis. Section 4 describes the numerical results. Section 5 is the conclusion and future scope of the paper.

2 System Model

This study investigates an RF EH NOMA Het-MEC network model consisting of a wireless power station (P), a limited energy and computational resources edge user (U), and two MES deployed at two points access (APs) in the presence of a passive eavesdropper (E), as described in Fig. 1. Specifically, U has to handle an L-bit task, where each bit is independent of the other, for a maximum delay of T. However, U lacks the power and computing to complete the task independently. Therefore, U uses the power service to collect radio energy from P; then it uses all the received energy for offloading tasks to the APs, where AP_1 and AP_2 are denoted for the far and the near AP, respectively. Furthermore, in the AP_2 installation area, an eavesdropping device, denoted by E, intends to steal important information transmitted from U to AP_2.

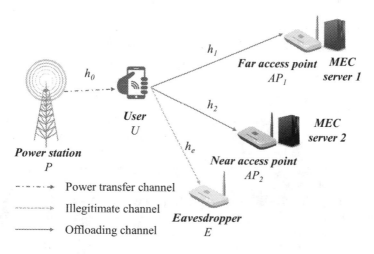

Fig. 1. The secrecy RF EH NOMA MEC system model.

Let h_0, h_1, h_2, and h_e be the channel coefficients from P to U, U to AP_1, U to AP_2, and U to E, respectively. Assume the devices in the proposed system are equipped with a single antenna, operating in a half-duplex mode under Rayleigh fading channel. Channels are characterized by an average channel gain of λ_Ω ($\Omega \in \{0, 1, 2, e\}$). The system is affected by the additive white Gaussian noise (AWGN). Let g_0, g_1, g_2, and g_e be the channel power gain from P to U and from U to AP_1, AP_2, and E, respectively. Note that $g_\Omega = |h_\Omega|^2$.

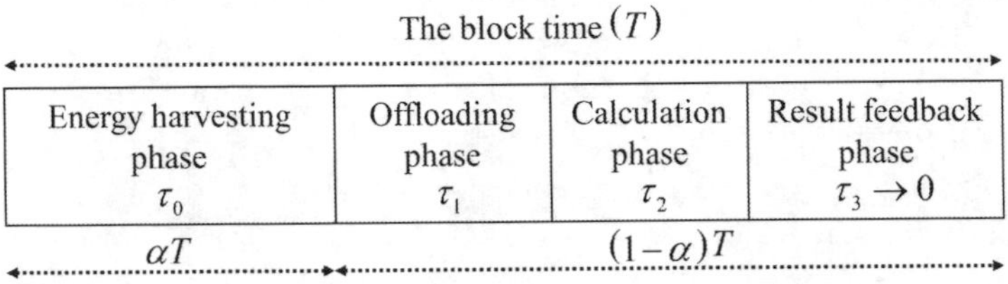

The block time (T)

Energy harvesting phase τ_0	Offloading phase τ_1	Calculation phase τ_2	Result feedback phase $\tau_3 \to 0$
αT		$(1-\alpha)T$	

Fig. 2. Time diagram for proposed system.

Based on the proposed system model, we develop a NOMA-based offloading protocol that ensures the system's latency, energy, and security requirements, namely NOLES. Precisely, NOLES which have time diagram at Fig. 2, consists of 4 phases, described in detail as follows:
- **Energy harvesting phase:** In this phase, the channel parameters are estimated. Then, U collects radio energy from P for $\tau_0 = \alpha T$, where α is the time switching ratio. The formula describing the energy U obtained in this phase is:

$$E_U = \eta P_0 g_0 \alpha T, \tag{1}$$

where η stand for energy conversion efficiency, P_0 is the transmit power of P.
- **The offloading phase:** U uses the energy obtained in the EH phase to send a superimposed signal to APs using the downlink NOMA scheme:

$$x = \sqrt{\rho} x_1 + \sqrt{1-\rho} x_2, \tag{2}$$

where x_1 and x_2 are tasks L_1 and L_2 bits are offloaded to AP_1 and AP_2 respectively; ρ stands for power allocation coefficient. Energy in NOMA-based systems is appropriately allocated to ensure user fairness; thus, the subtask x_1 that intends to offload for AP_1 will be allocated more power [11], i.e., $0.5 < \rho < 1$. During the offload period (τ_1), the signal is broadcast, so E also picks up the superimposed signal and tries to decode the important data at AP_2.
- **The computing phase:** In this context, the received signal at AP_1, AP_2, and E is as follow:

$$\begin{aligned} y_\Omega &= \sqrt{P_U} h_\Omega x + n_\Omega \\ &= \sqrt{P_U} h_\Omega (\sqrt{\rho} x_1 + \sqrt{1-\rho} x_2) + n_\Omega, \end{aligned} \tag{3}$$

where P_U is the transmit power of U, $P_U = \frac{E_U}{(1-\alpha)T - \tau} = \frac{\eta P_0 g_0 \alpha T}{(1-\alpha)T - \tau} = P_0 g_0 \mu$; $\mu = \frac{\eta \alpha T}{(1-\alpha)T - \tau}$; τ is the maximum computation time of APs, $\tau = \max\left\{ \frac{c_1 L_1}{f_1}, \frac{c_2 L_2}{f_2} \right\}$;

c_i and f_i are the number of CPU cycles required to process one input bit, and the operating frequency of the MES located at AP_i, $i \in \{1,2\}$, respectively; n_Ω is the AWGN has zero mean and variance δ^2, i.e., $n_i \sim \mathcal{CN}(0, \delta^2)$.

According to the NOMA scheme, APs apply SIC to decode the required signal. Since more power is allocated, x_1 is decoded directly. Then x_1 is removed from y, and the signal x_2 is decoded later. Therefore, the signal-to-interference-plus-noise ratio (SINR) at AP_1 used for decoding x_1 is as follow:

$$\gamma_1 = \frac{\gamma_0 \mu \rho g_0 g_1}{\gamma_0 \mu (1 - \rho) g_0 g_1 + 1}, \tag{4}$$

where $\gamma_o = \frac{P_0}{\delta^2}$.

The signal-to-noise ratio (SNR) at AP_2 used for decoding x_2 is:

$$\gamma_2 = \gamma_0 \mu (1 - \rho) g_0 g_2. \tag{5}$$

Suppose E has the same decoding abilities as AP_2, and it employs SIC to detect the signal received [16]. The SNR at E used to decode signal x_2 is:

$$\gamma_e = \gamma_0 \mu (1 - \rho) g_0 g_e. \tag{6}$$

- **The result feedback phase**: During this phase, the resultant calculation information is feedbacked to the U during τ_3. Following [8,11], τ_3 is significantly short compared to τ_0, τ_1 and τ_2, hence it is ignored.

The cumulative distribution function (CDF) and probability density function (PDF) of the channel power gain g_Ω, $\Omega \in \{1, 2, e\}$ are given as follows [5]:

$$F_{g_\Omega}(x) = 1 - \exp\left(-\frac{x}{\lambda_\Omega}\right), \tag{7}$$

$$f_{g_\Omega}(x) = \frac{1}{\lambda_\Omega} \exp\left(-\frac{x}{\lambda_\Omega}\right). \tag{8}$$

3 Performance Analysis

Different from the study [5,6,8], in this paper, we propose to use the secure successful computation probability (SSCP), denoted by ξ, which is the metric to evaluate the performance of the RF EH NOMA Het-MEC system. It is the probability that the security offload event occurs. Simply put, this event occurs when the system latency is lower than the maximum allowed time and the security capacity is above the secure data rate threshold.

$$\xi_S = \Pr\left(\max\left(\tau_1^{(i)} + \tau \le (1 - \alpha) T\right), C_{2e} > R\right), \tag{9}$$

where $\tau_1^{(i)}$ is the offloading time for task x to AP_i, $\tau_1^{(i)} = \frac{L}{C_i} = \frac{L}{(1-\alpha)B\log_2(1+\gamma_i)}$; C_{2e} is the secrecy capacity at AP_2, $C_{2e} = (1 - \alpha) B\log_2\left(\frac{1+\gamma_2}{1+\gamma_e}\right)$; and R is the secure data rate threshold, B is the bandwidth.

Thus, we state **Theorem** 1 describing the SSCP expression as follows.

Theorem 1. *The SSCP of the proposed RF EH NOMA Het-MEC system operating under the NOLES protocol over the Rayleigh fading channel is given by:*

$$
\xi_S = \begin{cases}
0, & \rho < 1 - \frac{1}{2^{\Lambda_1}} \\
2\left[\sqrt{\frac{b_1}{\lambda_0}}K_1\left(2\sqrt{\frac{b_1}{\lambda_0}}\right) - \sqrt{\frac{b_2}{\lambda_0}}K_1\left(2\sqrt{\frac{b_2}{\lambda_0}}\right)\right] & \\
\quad + \frac{2\lambda_2}{\lambda_0\left(\theta\lambda_e + \lambda_2\right)}\sqrt{b_3\lambda_0}K_1\left(2\sqrt{\frac{b_3}{\lambda_0}}\right), & \rho > 1 - \frac{1}{2^{\Lambda_1}}
\end{cases}
\tag{10}
$$

where $b_1 = \frac{\beta_1}{\lambda_1} + \frac{\beta_2}{\lambda_2}$, $b_2 = \frac{\beta_1}{\lambda_1} + \frac{\beta_2}{\lambda_2} + \frac{\beta_3}{\lambda_2}$, $b_3 = \omega_1 + \omega_2 + \frac{\beta_1}{\lambda_2}$, $\omega_1 = \frac{a_1}{\lambda_2}$, $\omega_2 = \beta_3\left(\frac{\theta}{\lambda_2} + \frac{1}{\lambda_e}\right)$, $a_1 = \frac{\theta-1}{\gamma_0\mu(1-\rho)}$, $\beta_1 = \frac{2^{\Lambda_1}-1}{\mu\gamma_0\left[2^{\Lambda_1}(1-\rho)+1\right]}$, $\beta_2 = \frac{2^{\Lambda_2}-1}{\mu\gamma_0(1-\rho)}$, $\beta_3 = \frac{\beta_2-a_1}{\theta}$, $\theta = 2^{\frac{R}{1-\alpha}}$, $\Lambda_1 = (1-\alpha)BT_1$, $\Lambda_2 = (1-\alpha)BT_2$, $T_1 = (1-\alpha)T - \frac{c_1L_1}{f_1}$, $T_2 = (1-\alpha)T - \frac{c_2L_2}{f_2}$.

Proof. Please see Appendix A. □

4   Numerical Results and Discussion

This section provides the numerical results regarding the SSCP of the RF EH NOMA Het-MEC downlink system. The Monte-Carlo simulations are employed to confirm the analytical results. Table 1 details the typical values of simulation parameters utilized in our work [5,8].

Table 1. Simulation Parameters.

Parameters	Notation	Typical Values
Environment		Rayleigh
Fading parameter	$\lambda_0, \lambda_1, \lambda_2$	1
The average transmit SNR	γ_0	0–20 dB
The time switching ratio	α	0.4
The energy conversion efficiency	η	0.75
The power allocation coefficient	ρ	0.7
The CPU-cycle frequency of MES at AP_1, AP_2	f_1, f_2	2 GHz, 1 GHz
The number of CPU cycles for computing each bit of MES at AP_1, AP_2	c_1, c_2	5, 2
Channel bandwidth	B	100 MHz
The threshold of latency	T	0.5 s
The length of sub-task 1, sub-task 2	L_1, L_2	2.5 Mbits
The secure data rate threshold	R	0.1 bps/Hz

In the first experiment, we investigated the impact of the time switching ratio (α) with different values of block time (T) on system performance, as shown in Fig. 3. Note that the smaller T is, the more stringent the real-time constraint corresponds to, and the worse the SSCP. It entirely agrees with the theoretical analysis presented in Section II. One more observation about the SSCP descriptive curve in this experiment shows that ξ_S is a function with extrema in α, i.e., there is a value $\alpha^\dagger$ such that maximum system performance. Therefore, when implementing the system in the real world, it is required to use strategies to determine $\alpha^\dagger$ so that EH time has a suitable value for U to collect sufficient operating energy and the remaining time is also enough for the process of offloading and computing to be performed.

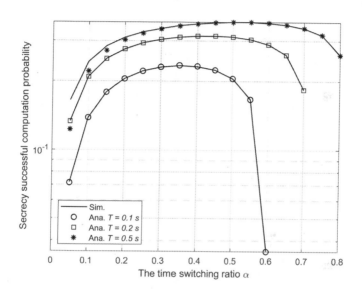

Fig. 3. SSCP vs. the time switching ratio with different values of block time.

In the next experiment, we investigate the impact of average transmit SNR (γ_0) with different bandwidth levels (B) on system performance, as shown in Fig. 4. Specifically, we examine three bandwidth levels, which are 50 MHz, 100 MHz, and 1 GHz. It is effortless to notice that the larger B or/and γ_0, the higher the SSCP. SSCP tends to saturate when γ_0 is greater than 15 dB and tends to saturate faster the larger B is. Therefore, depending on the bandwidth served for each application, we consider designing the transmit power accordingly.

Figure 5 depicts the curve of SSCP versus power allocation coefficient (ρ) with different task division ratios, denoted by ε, $\varepsilon = \frac{L_1}{L}$. We examine three cases, (i) $\varepsilon = 0.4$, (ii) $\varepsilon = 0.6$, and (iii) $\varepsilon = 0.8$. The graphs of all three cases show that the SSCP of the system is a function with extrema in ρ. It confirms that power allocation in a NOMA-based network is important for the best system performance. Furthermore, the correlation between the ε and ρ also gives us an exciting insight into the system behavior. The recommender system works well for case (i) with $0.5 < \rho < 0.65$. Meanwhile, in this range, (ii) makes SSCP low and (iii) makes the system outage. SSCP in (ii) is satisfactory only when

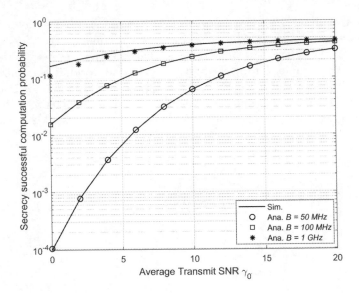

Fig. 4. SSCP vs. the average transmit SNR with different values of bandwidth.

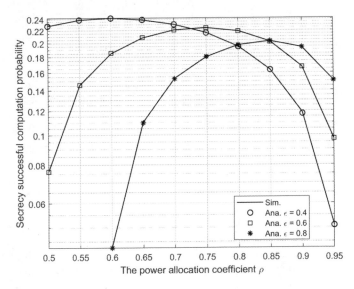

Fig. 5. SSCP vs. the power allocation coefficient with different task division ratios.

$0.7 < \rho < 0.8$, and (iii) is reasonable when $0.85 < \rho < 0.9$. Accordingly, with the Het-MEC network, it is necessary to have an optimal approach to offloading so that the system can achieve the highest performance corresponding to the available resources in the network. To put it succinctly, we need to clarify that tasks must be offloaded in the proper ratios for the system to be optimal.

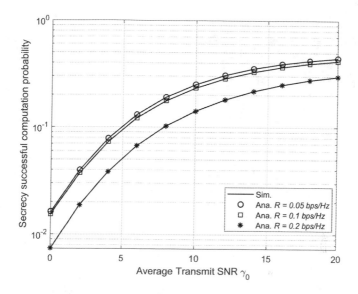

Fig. 6. SSCP vs. secure data rate thresholds.

In the final experiment, we studied the SSCP with different levels of secure data rate thresholds (R), 0.05 bps/Hz, 0.1 bps/Hz, and 0.2 bps/Hz, respectively, as Fig. 6. We conclude that increasing R can decrease SSCP. It is consistent with the definition of SSCP: as R increases, the possibility that the security capacity of the system will not meet the requirements also increases, leading to a decrease in SSCP.

Figure 3 to Fig. 6 all show that the simulated values match the computational theory. That proved the correctness of our study.

5   Conclusion

In this study, we evaluated the downlink RF EH NOMA Het-MEC network with the existence of a passive eavesdropper. Specifically, we consider the edge user to use the radio energy received from the power station to offload the task to two heterogeneous APs using NOMA over the Rayleigh channel. Accordingly, we propose the NOLES protocol for the system, ensuring it satisfies all three basic requirements of NOMA-MEC networks: delay time, energy, and security. We derive the exact closed-form expression of SSCP and perform system performance experiments versus essential system parameters. We give the following recommendations to improve system performance: (a) increase the transmit power of P, (b) increase the bandwidth for the application, (c) determine the optimal time switching ratio and/or power allocation coefficient.

In the next studies, we will deploy the low complexity optimization algorithms to determine the system parameters so that SSCP reaches the maximum value.

Acknowledgment. This research is funded by Vietnam National Foundation for Science and Technology Development (NAFOSTED) under grant number 102.04-2021.11.

PROOF OF THEOREM 1

Based on the definition formula, SSCP is rewritten as follows:

$$
\xi_S = \Pr\left(\underbrace{\frac{L}{C_1} \le (1-\alpha)T - \frac{c_1 L_1}{f_1}}_{T_1}, \underbrace{\frac{L}{C_2} \le (1-\alpha)T - \frac{c_2 L_2}{f_2}}_{T_2}, C_{2e} > R\right)
$$

$$
= \Pr\left(\gamma_1 > 2^{\Lambda_1} - 1, \gamma_2 > 2^{\Lambda_2} - 1, \frac{1+\gamma_2}{1+\gamma_e} > \underbrace{2^{\frac{R}{1-\alpha}}}_{\theta}\right)
\tag{A-1}
$$

$$
= \begin{cases} 0, & \rho < 1 - \frac{1}{2^{\Lambda_1}} \\ \Pr\left(g_1 > \frac{\beta_1}{g_0}, g_2 > \frac{\beta_2}{g_0}, g_2 > \frac{a_1}{g_o} + \theta g_e\right), & \rho > 1 - \frac{1}{2^{\Lambda_1}} \end{cases}
$$

where $a_1 = \frac{\theta-1}{\gamma_0 \mu(1-\rho)}$, $\beta_1 = \frac{2^{\Lambda_1}-1}{\mu\gamma_0[2^{\Lambda_1}(1-\rho)+1]}$, $\beta_2 = \frac{2^{\Lambda_2}-1}{\mu\gamma_0(1-\rho)}$, $\Lambda_1 = (1-\alpha)BT_1$, $\Lambda_2 = (1-\alpha)BT_2$.

We focus the case $\rho > 1 - \frac{1}{2^{\Lambda_1}}$, then the SSCP is:

$$
\xi_S = \Pr\left(g_1 > \frac{\beta_1}{g_0}, g_2 > \frac{\beta_2}{g_0}, g_2 > \frac{a_1}{g_0} + \theta g_e\right)
$$

$$
= \underbrace{\Pr\left(g_1 > \frac{\beta_1}{g_0}, g_2 > \frac{\beta_2}{g_0}, \frac{\beta_2}{g_0} > \frac{a_1}{g_0} + \theta g_e\right)}_{I_1}
\tag{A-2}
$$

$$
+ \underbrace{\Pr\left(g_1 > \frac{\beta_1}{g_0}, g_2 > \frac{a_1}{g_0} + \theta g_e, \frac{\beta_2}{g_0} < \frac{a_1}{g_0} + \theta g_e\right)}_{I_2}.
$$

We continue to present the calculation of I_1 as follows:

$$
I_1 = \Pr\left(g_1 > \frac{\beta_1}{g_0}, g_2 > \frac{\beta_2}{g_0}, g_e < \underbrace{\frac{\beta_2 - a_1}{\theta}}_{\beta_3}\frac{1}{g_0}\right)
$$

$$
= \int_0^\infty \left[1 - F_{g_1}\left(\frac{\beta_1}{x}\right)\right]\left[1 - F_{g_2}\left(\frac{\beta_2}{x}\right)\right] F_{g_e}\left(\frac{\beta_3}{x}\right) f_{g_0}(x)\, dx
\tag{A-3}
$$

$$
= 2\left[\sqrt{\frac{b_1}{\lambda_0}} K_1\left(2\sqrt{\frac{b_1}{\lambda_0}}\right) - \sqrt{\frac{b_2}{\lambda_0}} K_1\left(2\sqrt{\frac{b_2}{\lambda_0}}\right)\right],
$$

where $b_1 = \frac{\beta_1}{\lambda_1} + \frac{\beta_2}{\lambda_2}$, $b_2 = \frac{\beta_1}{\lambda_1} + \frac{\beta_2}{\lambda_2} + \frac{\beta_3}{\lambda_e}$.

Similarly, I_2 is calculated as follows:

$$
\begin{aligned}
I_2 &= \Pr\left(g_1 > \frac{\beta_1}{g_0}, g_2 > \frac{a_1}{g_o} + \theta g_e, g_e > \frac{\beta_3}{g_0}\right) \\
&= \int\limits_0^\infty \int\limits_{\beta_3/x}^\infty \left[1 - F_{g_1}\left(\frac{\beta_1}{x}\right)\right]\left[1 - F_{g_2}\left(\frac{a_1}{x} + \theta t\right)\right] f_{g_0}(x) f_{g_e}(t)\, dx dt \quad \text{(A-4)} \\
&= \frac{2\lambda_2}{\lambda_0(\theta\lambda_e + \lambda_2)}\sqrt{b_3\lambda_0} K_1\left(2\sqrt{\frac{b_3}{\lambda_0}}\right),
\end{aligned}
$$

where $b_3 = \omega_1 + \omega_2 + \frac{\beta_1}{\lambda_1}$, $\omega_1 = \frac{a_1}{\lambda_2}$, $\omega_2 = \beta_3\left(\frac{\theta}{\lambda_2} + \frac{1}{\lambda_e}\right)$.

Combining the results from (A-1) to (A-4), we get the result in **Theorem** 1. The proof is completed.

References

1. Parvez, I., Rahmati, A., Guvenc, I., Sarwat, A.I., Dai, H.: A survey on low latency towards 5G: RAN, core network and caching solutions. IEEE Commun. Surv. Tut. **20**(4), 3098–3130 (2018)
2. Siddiqi, M.A., Yu, H., Joung, J.: 5G ultra-reliable low-latency communication implementation challenges and operational issues with IoT devices. Electronics **8**(9), 981 (2019)
3. Xu, Y., Gui, G., Gacanin, H., Adachi, F.: A survey on resource allocation for 5G heterogeneous networks: current research, future trends, and challenges. IEEE Commun. Surv. Tut. **23**(2), 668–695 (2021)
4. Maray, M., Shuja, J.: Computation offloading in Mobile Cloud Computing and Mobile Edge Computing: survey, taxonomy, and open issues. Mobile Inform. Syst. **2022** (2022)
5. Truong, V.-T., Ha, D.-B., So-In, C., et al.: On the system performance of mobile edge computing in an uplink NOMA WSN with a multiantenna access point over Nakagami-m fading. IEEE/CAA J. Automatica Sinica **9**(4), 668–685 (2022)
6. Ha, D.-B., Truong, V.-T., Ha, D.-H.: A novel secure protocol for mobile edge computing network applied downlink NOMA. In: Vo, N.-S., Hoang, V.-P. (eds.) INISCOM 2020. LNICST, vol. 334, pp. 324–336. Springer, Cham (2020). https://doi.org/10.1007/978-3-030-63083-6_25
7. Ding, Z., Xu, D., Schober, R., Poor, H.V.: Hybrid NOMA offloading in multi-user MEC networks. IEEE Trans. Wireless Commun. (2022)
8. Truong, V.-T., Vo, M.-T., Ha, D.-B.: Performance analysis of mobile edge computing network applied uplink NOMA with RF energy harvesting. In: Vo, N.-S., Hoang, V.-P., Vien, Q.-T. (eds.) INISCOM 2021. LNICST, vol. 379, pp. 57–72. Springer, Cham (2021). https://doi.org/10.1007/978-3-030-77424-0_6
9. Qiu, H., Gao, S., Chen, Y., Tu, G.: Energy-efficient rate allocation for NOMA-MEC offloading under outage constraints. IEEE Commun. Lett. **26**(11), 2710–2714 (2022)
10. Pei, L., et al.: Energy-efficient D2D communications underlaying NOMA-based networks with energy harvesting. IEEE Commun. Lett. **22**(5), 914–917 (2018)

11. Truong, V.-T., Ha, D.-B.: Secured scheme for RF energy harvesting Mobile Edge Computing networks based on NOMA and access point selection. In: 7th NAFOS-TED Conference on Information and Computer Science (NICS), vol. 2020, pp. 7–12. IEEE (2020)

12. Do, D.-T., Van Nguyen, M.-S., Nguyen, T.N., Li, X., Choi, K.: Enabling multiple power beacons for uplink of NOMA-enabled mobile edge computing in wirelessly powered IoT. IEEE Access **8**, 148892–148905 (2020)

13. Mao, Y., You, C., Zhang, J., Huang, K., Letaief, K.B.: A survey on mobile edge computing: the communication perspective. IEEE Commun. Surveys Tut. **19**(4), 2322–2358 (2017)

14. Wang, K., Li, H., Ding, Z., Xiao, P.: Reinforcement learning based latency minimization in secure NOMA-MEC systems with hybrid SIC. IEEE Trans. Wireless Commun. (2022)

15. Wang, Q., Hu, H., Hu, R.Q., et al.: Secure and energy-efficient offloading and resource allocation in a NOMA-based MEC network. In: IEEE/ACM Symposium on Edge Computing (SEC), vol. 2020, pp. 420–424. IEEE (2020)

16. Xiang, Z., Yang, W., Cai, Y., Ding, Z., Song, Y., Zou, Y.: NOMA-assisted secure short-packet communications in IoT. IEEE Wireless Commun. **27**(4), 8–15 (2020)

An Application of Non Negative Matrix Factorization in Text Mining

Nguyen Bao Tran[✉], Thanh Son Huynh, Ba Lam To, and Luong Anh Tuan Nguyen

Information Technology Department, Vietnam Aviation Academy, Ho Chi Minh City 72200, Vietnam

{baotn,sonth,lamtb,nlatuan}@vaa.edu.vn

Abstract. The field of text mining has increasingly relied on Non-negative matrix factorization (NMF) for its ability to perform high-dimensional data reduction and visualization. This paper aims to employ NMF in analyzing a dataset of 1,500 documents and 12,419 words in bags-of-words format, obtained from the UCI Machine Learning Repository. Our analysis demonstrates the utility of NMF in effectively classifying ambiguous and sparse textual data into distinct topics and extracting meaningful contents through the identification of relevant keywords. Further, we demonstrate the robustness of NMF in topic clustering by exploring the semantic relationship between extracted keywords and the topics to which they belonged. Our findings offered valuable insights into the application of NMF in text mining and suggested that universities in Vietnam could leverage this technique to analyze feedback and suggestions from students.

Keywords: NMF · text mining · topic classification · bags-of-words

1 Introduction

The growth of high-dimensional data has led to an increased need for advanced techniques to extract and derive valuable information from large volumes of data [1]. In data mining, the main objectives of such techniques are generally focused on reducing high-dimensionality while preserving the majority of original information and clustering and interpreting underlying features from the original data, which can enable the exploitation of valuable knowledge and information thereafter [2]. Accordingly, various techniques based on data decomposition, such as Principal Component Analysis (PCA), Independent Component Analysis (ICA), Support Vector Machine (SVM), and Non-negative Matrix Factorization (NMF), have been utilized in data mining to extract pertinent information. Of these techniques, NMF has demonstrated robustness for non-negative data, which are naturally present in real-life datasets such as the number of pixels in an image, the number of occurrences of each word, and stock prices. The constraint of non-negative data in decomposed matrices leads to the part-based representation of NMF and improvement of interpretability [3, 4]. Therefore, NMF may be better suited for non-negative data and part-based representation compared to other techniques.

N.-S. Vo and H.-A. Tran (Eds.): INISCOM 2023, LNICST 531, pp. 287–295, 2023.
https://doi.org/10.1007/978-3-031-47359-3_21

NMF gained popularity after a seminal paper by Lee and Seung [5], which proposed an algorithm and highlighted the advantages of NMF, such as straightforward interpretability and potential ability of part-based representation. Indeed, NMF can effectively reduce the dimensionality of data with minimal information loss by approximately extracting high-dimensional data into low-rank matrices. Additionally, NMF automatically clusters the original data by sparse and meaningful features, which enables intuitive visualization of hidden correlations. As a result, NMF is a prominent tool to represent and factorize non-negative datasets in various fields, including signal processing, biomedical engineering, text mining, image processing, and more [6].

Due to the non-negative characteristic of word-document frequency of occurrence and NMF's automatic clustering abilities, NMF has proven effective and well-suited to analyze semantic and topic modeling in text mining [7]. Text mining can apply various applications, such as analyzing customer behaviors, conducting market research, and filtering malicious or spam content to enhance business performance [8]. Categorizing, interpreting, and discovering underlying features, word connections, and knowledge from a vast volume of text collections from document corpuses are considered as essential tasks in text mining. Topic clustering based on semantic might be the most prominent approach to text mining. To process data, text collections must undergo pre-processing, including tokenization and stop-word elimination under bags-of-words format. Then, NMF can automatically cluster meaningful topics by combining attributes in the two extracted matrices, resulting in low-dimensional data presentation. Given that the amount of textual data collections is growing larger and larger, such as on social network platforms (e.g., Facebook, Twitter, and Instagram) and email systems (Gmail and Yahoo), NMF applications in text mining are promising to uncover latent components and hidden topics of textual data by part-based representation.

In the context of university management, understanding students' viewpoints, reactions, and sentiments plays a vital role in enhancing educational quality and school facilities. The vast amount of feedback and comments sent from social media (e.g., Facebook and Twitter) and emails over the years should be made more compact, understandable, and intuitive to visualize, instead of becoming a burden for managers and staff. Accordingly, NMF can give the benefits of extracting the most concerned issues of students by topic clustering. In Vietnam, there are few studies in text mining that utilize NMF in text mining for education management in universities. Therefore, this paper aims to demonstrate the robustness of NMF in text mining by conducting an experiment from a data corpus. From the ambiguous and unstructured textual data, NMF might effectively cluster meaningful topics as well as gain insights into the underlying connections in terms of semantic between keywords within the clustered topics.

This study was structured into four main sections: Introduction, Methodology, Experiment, and Conclusions. The Introduction section presented an overview of the robustness of Non-negative Matrix Factorization (NMF) and its applications in text mining. In the Methodology section, a text mining process was proposed, which detailed the application of the NMF algorithm for topic clustering. The Experiment section provided a description of the dataset used, the experimental procedures employed for pre-processing the raw data, and the experimental results obtained. Finally, the Conclusions section outlined the significance of the study.

2 Methodology

2.1 Text Mining Process

In this study, a text mining process was proposed, which involved the application of the NMF algorithm (see Fig. 1). The process began with the pre-processing of raw data, which involved tokenization and stopword removal, and was referred to as the "Data Pre-processing" step in Fig. 1. The pre-processed data was then transformed into a bags-of-words format and transferred to a 2-dimensional matrix (n documents x m words), which served as the observed data, referred to as the "Text Transformation" step. The NMF algorithm was then applied to decompose the observed data into matrices, referred to as the "Applying NMF" step. Finally, the extracted topics accompanied by keywords within each topic were presented in the form of decomposed matrices, which constituted the "Text Mining" step.

Fig. 1. Proposed text mining process.

2.2 Non-negative Matrix Factorization Algorithm

From the algebraic perspective, NMF is relevant to matrix decomposition. Given a dataset consisting of non-negative elements, the NMF algorithm aims to approximate it as the product of two low-rank matrices, as shown in the following equation:

$$A \cong W \times H \qquad (1)$$

where A is the observed data (n x m), which n dimensions and m data points of each dimension, W is the basic matrix (n x k), and H is the coefficient matrix (k x m). Each data point in the A matrix can be approximated by a linear combination of the rows of W and the columns of H. The columns of W can be interpreted as basis vectors or "building blocks," while the rows of H present the coordinates of data points of W, used to approximately reconstruct the observed data.

The matrices W and H are initially randomized, and then determined through iterative updates based on the convergence of local optimal matrix factorization. The value of k ranges from 1 to the minimum of n and m. In other words, the original n dimensions are reduced to k.

Since NMF approximates the A matrix, we could evaluate the fit-goodness between the reconstructed and observed data. The reconstructed matrix R = W x H is calculated as follows:

$$R = \begin{bmatrix} w_{11} & w_{12} & \cdots & w_{1k} \\ w_{21} & w_{22} & \cdots & w_{2k} \\ \vdots & \vdots & \ddots & \vdots \\ w_{n1} & w_{n2} & \cdots & w_{nk} \end{bmatrix} \times \begin{bmatrix} h_{11} & h_{12} & \cdots & h_{1m} \\ h_{21} & h_{22} & \cdots & h_{2m} \\ \vdots & \vdots & \ddots & \vdots \\ h_{k1} & h_{k2} & \cdots & h_{km} \end{bmatrix} = W \times H \qquad (2)$$

Values in W and H are updated and terminated based on the minimum least-squares error (E) optimization between the original (A) and reconstructed (R) matrices.

$$E = \min \|D - R\|_F^2 \qquad (3)$$

3 Experiment

3.1 Data Set

For the experiment, we utilized a textual dataset obtained from the Neural Information Processing Systems (NIPS), a highly regarded machine learning conference. The dataset was obtained from the UCI Machine Learning Repository [9]. After initial processing steps such as tokenization and removal of stopwords, the dataset was transformed into bags-of-words format, and consisted of 12,419 words (n) in a vocabulary list and 1,500 documents (m), with approximately 2 million words in the colletion in total. Due to copyright restrictions, the name of each document was not provided, resulting in an untagged and ambiguous dataset, which was suitable for the purpose of topic clustering.

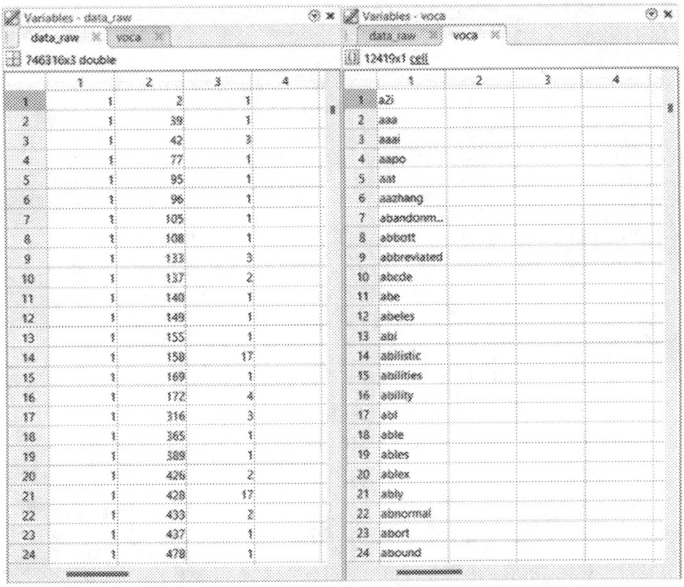

Fig. 2. The data obtained from NIPS and stored in Matlab. The left table presents the frequency of occurrence of each word in a single document. The right table presents the vocabulary list of 12,419 words.

3.2 Experimental Procedures

The raw data consisted of the vocabulary list of 12,419 words and the frequency of occurrence of each word in a single document. The latter was presented in the form of [docID wordID count], as illustrated in Fig. 2. For instance, the first line [1 2 1] indicates that the second word (wordID = 2, "aaa" – obtained to the vocabulary list) occurs once in the first document (docID = 1). From the raw data, we constructed a word-document matrix A of dimensions 12,419 x 1,500 to store and process information using the TF-IDF (Term Frequency-Inverse Document Frequency) normalization method. For example, A[1, 2] = 1 means that the second word ID (wordID = 2) appears once in the first document (docID = 1).

Following the application of Non-negative Matrix Factorization (NMF), we obtained two decomposed matrices, W and H. W is the basic matrix (12,419 words x k topics), while H is the coefficient matrix (k topics x 1,500 documents). We normalized matrix W by the maximum value in each column, and matrix H by the maximum value in each row. W and H provided insights into the initial word-document matrix, which lacked any class labels and was seemingly chaotic.

Each column of matrix W represented a basic vector, where higher values (from 0 to 1) indicated greater significance of a word (or term) in a topic, as well as a high degree of semantic association with other words in the same topic. We selected the top 20 most important words, which were corresponding to the 20 largest values in each column of W as representatives, to investigate the content of each topic. Meanwhile, values in each row of matrix H (i x j) indicated the extent to which document j belonged to topic i. A high value (from 0 to 1) indicated that document j was strongly associated with topic i.

The number of topics (k) was determined based on the semantic relationships and combined attributes between words in matrix W. After matrix decomposition, we obtained the following information: (1) the number of clustered topics, (2) the most significant words in each topic (from matrix W), and (3) the topic to which a document belonged (from matrix H).

To evaluate the performance of NMF, we analyzed the relationship between the semantic of 30 words that appeared most frequently in a document and the semantic of the top 20 most important words in the topic to which the document belonged. We selected five documents that belonged to the five extracted topics as representatives to confirm the robustness of NMF in terms of semantic similarity between keywords in the documents and topics. A clear explanation of the relationship between the most frequent words in a document and the keywords in the topic to which the document belonged confirmed the efficacy of NMF.

We used Matlab (Mathworks Inc.) to perform all kinds of data processing.

3.3 Experimental Results

Due to the relatively large and extremely sparse nature of the data in bags-of-words format, the coefficient of determination between the original and reconstructed data was found to be low. For instance, when we chose the number of topics was 100 topics, which was too large and unrealistic, the r^2 value was still relatively low, i.e. 0.41. As such, the selection of the appropriate value of the number of topics (k) was based on semantic similarity, rather than r^2. Specifically, the value of k was reduced until the topics were distinguishable, while maintaining semantic coherence. Ultimately, a value of $k = 5$ was chosen, resulting in a mean coefficient of determination (r^2) of 0.27.

Upon completion of the matrix decomposition, the basic matrix W was obtained with dimensions of 12,419 words by 5 topics. From this matrix, the 20 most important words were selected to represent each of the topics. The resulting five topics (A to E) are presented in Fig. 3, along with their respective most important words. Topic A seemed to focus on neural network architectures, such as inputs, outputs, training set, and the number of hidden layers to enhance performance. Meanwhile, Topic B was highly related to functions and algorithms, which focused on parameters such as the number of classes, weights, and training data sets. Topic C was relevant to models using control systems for speech or image recognition, such as the Hidden Markov model (with the keyword "hmm"), which can be controlled or modified by parameters and methods related to Gaussian probability distribution. Topic D appeared to describe the processing to neural information of the biological brain, such as synaptic responses, spike signals, firing, circuits, or stimulus. Finally, Topic E appears to be related to reinforcement learning with specific keywords related to learning algorithm as policiy, rule, states, and action, which enables to obtain an optimal controller applied for robot.

	A	B	C	D	E
1	network	function	model	neuron	learning
2	unit	algorithm	data	cell	action
3	neural	set	parameter	input	system
4	input	data	system	visual	control
5	training	error	distribution	system	algorithm
6	output	vector	object	circuit	task
7	weight	problem	recognition	function	reinforcement
8	hidden	training	set	response	policy
9	system	method	likelihood	pattern	function
10	set	number	mixture	synaptic	model
11	layer	result	gaussian	signal	dynamic
12	error	weight	image	output	problem
13	pattern	distribution	control	firing	learn
14	net	point	point	field	optimal
15	recognition	linear	method	direction	step
16	performance	parameter	neural	spike	states
17	trained	learning	speech	neural	robot
18	number	bound	hmm	activity	controller
19	architecture	case	probability	current	learned
20	problem	class	word	stimulus	rule

Fig. 3. The data of 5 extracted topics (5 columns) and the most 20 important words (20 rows) in each topic.

The coefficient matrix H, consisting of 5 topics and 1500 documents, facilitated the determination of a document's topic by identifying the highest value within a given column. Figure 4 presents three subsets of 15 representative documents each, specifically docID = 1 to 5, docID = 501 to 505, and docID = 1000 to 1005, which were used to represent the entire set of 1500 documents.

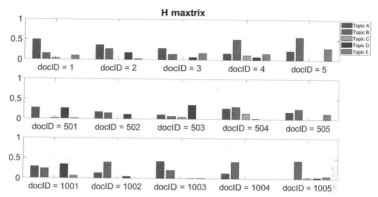

Fig. 4. The coefficient matrix H of 15 documents (docID from 1 to 5, 501 to 505, and 1000 to 1005) as representatives. The highest value of a bar means that document belonged to the topic.

As can be seen in Fig. 4, we could determine a document belonged to a certain topic based on the highest value of a column in the coefficient matrix H. For example, the first column of matrix H (docID = 1, see Fig. 4), the highest value was the first bar, which implied the first document (docID = 1) belonged to topic A.

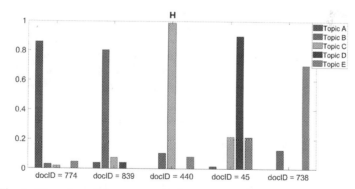

Fig. 5. Five selected documents which were apparently belonged to 5 topics.

To assess the efficacy of Non-negative Matrix Factorization (NMF) in topic cluster-ing, we chose five documents that clearly pertained to the five topics (i.e., those with a high value in matrix H, approaching unity) as representatives. As depicted in Fig. 5, the documents with docIDs of 774, 839, 440, 45, and 738 belonged to topics A, B, C, D, and E, respectively. Subsequently, we examined the semantic association between the 30 most frequent words in a given document and the top 20 important words in the corresponding topic to which the document belonged, as can be seen in Fig. 3 and Fig. 6.

Firstly, with regards to the document with a docID of 774, which belonged to topic A (Fig. 5), it was apparent that the top 30 most frequent words and the top 20 most important

	docID = 774	docID = 839	docID = 440	docID = 45	docID = 738
1	network	function	model	cell	skill
2	order	error	merging	potential	learning
3	output	bound	hmm	membrane	task
4	recurrent	rate	transition	light	action
5	neural	training	states	firing	reinforcement
6	number	problem	data	neuron	loss
7	problem	cross	prior	learning	policies
8	weight	sample	probability	model	function
9	finite	validation	baum	ganglion	algorithm
10	input	plot	algorithm	stimulus	domain
11	layer	generalization	likelihood	network	pay
12	machine	target	samples	alkon	description
13	states	approximation	welch	associative	length
14	multilayer	complexity	parameter	effect	performance
15	tdnn	estimation	number	input	policy
16	comparison	behavior	sample	control	order
17	experiment	model	posterior	discharge	problem
18	high	input	markov	hair	environment
19	nodes	structure	path	mechanism	learner
20	gamma	log	initial	response	states
21	node	theory	learning	threshold	denoted
22	training	data	size	background	multiple
23	result	examples	bayesian	exposure	paper
24	set	interval	emission	neural	structure
25	architecture	parameter	hidden	pulse	finding
26	local	selection	structure	pulses	number
27	narendra	number	search	resistance	single
28	quadratic	size	string	hermissenda	defined
29	system	term	distribution	order	discover
30	architectures	wide	induction	shunting	grid

Fig. 6. Thirty words which has the most frequent in the 5 documents as representatives. Bold and red words indicate that these words also appeared in the topic that a document belonged to. (Color figure online)

words in topic A shared a significant degree of semantic similarity. Specifically, both the document and topic A contained keywords that pertain to neural network architectures, including terms such as "input", "output", "training", "set", "weight", "number", and "layer".

Secondly, the document with a docID of 839, which was associated with topic B in Fig. 5, might be related to the generalization bound for neural networks. As such, this document shared certain keywords with topic B, such as "function", "training data", "parameter", and "bound".

Thirdly, the keywords of both the document with a docID of 440 and topic C were related to the Hidden Markov model ("HMM"), with various features such as "data", "parameter", "distribution", "probability", and "likelihood", leading to the document being grouped into topic C.

Moreover, both the document with a docID of 738 and topic D shared numerous keywords, including "cell", "firing", "neuron", "model", "stimulus", and "response". Therefore, it was suggested that the document may describe the nervous system in biology, and belonged to topic D.

Lastly, the document with a docID of 45 belonged to topic E (Fig. 5), and it was notable that the keywords in this document and topic E were related to reinforcement learning. Namely, certain terms such as "algorithm", "learning", "policiy", "function", "action", and "states" were employed to perform "task".

From the above-mentioned analyses of the five selected documents, it is apparent that the NMF technique is capable of reasonably handling topic clustering based on the semantic similarity of shared keywords.

4 Conclusions

This study seeks to examine the robustness of Non-negative Matrix Factorization (NMF) in topic clustering using a data corpus consisting of 1500 documents and 12419 words in the bags-of-words format. The study found that NMF was able to effectively cluster the relatively large and unstructured textual data into 5 meaningful topics and visually represent the topic context through keywords. Additionally, an investigation into the semantic relationship between the keywords of the documents and the corresponding extracted topics showed that NMF was an effective method for topic clustering. Thus, the study recommends the use of NMF as an efficient tool for education management in Vietnam.

References

1. Tan, P., Steinbach, M., Kumar, V.: Introduction to Data Mining, Pearson Addison Wesley (2006)
2. Xu, W., Liu, X., Gong, Y.: Document-clustering based on non-negative matrix factorization. In: Proceedings of SIGIR 2003, pp. 267–273. Toronto, CA (2003)
3. Wang, Y.-X., Zhang, Y.-J.: Nonnegative matrix factorization: a comprehensive review. IEEE Trans. Knowl. Data Eng. **25**(6), 1336–1353 (2013)
4. Ping, H., Xiaohua, X., Jie, D., Baichuan, F.: Low-rank nonnegative matrix factorization on Stiefel manifold. Inf. Sci. **514**, 131–148 (2020)
5. Lee, D.D., Seung, H.S.: Learning the parts of objects by non-negative matrix factorization. Nature **401**, 788–791 (1999)
6. Andrzej, C., Rafal, Z., Huy, P., Shunichi, A.: Nonnegative Matrix and Tensor Factorizations: Applications to Exploratory Multi-Way Data Analysis and Blind Source Separation. John Wiley & Sons (2009)
7. Athukorala, S., Mohotti, W.: An effective short-text topic modelling with neighbourhood assistance-driven NMF in Twitter. Soc. Netw. Anal. Min. **12** (89) (2022)
8. Gensler, S., Völckner, F., Egger, M., Fischbach, K., Schoder, D.: Listen to your customers: insights into brand image using online consumer-generated product reviews. Int. J. Electron. Commer. (20), 112–141 (2015)
9. Dua, D., Graff, C.: UCI Machine Learning Repository. University of California, School of Information and Computer Science, Irvine, CA (2019). [http://archive.ics.uci.edu/ml]

Mitigating and Analysis of Memory Usage Attack in IoE System

Zainab Alwaisi[1](✉), Simone Soderi[1,2], and Rocco De Nicola[1,2]

[1] IMT School for Advanced Studies, Lucca, Italy
{zainab.alwaisi,simone.soderi,rocco.denicola}@imtlucca.it
[2] CINI Cybersecurity Laboratory, Roma, Italy

Abstract. Internet of Everything (IoE) is a newly emerging trend, especially in homes. Marketing forces toward smart homes are also accelerating the spread of IoE devices in households. An obvious risk of the rapid adoption of these smart devices is that many lack controls for protecting the privacy and security of end users from attacks designed to disrupt lives and incur financial losses. Today the smart home is a system for managing the basic life support processes of both small systems, e.g., commercial, office premises, apartments, cottages, and largely automated complexes, e.g., commercial and industrial complexes. One of the critical tasks to be solved by the concept of a modern smart home is the problem of preventing the usage of IoE resources. Recently, there has been a rapid increase in attacks on consumer IoE devices.

Memory corruption vulnerabilities constitute a significant class of vulnerabilities in software security through which attackers can gain control of an entire system. Numerous memory corruption vulnerabilities have been found in IoE firmware already deployed in the consumer market. This paper aims to analyze and explain the resource usage attack and create a low-cost simulation environment to aid in the dynamic analysis of the attack. Further, we perform controlled resource usage attacks while measuring resource consumption on resource-constrained victims' IoE devices, such as CPU and memory utilization. We also build a lightweight algorithm to detect memory usage attacks in the IoE environment. The result shows high efficiency in detecting and mitigating memory usage attacks by detecting when the intruder starts and stops the attack.

Keywords: Smart Home (SH) · Internet of Everything (IoE) · memory usage attack · detection · security · resource constraint

1 Introduction

The Internet of Everything (IoE) encompasses data, people, the Internet of Things (IoT), and processes. IoE builds on IoT, which focuses on connecting network devices equipped with specialized sensors or actuators through the Internet [5]. The sensors and actuators can detect and respond to environmental changes, including light, temperature, sound, vibration, etc. IoE dramatically

N.-S. Vo and H.-A. Tran (Eds.): INISCOM 2023, LNICST 531, pp. 296–314, 2023.
https://doi.org/10.1007/978-3-031-47359-3_22

expands the scope of IoT by adding components that can provide richer experiences for businesses, individuals, and countries. For example, instead of simply relying on things to interact with their environments, as shown in Fig. 1, IoE can leverage all related data and processes to make IoT more relevant and valuable to people [19]. The ultimate goal of IoE is to boost operational efficiency, offer new business opportunities, and improve the quality of our lives. Better to relate to this idea; take the scenario of a person uncertain about closing a gas valve at home. An IoE solution allows a user to automatically check the gas valve's status and close it remotely if necessary [13,14].

Despite its potential rewards, IoE could pose significant security threats to its adopters. The number of IoE devices around us is steadily increasing, and IoE is starting to play a more critical role in our everyday lives. In particular, the link between the physical world and cyberspace established by IoE increases the risk of cyber attacks targeting smart devices since attacks against IoE can directly impact the health [11] and the welfare of their end users. Building on our gas value scenario, one can easily imagine a threat scenario in which an attacker causes a gas leak on purpose [20]. Even more alarming is that we are often oblivious to the quantity and nature of the IoE devices surrounding us, not to mention the potential security risks they represent. The recent security incidents resulting from IoE security vulnerabilities corroborate this observation. In particular, one of them is a Distributed Denial of Service (DDoS) attack against Dyn [2] in October 2016. This incident involved a botnet called Mirai, consisting of approximately 100,000 IoE hosts, including digital cameras and routers. The Mirai botnet launched DDoS attacks against Dyn, bringing down its Domain Name Servers (DNS), which resulted in an outage of major commercial

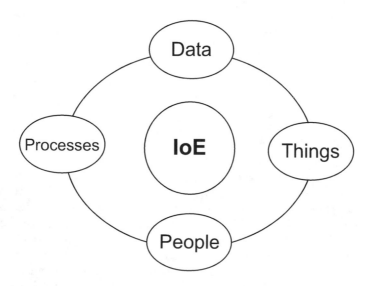

Fig. 1. The Definition of Internet of Everything (IoE).

websites, e.g., Netflix and CNN [7]. Another attack could affect the sensors and actuators' resources, making the smart devices unavailable to end-users.

Due to these emerging threats, it is imperative to raise awareness of potential IoE security risks [17] among end users through systematic risk assessment and effective visualizations. Home users are especially vulnerable because they are increasingly surrounded by IoE appliances, e.g., hands-free speakers, baby monitors, and security cameras. However, they lack the resources and skills to identify their IoE-related threats, remediate them, and minimize potential security risks. Therefore, in this paper, we mainly focus on analyzing the memory usage attack in smart devices and mitigating the effect of this attack by building a lightweight algorithm to detect memory usage attacks by calculating the memory usage of the smart device.

To accomplish this goal in home networks, we first identify memory usage attacks in smart home devices. Next, we analyze the effect of the attack by sending malicious attacks to affect the resources of the smart devices and calculate its effect on memory usage. We then elicit and document threats in the form of threat scenarios. Once specified, we build a lightweight algorithm to detect and mitigate the effect of the attack on memory usage.

1.1 Motivation and Contribution

IoE is a fast-growing field with capabilities to revolutionize the whole industry. As per market trends, more than 20 billion smart devices will be deployed in the next five years [10]. These interconnected devices will be generating sensitive data which needs to be protected. The field of IoE is making leaps and bounds technologically. There are multiple limitations while deploying IoE devices daily, e.g., battery life and lightweight computation. Therefore, building a novel security mechanism aims to protect the functionalities and privacy of sensitive IoE network environments, including healthcare, smart cities, etc. However, due to the substantial number of nodes in the environment and their restricted computing capabilities, securing smart nodes in the IoE environment is essential to protect the data and make the devices available to end-users. A lightweight mitigation technique should be considered to protect smart devices from resource-constraint attacks such as Denial of Services (DoS), Distributed Denial of Services (DDoS), and other malicious attacks. Our main contribution is building a lightweight technique to detect memory usage attacks in smart devices deployed directly at sensors. It applies real-time memory usage calculation to discriminate between different memory usage, e.g., read/write to memory. In this work, we consider different behaviors on the memory of smart devices. We measure the memory usage when there is read and write, under or without the attack, to evaluate the best detection of memory usage attack. We simulate the mitigation technique and assess the results by applying the proposed technique to smart devices, such as the Raspberry Pi[1] and Arduino. We measure the current memory usage of the smart device to monitor the memory usage to discriminate between normal

---

[1] https://www.raspberrypi.com/documentation/.

and abnormal behaviors. Therefore, this algorithm design is a protection strategy for IoE devices to maintain their integrity, seamlessly make them available to legitimate users, and protect them from memory attacks by considering their resource constraints.

1.2   Organization of the Paper

We organized this paper as follows. Section 2 presents a related work and background reading of resource-constrained attacks in IoT systems, e.g., memory usage attacks. We discuss the threat scenario and its analysis in Sects. 4 and 5. We describe our proposal, including metrics definition, methodology, and the detection algorithm, in Sect. 6.1. In Sect. 7, we show the results and discussions. Finally, Sect. 8 presents some concluding remarks and future works (Table 1).

Table 1. Memory Usage analysis before and after the attack.

Device	Status	% CPU Usage	% Memory Usage
Raspberry Pi	Idle	0.55 ÷ 0.88	10 ÷ 20
	Active	0.88 ÷ 1.50	20 ÷ 35
	Under Attack	1.5 ÷ 16.5	36 ÷ 66
Device	**Status**	**Thread Time [s]**	**% Memory Usage**
Arduino	Idle	1 ÷ 20	8 ÷ 11
	Active	21 ÷ 45	11 ÷ 16
	Under Attack	≥ 45	17 ÷ 45

2   Related Work

The IoE links people, data, things, and processes to make interconnections easier and more far-reaching than ever before [6]. As such, everyday appliances should be subjected to rigorous cyber security testing to the same degree that these appliances are tested and measured for traditional qualities, e.g., durability, fit-for-purpose, maintenance, etc. Unfortunately, standardized and independent verification of IoE devices is in its nascent stage, with IoE security being the focus of legislation and standard security criteria. Different authors tried to mitigate and detect attacks by analyzing the memory. Memory analysis has attracted several malware researchers. Vömel et al. in [16] surveyed the main memory acquisition and analysis techniques. In [12], Rathnayaka, et al. have observed that successful malware infection leaves a memory footprint. Zaki et al. in [18] studied the artifacts left by rootkits at the kernel level, such as driver, module, System Service Dispatch Table (SSDT) hook, Interrupt Descriptor Table (IDT) hook, and callback. The experiments proved that certain activities, such as callback functions, modified drivers, and attached devices, are the most suspicious activities at the kernel level. In [1], Aghaeikheirabady presented an analysis approach that extracts features available in memory, such as function calls, Dynamic-Link Libraries (DLLs), and registry, and compares the information available in different memory structures to increase the accuracy. The approach relies on the frequencies of the extracted features to classify them, and an overall accuracy of 98% is measured by applying Naïve Bayes. However, a significant drawback is the high False Positive Rate (FPR) that exceeded 16%.

Similarly, in [8], Mosli *et al.* introduced a technique that detects malware based on extracting three features from memory images; API calls, registry, and imported libraries. However, the experiments were performed on each feature individually, and maximum accuracy of 96% was achieved using the Support Vector Machines (SVM) classifier on the registry activities feature. Afterward, in their following work [9], Mosli *et al.* utilized the process handles available in memory to detect malware. The experiment has found that the handles used by malware are process handles, mutants, and section handles. However, when applying the random forest classifier, their approach achieved a modest accuracy slightly higher than 91%. Likewise, Duan *et al.* [4] presented an approach to extract live DLL is featured from memory and employed to detect malware variants that use the same DLLs. The experimental result showed an accuracy of 90% achieved using the hidden naïve bayes classifier. Furthermore, Dai *et al.* [3] proposed a malware detection and classification approach based on extracting memory images and converting them into fixed-size greyscale images. The approach then extracted the features from the images, using a gradient histogram, and used them to classify malware. An accuracy of 95.2% was obtained using the neural network classifier. Moreover, the authors of this work previously combined API calls from behavior analysis and memory analysis into one vector to represent each sample. A dataset was used, which consisted of 1200 malware and 400 benign files, to train the SVM classifier. The work confirmed that memory analysis could overcome the limitations of behavior analysis [15].

In this paper, we monitor the memory usage of the smart devices in the IoE environment to detect memory usage attacks and mitigate resource-constraints attacks. We also perform a testbed environment to measure the memory usage of the smart devices before and after attacking the IoE environment. In the experiments, the effectiveness of the proposed approach on memory usage attack detection and classification has been demonstrated and measured by three evaluations: classification accuracy, monitoring the memory usage, and detecting the attack. To the best of our knowledge, this is the first work to examine and detect such kind of memory usage attack in IoE systems.

3   Testbed Scenario

We used Raspberry Pi and Arduino as smart home devices in this experiment. We used different software tools for attacking data generation and collection.

On the adversary side, we used $Nmap^2$ to launch a network scan and identify devices' status, such as online or offline, IP address, and MAC address. Different tools can generate malicious attacks on the victim side, such as $hping3^3$. We used $tshark$ tool[4] to evaluate the impact of memory usage attacks on smart devices and capture WiFi traffic.

We also created a module inside the smart device to monitor memory usage and register all memory behaviors in the database (DB). The monitoring mode registers the behavior of the smart devices once it is *Idle, active,* and *under attack.* Different stages are used to run our experiment. In the first stage, we monitor the memory usage once the device is Idle, Active, and under attack. Then, we run a network scan to capture the port and device status. Once we ensure that the device is connected to the Internet, we send memory usage attacks for two purposes: first, to affect the memory, and second, to consume more memory usage and study the behavior of the attack. Then, we run memory usage monitoring to calculate the memory usage of the devices and study the devices' behaviors before and after the attack.

4   Threat Scenarios and Threat Model

This section will briefly discuss the design of memory usage attacks on IoE smart devices. The memory usage attack aims to affect the smart device's memory by sending malicious attacks such as DoS or DDoS attacks. In particular, memory usage attack targets a specific type of vulnerable IoE and embedded devices because these devices have very little build-in-security protection and suffer from resource-constraints problems.

4.1   Threat Scenario

The smart devices of IoE suffer from low computation problems such as low energy and memory. The resource-constraints problems encourage attackers to attack these devices by flooding the smart devices with malicious attacks. In this paper, we assume that the attacker has gained access to the control network and can communicate with the smart devices as an insider threat (e.g., a consumer who uses current or past authorized access to the smart devices to exceed or misuse) or an external hacker. A wide range of attacks, such as malicious attacks, will be available for the attacker when he/she gains access to a control network. In this paper, we study memory usage attacks on the smart devices of IoE systems (Fig. 2).

The threat scenario used in our experiment was first to scan the network and get different information about the port and devices' status. For scanning the network, we install *Nmap* on Kali-Linux. In this scenario, the attacker can send a malicious attack to the smart device to affect its resources in terms of

---

[2] https://nmap.org/.

[3] https://www.kali.org/tools/hping3/.

[4] https://www.wireshark.org/.

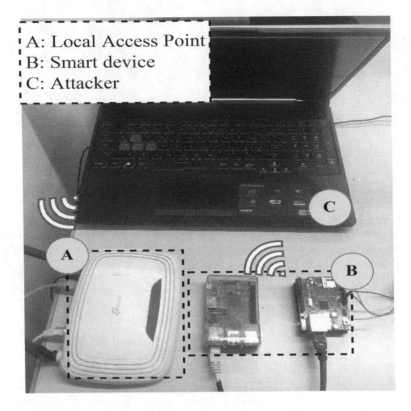

Fig. 2. Testbed scenario showing the devices used in our experiment.

memory. The IP address, port, and device status are stored in the DB for further calculation. After scanning the network, we start the monitoring mode of the smart device's memory usage; once the device is Idle and active, and when we send a malicious attack using *hping3* tools to the smart device. In this case, we study the memory behavior before and after attacking the smart devices. We also store all information about the memory, such as memory in total, memory usage, and CPU usage before and after attacking the smart devices.

In particular, the source code consists of three different parts:

– Memory usage attack: This module commences with the DoS and DDoS attack to send malicious attacks to the smart devices and affect their memory.
– Scanner: This module scans the network and gets different information about the smart devices. Also, it sends the IP address of the attacked smart devices for further calculation
– Memory-monitoring-mode: This module monitors the memory usage of the smart devices when it is Idle, active, and under attack. The monitoring mode helps to register different memory behaviors for detecting such attacks.

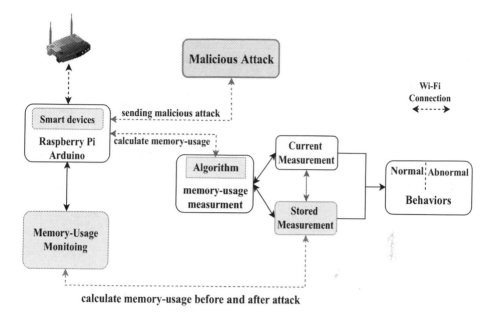

Fig. 3. Testing Environment.

4.2 Threat Model

We present a model of attacks on the memory usage of the smart devices of IoE systems, which can be used to understand the possible attack vectors intuitively and concisely. Also, to build lightweight algorithm[5] for detecting smart devices from these attacks. Let us assume ATK denotes the attacker while d denotes the smart devices, and MEM denotes the smart devices' memory usage. According to our model, every attack originates from an attacker ATK where $atk \in ATK$ by a means towards a target d. We can model this relationship as follows:

$$ATK \mapsto mem \rightarrow D \tag{1}$$

where $atk \in ATK, d \subset D, mem \in MEM$. The notation $\mapsto$ maps the attacker (ATK) to the victim's (D) memory (mem). For calculating the memory usage and CPU usage of the smart devices before and after attacking the memory, the following equation math represents this calculation. Let us describe the memory usage measurement (MEM) footprints considering the set of different device statuses in the attack's absence or presence.

$$MEM(d) = f(mem(d), ATK, n) \quad \text{and} \quad n \in [0, 1] \tag{2}$$

where (mem_d) the memory usage measurement (mem) of the smart device (d) at a point in time in the absence or presence of cyberattacks for a specific

---

[5] https://github.com/developerZA/MitigationMemoryAttack.git.

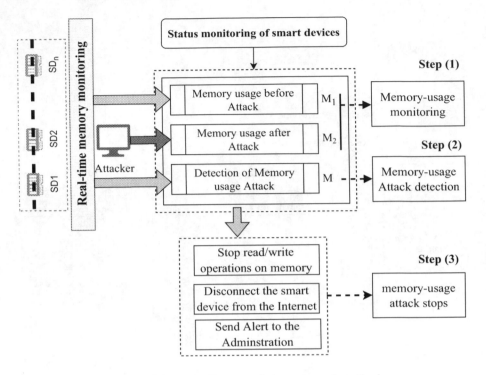

Fig. 4. Schematic diagram of the proposed method.

attack (ATK), and n is the number of memory usage measurements in a time interval, $f(mem(d), ATK, n) \in [0,1]$ where 0 is the minimum memory usage measurement, and 1 presents the maximum memory usage measurement in the absence or presence of the attack. The CPU (CPU) usage measurement is also calculated for the Raspberry Pi device as follows:

$$CPU(d) = f(cpu(d), ATK, n) \quad \text{and} \quad n \in [0,1] \tag{3}$$

where (cpu_d) is the CPU usage measurement (cpu) of the smart device (d) at a point in time in the absence or presence of cyberattacks for a specific attack (ATK), and n is the number of CPU usage measurements in a time interval, $f(cpu(d), ATK, n) \in [0,1]$ where 0 is the minimum CPU usage measurement, and 1 presents the maximum CPU usage measurement in the absence or presence of the attack (Fig. 4).

We do not calculate the CPU usage for the Arduino, as it is a microcontroller. We focus only on the maximum memory usage through or without the attack using a particular library called *MemoryFree* and *pgmStrToRAM*. And we also calculate *micros()* or *millis()* before and after sending the malicious attack. We also calculate the thread time for different statuses of the smart device, e.g., Idle, Active, and under attack.

5   Static Analysis of Resource Usage Attack

The smart devices used in this experiment were infected with malicious software used to carry out different malicious attacks on a target on an isolated network. During the experiments, the memory usage footprints of the smart devices were obtained under normal operating conditions, as well as when these smart devices carry out cyberattacks. Each memory usage footprint was obtained by taking measurements after 5 s within 1 minute when the smart device performs an attack and normal operation. A total of 10 minutes of calculation measurement of memory usage footprints of both in the presence of attacks and normal functioning smart devices were built.

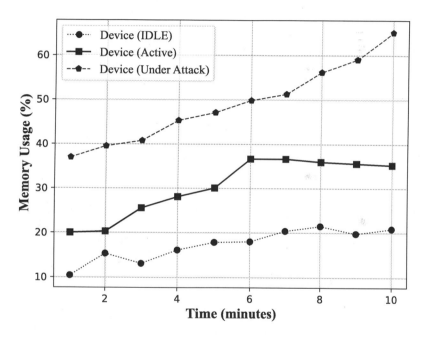

Fig. 5. Raspberry Pi (Memory Usage Before and After the attack).

During packet collection, the attacks are sent using the same Transmission Control Protocol (TCP) and User Datagram Protocol (UDP) flood commands. Using the topology as depicted by Fig. 3, the malicious TCP and UDP traffic are separately sent to the victim device, while all usage statistics are recorded on the victim device. Each attack is simulated for a duration of 1 minute, and all usage statistics are recorded for the same duration. No attacks are sent during the first period (10 minutes), and all usage statistics are recorded and saved in the DB. And also, the same things applied once the second period started after sending malicious attacks.

The result of this experiment shows the memory usage footprint when the device is Idle, Active, and under attack. Therefore, the normal usage of the memory of the Raspberry Pi device in the absence of the attack fluctuates between 10% to 36%. This percentage is divided between two different states of the smart device when it is Idle, the percentage is between 10 and 20%, and when it is Active, the percentage is more than 25% but less than 37% as shown in Fig. 5. Moreover, the percentage of memory usage changed after sending the malicious attack, and the percentage changed to be more than 66% per minute. We also calculate the CPU usage of the smart devices to check the CPU status before and after attacking the memory of the smart devices. Figure 6 shows the normal CPU usage for Idle and Active statuses of the Raspberry Pi device. The normal CPU usage for Idle devices is between 0.55% to 0.88%. The memory usage of the Active smart devices is between 0.88% to 1.50%. At the same time, the CPU usage is more than 1.5% once we send the malicious attack to the smart devices. We also calculate the memory usage of another smart device (Arduino). The main purpose of using two different devices is to show how the algorithm works for different devices which implement different architectures. For printing the memory usage of the Arduino device, we used a specific library to get the free usage memory for different statuses of the smart device, e.g., Idle, Active, under attack. Therefore, the memory usage for the first status, as shown in Fig. 7, fluctuates between 8.1% to 11%, and for the Active status, it is between 11% to less than 16%. The memory usage percentage changes to more than 17% and less than 50% once we send a malicious attack to the smart device.

The results and analyzes of this experiment assisted us in understanding the impact of the memory usage attack on smart devices and building a lightweight algorithm to protect these devices from such an attack. The following section describes the detection algorithm and presents some results.

6   Threat Mitigation

This paper introduces a detection mechanism and response to cyber-attacks on smart devices' memory usage. We also propose a lightweight algorithm to detect such memory changes inside smart devices by monitoring memory usage. Once the attack is detected, the algorithm will force the memory to stop listening to such an attack (e.g., stop reading and writing to memory). We also disconnect the victim devices from the Internet automatically. We implement this algorithm in the smart devices themselves. The presented mechanism records the response of the attack, and memory usage, for different states such as Idle, Active, under attack. The detection algorithm detects any breach in the memory usage of smart devices.

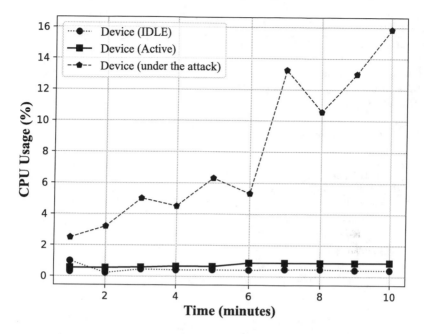

Fig. 6. Raspberry Pi (CPU Usage Before and After the attack).

6.1 Proposed Algorithm

The attacker aims to consume more memory usage of the smart device, and the monitoring mode of the presented algorithm updates and registers all different cases of memory behaviors before and after the attack. We record the change on memory for every 3 second for 1 minute. According to the data obtained from the testbed, the attacker can change the memory usage within 67% of wrong values during 10 minutes in total.

This Algorithm 6.1 takes the recorded readings from the DB for each smart device in the IoE system. The variable $Diff$ stores the subtraction of previous (*before sending such attack*) and current (*after sending malicious attack*) smart devices reading. For instance, the maximum memory usage of the smart devices for Idle and Active smart devices are given in Fig. 5. The variable $Diff$ stores the subtraction of the previous and current memory usage readings. For instance, the maximum sudden memory usage change expected in the memory of the smart device is given by subtracting the value of the maximum memory usage when the device is under attack minus the minimum memory usage when the device is Active and Idle before sending any attack.

$$Reading_{Threshold} = Max_{usage(MEM)} - Min_{usage(MEM)} \qquad (4)$$

When the variable $Diff$ exceeds the expected value, the variable $T1$ *"Timer"* is reset, and we verify whether the alert message has been sent to the adminis- tration. If not, we increase the *counter*1 variable, which records the number of

---

Algorithm 1 A Technique to detect Memory Usage Attack

1: Input: $d, Diff, C1, T1, Alert$
2: Output1: Normal($M1$)
3: Output2: Abnormal ($M2$)
4: Final Result: Output1 *or* Output2
5: $M1 : Reading_{memory-usage}$
6: $MEM(d) = f(mem(d), ATK, n)$
7: $M2 : Reading_{memory-usage}$
8: $Reading_{Threshold} = Max_{usage(MEM)} - Min_{usage(MEM)}$
9: $Diff = M1 - M2$
10: **if** $M2 = M1$ **then**
11:     **if** $Diff > Reading_{Threshold}$ **then**
12:         $ResetT1$
13:         **if** $Alert =='On'$ **then**
14:             monitor memory
15:         **else**
16:             $C1 = C1 + 1$
17:             **if** $C1 > Max_{(memory-usage)}$ **then**
18:                 $Alert =='On'$
19:                 Attack detected
20:                 Detect the main source (X)
21:                 Stopped Reading/Writing on Memory from (X)
22:                 Disconnect the smart device (d) from the Internet
23:             **else**
24:                 Return back to monitor memory
25:     **else**
26:         **if** $C1 > 0$ **then**
27:             $T1 = T1 + 1$
28:             **if** $T1 > Threshold_T$ **then**
29:                 Reset Alert
30:                 Reset C1
31:                 Reset C1
32:                 Attack stopped
33:             **else**
34:                 return back to monitor memory

---

times the difference between previous and current memory usage reading exceeds the maximum allowed value. When the *counter*1 variable is greater than the maximum allowed value, it sends the alert message indicating that the space of memory usage addressed to that smart device is under memory usage attack. At this stage, we stop any reading/writing operations to and from memory and disconnect the smart device from the Internet, as all victim device's IPs are stored in the black-list of our DB.

Through experimentation, we consider the scenario when the attacker stops the attack. When the $Diff$ value is less than $Reading_{threshold}$ value, we compare whether the variable counter is greater than *zero*, then we increase $T1$. We can

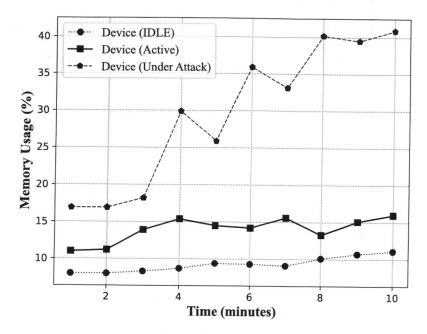

Fig. 7. Arduino (Memory Usage Before and After the attack).

assume the attack stops if the variable is greater than the $Time_{Threshold}$ variable. Finally, we reset the alert: $counter1$ and $T1$ variables.

After detecting the memory usage attack of such a device (d), we put all the victim devices on a black-list. Then, once the attack is detected on such a device, we first stop any operation on the memory, e.g., read and write on memory. We disconnect the Internet connection of the smart device (d) to prevent any further attack on the smart device's memory usage. The next section presents different results regarding detecting memory usage attacks.

Therefore, the mitigation is summarized in the following steps:

1. add the victim smart devices' IP to a black-list;
2. stop any reading/writing to the smart device;
3. disconnect the smart device from the Internet.

7 Experimentation and Discussion

7.1 Results

We ran malicious attacks on the smart device to check the memory usage before and after the attack. Figure 8 shows the mechanisms of our algorithm to fetch the attack once it is started. The monitoring mode of the memory usage sends memory usage readings to the algorithm, and inside the algorithm, there is a statistics comparison between normal and abnormal cases. As described in

Sect. 4, we first check the behavior of the smart devices once there is an attack, and we register all different cases for memory usage, e.g., Idle, Active, under attack. The main purpose of this analysis is to study the attack first and then to build a mitigation mechanism to detect memory attacks.

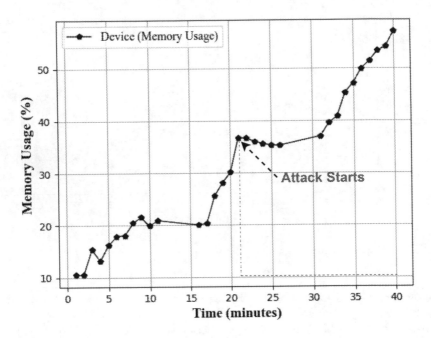

Fig. 8. Raspberry Pi (Detecting the memory usage Attack.).

Figures 8 and 9 shows the presented results of detecting the attack once it starts; we can notice that the attack starts when the memory usage is greater than 37%, and the $Diff$ variable is greater than the expected memory usage value. At this stage, the smart device d is passed through different operations, e.g., stop reading/writing on d, disconnect d from the Internet to stop any further attack, and send an alert to the administration about the status of the smart device.

The detection algorithm also notified the administration once the attack stopped. This stage will help with further operations. Through this experiment, we also studied the behavior of the CPU usage of the Raspberry Pi device under the same attack. Figure 10 shows the behavior of the CPU usage before and after attacking the memory of the smart devices. We also applied the same detection algorithm to study the behavior of the mitigation algorithm on the CPU and whether this algorithm detects the attack or not.

The same calculation is applied to the Arduino, and the detection algorithm records different variables about the attack once it is started and stopped. Figure 11 shows the recorded results of detecting the attack. We can notice that

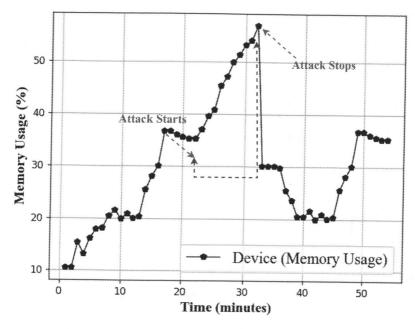

Fig. 9. Raspberry Pi (Detecting the memory usage once the attack starts and when it stops).

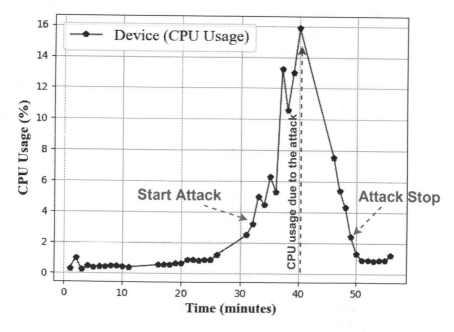

Fig. 10. CPU Usage during the attack when it started and stopped (Raspberry Pi).

the attack started when the memory usage percentage increased to be more than 16%, and for detecting the attack when it is stopped, once the memory usage percentage decreased to be less than 20%. Once the system detects that the attack is stopped on the smart device d, the system might disconnect the smart device from the Internet, or the actual attack is stopped from the main source.

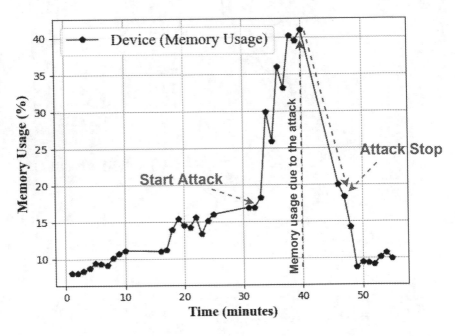

Fig. 11. Arduino (Detecting the memory usage once the attack starts and when it stops).

The algorithm also stores all victim devices' IPs in the black-list, so when there is an attack on the smart device, we disconnect the smart device to prevent any further attack. We also prevent further access to the database until the administration team solves the issue.

8   Conclusion and Future Work

The Internet of Everything is the beginning of a new era of technology in Internet-based smart communication and connecting smart devices. The security of IoE pillars is important as some suffer from resource-constraints problems. This paper proposed an approach that can detect and classify memory usage attacks using memory-based features extracted from the memory usage of the smart device. The approach represents a mitigation method to detect the attack once it appears in the memory usage of the smart devices. First, we monitor memory usage by using a specific tool in *Python* script and *C* language to fetch different data about memory usage. Then, all the fetched data is stored in the DB for further calculation. Second, we studied the attack behavior and registered the memory usage readings before and after the attack. In this work, we conduct static and dynamic analysis of the memory usage attack. In particular, we have conducted all the experiments in an isolated and cost-efficient experimental setup. It is observed that malicious attacks, e.g., flooding attacks have a significant impact on the resources of the IoE smart devices. When an IoE edge device is flooded with malicious attacks, there are significant increases in CPU and memory usage. This analysis helps in building the detection algorithm. The detection method relies on monitoring the memory usage to compare different variables of the memory reading. It is also able to detect the attack on time once it happens. Moreover, it can detect if the intruder stops the attack or not. We also build an alert message inside the algorithm to send different notifications to the administration once the attack is detected. Moreover, all victim devices are disconnected from the Internet, and all read/write operations to and from memory are also stopped. In the future, we will focus on detecting the main sources of memory usage attacks in the IoE environment.

References

1. Aghaeikheirabady, M., Farshchi, S.M.R., Shirazi, H.: A new approach to malware detection by comparative analysis of data structures in a memory image. In: 2014 International Congress on Technology, Communication and Knowledge (ICTCK), pp. 1–4. IEEE (2014)
2. Attack, D.: DDoS attack that disrupted internet was largest of its kind in history, experts say (2016). https://www.theguardian.com/technology/2016/oct/26/ddos-attack-dyn-mirai-botnet
3. Dai, Y., Li, H., Qian, Y., Lu, X.: A malware classification method based on memory dump grayscale image. Digit. Investig. **27**, 30–37 (2018)
4. Duan, Y., Fu, X., Luo, B., Wang, Z., Shi, J., Du, X.: Detective: automatically identify and analyze malware processes in forensic scenarios via DLLs. In: 2015 IEEE International Conference on Communications (ICC), pp. 5691–5696. IEEE (2015)
5. Jamil, B., Ijaz, H., Shojafar, M., Munir, K., Buyya, R.: Resource allocation and task scheduling in fog computing and internet of everything environments: a taxonomy, review, and future directions. ACM Comput. Surv. **54**, 1–38 (2022)
6. Jara, A.J., Ladid, L., Skarmeta, A.: The internet of everything through IPv6: an analysis of challenges, solutions and opportunities. J. Wirel. Mob. Networks Ubiquitous Comput. Dependable Appl. **4**, 97–118 (2013)
7. Kathole, A.B., et al.: Energy-aware UAV based on blockchain model using IoE application in 6g network-driven Cybertwin. Energies **15**(21), 8304 (2022)
8. Mosli, R., Li, R., Yuan, B., Pan, Y.: Automated malware detection using artifacts in forensic memory images. In: 2016 IEEE Symposium on Technologies for Homeland Security (HST), pp. 1–6. IEEE (2016)
9. Mosli, R., Li, R., Yuan, B., Pan, Y.: A behavior-based approach for malware detection. In: DigitalForensics 2017. IAICT, vol. 511, pp. 187–201. Springer, Cham (2017). https://doi.org/10.1007/978-3-319-67208-3_11

10. Murtuza, S.: Internet of everything: Application and various challenges analysis a survey. In: 2022 1st International Conference on Informatics (ICI), pp. 250–252 (2022). https://doi.org/10.1109/ICI53355.2022.9786891
11. Rani, R., et al.: Towards green computing oriented security: a lightweight postquantum signature for IoE. Sensors **21**(5), 1883 (2021)
12. Rathnayaka, C., Jamdagni, A.: An efficient approach for advanced malware analysis using memory forensic technique. In: 2017 IEEE Trustcom/BigDataSE/ICESS, pp. 1145–1150. IEEE (2017)
13. Ryoo, J., Kim, S., Cho, J., Kim, H., Tjoa, S., Derobertis, C.: IoE security threats and you. In: 2017 International Conference on Software Security and Assurance (ICSSA), pp. 13–19 (2017). https://doi.org/10.1109/ICSSA.2017.28
14. Shi, W., Xu, W., You, X., Zhao, C., Wei, K.: Intelligent reflection enabling technologies for integrated and green internet-of-everything beyond 5G: communication, sensing, and security. IEEE Wirel. Commun. **30**, 147–154 (2022)
15. Sihwail, R., Omar, K., Zainol Ariffin, K.A., Al Afghani, S.: Malware detection approach based on artifacts in memory image and dynamic analysis. Appl. Sci. **9**(18), 3680 (2019)
16. Vomel, S., Freiling, F.C.: A survey of main memory acquisition and analysis techniques for the windows operating system. Digit. Investig. **8**(1), 3–22 (2011)
17. Wei, L., Wu, J., Long, C., Lin, Y.B.: The convergence of IoE and blockchain: security challenges. IT Prof. **21**(5), 26–32 (2019)
18. Zaki, A., Humphrey, B.: Unveiling the kernel: rootkit discovery using selective automated kernel memory differencing. Virus Bull. 239–256 (2014)
19. Zhan, J., Dong, S., Hu, W.: IoE-supported smart logistics network communication with optimization and security. Sustain. Energy Technol. Assess. **52**, 102052 (2022)
20. Zhang, H., Shlezinger, N., Guidi, F., Dardari, D., Imani, M.F., Eldar, Y.C.: Near-field wireless power transfer for 6G internet of everything mobile networks: opportunities and challenges. IEEE Commun. Mag. **60**(3), 12–18 (2022)

Physical Layer Security of Heterogenous Networks with Unreliable Wireless Backhaul and Small Cell Selections

Eoin O'Boyle[1]([✉]), Xinkai Cheng[2], and Cheng Yin[3]

[1] Queen's University, Belfast, UK
eoboyle11@qub.ac.uk
[2] Wuhan University of Science and Technology, Wuhan, China
[3] University of Surrey, Guildford, UK
c.yin@surrey.ac.uk

Abstract. In this study, we propose a novel secure heterogeneous network system model that incorporates an unreliable wireless backhaul and perfect channel estimation across identical Rayleigh fading channels. Our approach employs three transmission schemes: Sub-Optimum Selection (SS), Optimum Selection (OS), and Minimum-Eavesdropping Selection (MES), with the goal of improving the secrecy performance of the system. We derive advanced closed-form expressions for the Secrecy Outage Probability (SOP) for these three selection schemes in both practical and ideal scenarios. We investigate the influence of uncertainties in wireless backhaul and perfect Channel State Information (CSI) on the system's secrecy performance. Furthermore, we examine how the number of small-cell transmitters impacts the system's secrecy performance. By conducting Monte-Carlo simulations, we validate the accuracy of our analytical results. This verification ensures the correctness of our expressions and strengthens the reliability of our findings.

Keywords: Physical layer security · Rayleigh fading · Secrecy outage probability · Wireless backhaul

1 Introduction

Physical layer security has been considered as a promising technology to build the security of wireless networks [1]. The fundamental concept behind physical layer security involves leveraging the inherent properties of wireless channels to ensure message security from an information-theoretical perspective. A seminal study by Wyner demonstrated that when the primary channel between the source and destination surpasses the eavesdropping channel, it is possible to achieve flawless message security at a nonzero transmission rate. In this context, employing small cell transmitter selection schemes proves to be an efficient approach [2–6].

The rising wireless data traffic demand leads networks being more dense and heterogeneous. Heterogeneous networks supply effective methods of accommodating current

N.-S. Vo and H.-A. Tran (Eds.): INISCOM 2023, LNICST 531, pp. 315–326, 2023.
https://doi.org/10.1007/978-3-031-47359-3_23

data traffic growth by building macro base stations with small-cells and access points [6]. Macro base stations are typically erected on towers to facilitate extensive transmission coverage using low-frequency bands. On the other hand, small cells operate on higher frequency bands and offer radio coverage within a shorter range compared to macro cells. Despite their smaller coverage area, small cells provide highly reliable connections characterized by low latency and high speed. In order to meet the increasing data traffic demands, both macro base stations and small cells are integrated to create heterogeneous networks. These networks are designed to address future communication requirements. The backhaul plays a crucial role by establishing connections between the macro base station and the small cells. Wireless backhaul has emerged as a solution for establishing communication connections between small cells and access points in outdoor where wired connections are not avaliable. Although wireless backhaul encounters occasional unreliability, it has proven to be a viable method for ensuring seamless communication in such scenarios [11]. The deployment of a two-tier network configuration was explored, involving a macro base station that establishes a connection with the cloud. In this setup, small cells have the capability to connect wirelessly to either the macro base station or the core network by utilizing backhaul links [11–13]. The demand for high connectivity in heterogeneous networks has led to a proliferation of devices, thereby posing significant challenges to wireless security. Furthermore, the inherent uncertainties in wireless communication make these networks even more susceptible to various attacks. Consequently, the research focus has shifted towards exploring secure heterogeneous networks that can effectively address the issue of wireless backhaul unreliability.

In this paper, we assume that transmission links follow Rayleigh fading channel, which is a special case of Nakagami-m fading [14]. Additionally, we propose different transmitter selection schemes to enhance the secrecy performance under perfect channel estimation and wireless backhaul uncertainties. This study proposes an advanced design for a secure heterogeneous system based on Physical Layer Security (PLS). The investigation focuses on the impact of unreliable wireless backhaul and perfect channel estimation in the presence of Rayleigh fading. To enhance the secrecy performance of the system, three small-cell transmitter selection schemes are introduced: SS, OS and MES. These selection schemes are implemented to improve the overall security of the system.

2 System Model

The considered system model is in Fig. 1. It consists of K small-cells transmitters, $\{T_1,...,T_k,..., T_K\}$, connecting to a macro-base station, BS, through unreliable backhaul links, b_k, a secondary destination, D, and an eavesdropper, E. We assume $T - D$ and undergo independent and identically distributed Rayleigh fading [2].

The best transmitter is chosen among K small-cell transmitters in the considered system. When the information is sent to small-cell transmitters, there is a certain probability that the backhaul fails to convey the transmission. We model the backhaul reliability as a Bernoulli process, I_k. The success probability of Bernoulli process is defined as s, and failure probability is defined as $1 - s$ [6].

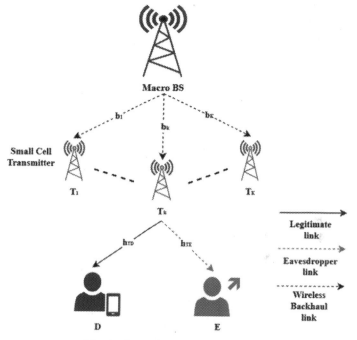

Fig. 1. Secure heterogenous network.

The CDF and PDF of the random variable X is

$$F_X(x) = 1 - exp\left(-\frac{x^2}{2\sigma^2}\right), for\ x \in [0, \infty]$$

$$f_X(x) = \frac{x}{\sigma^2} exp\left(-\frac{x^2}{2\sigma^2}\right), for\ x \geq 0 \tag{1}$$

The connection between the small-cell transmitters and the macro BS is established through backhaul. The received signals at D and E can be expressed as follows:

$$
\begin{aligned}
Fy_D &= \sqrt{P_T}\, h_{T_kD} \mathbb{I}_k x + z, \\
y_E &= \sqrt{P_T}\, h_{T_kE} x + z,
\end{aligned}
\quad F \tag{2}
$$

where $h_{T_{kD}}$ and h_{T_kE} are channel coefficients from T_k to D and from T_k to E. In addition, x is the power transmitted symbol and P_T is the transmitted power of T_k. It is assumed that D and E encounter the complex additive white Gaussian Noise, i.e., $z \sim CN\left(0, \sigma^2\right)$. The relationship between the estimated channel coefficients $\hat{h}_{T_kD}, \hat{h}_{T_kE}$ and real channel coefficients h_{T_kD}, h_{T_kE} are given as

$$
\begin{aligned}
\hat{h}_{T_kD} &= h_{T_kD}, \\
\hat{h}_{T_kE} &= h_{T_kE}.
\end{aligned}
\tag{3}
$$

Then, the received signals are rewritten as

$$y_D = \sqrt{P_T}\hat{h}_{T_kD}\mathbb{I}_k x + z,$$
$$y_E = \sqrt{P_T}\hat{h}_{T_kE}x + z. \tag{4}$$

In consonance with (4), the SNRs at D and E are,

$$SNR_{TD} = \frac{P_T|h_{TD}|^2\mathbb{I}_k}{\sigma^2} = \gamma_m|h_{TD}|^2\mathbb{I}_k,$$

$$SNR_{TE} = \frac{P_T|h_{TE}|^2}{\sigma^2} = \gamma_m|h_{TE}|^2, \tag{5}$$

where $\gamma_m = \frac{P_T}{\sigma^2}$. To improve the system secrecy performance, the best transmitter T_{k*} is chosen from the K transmitters. The SNRs at D and E with the selected T_{k*} are

$$SNR_{T_{k*}D} = \frac{P_T|h_{T_{k*}D}|^2\mathbb{I}_{k*}}{\sigma^2} = \gamma_m|h_{T_{k*}D}|^2\mathbb{I}_{k*},$$

$$SNR_{T_{k*}E} = \frac{P_T|h_{T_{k*}E}|^2}{\sigma^2} = \gamma_m|h_{T_{k*}E}|^2, \tag{6}$$

where $|h_{T_{k*}D}|^2$ and $|h_{T_{k*}E}|^2$ are the channel coefficients of the chosen transmitter T_{k*} to D and E. $\mathbb{I}_{k*}$ represents the backhaul reliability from the macro-BS to T_{k*}.

3   Small Cell Transmitter Selection Schemes

This section presents the three small-cell selection schemes, which are expressed as follows.

A. *Sub-optimum Selection (SS)*
   By using T_k-D links, the SS scheme chooses the transmitter by calculating the maximum power gain as

$$k^* = arg \max_{1 \leq k \leq K} \gamma_m|h_{T_kD}|^2\mathbb{I}_k, \tag{7}$$

   where k^* indicates the index of the chosen transmitter.
B. *Optimum Selection (OS)*
   The OS requires global CSI of the considered system and the system secrecy capacity is given as

$$C_s = \left[log_2(1 + SNR_{TD}) - log_2(1 + SNR_{TE})\right]^+, \tag{8}$$

   where $[x]^+$=max$(x, 0)$ and the definitions of SNR_{TD} and SNR_{TE} are illustrated in (5).

$$k^* = argmax C_s^k, \tag{9}$$

   where $C_s^k = \left[log_2(1 + SNR_{T_{k*}D}) - log_2(1 + SNR_{T_{k*}E})\right]^+$ and the definitions of $SNR_{T_{k*}D}$ and $SNR_{T_{k*}E}$ can be found in (6).

C. Minimum-Eavesdropping Selection (MES)

The MES scheme is considered to select the smallest channel gain from T_k to E. The transmitter T_{k^*} is chosen by searching the worst $T_k - E$ link. This scheme can be written mathematically as

$$k^* = arg \min_{1 \le k \le K} \left| h_{T_k E} \right|^2. \tag{10}$$

4 Performance Analysis

The system performance is analysed by deriving SOP expressions including uncertainties from wireless backhaul unreliability. The definition of SOP is mathematically written as [8]

$$\mathbb{P}_{out}(\theta) = \mathbb{P}_{out}(C_s < \theta)$$

$$= \int_0^\infty F_{T_{k^*}D}(\rho(1+x) - 1) f_E(x) dx. \tag{11}$$

where $F_{T_{k^*}D}(\rho(1+x) - 1)$ is the CDF, $f_E(x)$ is the PDF and $\rho = 2^\theta$.

The CDF and PDF of random variable $\mathbb{I}_k X$ for the $T - D$ link is given as

$$F_{|h_{TD}|^2 \mathbb{I}_k X}(x) = \int_0^t (1-s)\delta(x) + s\lambda_{TD} exp(-\lambda_{TD} x) dt. = 1 - s exp\left(-\lambda_{TD}\frac{x}{\gamma_m}\right)$$

$$f_{|h_{TD}|^2 \mathbb{I}_k X}(x) = (1-s)\delta(x) + s\lambda_{TD} exp(-\lambda_{TD} x) \tag{12}$$

The PDF expression of random variable $\mathbb{I}_k X$ for the T-E link is

$$f_E(x) = \frac{\lambda_{TE}}{\gamma_m} exp\left(-\lambda_{TE}\frac{x}{\gamma_m}\right) \tag{13}$$

where $\gamma_m = P_T / \sigma^2$.

1) *Sub-optimum Selection:*

Firstly, we derive the SOP of the SS scheme. Conforming to the selection rules in (7), the SOP expression of the SS scheme is,

$$\mathbb{P}_{out}(\theta) = \mathbb{P}_{out}(C_s < \theta)$$

$$= \int_0^\infty F_{T_{k^*}D}(\rho(1+x) - 1) f_E(x) dx. \tag{14}$$

The CDF and PDF are,

$$F_{T_k^* D} = F_{TD}^k = \left[1 - s exp\left(-\lambda_{TD}\frac{x}{\gamma_m}\right)\right]^k$$

$$= 1 + \sum_{k=1}^{K} (-1)^k \binom{K}{k} s^k exp\left(-\frac{\lambda_{TD} k x}{\gamma_m}\right) \tag{15}$$

Substituting this equation into $\mathbb{P}_{out}(\theta)$ leads to the corresponding CDF,

$$F_{T_{k^*}D}(\rho(1+x) - 1) = 1 + \sum_{k=1}^{K} (-1)^k \binom{K}{k} s^k exp\left(-\frac{\lambda_{TD} k(\rho(1+x) - 1)}{\gamma_m}\right)$$

The PDF part is written mathematically as,

$$f_E(x) = \frac{\lambda_{TE}}{\gamma_m} exp\left(-\lambda_{TE}\frac{x}{\gamma_m}\right)$$

Therefore, the final SOP of the SS scheme is given as,

$$\mathbb{P}_r(C_s < \theta) = \int_0^\infty 1 + \sum_{k=0}^{K} \binom{K}{k} (-1)^k s^k exp\left(-\frac{\lambda_{TD} k(\rho(1+x) - 1)}{\gamma_m}\right) \frac{\lambda_{TE}}{\gamma_m} exp\left(-\lambda_{TE}\frac{x}{\gamma_m}\right)$$

$$= 1 + \sum_{k=0}^{K} \binom{K}{k} (-1)^k s^k \frac{\lambda_{TE}}{\gamma_m} \int_0^\infty exp\left(-\frac{\lambda_{TD} k(\rho(1+x) - 1)}{\gamma_m}\right) exp\left(-\lambda_{TE}\frac{x}{\gamma_m}\right)$$

$$= 1 + \sum_{k=0}^{K} \binom{K}{k} (-1)^k s^k \frac{\lambda_{TE}}{\gamma_m} \int_0^\infty exp\left(-\frac{\lambda_{TD} k(\rho(1+x) - 1) - \lambda_{TE} x}{\gamma_m}\right)$$

$$= 1 + \sum_{k=0}^{K} \binom{K}{k} (-1)^k s^k \frac{\lambda_{TE}}{\gamma_m} \frac{\gamma_m}{\lambda_{TD} \rho k + \lambda_{TE}} exp\left(-\frac{\lambda_{TD} k(\rho(1+0) - 1) - \lambda_{TE}(0)}{\gamma_m}\right)$$

$$= 1 + \sum_{k=0}^{K} \binom{K}{k} (-1)^k s^k \frac{\lambda_{TE}}{\gamma_m} \frac{\gamma_m}{\lambda_{TD} \rho k + \lambda_{TE}} exp\left(-\frac{\lambda_{TD} \rho k - \lambda_{TD} k}{\gamma_m}\right)$$

Thus, the SOP for SS is written mathematically as,

$$\mathbb{P}_{out}^{SS} = 1 + \sum_{k=0}^{K} \binom{K}{k} (-1)^k s^k \left(\frac{\lambda_{TE}}{\lambda_{TD} \rho k + \lambda_{TE}}\right) exp\left(-\frac{\lambda_{TD} k \rho - \lambda_{TD} k}{\gamma_m}\right) \tag{16}$$

2) *Optimum Selection:*

Firstly, the CDF and PDF of the OS scheme are,

$$F_{TD} = 1 - s exp\left(-\lambda_{TD}\frac{x}{\gamma_m}\right)$$

$$f_E(x) = \frac{\lambda_{TE}}{\gamma_m} exp\left(-\frac{\lambda_{TE} x}{\gamma_m}\right) \tag{17}$$

Then, substituting the above equations into (11) and we can obtain the following integral,

$$\mathbb{P}_r(C_s < \theta) = \int_0^\infty F_{TD}(\rho(1+x) - 1) f_E(x) dx.$$

$$= \int_0^\infty \left[1 - sexp\left(-\lambda_{TD} \frac{(\rho(1+x) - 1)}{\gamma_m} \right) \right] \frac{\lambda_{TE}}{\gamma_m} exp\left(-\lambda_{TD} \frac{\lambda_{TE}x}{\gamma_m} \right) dx.$$

$$= 1 - s \frac{\lambda_E}{\gamma_m} exp\left(\frac{-\lambda_{TD}}{\gamma_m} \rho + \frac{\lambda_{TD}}{\gamma_m} \right) \int_0^\infty exp\left(-\frac{\lambda_{TD}}{\gamma_m} \rho x - \frac{\lambda_E}{\gamma_m} \right) dx.$$

Recall the selection rules in (9), we obtain

$$\mathbb{P}_r(C_s < \theta) = \int_0^\infty F_{TD}(\rho(1+x) - 1) f_E(x) dx.$$

$$= \left[1 - \frac{s\lambda_E}{\lambda_{TD}\rho + \lambda_{TE}} exp\left(-\frac{\lambda_{TD}\rho + \lambda_{TD}}{\gamma_m} \right) \right]^k$$

The SOP of the OS scheme is expressed as

$$\mathbb{P}_{out}^{OS} = \sum_{k=0}^K \binom{K}{k} (-1)^k s^k \left(\frac{\lambda_{TE}}{\lambda_{TD}\rho + \lambda_{TE}} \right)^k exp\left(-\frac{\lambda_{TD}k\rho + \lambda_{TD}k}{\gamma_m} \right) \qquad (18)$$

3) *Minimum Eavesdropping Selection:*

The CDF and PDF of the MES scheme are:

$$F_{TD} = 1 - sexp\left(-\lambda_{TD} \frac{x}{\gamma_m} \right)$$

$$f_E(x) = \frac{\lambda_{TE}}{\gamma_m} kexp\left(-\frac{\lambda_{TE}}{\gamma_m} kx \right) \qquad (19)$$

Based on the selection rule of the MES scheme in (10) we could obtain

$$\mathbb{P}_r(C_s < \theta) = \int_0^\infty (1 - sexp(-\lambda_{TD} \frac{(\rho(1+x) - 1)}{\gamma_m}) \frac{\lambda_{TE}k}{\gamma_m} exp\left(-\frac{\lambda_{TE}}{\gamma_m} kx \right) dx.$$

$$= 1 - s \frac{\lambda_{TE}k}{\gamma_m} \int_0^\infty exp(-\lambda_{TD} \frac{(\rho(1+x) - 1)}{\gamma_m}) exp\left(-\frac{\lambda_{TE}}{\gamma_m} kx \right) dx.$$

$$= 1 - s \frac{\lambda_{TE}k}{\gamma_m} \int_0^\infty exp(-\lambda_{TD} \frac{(\rho(1+x) - 1) - \lambda_{TE}kx}{\gamma_m}) dx.$$

$$= 1 - s \frac{\lambda_{TE}k}{\gamma_m} \frac{\gamma_m}{\lambda_{TD}\rho + \lambda_{TE}k} exp\left(-\frac{\lambda_{TD}(\rho(1+0) - 1) - \lambda_{TE}k(0)}{\gamma_m} \right)$$

$$= 1 - \left(\frac{s\lambda_{TE}k}{\lambda_{TD}\rho + \lambda_{TE}k} \right) exp\left(-\frac{\lambda_{TD}\rho + \lambda_{TD}}{\gamma_m} \right)$$

The closed-form expression of the MES scheme is obtained as

$$\mathbb{P}_{out}^{MES} = 1 - \left(\frac{s\lambda_{TE}k}{\lambda_{TD}\rho + \lambda_{TE}k} \right) exp\left(-\frac{\lambda_{TD}\rho + \lambda_{TD}}{\gamma_m} \right) \qquad (20)$$

5   Numerical and Simulation Results

We employ Monte Carlo simulations to illustrate the numerical and simulation outcomes, showcasing the system's secrecy performance in the presence of wireless backhaul uncertainties and perfect channel estimation. Additionally, we conduct a comparative analysis of the system's secrecy performance across different selection schemes in both practical and ideal scenarios. By comparing the simulation curves and the analysis results, we observe a close correspondence, thereby validating the accuracy and reliability of our theoretical analysis. Threshold, θ, is set at 1bits/s/Hz. We assume that transmitters, receiver and eavesdropper are located at $T_k = (0,0)$, $D = (1,0)$ and $E = (4,1)$ in Cartesian coordinate system. The path loss pl is assumed as 4 [10].

   Figure 2 below presents SOP against SNR (γ_m). Parameter s is set at 0.99. Among the selection schemes considered, the OS outperforms the others due to its utilization of global CSI and wireless backhaul information. This comprehensive approach results in superior secrecy performance. On the other hand, the SS scheme, which only relies on partial CSI combined with backhaul information, exhibits lower secrecy performance compared to the OS scheme. The MES scheme performs poorly as it solely relies on the CSI of the wiretap channel. Generally, system performance is hindered by K, s, and the other parameters, reaching the asymptotic limits eventually. The secrecy performance for all schemes improves with an increase in the parameter K, as it enhances the achieved diversity by increasing the number of small cell transmitters. Both the SS and OS schemes exhibit remarkable enhancements in secrecy performance due to a higher likelihood of selecting a small-cell transmitter with superior channel conditions. However, the MES scheme shows only marginal improvement with an increase in the number of small-cell transmitters. The SOP relies on the probability that the legitimate channel possesses better quality than the wiretap channel. While increasing K results in a higher probability of selecting a weaker channel for the eavesdropper in the MES scheme, it does not lead to an improvement in the main channel from the small-cell transmitter to the destination, unlike the other two schemes. As a result, the MES scheme does not exhibit a clear overall enhancement in secrecy performance.

   Figure 3 shows SOP versus γ_m for different backhaul reliability values. Similar to Fig. 2, the MES scheme demonstrates the poorest performance among the three schemes. It is evident that the SOP experiences a sudden decrease for the SS and OS schemes, while it decreases gradually for the MES scheme and eventually converges to a constant value at approximately 30dB for all schemes.

   Figure 4 shows the impact of the distance between the E and T_k, d_{T_kE}, on SOP with parameters, $K = 3$ and $s = 0.90$. We assume that, d_{T_kD}, is unity as $d_{T_kD}=1.0$. We consider the following four cases: 1. $d_{T_kE} = 1.0$; 2. $d_{T_kE} = 2.0$; 3. $d_{T_kE} = 10.0$; 4. $d_{T_kE} = 0.5$. In these sets of parameters, we observe from *Fig. 4* that the SOP decreases when the eavesdropper locates further from the transmitter.

   Moreover, SOP exhibits significantly high values when the distance between T_k and E is equal to or smaller than that between T_k and D, at distances of 0.5 and 1.0. This implies that the wiretap channel quality surpasses that of the legitimate channel. On the contrary, PLS can be achieved when E is positioned further to T_k than D. As outlined in Fig. 4, it is evident that the OS scheme outperforms the SS scheme due to the additional channel knowledge utilized in the proposed system. Notably, when the distance between

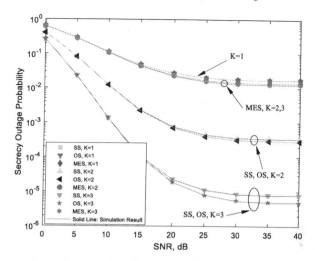

Fig. 2. Impact of number of K on SOP for K = 1, 2, 3.

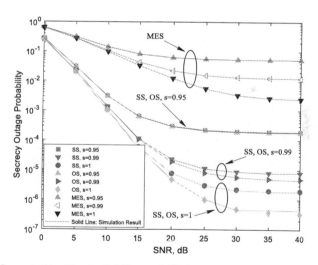

Fig. 3. Impact of backhaul reliability on SOP for s = 0.95, s = 0.99 and s = 1.00.

E and T_k becomes extremely large ($d_{T_kE} = 10.0$), the SOP curves of SS and OS nearly coincide. This indicates that considering the wiretap CSI in the transmitter selection has minimal impact on enhancing the secrecy performance when the wiretap channel quality is severely inadequate, such as when E is located far away from T_k.

The SOP versus s is provided with various values of P_o, i.e., P_o=5 dB and P_o=30 dB in Fig. 5. As the reliability of the backhaul increases, the SOP decreases for all three schemes, reaching its minimum when the backhaul is perfect. This observation underscores the significant impact of wireless backhaul reliability on system performance. Consequently, it becomes crucial to account for this imperfection when designing future heterogeneous system models.

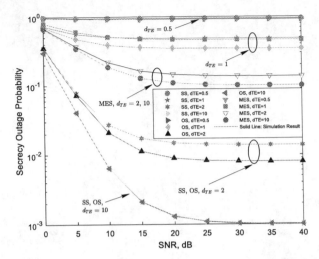

Fig. 4. Impact of different distances between T and E on SOP: d_{TE}=0.5, 1, 2 and 1.

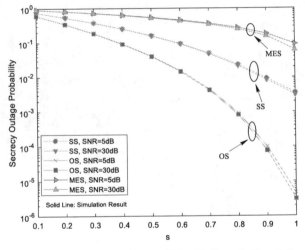

Fig. 5. Impact of backhaul reliability on SOP with $Po = 5$ dB and $Po = 30$ dB.

6   Conclusion

We evaluated the effectiveness of a heterogeneous network incorporating an unreliable backhaul in maintaining secrecy by proposing three transmitter selection schemes for small-cell networks. We derived closed-form expressions for the SOP and investigated the impact of uncertain backhaul connections on the network's ability to maintain secrecy. Our innovative theoretical analysis and simulations demonstrated that the OS scheme outperformed the SS scheme in scenarios where additional CSI knowledge was available. However, this advantage diminished significantly when the quality of the wiretap channel was extremely poor. Conversely, the MES scheme exhibited the weakest performance as it relied solely on the channel knowledge of the eavesdropper's link. Furthermore, increasing the number of small-cell transmitters had a positive impact on the system's secrecy performance with the OS and SS schemes. However, the MES scheme showed minimal sensitivity to changes in the number of small-cell transmitters. Additionally, the influence of wireless backhauls impairments on the system's secrecy performance varied depending on the number of small-cell transmitters in the SS and OS schemes. In contrast, the MES scheme demonstrated less susceptibility to the number of small-cell transmitters.

References

1. Tang, W., Feng, S., Ding, Y., Liu, Y.: Physical layer security in heterogeneous networks with jammer selection and full-duplex users. IEEE Trans. Wireless Commun. 16(12), 7982–7995 (2017)
2. Yin, C., Duong, T.Q., Xiao, P.: Secrecy performance of small-cell networks over nakagami-m fading in the presence of unreliable backhaul and imperfect CSI. IEEE 18th International Conference on Wireless and Mobile Computing, Networking and Communication, pp. 257–261 (2022)
3. Yin, C., Garcia-Palacios, E., Xiao, P., Sharma, V., Dobre, O.A., Duong, T.Q.: Secrecy performance analysis of heterogeneous networks with unreliable wireless backhaul and imperfect channel estimation. IEEE Transactions on Vehicular Technology (2023)
4. Kotwal, S.B., Kundu, C., Modem, S., Dubey, A., Flanagan, M.F.: Transmitter selection for secrecy in a frequency selective fading channel with unreliable Backhaul. IEEE 93rd Vehicular Technology Conference (VTC2021-Spring) (2021)
5. Wafai, B., Kundu, C., Dubey, A., Zhang, J., Flanagan, M.F.: Transmitter selection for secrecy in cognitive small-cell networks with Backhaul knowledge. IEEE 93rd Vehicular Technology Conference (VTC2021-Spring) (2021)
6. Yin, C., Garcia-Palacios, E.: Performance analysis for secure cooperative systems under unreliable backhaul over Nakagami-m channels. Mobile Networks and Appl. 24, pp. 480-490 (2018)
7. Yin, C., Garcia-Palacios, E., Vo, N.-S., Duong, T.Q.: Cognitive heterogeneous networks with multiple primary users and unreliable backhaul connections. IEEE Acccss 7, 3644–3655 (2019)
8. Yang, N., Suraweera, H.A., Collings, I.B., Yuen, C.: Physical layer security of TAS/MRC with antenna correlation. IEEE Trans. Inf. Forensics Secur. 8(1), 254–259 (2013)
9. Li, X., Huang, M., Li, J., Yu, Q., Rabie, K., Cavalcante, C.C.: Secure analysis of multi-antenna cooperative networks with residual transceiver HIs and CEEs. IET Commun. 13(17), 2649–2659 (2019)
10. Yin, C., Cheng, X., Li, Y., Liu, H.: Impact of wireless backhaul and imperfect channel estimation on secure communication networks. Lecture Notes of the Institute for Computer Sciences, Social Informatics and Telecommunications Engineering, pp. 231–240 (2022)
11. Elsawy, H., Hossain, E., Kim, D.: HetNets with cognitive small cells: user offloading and distributed channel access techniques. IEEE Commun. Mag. 51(6), 28–36 (2013)
12. ElSawy, H., Hossain, E.: Two-Tier hetnets with cognitive femtocells: downlink performance modeling and analysis in a multichannel environment. IEEE Trans. Mob. Comput. 13(3), 649–663 (2014)

E. O'Boyle et al.

13. Yin, C., Nguyen, H.T., Kundu, C., Kaleem, Z., Garcia-Palacios, E., Duong, T.Q.: Secure energy harvesting relay networks with unreliable backhaul connections. IEEE Access **6**, 12074–12084 (2018)
14. Nakagami, M.: The m-distribution—a general formula of intensity distribution of rapid fading. ScienceDirect (1960)

Author Index

N.-S. Vo and H.-A. Tran (Eds.): INISCOM 2023, LNICST 531, pp. 327–328, 2023.
https://doi.org/10.1007/978-3-031-47359-3

Printed in the United States
by Baker & Taylor Publisher Services